Hymns
of the
Saints

Hymns
of the
Saints

Reorganized Church of Jesus Christ
of Latter Day Saints

Reprint Restrictions

Most hymns in this hymnal may be reproduced for onetime use only (e.g., in worship service bulletins). Following is a list of hymns that **cannot** be reproduced without specific written permission from the copyright holders:

Text: 44, 107, 153, 156, 171, 182, 197, 227, 300, 308, 315, 327, 331, 367, 452, 491, 493

Tune: 85, 108, 111, 163, 170, 202, 218, 297, 301, 356; (descant) 142

Both: 74, 79, 187, 285, 290, 322, 377, 382, 388, 420, 466

Please send two (2) copies of all reproduced hymns to Music Office, the Auditorium, Independence, MO 64051. Extensive efforts have been made to contact and acknowledge copyright owners. Errors or omissions, sent to the above address, will be corrected in subsequent printings.

10   9   8   7   6   5   4   3   85   86   87   88   89

Copyright © 1981   Corrected printing, 1982.

Herald Publishing House
Independence, Missouri

ISBN 0-8309-0326-7
Printed in the United States of America

Contents

Lord's Prayer

Our Father who art in heaven, Hallowed be thy name. Thy kingdom come. Thy will be done on earth, as it is done in heaven. Give us this day, our daily bread. And forgive us our trespasses, as we forgive those who trespass against us. And suffer us not to be led into temptation, but deliver us from evil. For thine is the kingdom, and the power, and the glory, forever and ever, Amen.

—*Matthew 6:10-15 (Inspired Version)*

Communion Prayers

BREAD

O God, the eternal Father, we ask thee in the name of thy Son Jesus Christ, to bless and sanctify this bread to the souls of all those who partake of it, that they may eat in remembrance of the body of thy Son, and witness unto thee, O God, the eternal Father, that they are willing to take upon them the name of thy Son, and always remember him and keep his commandments which he has given them, that they may always have his Spirit to be with them. Amen.

—*Doctrine and Covenants 17:22d*

WINE

O God, the eternal Father, we ask thee in the name of thy Son Jesus Christ, to bless and sanctify this wine to the souls of all those who drink of it, that they may do it in remembrance of the blood of thy Son which was shed for them, that they may witness unto thee, O God, the eternal Father, that they do always remember him, that they may have his Spirit to be with them. Amen.

—*Doctrine and Covenants 17:23b*

Foreword

It is with considerable pleasure that we present *Hymns of the Saints* to the church.

The publication of a new hymnal is a major event and has potential for enormous impact on the membership. A hymnal stands alongside the scriptures as a vital resource for the church's worship. Hymn singing is the principal form, or in some places the only form, by which we speak our faith together. It is a means whereby Saints around the world can experience a sense of unity as we sing the well-loved hymns of the church.

In order to express appropriately our best understanding and experience of the gospel it is necessary on occasion to revise our hymnal—introducing new hymns and discarding some old ones. By producing a new hymnal at this time we are responding to the invitation "Sing unto the Lord a new song" (Isaiah 42:10).

This hymnal is the culmination of many years of intensive work involving hymn selection and production of the book itself. The hymn selection committee was chaired by Harold Neal who from 1969 to 1978 served as Director of the Music Department (now Music Office). In 1978 Brother Neal was named Director of Ensembles and Fine Arts Consultant for the church. One of his continuing responsibilities has been to conduct the annual performance of *Messiah*, broadcasts of which are heard around the world. His previous musical experience includes membership in the London, Ontario, Symphony Orchestra, various conducting and choral responsibilities in church and community, and fifteen years on the Graceland College faculty. Brother Neal ably facilitated the work of the committee throughout its tenure.

The following persons served as members of the committee under Brother Neal's competent leadership:

Rosalee Elser is an accomplished organist and music theorist. Her natural talents and professional training have been enhanced by industrious application. As a result many hymns are richer in sound because of her skill as a harmonizer and arranger.

Barbara Higdon has taught English at Graceland College and other institutions of higher education. She is presently Vice President/Dean of Academic Affairs at Park College in Parkville, Missouri. Her skills in the use of the English language greatly facilitated the work of the committee.

Barbara Howard, a Herald House editor, made an imaginative and stimulating contribution to the theological integrity and poetic quality of hymn texts. She was one whose hymn-writing talents blossomed in response to need.

In the fall of 1975 Peter Judd was invited to join the committee by virtue of his appointment as Director of the Worship Office. His inquiring mind and mediating spirit strengthened the work of the committee.

The effectiveness of Aleta Runkle Page's contribution was consistent with her lifelong service in many areas of the church. She was a staff member on numerous occasions between 1956 and 1969 at music camps sponsored by the Music Department. She was employed for a number of years as Supervisor of

Elementary School Music in Independence, Missouri. She served on the Board of Trustees of Graceland College from 1974 to 1980.

Roger A. Revell served as administrative assistant in the Music Department from 1971 to 1978, when he was named Director of the Music Office. His background in music education, youth ministries, management, and copyright law enabled him to make valuable contributions to the committee.

Ammon Roberson, a music educator, has served the church for many years as a choir director. In 1978 he received the Distinguished Music Alumnus Award from the Central Missouri State University, and retired in 1980 from their music department with the rank of Professor Emeritus. He brought a viewpoint to the committee that combined traditional RLDS sentiments with universal concepts.

Geoffrey Spencer has served the church as an appointee minister in many capacities. He is now President of the High Priest's Quorum and of the Temple School. His keen theological and historical insights were invaluable to the committee's work. One of the exciting aspects of the work of the committee was the discovery and stimulation of Brother Spencer's talent as hymn writer.

John Thumm, a former high school music teacher, is currently an appointee seventy. His musical background and field experience enabled him to make an important contribution to the process.

For many years Alta Topham has been a piano teacher, organist, and music director for the Shenandoah, Iowa, congregation. Her utter devotion and loyal support were an inspiration to the rest of the committee. Her practical experience, participation, and influence were characterized by a graciousness and gentleness of spirit that helped immeasurably.

Alan Tyree as a linguist, hymn-writer, theologian, and musician has made many contributions to the work of the committee. As a member of the Quorum of Twelve Apostles since 1966, his considerable contact with the church membership helped raise the committee's awareness of the worldwide needs of the church.

Richard Clothier and Kenneth Cooper both served on the committee between 1971 and 1975 while on the Graceland Music Faculty.

John Obetz, Auditorium organist, assisted the committee as a member of the music subcommittee. Doris Harding Criss served as the principal accompanist for the committee. From 1978 to 1980 Carol Cavin served as the committee's executive secretary.

Other persons and groups assisting in this project are named in the acknowledgments.

We express our appreciation to these people for their efforts and commend this hymnal to the church. May we indeed "sing to the Lord a new song" as we use *Hymns of the Saints* in our corporate worship.

The First Presidency

Wallace B. Smith
Duane E. Couey
Howard S. Sheehy, Jr.

May 1981

Preface

In 1971 a Committee on Congregational Music was established to study the need for a new hymnal. This committee superseded an earlier standing committee of the Music Department which had been evaluating hymn texts and tunes that were brought to its attention. The 1971 committee was formed in response to many written and verbal requests to consider the publication of a new official hymnal for the church.

The early 1970s saw considerable ferment, even turmoil, in contemporary hymn-writing and usage. The committee monitored and studied these phenomena while directing its efforts toward the production of two supplements to The Hymnal (1956). Published in 1974 and 1976, these supplements contained a total of twenty-five new hymns, some of a contemporary style. The response of the church was such that the First Presidency approved plans to publish an entirely new hymnal. The committee's name was then changed to the 1981 Hymnal Committee.

The task of hymn selection has been a formidable one. The committee recognized that since the early 1960s organized religion, including our own church, has passed through a sort of crucible characterized by changing theological concepts, the searching eye of historical research, shifting modes of expression, and increased sensitivity to the sanctity of personhood. The committee was also very much aware that the range of musical taste in the church had widened considerably during the past two decades. That the committee faced its task unflinchingly and brought it to fruition is a testimony of the members' individual and collective devotion and endurance. Theirs is an accomplishment that exacted virtually years of dedicated and ofttimes heart-rending service.

Hymns of the Saints contains a total of 501 hymns. These are organized in four major sections: Praise and Thanksgiving (78 hymns), Contemplation and Renewal (107 hymns), God's Word for Us (183 hymns), and Commission and Commitment (133 hymns). Each section is divided into categories for the purpose of ordering the hymns in the hymnal. Users of the hymnal are advised, however, to make frequent use of the topical index rather than to rely solely on the category designations that appear at the top of each hymn page. The topical index is extensive, and each hymn is included under several topics in addition to the category on the page. Regular use of this index will increase the versatility and usefulness of the entire hymnal and each individual hymn.

Of the 501 hymns, 292 were included in The Hymnal (1956). Four hymns were in the 1933 Saints Hymnal but not in The Hymnal (1956) or its supplements. Twenty-one appeared in the First and Second Supplements. One hundred and eighty-four are entirely new hymns not previously appearing in RLDS hymnals.

In total, 127 hymns have texts written in whole or in part by RLDS authors, and 88 hymn tunes were written, harmonized, or adapted by RLDS composers.

Criteria for hymn text selection focused on the extent to which texts expressed the faith of the Saints as best understood by the committee. Most hymns in The Hymnal (1956) that were not chosen for inclusion in this hymnal were omitted because they are seldom used, or because the text does not adequately express the church's best current understanding of the gospel. In some cases, an infrequently used hymn was thought to express important concepts and so was matched with a new tune. Some hymns from *The Hymnal* (1956) were retained with text changes. In some cases only a word or two was changed. In other cases major rewriting was necessary to make the hymn reflect adequately the best thinking of the church theologically and linguistically. The hymn texts generally reflect the "Policy of Inclusive Language" for church publications approved by the First Presidency in 1978.

Hymns of the Saints contains no identifiable children's or youth hymns. The committee has sought diligently for hymns that are representative of the expressions of all ages—hymns which can have meaning and be sung joyfully by all worshipers regardless of chronological age.

The image of the church as a world organization has been enhanced by the inclusion of a number of hymns from other than English-speaking countries. For practical purposes these texts have been translated into English. The committee also intentionally tried to include hymns that are meaningful to the Saints in all English-speaking countries where the hymnal will be used. It is recognized, however, that church members as they gather for worship in various places may wish to supplement this hymnal with hymns of their own choosing from other sources.

The hymnal offers new hymns in the traditional style, some in an unfamiliar setting, some folk and modern gospel hymns, and some in the contemporary classical style. Within this rich variety, a sense of unity can be felt by using hymns that express diversity of need and cultural background. As the Saints share in this pluralism of musical and poetic ministry, they may find their spiritual awareness enlarged and enriched.

The intent of the committee was to assemble a body of hymnody that can have wide usage throughout the church without trying to include all the hymns that the various jurisdictions of the church in various places may wish to use.

Every effort has been made to keep the hymns as simple to sing as possible, consistent with music's integrity as an art. Some who enjoy part singing (alto, tenor, bass) may encounter difficulty with some new tunes at first. The desire to provide music of warmth and vitality has resulted in the use of slightly complex rhythms, moving harmonies, and lyric-style melodies, some of which are intended to be sung in unison. However, as many of these "unison" tunes as possible have been given four-part settings.

The editors of the hymnal have arranged the page layout for maximum readability. The following features appear on the hymn pages:

1. The broad *category* in which the hymn is found appears at the top outside corner of the page. For maximum flexibility in the use of hymns, make regular use of the topical index when choosing hymns.

2. The hymn *number* appears immediately below the category designation.

3. The hymn *title* (first line) appears at the top of the hymn opposite the number, on the inside of the page.

4. Two *scriptures* are listed at the top left of each hymn. Where Inspired Version versification differs from that of other versions, *the I.V. verses are listed first, with those for other versions in parentheses.* See also scripture index.

5. The *tune name and meter* are listed at the top right of each hymn. When the same text is set to two different tunes, the hymns have adjacent

but separate numbers. The other hymn is listed immediately below the tune name and meter as an alternate hymn. When it is suggested that a tune found elsewhere in the hymnal may be used appropriately with a particular text, this tune name and number is listed as an alternate tune.

When a tune is found elsewhere in the hymnal at a higher or lower setting (key), a note to this effect is included. A few hymns have descant, faux bourdon (melody in the tenor), or canon (round) settings in addition to the regular arrangement. These are provided to enhance the musical possibilities in the hymnal.

6. *Guitar chords* have been provided above the staff lines of some hymns. These do *not* apply to keyboard accompaniment, and it is not anticipated that keyboard instruments will be used simultaneously with guitars. Capital (upper case) letters are used to designate major chords. Small (lower case) letters are used to designate minor chords.

7. *Time signatures* are included in most hymns according to conventional notation and use. A few hymns have no time signature because the measures (bars) are of unequal length. In most of these cases an instructional note appears immediately above the top staff line of the hymn.

8. *Amens* are placed at the end of certain prayer hymns, and with those whose melodic and harmonic structures indicate the use of amens. The responsibility of deciding when the use of an amen is appropriate rests with the persons planning the worship service.

9. *Credit lines* appear below each hymn. Complete information is included regarding the sources of texts and tunes.

Copyrighted hymns include the words "copyright," "by permission," or the equivalent. Some of these copyrighted hymns may be reproduced for one-time use in worship bulletins. Others may not be reproduced without specific permission from the copyright holder. *A list of hymns that may not be reproduced without further permission appears on the copyright page at the front of this hymnal. Unauthorized reproduction of hymn texts or tunes for any purpose can result in legal action by the owners of the material.* For up-to-date information on the copyright status of a specific hymn contact the Music Office, the Auditorium, Independence, MO 64051.

The following abbreviations are used in the credit lines:

Abr.	- Abbreviated
Adapt.	- Adapted
Alt.	- Altered
Arr.	- Arranged
Attr.	- Attributed to
C.	- Circa
Coll.	- Collected
Harm.	- Harmonized
Rev.	- Revised
Tr., Trans.	- Translated or Translator

Additional information on the content and use of *Hymns of the Saints* can be found in the paperback book *Hymns in Worship: A Guide to "Hymns of the Saints"* by Roger A. Revell, Herald House 1981.

Harold Neal, Chairman, 1981 Hymnal Committee
Peter A. Judd, Director, Worship Office
Roger A. Revell, Director, Music Office

Acknowledgments

The work of production of the hymnal was coordinated by Peter Judd and Roger A. Revell. Carol Cavin prepared the copy for typesetting and handled the copyright and permissions arrangements. The engraving (typesetting) of the words and music on the hymn pages was done by the following employees of White Harvest Music Corporation: Dale G. Rider, Twila Hidy Rider, Doris Harding Criss, Edward Grove Mason, and William T. Stewart. Proofreading was by Norma Smith Coberly, Blake West, John Davies, Patricia Ballinger, and Marsha Morgan. Cover design and non-hymnic layout was prepared by the Office of Graphic Arts at the Auditorium. Hymn titles, indexes, and other non-hymnic text was set by Herald House, which also printed and published the hymnal. Others assisting in the project include Nadine Woods, Barbara Bryant Thatcher, Evelyn Maples, Bethany Andrews, Stephen Goff, David C. Hawley, Delores Fitzpatrick, and Mary Fincham.

Praise and Thanksgiving

O Lord, Grace Our Communion

Matthew 11:29, 30
D. and C. 119:6c

HOLY WINGS 7.6.7.6.D.

1

1. O Lord, grace our com - mun-ion In the prom-ise of this hour.
2. In-to lives weighed down by sor -row Let thy Spir - it gent - ly flow;

We a - wait some con - fir - ma -tion Of thy lib - er - a - ting power.
May the bruised and bro - ken - heart-ed, Re-sur - rec -tion sure - ly know.

E - ven though thy Saints here gath-ered The hu - man bur - den share,
And so, re - newed in spir - it, With new-born hearts a - flame,

In the warmth of thy com - pas-sion, How can our hearts de - spair?
Let this wait - ing con - gre - ga -tion Rise up and praise thy name.

Text: Geoffrey F. Spencer, 1927 - ; copyright 1980 Reorganized Church of Jesus Christ of Latter Day Saints.
Tune: Swedish Folk Melody; harm. Mark S. Dickey, 1885-1961; alt.

2 Met in Thy Sacred Name, O Lord

D. and C. 6:15, 16a
Matthew 18:20

MANOAH C.M.

1. Met in thy sa-cred name, O Lord, To wor-ship thee be-low, Grant
   that each soul with joy may thrill, With love each bos-om glow.
2. Thy cheer-ing prom-ise, Lord, we wait:"Wher-ev-er two or three Shall
   in my name to-geth-er meet, There will I choose to be."
3. In-spire our praise, di-rect our prayer, Thy Spir-it fill each heart; Clothe
   thou with power each thought and word; To all thy grace im-part. A-men.

Text: Mark H. Forscutt, 1834-1903.
Tune: Arr. from Gioacchino A. Rossini, 1792-1868, in Henry W. Greatorex's *Collection of Church Music*, 1851.

3 With Thankful Hearts We Meet, O Lord

I Nephi 7:56-59
D. and C. 34:6

HICKS L.M.

1. With thank-ful hearts we meet, O Lord, To sing thy
   praise, to hear thy word, To seek thy face in ear-nest
2. Dear Shep-herd of thy cho-sen flock, Thy peo-ple's
   shield, their shad-ow-ing rock, Once more we meet to hear thy
3. Thy pres-ence, Sav-ior, now we seek; Con-firm the
   strong, sus-tain the weak; Way-worn and tired we hith-er

prayer, To cast on thee each earth - ly care.
voice, Once more be - fore thee to re - joice.
come; Give us a fore - taste of our home. A - men.

Text: Mary Bowly Peters, 1813-1856.
Tune: Arthur H. Mills, 1870-1943.

Sweet the Time, Exceeding Sweet   4

Psalm 50:5, 6   HENDON 7.7.7.7.7.
John 4:25, 26 (23-24)

1. Sweet the time, ex - ceed-ing sweet, When the Saints to -
2. Sing the Son's a - maz - ing love— How he left the
3. Sweet the place, ex - ceed-ing sweet, Where the Saints in

geth - er meet, When the Sav - ior is the theme, When they
realms a - bove, Took our na - ture and our place, Lived and
glo - ry meet, Where the Sav - ior's still the theme, Where they

joy to sing of him; When they joy to sing of him.
died to save our race; Lived and died to save our race.
see and sing of him; Where they see and sing of him.

Text: George Burder, 1752-1832.
Tune: Henri Abraham César Malan, 1787-1864.

5

Isaiah 58:13, 14
D. and C. 29:2d, e

In God's Most Holy Presence

EWING 7.6.7.6.D.

1. In God's most ho-ly pres-ence We meet with one ac-cord
2. Our wor-ship will be fruit-less, And all our prayers be vain,
3. If we but love Thee tru-ly, Our love is not con-fined

To grasp the hand of friend-ship And learn of Christ, our Lord.
If, hold-ing this day sa-cred, We make the week pro-fane.
To Thee but grows ex-pan-sive, Em-brac-ing hu-man-kind.

We leave the week be-hind us, With all its toil and strain,
In ev-ery dai-ly du-ty High pur-pose we must show,
Help us in mu-tual ser-vice For all, a-broad, at home,

With grate-ful hearts to wel-come The Sab-bath once a-gain.
And as we hope for heav-en Make earth a heaven be-low.
To share the con-quering tra-vail That makes Thy king-dom come.

Text: Ernest Dodgshun, 1876-1944.
Tune: Alexander Ewing, 1830-1895.

Lord, Thou Hast Brought Us to This Place   6

D. and C. 59:1a, b
Psalm 24:1-5

MELITA 8.8.8.D.

1. Lord, thou hast brought us to this place As sure-ly as thy
2. Be still and won-der at God's grace That he for us did
3. The streams and wood-lands, flowers and trees, High hills and sun-shine,
4. We can-not give thee what is thine, So sim-ply pray that

cho-sen race Was led to Is-rael's prom-ised land, Where
choose this place, And here in love he deigns to share His
cool-ing breeze—Thou mad-est all— A set-ting fine For
light may shine From out this place, that all may see Thy

bless-ings flowed on ev-ery hand. Al-might-y God, we
peace— and joys be-yond com-pare. Al-might-y God, we
this thy house is tru-ly thine. Al-might-y God, for
love for us and ours for thee. Al-might-y God, with

dare to pray That thou wilt bless thy house this day.
praise thy name, Thy won-drous prov-i-dence ac-claim.
this place fair Ac-cept our hum-ble, thank-ful prayer.
strength en-dow Thy chil-dren for their wit-ness now. A-men.

Text: Dennis Aldridge, 1934 - ; copyright 1980 Reorganized Church of Jesus Christ of Latter Day Saints.
Tune: John B. Dykes, 1823-1876.

7 O Lord, Around Thine Altar Now

D. and C. 85:16b-e
Philippians 4:6, 7

ARLINGTON C.M.

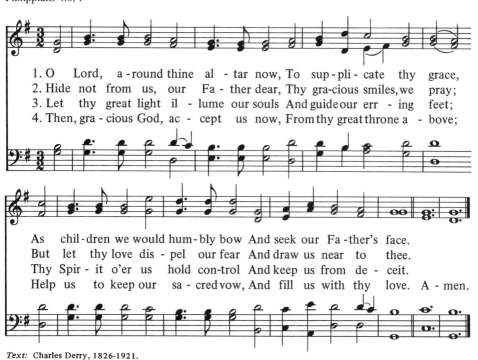

1. O Lord, a - round thine al - tar now, To sup - pli - cate thy grace,
2. Hide not from us, our Fa - ther dear, Thy gra-cious smiles, we pray;
3. Let thy great light il - lume our souls And guide our err - ing feet;
4. Then, gra - cious God, ac - cept us now, From thy great throne a - bove;

As chil - dren we would hum - bly bow And seek our Fa - ther's face.
But let thy love dis - pel our fear And draw us near to thee.
Thy Spir - it o'er us hold con - trol And keep us from de - ceit.
Help us to keep our sa - cred vow, And fill us with thy love. A - men.

Text: Charles Derry, 1826-1921.
Tune: Thomas A. Arne, 1710-1778.

8 You May Sing of the Beauty

II Nephi 8:19
Psalm 122:1

FELLOWSHIP 12.12.12.12.

1. You may sing of the beau - ty of moun-tain and dale, Of the sil - ver - y
2. You may boast of the sweet-ness of day's ear - ly dawn, Of the skies' soft-ening
3. You may val - ue the friend-ship of youth and of age, And se - lect for your

stream - let and flowers of the vale, But the place most de - light - ful this
grac - es where day is just gone, But there's no oth - er sea - son or
com - rades the no - ble and sage, But the friends that most cheer me on

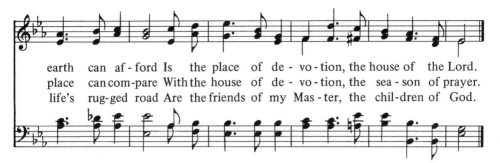

earth can af-ford Is the place of de-vo-tion, the house of the Lord.
place can com-pare With the house of de-vo-tion, the sea-son of prayer.
life's rug-ged road Are the friends of my Mas-ter, the chil-dren of God.

Text: David Hyrum Smith, 1844-1904.
Tune: Ascribed to Norman W. Smith, 1833-1917.

Within the Shelter of Our Walls 9

Alma 16:219-222
D. and C. 119:2

LOBT GOTT, IHR CHRISTEN
8.6.8.8.6.

1. With - in the shel - ter of our walls, Be pres - ent, Lord, to
2. Trans-form our spir - its as we learn Thy lov - ing dis - ci -
3. Make dai - ly bread a sac - ra - ment Which Thou, O Lord, might

guide. Where work is planned, where plea - sure calls, Where hearts keep
pline. When tasks are hard or du - ty stern, Give us the
share. Give con - ver - sa - tion high in - tent; Our dai - ly

ho - ly fes - ti - vals, Find wel - come, and a - bide.
wis - dom to dis - cern Thy com - rade - ship with - in.
strength for thee be spent With thought and lov - ing care. A - men.

Text: Elinor Lennen; copyright 1961 Hymn Society of America; used by permission.
Tune: Nicolaus Hermann, c. 1485-1561; harm. Austin C. Lovelace, 1919 - ; harm. copyright 1965 Abingdon Press.
Used by permission.

10
Lord, We Come Before Thee Now

D. and C. 10:3
Isaiah 26:3, 4

INVOCATION 7.7.7.7.D.

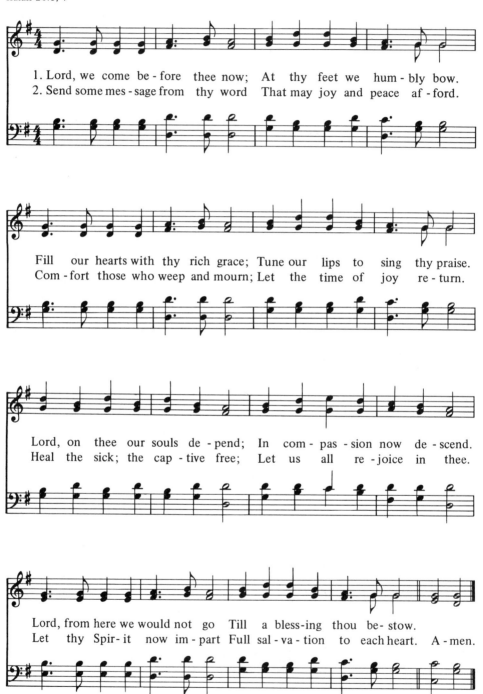

1. Lord, we come be-fore thee now; At thy feet we hum-bly bow.
2. Send some mes-sage from thy word That may joy and peace af-ford.

Fill our hearts with thy rich grace; Tune our lips to sing thy praise.
Com-fort those who weep and mourn; Let the time of joy re-turn.

Lord, on thee our souls de-pend; In com-pas-sion now de-scend.
Heal the sick; the cap-tive free; Let us all re-joice in thee.

Lord, from here we would not go Till a bless-ing thou be-stow.
Let thy Spir-it now im-part Full sal-va-tion to each heart. A-men.

Text: William Hammond, 1719-1783, alt.
Tune: Old Tune.

We Gather Together

11

I Corinthians 15:57, 58
D. and C. 59:1

KREMSER 12.11.12.11.

1. We gath - er to - geth - er to ask the Lord's bless - ing;
2. Be - side us to guide us, our God with us join - ing,
3. We all do ex - tol thee, thou lead - er tri - umph - ant,

He chas - tens and has - tens his will to make known;
Or - dain - ing, main - tain - ing his king - dom di - vine;
And pray that thou still our de - fend - er wilt be.

The wick - ed op - press - ing cease them from dis - tress - ing.
So from the be - gin - ning the fight we were win - ning;
Let thy con - gre - ga - tion es - cape trib - u - la - tion.

Sing prais - es to his name; he for - gets not his own.
Thou, Lord, wast at our side; the glo - ry be thine!
Thy name be ev - er praised! O Lord, make us free! A - men.

Text: Netherlands Folk Song; trans. by Theodore Baker, 1851-1934.
Tune: Traditional Netherlands Melody, publ. 1625; arr. by Edward Kremser, 1838-1914.

12 Sovereign and Transforming Grace

Moroni 10:29, 30
D. and C. 90:3b, c

GOTTSCHALK (Mercy) 7.7.7.7.

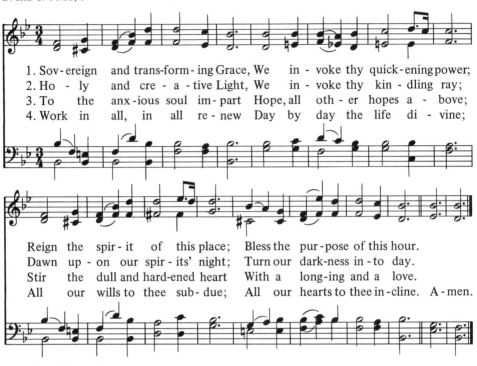

1. Sov-ereign and trans-form-ing Grace, We in-voke thy quick-ening power;
2. Ho-ly and cre-a-tive Light, We in-voke thy kin-dling ray;
3. To the anx-ious soul im-part Hope, all oth-er hopes a-bove;
4. Work in all, in all re-new Day by day the life di-vine;

Reign the spir-it of this place; Bless the pur-pose of this hour.
Dawn up-on our spir-its' night; Turn our dark-ness in-to day.
Stir the dull and hard-ened heart With a long-ing and a love.
All our wills to thee sub-due; All our hearts to thee in-cline. A-men.

Text: Frederick Henry Hedge, 1805-1890.
Tune: Arr. from Louis M. Gottschalk, 1829-1869.

13 Great God, as Followers of Thy Son

D. and C. 76:2a, b
Romans 8:16, 17

HEBRON L.M.

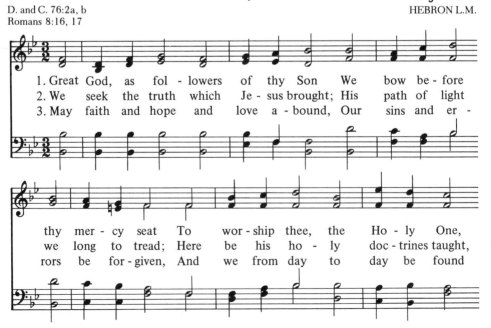

1. Great God, as fol-lowers of thy Son We bow be-fore
2. We seek the truth which Je-sus brought; His path of light
3. May faith and hope and love a-bound, Our sins and er-

thy mer-cy seat To wor-ship thee, the Ho-ly One,
we long to tread; Here be his ho-ly doc-trines taught,
rors be for-given, And we from day to day be found

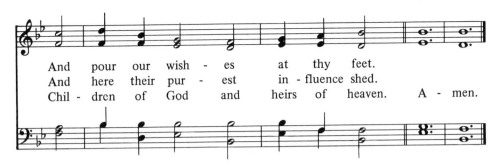

And pour our wish - es at thy feet.
And here their pur - est in - fluence shed.
Chil - dren of God and heirs of heaven. A - men.

Text: Henry Ware, 1793-1843.
Tune: Lowell Mason, 1792-1872.

O God, Whose Presence Glows in All 14

I Thessalonians 2:19
D. and C. 18:6

HURSLEY L.M.

1. O God, whose pres - ence glows in all— With - in, a -
2. Thy truth be with the heart be - lieved By all who
3. Thy love its ho - ly in - fluence pour To keep us
4. Send down its an - gels to our side; Send in its

round us, and a - bove— Thy word we bless, thy name we
seek this sa - cred place; With power pro - claimed, in peace re -
meek and make us free, And throw its bind - ing bless - ing
calm up - on each breast; For we would know no oth - er

call, Whose word is Truth, whose name is Love.
ceived, Our spir - its' light thy Spir - it's grace.
more Round each with all, and all with thee.
guide, And we can need no oth - er rest. A - men.

Text: Nathaniel L. Frothingham, 1793-1870.
Tune: Allgemeines Katholisches Gesangbuch, Vienna, 1774; arr. William Henry Monk, 1823-1889.

15

Psalm 96:9
I Chronicles 16:29

O Worship the Lord

PORTER 13.8.

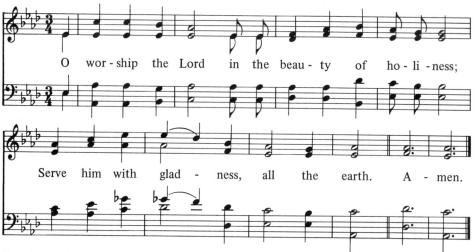

O wor-ship the Lord in the beau-ty of ho-li-ness;

Serve him with glad - ness, all the earth. A - men.

Text: Adapted from Psalm 96:9.
Tune: Robert Guy McCutchan, 1877-1958.

16

Psalm 65:1, 2
D. and C. 28:2b

O Thou Who Hearest

MORECAMBE 10.10.10.10.
See 181 for a higher setting.

O thou who hear - est ev -ery heart-felt prayer, With thy rich

grace, Lord, all our hearts pre - pare; Thou art our life, thou art our

love and light; O let this Sab-bath hour with thee be bright. A-men.

Text: Unknown.
Tune: Frederick Cook Atkinson, 1841-1897.

Lord, Whose Love Through Humble Service   17

Mark 10:42-45
Alma 14:82, 96

HYFRYDOL 8.7.8.7.D.

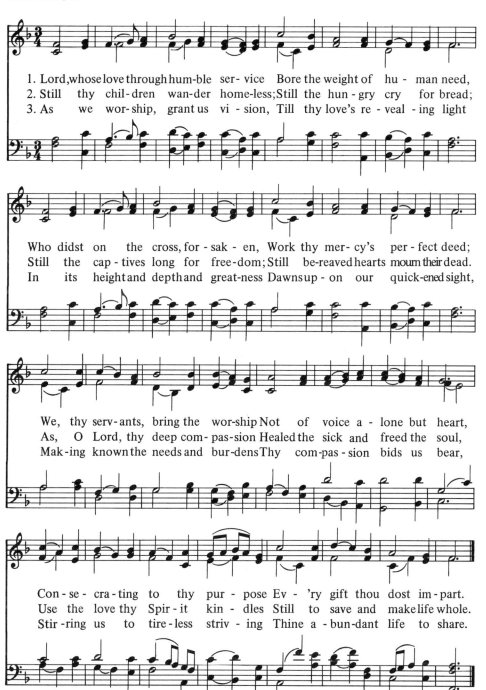

1. Lord, whose love through hum-ble ser-vice Bore the weight of hu - man need,
2. Still thy chil-dren wan-der home-less; Still the hun-gry cry for bread;
3. As we wor-ship, grant us vi - sion, Till thy love's re - veal-ing light

Who didst on the cross, for - sak - en, Work thy mer - cy's per - fect deed;
Still the cap - tives long for free-dom; Still be-reaved hearts mourn their dead.
In its height and depth and great-ness Dawns up - on our quick-ened sight,

We, thy serv-ants, bring the wor-ship Not of voice a - lone but heart,
As, O Lord, thy deep com-pas-sion Healed the sick and freed the soul,
Mak-ing known the needs and bur-dens Thy com-pas - sion bids us bear,

Con - se - cra-ting to thy pur - pose Ev - 'ry gift thou dost im-part.
Use the love thy Spir - it kin - dles Still to save and make life whole.
Stir-ring us to tire-less striv - ing Thine a - bun-dant life to share.

Text: Albert F. Bayly, 1901 - ; alt. by author, 1975. Copyright 1961 by Albert F. Bayly; used by permission.
Tune: Rowland Hugh Prichard, 1811-1887.

18 All Things Bright and Beautiful

I Chronicles 16:23-29

D. and C. 59:4

ROYAL OAK 7.6.7.6. with refrain

Refrain

All things bright and beau-ti-ful, All crea-tures great and small,

All things wise and won-der-ful, The Lord God made them all.

Fine

1. Each lit-tle flower that o-pens, Each lit-tle bird that sings,
2. The pur-ple-head-ed moun-tain, The riv-er run-ning by,
3. The cold wind in the win-ter, The pleas-ant sum-mer sun,
4. He gave us eyes to see them, And lips that we might tell

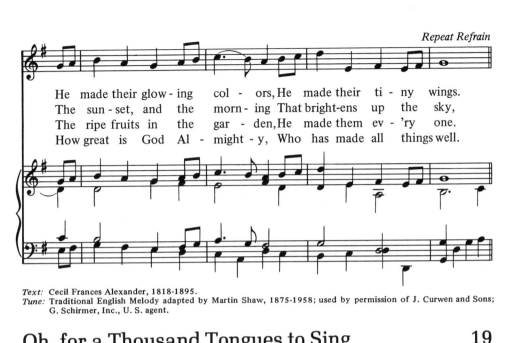

Repeat Refrain

He made their glow-ing col - ors, He made their ti - ny wings.
The sun-set, and the morn-ing That bright-ens up the sky,
The ripe fruits in the gar - den, He made them ev - 'ry one.
How great is God Al - might-y, Who has made all things well.

Text: Cecil Frances Alexander, 1818-1895.
Tune: Traditional English Melody adapted by Martin Shaw, 1875-1958; used by permission of J. Curwen and Sons;
    G. Schirmer, Inc., U. S. agent.

Oh, for a Thousand Tongues to Sing   19

D. and C. 22:23
Psalm 30:1-4

AZMON C.M.

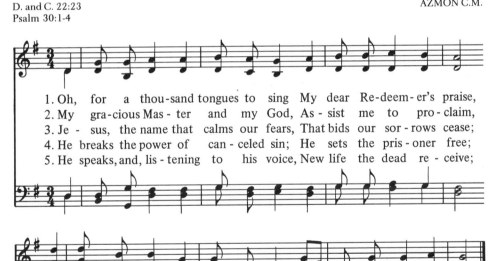

1. Oh, for a thou-sand tongues to sing My dear Re-deem-er's praise,
2. My gra-cious Mas - ter and my God, As - sist me to pro-claim,
3. Je - sus, the name that calms our fears, That bids our sor - rows cease;
4. He breaks the power of can - celed sin; He sets the pris - oner free;
5. He speaks, and, lis - tening to his voice, New life the dead re - ceive;

The glo - ries of my God and King, The tri-umphs of his grace!
To spread through all the earth a - broad, The hon - ors of thy name.
'Tis mu - sic in the sin - ner's ears, 'Tis life and health and peace.
His blood can make the foul - est clean; His love a - vails for me.
The mourn-ful, bro - ken hearts re - joice; The hum - ble poor be - lieve.

Text: Charles Wesley, 1707-1788.
Tune: Carl G. Gläser, 1784-1839; arr. Lowell Mason, 1792-1872.

20 Joyful, Joyful, We Adore Thee

II Nephi 9:133-137
Psalm 150

HYMN TO JOY 8.7.8.7.D.

1. Joy - ful, joy - ful, we a - dore thee, God of glo - ry, Lord of love;
2. All thy works with joy sur-round thee; Earth and heaven re -flect thy rays.
3. Thou art giv - ing and for - giv - ing, Ev - er bless - ing, ev - er blest,

Hearts un - fold like flowers be - fore thee, Hail thee as the sun a - bove.
Stars and an - gels sing a - round thee, Cen - ter of un - bro - ken praise;
Well- spring of the joy of liv - ing, O - cean depth of hap - py rest!

Melt the clouds of sin and sad - ness; Drive the dark of doubt a - way;
Field and for - est, vale and moun - tain, Blos - soming mead-ow, flash-ing sea,
Thou our Fa - ther, Christ our broth-er, All who live in love are thine;

Giv - er of im - mor - tal glad-ness, Fill us with the light of day!
Chant-ing bird and flow-ing foun-tain Call us to re -joice in thee.
Teach us how to love each oth - er; Lift us to the joy di - vine. A-men.

Text: From *The Poems of Henry Van Dyke* by Henry Van Dyke, 1852-1933. Copyright 1902, 1911 Charles Scrib-ner's Sons; copyright renewed. Reprinted by permission of the publisher.
Tune: Arr. from Ludwig van Beethoven, 1770-1827, by Edward Hodges, 1796-1867.

Declare, O Heavens, the Lord of Space

21

Colossians 1:16-18
Alma 14:124, 125

LASST UNS ERFREUEN
8.8.8.8.8. with alleluias

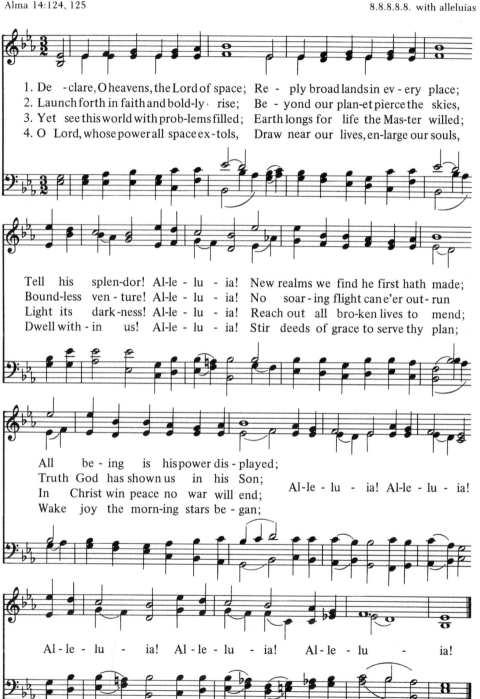

1. De -clare, O heavens, the Lord of space; Re - ply broad lands in ev - ery place;
2. Launch forth in faith and bold-ly rise; Be - yond our plan-et pierce the skies,
3. Yet see this world with prob-lems filled; Earth longs for life the Mas-ter willed;
4. O Lord, whose power all space ex-tols, Draw near our lives, en-large our souls,

Tell his splen-dor! Al-le - lu - ia! New realms we find he first hath made;
Bound-less ven - ture! Al-le - lu - ia! No soar-ing flight can e'er out-run
Light its dark-ness! Al-le - lu - ia! Reach out all bro-ken lives to mend;
Dwell with - in us! Al-le - lu - ia! Stir deeds of grace to serve thy plan;

All be - ing is his power dis - played;
Truth God has shown us in his Son;
In Christ win peace no war will end;
Wake joy the morn-ing stars be - gan;

Al-le - lu - ia! Al-le - lu - ia!

Al - le - lu - ia! Al - le - lu - ia! Al - le - lu - ia!

Text: Robert Lansing Edwards, 1915 - ; alt.; Copyright 1962 The Hymn Society of America. Used by permission.
Tune: Geistliche Kirchengesäng, Cologne, 1623; arr. Ralph Vaughan Williams, 1872-1958. From *The English Hymnal*
by permission of Oxford University Press.

22 Morning Has Broken

II Peter 1:4-8
Psalm 62:1, 2, 5-8

BUNESSAN 5.5.5.4.D.

1. Morn-ing has bro - ken Like the first morn - ing; Black-bird has
2. Sweet the rain's new fall Sun - lit from heav - en, Like the first
3. Mine is the sun - light! Mine is the morn - ing Born of the

spo - ken Like the first bird. Praise for the sing - ing!
dew fall On the first grass. Praise for the sweet - ness
one light E - den saw play! Praise with e - la - tion,

Praise for the morn - ing! Praise for them, spring-ing Fresh from the Word!
Of the wet gar - den, Sprung in com-plete-ness Where his feet pass.
Praise ev -ery morn - ing, God's re -cre - a - tion Of the new day!

Text: Eleanor Farjeon, 1881-1965. Used by permission of David Higham Associates Ltd.
Tune: Gaelic melody; harm. by David Evans, 1874-1948; from *The Revised Church Hymnary* by permission of Oxford University Press.

All Glory, Laud, and Honor

23

Mark 11:9-12 (9, 10)
II Nephi 3:61, 65, 66

ST. THEODULPH 7.6.7.6.D.

1. All glo - ry, laud, and hon - or To thee, Re - deem - er, King,
2. The com - pa - ny of an - gels Are prais - ing thee on high,
3. To thee, be - fore thy pas - sion, They sang their hymns of praise;

To whom the lips of chil - dren Made sweet ho - san - nas ring.
Cre - a - tion and all mor - tals In cho - rus make re - ply.
To thee, now high ex - alt - ed, Our mel - o - dy we raise.

Thou art the King of Is - rael, Thou Da - vid's roy - al Son,
The mul - ti - tude of peo - ple With palms be - fore thee went;
Thou didst ac - cept their prais - es; Ac - cept the praise we bring,

Who in the Lord's name com - est, The King and Bless - ed One.
Our praise and prayer and an - thems Be - fore thee we pre - sent.
Who in all good de - light - est, Thou good and gra - cious King.

Text: Theodulph of Orleans, c. 760-821; trans. by John M. Neale, 1818-1866, alt.
Tune: Melchior Teschner, 1584-1635.

24 Blest Be Thou, O God of Israel

I Chronicles 29:10, 11
II Nephi 6:41, 42

NORMAN 8.7.8.7.

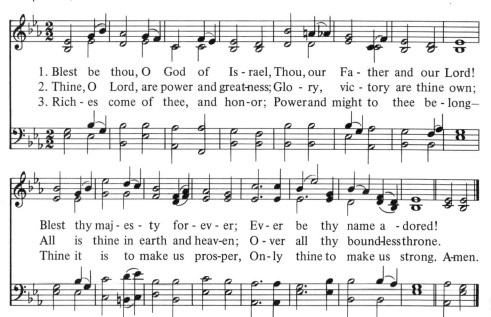

1. Blest be thou, O God of Is - rael, Thou, our Fa - ther and our Lord!
2. Thine, O Lord, are power and great-ness; Glo - ry, vic - tory are thine own;
3. Rich - es come of thee, and hon-or; Power and might to thee be - long—

Blest thy maj - es - ty for - ev - er; Ev - er be thy name a - dored!
All is thine in earth and heav-en; O - ver all thy bound-less throne.
Thine it is to make us pros-per, On-ly thine to make us strong. A-men.

Text: Attr. to Henry U. Onderdonk, 1789-1858.
Tune: Mark H. Forscutt, 1834-1903.

25 The Lord Jehovah Reigns

Psalm 47:1-7
I Nephi 5:126, 127, 130

SUTHERLAND 6.6.6.6.8.8.

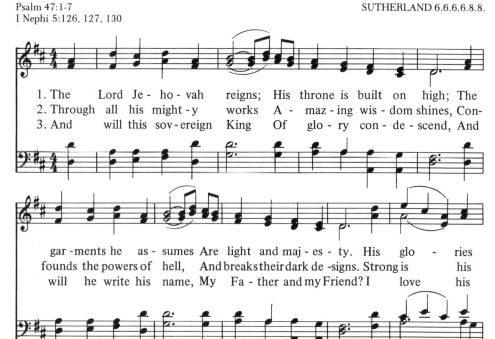

1. The Lord Je - ho - vah reigns; His throne is built on high; The
2. Through all his might - y works A - maz - ing wis - dom shines, Con-
3. And will this sov - ereign King Of glo - ry con - de - scend, And

gar -ments he as - sumes Are light and maj - es - ty. His glo - ries
founds the powers of hell, And breaks their dark de -signs. Strong is his
will he write his name, My Fa - ther and my Friend? I love his

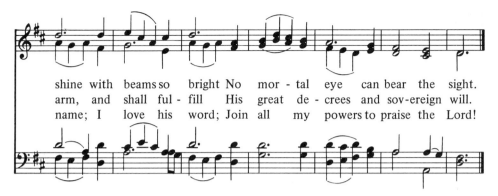

shine with beams so bright No mor - tal eye can bear the sight.
arm, and shall ful - fill His great de - crees and sov-ereign will.
name; I love his word; Join all my powers to praise the Lord!

Text: Isaac Watts, 1674-1748.
Tune: William B. Bradbury, 1816-1868.

Lord, May Our Hearts Be Tuned to Sing   26

Psalm 96:7-9
Alma 14:97

GRATEFULNESS L.M.

1. Lord, may our hearts be tuned to sing Thy great and
2. Great God, thy good - ness we a - dore; Help us to
3. Our sa - cred vows we now re - new, Our lives a -

ev - er - last - ing praise, Our will - ing hands an of - fering
sing thy bound-less love, Own thee as God for - ev - er -
fresh to thee de - vote; Help us to keep each prom - ise

bring To thee on this the chief of days.
more, And swell thy praise in realms a - bove.
true, And seek thy glo - ry to pro - mote. A - men.

Text: Charles Derry, 1826-1921.
Tune: Mary A. Bradford, 1821-1902.

27

Psalm 145:9, 10
D. and C. 76:1

O Worship the King

LYONS 10.10.11.11.
Alternate hymn: 28

1. O wor - ship the King, all glo - rious a - bove,
2. His boun - ti - ful care what tongue can re - cite?
3. O tell of his might, O sing of his grace,

O grate - ful - ly sing his power and his love;
It breathes in the air, it shines in the light,
Whose robe is the light, whose can - o - py, space;

Our Shield and De - fend - er, the An - cient of Days,
It streams from the hills, it de - scends to the plain,
His mer - cies how ten - der, how firm to the end;

Pa - vil - ioned in splen - dor and gird - ed with praise.
And sweet - ly dis - tills in the dew and the rain.
Our Mak - er, De - fend - er, Re - deem - er, and Friend!

Text: Robert Grant, 1785-1838, alt.
Tune: J. Michael Haydn, 1737-1806.

O Worship the King

28

Psalm 145:9, 10
D. and C. 76:1

HANOVER 10.10.11.11.
Alternate hymn: 27

1. O wor - ship the King, all glo - rious a - bove,
2. His boun - ti - ful care what tongue can re - cite?
3. O tell of his might, O sing of his grace,

O grate - ful - ly sing his power and his love;
It breathes in the air, it shines in the light,
Whose robe is the light, whose can - o - py, space;

Our Shield and De - fend - er, the An - cient of Days,
It streams from the hills, it de - scends to the plain,
His mer - cies how ten - der, how firm to the end;

Pa - vil - ioned in splen - dor and gird - ed with praise.
And sweet - ly dis - tills in the dew and the rain.
Our Mak - er, De - fend - er, Re - deem - er and Friend!

Text: Robert Grant, 1785-1838, alt.
Tune: William Croft, 1678-1727.

29

With Happy Voices Ringing

D. and C. 85:17, 18
II Nephi 5:90, 91

FAITHFUL 7.6.7.6.D.

1. With hap - py voic - es ring - ing, Thy chil - dren, Lord, ap - pear,
2. What though no eye be - holds thee, No hand thy touch may feel,
3. And shall we not a - dore thee With more than joy - ous song,

Their joy - ous prais - es bring - ing In an - thems full and clear.
Thy u - ni - verse un - folds thee, Thy star - ry heavens re - veal.
And live in truth be - fore thee, All beau - ti - ful and strong?

For skies of gold - en splen - dor, For az - ure roll - ing sea,
The earth and all its glo - ry, Our homes and all we love,
Lord, bless our souls' en - deav - or Thy ser - vants true to be,

For blos - soms sweet and ten - der, O Lord, we wor - ship thee.
Tell forth the won - drous sto - ry Of One who reigns a - bove.
And through all life, for - ev - er, To live our praise to thee. A - men.

Text: William G. Tarrant, 1853-1928.
Tune: Johann Sebastian Bach, 1685-1750.

Let All the World in Every Corner Sing

30

Psalm 149:1, 2
II Nephi 9:136, 137

LIVINGSTON 10.4.6.6.6.6.10.4.

1. Let all the world in ev-ery cor-ner sing, My God and King!
2. Let all the world in ev-ery cor-ner sing, My God and King!

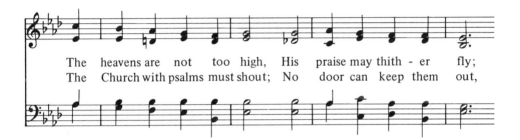

The heavens are not too high, His praise may thith - er fly;
The Church with psalms must shout; No door can keep them out,

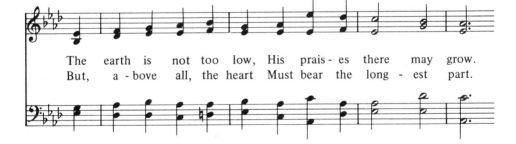

The earth is not too low, His prais - es there may grow.
But, a - bove all, the heart Must bear the long - est part.

Let all the world in ev - ery cor - ner sing, My God and King!
Let all the world in ev - ery cor - ner sing, My God and King!

Text: George Herbert, 1593-1632.
Tune: Franklyn S. Weddle, 1905- . Copyright 1956 by Herald Publishing House.

31 Come Thou Fount of Every Blessing

D. and C. 83:17c
Psalm 135:1-3

NETTLETON 8.7.8.7.D.

1. Come thou Fount of ev - ery bless-ing, Tune my heart to sing thy grace;
2. Here I raise mine Eb - en - e - zer; Hith - er by thy help I'm come;
3. Oh, to grace how great a debt- or Dai -ly I'm con-strained to be!

Streams of mer - cy, nev - er ceas - ing, Call for songs of loud-est praise.
And I hope, by thy good pleas - ure, Safe- ly to ar - rive at home.
Let thy good - ness like a fet - ter Bind my wan -dering heart to thee.

Teach me some me - lo - dious son - net Sung by flam - ing tongues a-bove;
Je - sus sought me when a stran-ger, Wan- dering from the fold of God;
Prone to wan - der, Lord, I feel it, Prone to leave the God I love;

Praise the mount-I'm fixed up-on it—Mount of thy re-deem-ing love.
He, to res - cue me from dan -ger, In - ter-posed his pre-cious blood.
Here's my heart, O take and seal it, Seal it for thy courts a - bove. A-men.

Text: Robert Robinson, 1735-1790.
Tune: John Wyeth, 1770-1858.

Immortal, Invisible, God Only Wise

32

Colossians 1:2, 14-17
D. and C. 85:16, 18

ST. DENIO 11.11.11.11.

1. Im - mor - tal, in - vis - i - ble, God on - ly wise,
2. Un - rest - ing, un - hast - ing, and si - lent as light,
3. To all, life thou giv - est— to both great and small;
4. Thou dwell - est in glo - ry, thou reign - est in light;

In light in - ac - ces - si - ble hid from our eyes,
Nor want - ing, nor wast - ing, thou rul - est in might,
In all life thou liv - est, the true life of all;
Thine an - gels a - dore thee, all veil - ing their sight;

Most bless - ed, most glo - rious, the An - cient of Days,
Thy jus - tice like moun - tains high soar - ing a - bove
We blos - som and flour - ish as leaves on the tree,
All praise we should ren - der; O help us to see

Al - might - y, vic - to - rious, thy great name we praise.
Thy clouds which are foun - tains of good - ness and love.
And with - er and per - ish— but naught chang - eth thee.
'Tis on - ly the splen - dor of light hid - eth thee!

Text: Walter Chalmers Smith, 1825-1908, alt.
Tune: Welsh Hymn Melody, John Roberts' *Canaidau y Cyssegr*, 1839.

33 The Spirit of God Like a Fire Is Burning

III Nephi 8:25, 26
D. and C. 85:18

PARACLETE 12.11.12.11. with refrain

1. The Spir - it of God like a fire is burn - ing;
2. The Lord is ex - tend - ing his saints' un - der - stand - ing,
3. We call in our sol - emn as - sem - blies, in spir - it,

The lat - ter - day glo - ry be - gins to come forth;
Re - stor - ing their judg - es and all as at first;
To spread forth the king - dom of heav - en a - broad,

The vi - sions and bless - ings of old are re - turn - ing;
The knowl - edge and pow - er of God are ex - pand - ing;
That we through our faith may be - gin to in - her - it

The an - gels are com - ing to vis - it the earth.
The veil o'er the earth is be - gin - ning to burst.
The vi - sions and bless - ings and glo - ries of God.

Refrain

We'll sing and we'll shout with the ar - mies of heav - en,

"Ho - san - nah, ho - san - nah, to God and the Lamb!" Let

glo - ry to them in the high - est be giv - en

Hence - forth and for - ev - er! A - men, and a - men!

Text: W. W. Phelps, 1792-1872.
Tune: English Tune.

Sung at the dedication of Kirtland Temple.

34

Hosanna to the Lamb

Matthew 21:7, 13 (9, 15)
Mark 11:10

TANDY 6.7.

Ho - san - na   to the Lamb, Al - le - lu - i - a, _____ A - men.

Text and Tune: F. Phillip Tandy, 1943 - ; copyright 1980 Reorganized Church of Jesus Christ of Latter Day Saints.

35

When Morning Gilds the Skies

Alma 14:88
Revelation 5:13

LAUDES DOMINI 6.6.6.D.

1. When morn - ing gilds the   skies,   My   heart a - wak - ing   cries,
2. Let   earth's wide cir - cle   round   In   joy - ful notes re - sound,
3. Be   this, while life   is   mine,   My   can - ti - cle   di - vine,

May Je - sus Christ   be   praised; A - like   at   work   and   prayer
May Je - sus Christ   be   praised! Let   air   and   sea   and   sky
May Je - sus Christ   be   praised; Be   this   the e - ter - nal   song

To   Je - sus   I   re - pair;   May   Je - sus Christ   be   praised!
From   depth to height re - ply,   May   Je - sus Christ   be   praised!
Through   all   the   a - ges   long,   May   Je - sus Christ   be   praised!

Text: From the German, 19th century; trans. Edward Caswall, 1814-1878.
Tune: Joseph Barnby, 1838-1896.

Rejoice, Ye Saints of Latter Days

36

Isaiah 60:1-3
D. and C. 85:2

SAINTLY PRAISE C.M.D.

1. Re-joice, ye Saints of lat-ter days, Lift up your heads and sing!
2. The Ho-ly Spir-it is sent down As in the days of old

With one ac-cord u-nite to praise Your ev-er-last-ing King.
To bring to mind things that are past And things to come un-fold.

No more in dark-ness need you walk, Nor tread in er-ror's night,
Oh, may it rest up-on us now While we're as-sem-bled here,

Refrain after second stanza only.
Oh, may it ev-er guide our feet In ways of right-eous-ness

For the Most High a-gain has called The dark-ness in-to light.
Bring con-so-la-tion to our souls, Our droop-ing spir-its cheer.

That we may be ac-count-ed meet To dwell in bless-ed-ness.

Text: Old Edition.
Tune: Old Tune.

37 Come, Ye Thankful People, Come

D. and C. 46:9
James 1:17

BENEVENTO 7.7.7.7.D.
Alternate hymn:38

1. Come, ye thank-ful peo-ple, come, Raise the song of har-vest home.
2. All the bless-ings of the field, All the stores the gar-dens yield,
3. These to thee, our God, we owe, Source whence all our bless-ings flow,

All is safe-ly gath-ered in Ere the win-ter storms be-gin;
All the fruits in full sup-ply, Rip-ened 'neath the sum-mer sky,
And for these our souls shall raise Grate-ful vows and sol-emn praise.

God, our Mak-er, doth pro-vide For our wants to be sup-plied;
All that spring with boun-teous hand Scat-ters o'er the smil-ing land,
Come, then, thank-ful peo-ple, come, Raise the song of har-vest home;

Come to God's own tem-ple, come, Raise the song of har-vest home.
All that lib-eral au-tumn pours From her rich o'er-flow-ing stores—
Come to God's own tem-ple, come, Raise the song of har-vest home.

Text: Henry Alford, 1810-1871; alt. by Hugh Hartshorne, 1915.
Tune: Samuel Webbe, 1740-1816.

Come, Ye Thankful People, Come

38

D. and C. 46:9
James 1:17

ST. GEORGE'S WINDSOR 7.7.7.7.D.
Alternate hymn: 37

1. Come, ye thank-ful peo-ple, come, Raise the song of har-vest home.
2. All the bless-ings of the field, All the stores the gar-dens yield,
3. These to thee, our God, we owe, Source whence all our bless-ings flow,

All is safe-ly gath-ered in Ere the win-ter storms be-gin;
All the fruits in full sup-ply, Rip-ened 'neath the sum-mer sky,
And for these our souls shall raise Grate-ful vows and sol-emn praise.

God, our Ma-ker, doth pro-vide For our wants to be sup-plied;
All that spring with boun-teous hand Scat-ters o'er the smil-ing land,
Come, then, thank-ful peo-ple, come, Raise the song of har-vest home;

Come to God's own tem-ple, come, Raise the song of har-vest home.
All that lib-eral au-tumn pours From her rich o'er-flow-ing stores—
Come to God's own tem-ple, come, Raise the song of har-vest home.

Text: Henry Alford, 1810-1871; alt. by Hugh Hartshorne, 1915.
Tune: George J. Elvey, 1816-1893.

39
God Himself Is with Us

Zechariah 2:13
Habakkuk 2:20

WUNDERBARER KÖNIG (Arnsberg) 6.6.8.6.6.8.6.6.6.

God him-self is with us: Let us now a-dore him, And with awe ap-pear be-fore him. God is in his tem - ple: All with-in keep si - lence, And be-fore him bow with rev - erence. Him a - lone, God we own; To our Lord and Sav - ior Prais - es sing for - ev - er.

Text: Gerhard Tersteegen, 1697-1769; tr. composite.
Tune: Joachim Neander, 1650-1680.

Sing Praise to God, Who Reigns Supreme

40

Alma 21:2
Psalm 66:1,2

MIT FREUDEN ZART 8.7.8.7.8.8.7.

This hymn is most effectively sung at a steady tempo and in a stately manner.

1. Sing praise to God, who reigns su-preme, the au-thor of cre - a - tion,
2. All you who name Christ's ho-ly name, give God all praise and glo - ry;

The God of power, the God of love, the God of our sal - va - tion;
All you who own his power pro-claim a - loud the won - drous sto - ry!

With - in the king - dom of his might All things are just and
Cast each false i - dol from its throne; The Lord is God, the

good and right: To God all praise and glo - ry.
Lord a - lone: To God all praise and glo - ry. A - men.

Text: Johann J. Schutz, 1640-1690; trans. F. E. Cox, 1812-1897; rev. Barbara McFarlane Higdon, 1930 -; Copyright 1980 Reorganized Church of Jesus Christ of Latter Day Saints.
Tune: Bohemian Brethren's *Kirchengesänge,* 1566.

41 Praise, My Soul, the King of Heaven

Titus 3:3-7
Jacob 3:9-16

LAUDA ANIMA 8.7.8.7.8.7.

This hymn has three settings. The second (four-part) setting may be used for all stanzas.

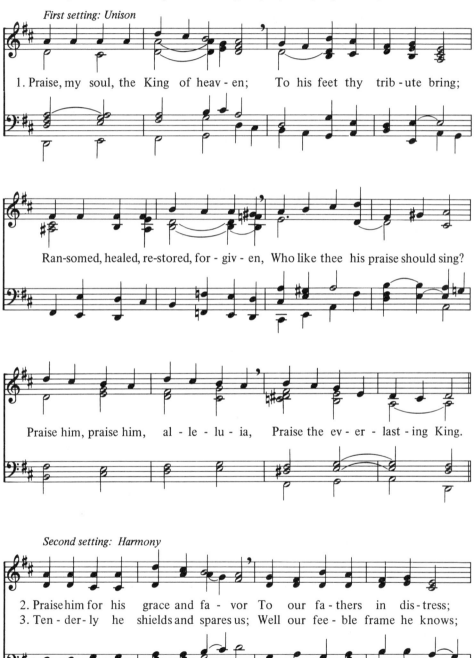

First setting: Unison

1. Praise, my soul, the King of heav-en; To his feet thy trib-ute bring;

Ran-somed, healed, re-stored, for-giv-en, Who like thee his praise should sing?

Praise him, praise him, al-le-lu-ia, Praise the ev-er-last-ing King.

Second setting: Harmony

2. Praise him for his grace and fa-vor To our fa-thers in dis-tress;
3. Ten-der-ly he shields and spares us; Well our fee-ble frame he knows;

Praise him, still the same for - ev - er, Slow to chide and swift to bless;
In his hands he gent - ly bears us, Res - cues us from all our foes:

Praise him, praise him, al - le - lu - ia, Glo - rious in his faith - ful - ness.
Praise him, praise him, al - le - lu - ia, Wide - ly as his mer - cy flows.

Third setting

4. An - gels, help us to a - dore him: Ye be - hold him face to face;

Sun and moon bow down be - fore him: Dwell-ers all in time and space,

Praise him, praise him, al - le - lu - ia, Praise with us the God of grace.

Text: Henry Francis Lyte, 1793-1847.
Tune: John Goss, 1800-1880.

42   O Sing the Mighty Power of God

Genesis 1:3, 12, 19, 20, 29 (9, 16-18, 26)
Mormon 4:77, 78

BRIDGMAN C.M.

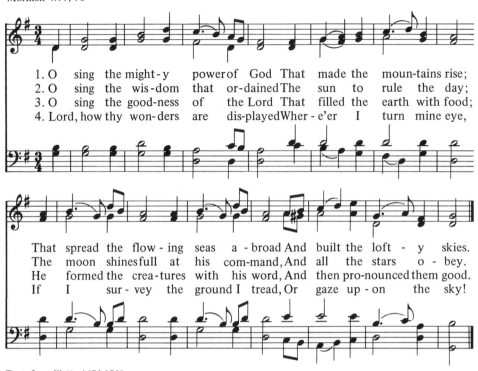

1. O sing the might-y power of God That made the moun-tains rise;
2. O sing the wis-dom that or-dained The sun to rule the day;
3. O sing the good-ness of the Lord That filled the earth with food;
4. Lord, how thy won-ders are dis-played Wher - e'er I turn mine eye,

That spread the flow - ing seas a - broad And built the loft - y skies.
The moon shines full at his com-mand, And all the stars o - bey.
He formed the crea-tures with his word, And then pro-nounced them good.
If I sur - vey the ground I tread, Or gaze up - on the sky!

Text: Isaac Watts, 1674-1748.
Tune: Ludwig van Beethoven, 1770-1827; arr. George Kingsley, 1811-1884.

43   Praise God, from Whom All Blessings Flow

Psalm 69:34
I Chronicles 16:31

OLD HUNDREDTH L.M.

Praise God, from whom all bless-ings flow; Praise him, all crea-tures here be - low;

Praise him a-bove, ye heav'n - ly host; Praise Fa-ther, Son, and Ho-ly Ghost. A-men.

Text: Thomas Ken, 1637-1711.
Tune: Genevan Psalter, 1551, attr. to Louis Bourgeois, c. 1510-1561.

Come, Rejoice Before Your Maker 44

II Nephi 9:133-137
Psalm 16:8, 9, 11

BRYN CALFARIA 8.7.8.7.4.4.4.7.7.
Alternate tune: HYMN OF PRAISE* (53)

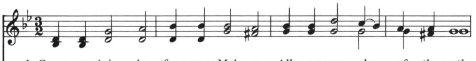

1. Come, re - joice be - fore your Mak - er, All you peo - ples of the earth;
2. Know for cer - tain that Je - ho - vah Is the true and on - ly God;
3. Come with grate - ful hearts be - fore Him; En - ter now His courts with praise;
4. For the Lord our God is gra - cious—Ev - er - last - ing in His love.

Serve the Lord your God with glad - ness; Come be - fore Him with a song!
We are His, for He has made us— We are sheep with - in His fold.
Show your thank-ful - ness to - ward Him; Give due hon - or to His name.
And to ev - ery gen - er - a - tion His great faith - ful - ness en - dures.

Al - le - lu - ia, Al - le - lu - ia, Al - le - lu - ia!

Come be -
We are
Give due
His great

fore Him with a song, Come be - fore Him with a song!
sheep with - in His fold, We are sheep with - in His fold.
hon - or to His name, Give due hon - or to His name.
faith - ful - ness en - dures, His great faith - ful - ness en - dures.

Text: Michael A. Baughen; copyright 1973 Church Pastoral Aid Society, England; GIA Publ., Inc., U. S. Agent.
Used by permission.
Tune: William Owen, 1814-1893.

* Sing first two lines only.

45

Day Is Dying in the West

D. and C. 6:10
Psalm 104:1-5

CHAUTAUQUA 7.7.7.7.4. with refrain

1. Day is dy - ing in the west; Heaven is touch - ing earth with rest; Wait and wor - ship while the night Sets the eve - ning lamps a - light Through all the sky.

2. Lord of life, be - neath the dome Of the u - ni - verse, thy home, Gath - er us who seek thy face To the fold of thine em - brace, For thou art nigh.

3. While the deepen - ing sha - dows fall, Heart of Love, en - fold - ing all, Through the glo - ry and the grace Of the stars that veil thy face, Our hearts as - cend.

Refrain

Ho - ly, ho - ly, ho - ly, Lord God of hosts! Heaven and earth are full of thee! Heaven and earth are prais - ing thee, O Lord most high!

Text: Mary A. Lathbury, 1841-1913.
Tune: William F. Sherwin, 1826-1888.

Sing to the Lord of Harvest

46

James 1:17
Psalm 103:1-4

WIE LIEBLICH IST DER MAIEN 7.6.7.6.D.

1. Sing to the Lord of har - vest, Sing songs of love and praise;
2. God makes the clouds bring fresh - ness, The des - erts bloom and spring,
3. Bring to this sa - cred al - tar The gifts his good - ness gave,

With joy - ful hearts and voic - es Our al - le - lu - ias raise.
The hills leap up in glad - ness, The val - leys laugh and sing.
The gold - en sheaves of har - vest, The souls Christ died to save.

By him the roll - ing sea - sons In fruit - ful or - der move;
God fills them with his full - ness, All things with large in - crease;
Our hearts lay down be - fore him When at his feet we fall,

Sing to the Lord of har - vest A joy - ous song of love.
He crowns the year with good - ness, With plen - ty and with peace.
And with our lives a - dore him Who gave his life for all.

Text: John S. B. Monsell, 1811-1875, alt.
Tune: Johann Steurlein, 1546-1613; arr. Rosalee Elser, 1925 - ; copyright 1980 Rosalee Elser; used by permission.

47 Praise to the Living God

Moroni 8:19
I Corinthians 8:6

LEONI 12.12.12.12.

1. Praise to the liv-ing God! All prais-ed be thy name
2. Thy Spir-it flow-eth free, high surg-ing where it will,
3. E-ter-nal life hast thou im-plant-ed in the soul;

Who e'er hast been and e'er shalt be, and still the same.
In proph-et's word re-vealed of old and liv-ing still.
Thy love shall be our strength and stay while a-ges roll.

The one e-ter-nal God ere aught that now ap-pears:
Es-tab-lished is thy law, and change-less it shall stand,
Praise to the liv-ing God, all prais-ed be thy name

The first, the last, be-yond all thought through time-less years!
Deep writ up-on the hu-man heart, on sea or land.
Who e'er hast been and e'er shalt be, and still the same.

Text: Based on the Yigdal of Daniel Ben Judah, 14th century; tr. Max Landsberg, 1845-1928, and Newton Mann, 1836-1926; alt.; used with permission of the Ecumenical Women's Center, Chicago, IL, *Because We Are One People.*
Tune: Hebrew Melody; arr. Meyer Lyon, 1751-1797.

Great and Marvelous Are Thy Works

48

Psalm 97:1, 6, 12
Romans 16:25-27

SING OF HIS MIGHTY LOVE L.M. with refrain

Unison (or harmony)

1. Great and mar-vel-ous are thy works, O Lord of hosts, al-might-y One!
2. Thou hast fash-ioned with thine own hand The earth be-low, the heavens a-bove;
3. O thou in-fi-nite, liv-ing God, Up-on us now thy Spir-it pour;

Earth and fir-ma-ment speak thy praise, Thy name is writ-ten in the sun.
Oh, how won-der-ful is thy power, And yet how ten-der is thy love.
We would wor-ship thee, laud and praise Thy ho-ly name for-ev-er-more.

Refrain

Sing of his might-y love, for it is won-der-ful;

Let his praise through all the earth re-sound; Hon-or and maj-es-ty

now and for-ev-er be Un-to God whose love and mer-cy have no bound.

Text: Charlotte G. Homer.
Tune: Charles H. Gabriel, 1856-1932.

49
Earth and All Stars

I Chronicles 16:23-29
Isaiah 61:10, 11

EARTH AND ALL STARS 9.7.9.7. with refrain

Unison (or harmony)

1. Earth and all stars, Loud rush-ing plan-ets
2. Hail, wind, and rain, Loud blow-ing snow-storm
3. Trum-pet and pipes, Loud clash-ing cym-bals
4. En-gines and steel, Loud pound-ing ham-mers

Sing to the

Lord a new song!

     O vic-to-ry, Loud shout-ing
Flow-ers and trees, Loud rus-tling
Harp, lute, and lyre, Loud hum-ming
Lime-stone and beams, Loud build-ing

ar - my
dry leaves
cel - los
work - men

Sing to the Lord a new song!

Refrain

He has done mar - vel - ous things.

I, too, will praise him with a new song!

Text: Herbert Brokering, 1926 - .
Tune: David N. Johnson, 1922 - .
Text and tune from *Twelve Folksongs and Spirituals*, copyright 1968 Augsburg Publishing House; used with permission.

From All That Dwell Below the Skies 50

Psalm 117   DUKE STREET L.M.
II Nephi 3:50

1. From all that dwell be - low the skies, Let the Cre -
2. E - ter - nal are thy mer - cies, Lord; E - ter - nal
3. Your loft - y themes, ye mor - tals, bring; Your songs of
4. In ev - ery land be - gin the song; To ev - ery

a - tor's praise a - rise; Let the Re - deem - er's
truth at - tends thy word: Thy praise shall sound from
praise di - vine - ly sing; The great sal - va - tion
land the strains be - long; In cheer - ful sound all

name be sung Through ev - ery land, by ev - ery tongue.
shore to shore, Till suns shall rise and set no more.
loud pro - claim, And shout for joy the Sav - ior's name.
voic - es raise, And fill the world with loud - est praise.

Text: Isaac Watts, 1674-1748, Sts. 1, 2; Sts. 3, 4 Anonymous.
Tune: John Hatton, (?)-1793.

51 Heaven and Earth and Sea and Air

Psalm 104:31-33
I Nephi 5:126, 130, 131

MAIDSTONE 7.7.7.7.D.

1. Heaven and earth and sea and air God's e - ter - nal praise de - clare;
2. See how earth, with beau - ty decked, Tells a heaven-ly Arch - i - tect;
3. See the bil - lows tum-bling o'er, Chaf-ing with in - ces - sant roar;

Up, my soul, a - wake and raise Grate - ful hymns and songs of praise.
Woods and fields, with low - ing kine, Show their Mak - er all di - vine.
Hear them as they sink and swell Loud their Mak - er's prais - es tell.

See the sun with glo - rious ray Pierce the clouds at open - ing day;
See the birds, how, pair by pair, Swift they cleave the yield - ing air;
Through the world, great God, I trace Won - ders of thy power and grace.

Moon and stars in splen-dor bright Praise their God through si - lent night.
Thun - der, light - ning, storm, and wind God doth at his will un - bind.
Write more deep - ly on my heart What I am, and what thou art.

Text: From Psalm 19 by Joachim Neander, 1650-1680; tr. by Frances Elizabeth Cox, 1812-1897.
Tune: Walter B. Gilbert, 1829-1910·

This Is My Father's World

Isaiah 41:10
D. and C. 98:5j

TERRA BEATA S.M.D.

1. This is my Fa-ther's world, And to my lis-tening ears
2. This is my Fa-ther's world; The birds their car-ols raise,
3. This is my Fa-ther's world; O let me ne'er for-get

All na-ture sings, and round me rings The mu-sic of the spheres.
The morn-ing light, the o-cean's might De-clare their Mak-er's praise.
That though the wrong seems oft so strong, God is the Rul-er yet.

This is my Fa-ther's world; I rest me in the thought
This is my Fa-ther's world; He moves in all I see.
This is my Fa-ther's world; Why should my heart be sad?

Of rocks and trees, of skies and seas, His hand the won-ders wrought.
In rus-tling grass I hear him pass; He's al-ways near to me.
The Lord is King, let the heav-ens ring; God reigns, let earth be glad!

Text: Maltbie D. Babcock, 1858-1901.
Tune: Traditional English Melody, adapted by Franklin L. Sheppard, 1852-1930.

53 Hallelujah! Hallelujah!

Psalm 150
II Chronicles 5:13

HYMN OF PRAISE 8.7.8.7.

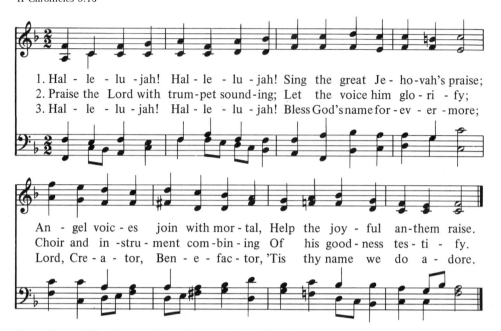

1. Hal - le - lu - jah! Hal - le - lu - jah! Sing the great Je - ho-vah's praise;
2. Praise the Lord with trum-pet sound-ing; Let the voice him glo - ri - fy;
3. Hal - le - lu - jah! Hal - le - lu - jah! Bless God's name for - ev - er -more;

An - gel voic - es join with mor - tal, Help the joy - ful an-them raise.
Choir and in -stru - ment com - bin - ing Of his good - ness tes - ti - fy.
Lord, Cre - a - tor, Ben - e - fac - tor, 'Tis thy name we do a - dore.

Text and Tune: William Graves, 1915 - ; alt.; copyright 1956 Herald Publishing House.

54 Come, Thou Almighty King

I Timothy 1:15-17
John 4:25, 26 (23, 24)

ITALIAN HYMN 6.6.4.6.6.6.4.

1. Come, thou Al - might - y King, Help us thy name to sing,
2. Je - sus, our Lord, come near; In ris - en glo - ry ap - pear.
3. Come, Ho - ly Com - fort - er, Thy sa - cred wit - ness bear

Help us to praise! Fa - ther all glo - ri - ous, O'er all vic -
With sweet ac - cord May thy re - deem - ing grace Be known in
In this glad hour; Thou who Al - might - y art, Now rule in

to - ri - ous, Come and reign o - ver us, Al - pha of Days!
ev - ery place Till all cre - a - tion's face Hon - ors its Lord.
ev - ery heart, And ne'er from us de - part, Spir - it of power.

Text: Ascribed to Charles Wesley, 1707-1788, Sts. 1, 3; Geoffrey F. Spencer, 1927 - , St. 2, copyright 1980 Reorganized Church of Jesus Christ of Latter Day Saints.
Tune: Felice de Giardini, 1716-1796.

Sing to the Lord a Joyful Song 55

Revelation 19:1, 5, 6
Romans 11:33-36

AGINCOURT L.M.

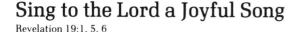

Unison

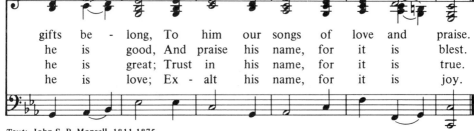

1. Sing to the Lord a joy - ful song; Lift up
2. For life and love, for home and food, For dai -
3. For strength to those who on him wait His truth
4. For joys un - told, that from a - bove Cheer those

your hearts, your voic - es raise; To us his gra - cious
ly help and night - ly rest, Sing to the Lord, for
to prove, his will to do, Praise ye our God, for
who love his high em - ploy, Sing to our God, for

gifts be - long, To him our songs of love and praise.
he is good, And praise his name, for it is blest.
he is great; Trust in his name, for it is true.
he is love; Ex - alt his name, for it is joy.

Text: John S. B. Monsell, 1811-1875.
Tune: "The Agincourt Song," 15th Century.

56

Holy, Holy, Holy! Lord God Almighty

Isaiah 6:1-5
Omni 1:46, 47

NICAEA 11.12.12.10.

1. Ho - ly, ho - ly, ho - ly! Lord God Al - might - y!
2. Ho - ly, ho - ly, ho - ly! All the saints a - dore thee,
3. Ho - ly, ho - ly, ho - ly! Though dark - ness hide thee,
4. Ho - ly, ho - ly, ho - ly! Lord God Al - might - y!

Ear - ly in the morn - ing our song shall rise to thee;
Cast - ing down their gold - en crowns a - round the glass - y sea;
Though the eye made blind by sin thy glo - ry may not see,
All thy works shall praise thy name in earth and sky and sea;

Ho - ly, ho - ly, ho - ly, mer - ci - ful and might - y!
Cher - u - bim and ser - a - phim fall - ing down be - fore thee,
On - ly thou art ho - ly, there is none be - side thee,
Ho - ly, ho - ly, ho - ly, mer - ci - ful and might - y!

God in Three Per - sons, bless - ed Trin - i - ty!
Which wert and art and ev - er - more shalt be.
Per - fect in power, in love, and pu - ri - ty.
God in Three Per - sons, bless - ed Trin - i - ty! A - men.

Text: Reginald Heber, 1783-1826, alt.
Tune: John B. Dykes, 1823-1876.

Holy, Holy, Holy Is the Lord

57

Isaiah 12:2-6
Psalm 97:1, 6, 9, 11, 12

SABAOTH 9.10.9.D. with refrain

1. Ho - ly, ho - ly, ho - ly is the Lord! Sing, O ye peo - ple, glad - ly a - dore him; Let the moun - tains trem - ble at his word; Let the hills be joy - ful be - fore him. Might - y in wis - dom, bound - less in mer - cy, Great is Je - ho - vah, king o - ver all.

2. Praise him, praise him! Shout a - loud for joy! Chil - dren of Zi - on, her - ald the sto - ry; Sin and death his king - dom shall de - stroy; All the earth shall sing of his glo - ry. Praise him, ye an - gels, ye who be - hold him Robed in his splen - dor, match - less, di - vine.

Refrain *a tempo*

Ho - ly, ho - ly, ho - ly is the Lord! Let the hills be joy - ful be - fore him.

Text: Fanny J. Crosby, 1820-1915, alt.
Tune: William B. Bradbury, 1816-1868.

58

Now in This Moment

Romans 5:1-5
D. and C. 85:16a-e

ASSURANCE 9.10.9.9 with refrain

Joyously

1. Now in this mo - ment, now in this day, God is cre -
2. Past, pre - sent, fu - ture, joy, sor - row, hope, We write the

at - ing and lead - ing the way; Life is be - hind us,
sto - ry, and life is its scope. God's love as - sures us

life is be - fore; We write the sto - ry not heard be - fore.
through the un - known, God's grace sus - tains us, we're not a - lone.

Refrain

This is our sto - ry, this is our song, Prais - ing our

Sav - ior all the day long. This is our sto - ry,

this is our song, Prais-ing our Sav - ior all the day long.

Text: Stanzas by Richard P. Howard, 1929 - , and Barbara Howard, 1930 - ; copyright 1980 Reorganized Church of Jesus Christ of Latter Day Saints. Refrain by Fanny J. Crosby, 1820-1915.
Tune: Phoebe P. Knapp, 1839-1908.

Great God, Attend While Zion Sings 59

Alma 14:88
Psalm 84:10-12

UXBRIDGE L.M.

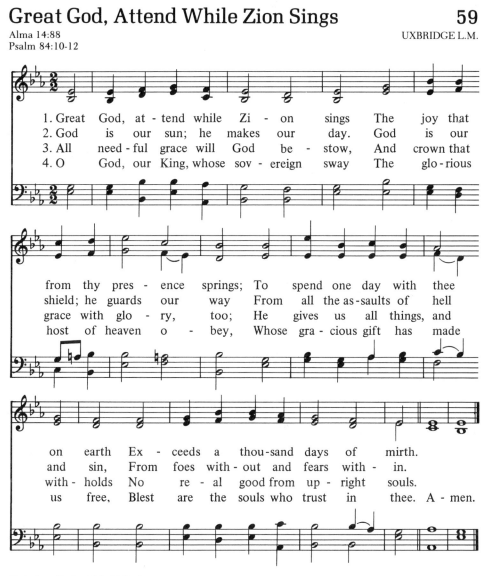

1. Great God, at - tend while Zi - on sings The joy that
2. God is our sun; he makes our day. God is our
3. All need - ful grace will God be - stow, And crown that
4. O God, our King, whose sov - ereign sway The glo - rious

from thy pres - ence springs; To spend one day with thee
shield; he guards our way From all the as - saults of hell
grace with glo - ry, too; He gives us all things, and
host of heaven o - bey, Whose gra - cious gift has made

on earth Ex - ceeds a thou-sand days of mirth.
and sin, From foes with - out and fears with - in.
with - holds No re - al good from up - right souls.
us free, Blest are the souls who trust in thee. A - men.

Text: Isaac Watts, 1674-1748; alt.
Tune: Lowell Mason, 1792-1872.

60

Now Thank We All Our God

Psalm 107:1-6
D. and C. 59:2d-h

NUN DANKET ALLE GOTT 6.7.6.7.6.6.6.6.

1. Now thank we all our God With heart and hands and voic - es,
2. Oh, may this boun -teous God Through all our life be near us,
3. All praise and thanks to God, The Fa - ther, now be giv - en,

Who won-drous things hath done, In whom his world re - joic - es,
With ev - er joy - ful hearts And bless- ed peace to cheer us;
The Son, and him who reigns With them in high - est heav - en,

Who from our moth - ers' arms Hath blessed us on our way
And keep us in his grace, And guide us when per - plexed,
The one e - ter - nal God, Whom earth and heaven a - dore;

With count - less gifts of love, And still is ours to - day.
And free us from all ills In this world and the next.
For thus it was, is now, And shall be ev - er - more.

Text: Martin Rinkart, 1586-1649; trans. by Catherine Winkworth, 1827-1878.
Tune: From *Praxis Pietatis Melica*, c. 1647, by Johann Crüger, 1598-1662.

My Soul, Praise the Lord

61

D. and C. 17:4a
Mosiah 2:13, 14

PADERBORN 10.10.11.11.

1. My soul, praise the Lord! O God, thou art great;
2. The earth where we dwell That journeys through space
3. O God, thou art great! My pleasure shall be

The earth and all things Thyself didst create.
Turns countries around To see the sun's face;
To muse on the good And greatness I see.

Thou laidst the foundation Of seas and of lands,
And high o'er the mountains The clouds gather rain
My full adoration I gladly shall give.

And stretched out the heavens As works of thy hand.
To drop o'er the valleys In blessings again.
My soul, praise the Lord now And long as I live.

Text: William Kethe, d. 1594. Alt. by Roy A. Cheville, 1897 - .
Tune: Paderborn 'Gesangbuch' 1765.

62

Praise Ye the Lord

Psalm 148
II Nephi 1:95

PRAISE L.M.
Alternate hymn: 63

1. Praise ye the Lord! 'Tis good to raise Your hearts and
2. He formed the stars, those heaven-ly flames; He counts their
3. Sing to the Lord! Ex - tol him high Who spreads his
4. He makes the grass the hills a - dorn, And clothes the
5. His saints are love - ly in his sight; He views his

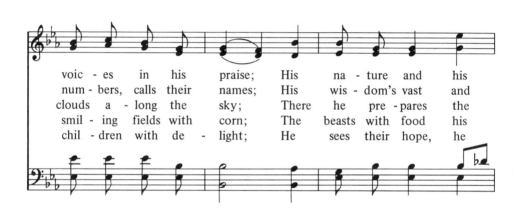

voic - es in his praise; His na - ture and his
num - bers, calls their names; His wis - dom's vast and
clouds a - long the sky; There he pre - pares the
smil - ing fields with corn; The beasts with food his
chil - dren with de - light; He sees their hope, he

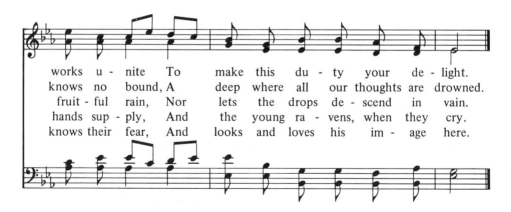

works u - nite To make this du - ty your de - light.
knows no bound, A deep where all our thoughts are drowned.
fruit - ful rain, Nor lets the drops de - scend in vain.
hands sup - ply, And the young ra - vens, when they cry.
knows their fear, And looks and loves his im - age here.

Text: Isaac Watts, 1674-1748.
Tune: Anonymous.

Praise Ye the Lord

63

Psalm 148
II Nephi 1:95

RIMINGTON L.M.
Alternate hymn: 62

1. Praise ye the Lord! 'Tis good to raise Your hearts and
2. He formed the stars, those heaven - ly flames; He counts their
3. Sing to the Lord! Ex - tol him high Who spreads his
4. He makes the grass the hills a - dorn, And clothes the
5. His saints are love - ly in his sight; He views his

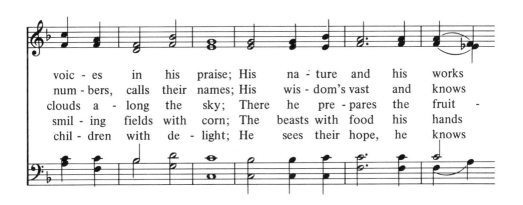

voic - es in his praise; His na - ture and his works
num - bers, calls their names; His wis - dom's vast and knows
clouds a - long the sky; There he pre - pares the fruit -
smil - ing fields with corn; The beasts with food his hands
chil - dren with de - light; He sees their hope, he knows

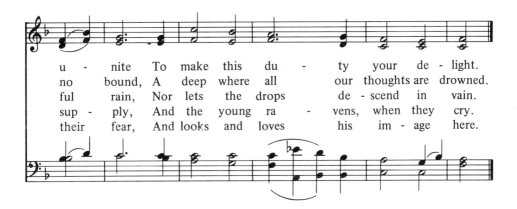

u - nite To make this du - ty your de - light.
no bound, A deep where all our thoughts are drowned.
ful rain, Nor lets the drops de - scend in vain.
sup - ply, And the young ra - vens, when they cry.
their fear, And looks and loves his im - age here.

Text: Isaac Watts, 1674-1748.
Tune: Francis Duckworth, 1862-1941; copyright; used by permission of Mrs. B. A. Duckworth.

64
O Jesus, the Giver of All We Enjoy

Ecclesiastes 5:19, 20
D. and C. 17:4a, b

O JESUS, THE GIVER 11.11.11.11.

1. O Jesus, the giver of all we enjoy,
2. With joy we remember the dawn of that day
3. We now are enlisted in Jesus' blest cause,

Our lives to thy honor we wish to employ;
When, led by the Spirit the truth to obey,
Divinely assisted to conquer his foes;

With praises unceasing we'll sing of thy name,
The light dawned upon us and filled us with love,
His grace will support us, his goodness we'll prove

Thy goodness ne'er ceasing, thy love we'll proclaim.
The Spirit's sure witness sent down from above.
In Zion's redemption through labors of love.

Text: W. W. Phelps, 1792-1872; stanza 3 adapted by Roy Cheville, 1897 - .
Tune: Ralph Bradshaw. Copyright 1927 by the Corporation of the President of the Church of Jesus Christ of Latter Day Saints. Adapted by Franklyn S. Weddle, 1905 - . Used by permission.

God of the Earth, the Sky, the Sea

65

Jacob 3:11-14
Psalm 139:7-10, 14

OLD 113th 8.8.8.D.

1. God of the earth, the sky, the sea! Mak - er of all
2. Thy love is in the sun - shine's glow; Thy life is in
3. We feel thy calm at eve - ning's hour, Thy gran - deur in

a - bove, be - low! Cre - a - tion lives and moves in thee;
the quick-ening air; When light - nings flash and storm winds blow,
the march of night; And when thy morn - ing breaks in power,

Thy pres - ent life through all doth flow.
There is thy power; thy law is there. We give thee thanks,
We hear thy word, "Let there be light."

Thy name we sing, Al - might - y Fa - ther, heaven-ly King. A - men.

Text: Samuel Longfellow, 1819-1892.
Tune: Strassburger Kirchenamt, 1525; probably by Matthäus Greiter, c. 1500-1552; harm. V. Earle Copes, 1921 - .
Harm. copyright 1964 Abingdon Press. Used by permission.

66 Praise the Lord, Ye Heavens, Adore Him

Psalm 19:1, 14
Isaiah 44:23

HYFRYDOL 8.7.8.7.D.

1. Praise the Lord, ye heavens, a - dore him; Praise him, an - gels, in the height;
2. Praise the Lord, for he is glo - rious; Nev - er shall his prom-ise fail:

Sun and moon, re - joice be - fore him; Praise him, all ye stars and light.
God hath made his saints vic- to - rious; Sin and death shall not pre-vail.

Praise the Lord, for he hath spo - ken; Worlds his might-y voice o - beyed;
Praise the God of our sal- va - tion; Hosts on high, his power pro-claim;

Laws which nev - er shall be bro - ken For their guid-ance hath he made.
Heaven and earth and all cre - a - tion Laud and mag - ni - fy his name.

Text: From Psalm 148. Foundling Hospital Collection, 1796.
Tune: Rowland Hugh Prichard, 1811-1887.

Praise to the Lord, the Almighty

67

Psalm 103:1, 2
Mosiah 2:18-20

LOBE DEN HERREN 14.14.4.7.8.

1. Praise to the Lord, the Al-might-y, the King of cre-a-tion! O my soul, praise him, for he is thy health and sal-va-tion! All ye who hear, Now to his tem-ple draw near, Praise him in glad ad-o-ra-tion!

2. Praise to the Lord, who doth pros-per thy work and de-fend thee; Sure-ly his good-ness and mer-cy here dai-ly at-tend thee! Pon-der a-new What the Al-might-y can do, If with his love he be-friend thee!

3. Praise to the Lord! O let all that is in me a-dore him! All that hath life and breath, come now with prais-es be-fore him! Let the A-men Sound from his peo-ple a-gain: Glad-ly for-ev-er a-dore him.

Text: Joachim Neander, 1650-1680; trans. by Catherine Winkworth, 1827-1878.
Tune: Stralsund Gesangbuch, 1665; harm. by F. S. Weddle, 1905 - , alt. Harm. copyright 1956 by Herald Publishing House.

68

Psalm 103:1, 2
Titus 2:13, 14

Praise Him, Praise Him

PRAISE HIM, PRAISE HIM 12.10.12.10.11.10. with refrain

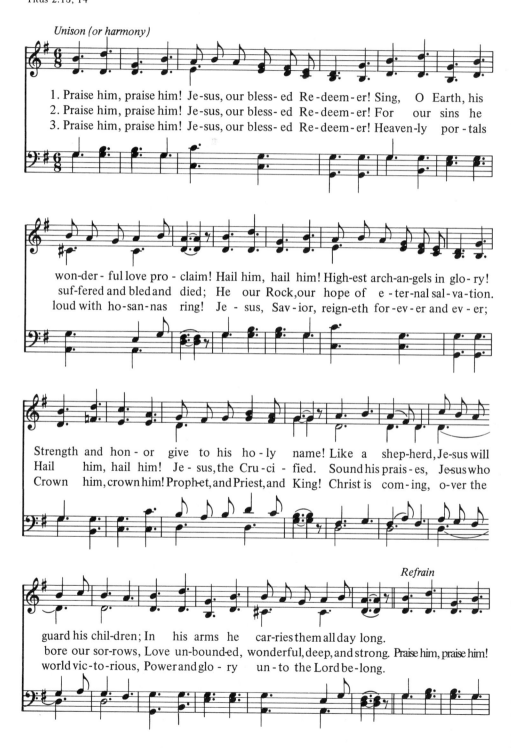

Unison (or harmony)

1. Praise him, praise him! Je-sus, our bless-ed Re-deem-er! Sing, O Earth, his
2. Praise him, praise him! Je-sus, our bless-ed Re-deem-er! For our sins he
3. Praise him, praise him! Je-sus, our bless-ed Re-deem-er! Heaven-ly por-tals

won-der-ful love pro-claim! Hail him, hail him! High-est arch-an-gels in glo-ry!
suf-fered and bled and died; He our Rock, our hope of e-ter-nal sal-va-tion.
loud with ho-san-nas ring! Je-sus, Sav-ior, reign-eth for-ev-er and ev-er;

Strength and hon-or give to his ho-ly name! Like a shep-herd, Je-sus will
Hail him, hail him! Je-sus, the Cru-ci-fied. Sound his prais-es, Je-sus who
Crown him, crown him! Proph-et, and Priest, and King! Christ is com-ing, o-ver the

Refrain

guard his chil-dren; In his arms he car-ries them all day long.
bore our sor-rows, Love un-bound-ed, wonderful, deep, and strong. Praise him, praise him!
world vic-to-rious, Power and glo-ry un-to the Lord be-long.

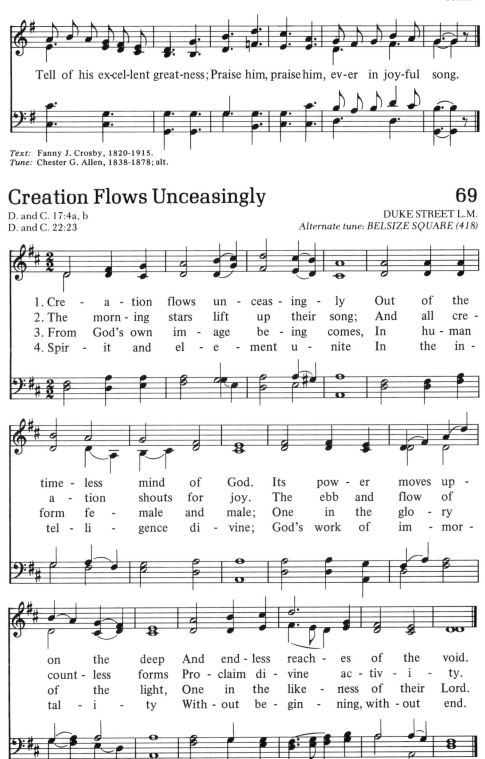

Tell of his ex-cel-lent great-ness; Praise him, praise him, ev-er in joy-ful song.

Text: Fanny J. Crosby, 1820-1915.
Tune: Chester G. Allen, 1838-1878; alt.

Creation Flows Unceasingly 69

D. and C. 17:4a, b
D. and C. 22:23

DUKE STREET L.M.
Alternate tune: BELSIZE SQUARE (418)

1. Cre - a - tion flows un - ceas - ing - ly Out of the
2. The morn - ing stars lift up their song; And all cre -
3. From God's own im - age be - ing comes, In hu - man
4. Spir - it and el - e - ment u - nite In the in -

time - less mind of God. Its pow - er moves up -
a - tion shouts for joy. The ebb and flow of
form fe - male and male; One in the glo - ry
tel - li - gence di - vine; God's work of im - mor -

on the deep And end - less reach - es of the void.
count - less forms Pro - claim di - vine ac - tiv - i - ty.
of the light, One in the like - ness of their Lord.
tal - i - ty With - out be - gin - ning, with - out end.

Text: Barbara McFarlane Higdon, 1930 - ; copyright 1980 Reorganized Church of Jesus Christ of Latter Day Saints.
Tune: John C. Hatton, ?-1793.

70   All Hail the Power of Jesus' Name

Isaiah 11:1, 2
Philippians 2:9-11

DIADEM 8.6.6.8. with refrain
Alternate hymn: 71

1. All hail the power of Je - sus' name! Let an-gels pros-trate fall; Let an - gels pros - trate fall; Bring forth the roy - al di - a - dem
2. Crown him, ye mar - tyrs of our God, Who from his al -tar call; Who from his al - tar call; Ex - tol the stem of Jes - se's rod
3. Ye cho - sen seed of Is - rael's race, Ye rem-nant weak and small, Ye rem - nant weak and small, Hail him who saves you by his grace
4. Let ev - ery kin - dred, ev - ery tribe On this ter-res-trial ball, On this ter - res - trial ball, To him all maj - es - ty as - cribe
5. Oh, that with yon - der sa - cred throng We at his feet may fall! We at his feet may fall! We'll join the ev - er- last - ing song

And crown ____ him,
And crown him, crown him, crown him, crown him, crown ____

crown him, crown him, crown him, And crown him Lord of all.

____ him.

Text: Edward Perronet, 1726-1792.
Tune: James Ellor, 1819-1899.

All Hail the Power of Jesus' Name

71

Revelation 5:12, 13
I Chronicles 29:11-13

CORONATION 8.6.8.6.8.6.
Alternate hymn: 70

1. All hail the power of Je-sus' name! Let an-gels pros-trate fall!
2. Crown him, ye mar-tyrs of our God, Who from his al-tar call;
3. Ye cho-sen seed of Is-rael's race, Ye rem-nant weak and small,
4. Let ev-ery kin-dred, ev-ery tribe On this ter-res-trial ball
5. Oh, that with yon-der sa-cred throng We at his feet may fall!

Descant, stanzas 4 and 5

4. To him all maj-es-ty as-cribe And crown him Lord of all;
5. We'll join the ev-er-last-ing song And crown him Lord of all;

Bring forth the roy-al di-a-dem And crown him Lord of all;
Ex-tol the stem of Jes-se's rod And crown him Lord of all;
Hail him who saves you by his grace And crown him Lord of all;
To him all maj-es-ty as-cribe And crown him Lord of all;
We'll join the ev-er-last-ing song And crown him Lord of all;

To him all maj-es-ty as-cribe And crown him Lord of all.
We'll join the ev-er-last-ing song And crown him Lord of all.

Bring forth the roy-al di-a-dem And crown him Lord of all.
Ex-tol the stem of Jes-se's rod And crown him Lord of all.
Hail him who saves you by his grace And crown him Lord of all.
To him all maj-es-ty as-cribe And crown him Lord of all.
We'll join the ev-er-last-ing song And crown him Lord of all.

Text: Edward Perronet, 1726-1792.
Tune: Oliver Holden, 1765-1844; descant by Lawrence Curry, 1906 - ; descant copyright, 1941, by the Presbyterian Board of Christian Education; renewed, 1969; from *The Hymnal for Youth.* Used by permission of The Westminster Press.

72 All Creatures of Our God and King

Psalm 148
I Nephi 5:127, 128, 130, 131

LASST UNS ERFREUEN 8.8.8.8.8.6. with refrain

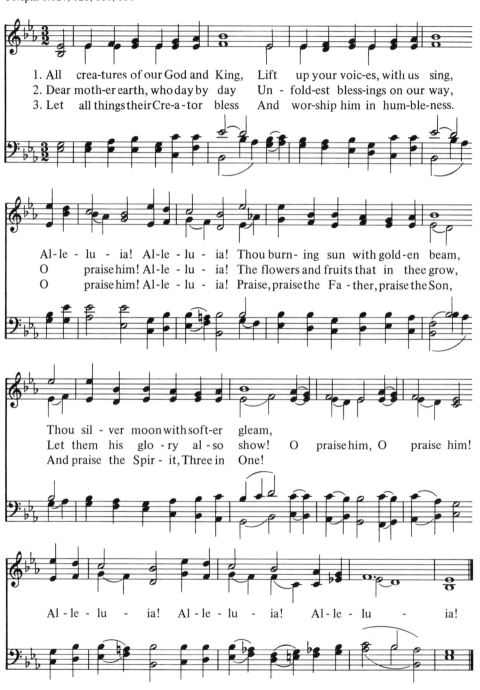

1. All crea-tures of our God and King, Lift up your voic-es, with us sing,
2. Dear moth-er earth, who day by day Un - fold-est bless-ings on our way,
3. Let all things their Cre-a-tor bless And wor-ship him in hum-ble-ness.

Al-le - lu - ia! Al-le - lu - ia! Thou burn- ing sun with gold-en beam,
O praise him! Al-le - lu - ia! The flowers and fruits that in thee grow,
O praise him! Al-le - lu - ia! Praise, praise the Fa - ther, praise the Son,

Thou sil - ver moon with soft-er gleam, O praise him, O praise him!
Let them his glo - ry al - so show!
And praise the Spir - it, Three in One!

Al - le - lu - ia! Al - le - lu - ia! Al - le - lu - ia!

Text: St. Francis of Assisi, 1182-1226; tr. William H. Draper, 1855-1933. Copyright J. Curwen & Sons. Used by permission of G. Schirmer, Inc.
Tune: Melody from *Geistliche Kirchengesäng*, Cologne, 1623; arr. & harm. Ralph Vaughan Williams, 1872-1958. From *The English Hymnal* by permission of Oxford University Press.

For the Fruits of All Creation

73

D. and C. 59:4
Matthew 9:43, 44 (37, 38)

EAST ACKLAM 8.4.8.4.8.8.8.4.

Unison (or harmony)

1. For the fruits of all cre - a - tion, thanks be to God;
2. In the just re - ward of la - bor, God's will is done;
3. For the har - vests of the Spir - it, thanks be to God;

For these gifts to ev - ery na - tion, thanks be to God;
In the help we give our neigh - bor, God's will is done;
For the good we all in - her - it, thanks be to God;

For the plough - ing, sow - ing, reap - ing, Si - lent growth while we are sleep - ing,
In our world - wide task of car - ing For the hun - gry and de - spair - ing,
For the won - ders that as - tound us, For the truths that still con - found us,

Fu - ture needs in earth's safe - keep - ing, thanks be to God!
In the har - vests we are shar - ing, God's will is done.
Most of all, that love has found us, thanks be to God!

Text: F. Pratt Green, 1903 - ; alt.; used by permission of Oxford University Press.
Tune: Francis Jackson, 1917 - ; used by permission of the composer.

74

Thank You for Giving Me the Morning

II Corinthians 9:15
Hebrews 13:15

THANK YOU 9.8.9.5.

After stanza 1, any number and order of stanzas is appropriate.

1. Thank You for giv-ing me the morn-ing; Thank You for ev-ery
2. Thank You— I have my oc-cu-pa-tion; Thank You for ev-ery
3. Thank You for man-y lit-tle sor-rows; Thank You for ev-ery

day that's new; Thank You that I can know my wor-ries
pleas-ure small; Thank You for mu-sic, light, and glad-ness;
kind-ly word; Thank You that ev-ery-where Your gui-dance

Can be cast on You.
Thank You for them all.
Reach-es ev-ery land.

4. Thank You— I see Your
5. Thank You, O Lord--You
6. Thank You, O Lord-Your

Word has mean-ing; Thank You— I know Your Spir-it here;
spoke un-to us; Thank You that for our words You care;
love is bound-less; Thank You that I am full of You;

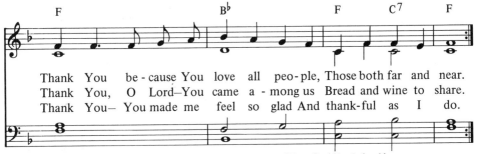

Thank You be-cause You love all peo-ple, Those both far and near.
Thank You, O Lord—You came a-mong us Bread and wine to share.
Thank You— You made me feel so glad And thank-ful as I do.

Text: Martin G. Schneider; English words by Walter Van Der Haas and Peter-Paul Van Lelyveld.
Tune: Martin G. Schneider.
© Copyright 1964, 1969 by Gustav Bosse Verlag, Regensburg, Germany. Assigned to Bosworth & Co. Ltd. for British Commonwealth and U. S. A. Sole selling agent—MCA Music, a division of MCA, Inc., N. Y., N. Y. Used by permission. All rights reserved.

For the Beauty of the Earth 75

II Nephi 9:135-137
Philippians 4:19, 20

DIX 7.7.7.7. with refrain

1. For the beau-ty of the earth, For the glo-ry of the skies,
2. For the joy of hu-man love, Broth-er, sis-ter, par-ent, child,
3. For thy church that ev-er-more Lift-eth ho-ly hands a-bove,
4. For thy-self, best Gift Di-vine To our race so free-ly given,

For the love which from our birth O-ver and a-round us lies:
Friends on earth and friends a-bove, For all gen-tle thoughts and mild:
Of-fering up on ev-ery shore Her pure sac-ri-fice of love:
For that great, great love of thine, Peace on earth, and joy in heaven:

Refrain

Lord of all, to thee we raise This our hymn of grate-ful praise. A-men.

Text: Folliot S. Pierpoint, 1835-1917.
Tune: Arr. from Conrad Kocher, 1786-1872, by W. H. Monk, 1823-1889.

76 We Plow the Fields and Scatter

Psalm 147:12-19
D. and C. 59:4

WIR PFLÜGEN 7.6.7.6.D with refrain

1. We plow the fields and scatter The good seed on the land,
2. He only is the Maker Of all things near and far;
3. We thank thee then, O Father, For all things bright and good:

But it is fed and watered By God's almighty hand.
He paints the wayside flower, He lights the evening star.
The seed-time and the harvest, Our life, our health, our food.

He sends the snow in winter, The warmth to swell the grain,
The winds and waves obey him, By him the birds are fed;
No gifts have we to offer For all thy love imparts,

The breezes and the sunshine, And soft, refreshing rain.
Much more to us, his children, He gives our daily bread.
But that which thou desirest, Our humble, thankful hearts.

All good gifts a - round us Are sent from heaven a - bove;

Then thank the Lord, O thank the Lord For all his love. A-men.

Text: Matthias Claudius, 1740-1815; tr. Jane M. Campbell, 1817-1878.
Tune: Johann A. P. Schulz, 1747-1800.

O Lord of Heaven and Earth and Sea 77

Acts 5:30, 31
D. and C. 17:5

ALMSGIVING 8.8.8.4.

1. O Lord of heaven and earth and sea, To thee all praise and glo -
2. Thou didst not spare thine on - ly Son, But gavest him for a world
3. For souls re - deemed, for sins for - given, For means of grace and hopes

ry be! How shall we show our love to thee, Who giv-est all?
un - done, And free-ly with that bless - ed One Thou giv-est all.
of heaven, What can to thee, O Lord, be given, Who giv-est all? A- men.

Text: Christopher Wordsworth, 1807-1885.
Tune: John B. Dykes, 1823-1876.

78 We Thank You, Lord, for Strength of Arm

I John 3:16-18
Psalm 92:1, 2

O JESU 8.4.8.4.8.8.

1. We thank you, Lord, for strength of arm To win our bread, And that, be-yond our need, is meat For friends un-fed: We thank you much for bread to live; We thank you more for bread to give.

2. We thank you, Lord, for shel-tered home In cold and storm, And that, be-yond our need, is room For friends for-lorn: We thank you much for place to rest, But more for shel-ter for our guest.

3. We thank you, Lord, for lav-ish love On us be-stowed, E-nough to share with love-less folk To ease their load: Your love to us we ill could spare, Yet dear-er is your love we share. A-men.

Text: Robert Davis, 1881-1950; alt.
Tune: Hirschberg Gesangbuch, 1741; Attr. to Johann Balthasar Reimann, 1702-1749; alt.

Contemplation and Renewal

Come Ye Apart

79

D. and C. 85:36
Mark 6:32, 33 (31, 32)

CHISHOLM 11.10.11.10.

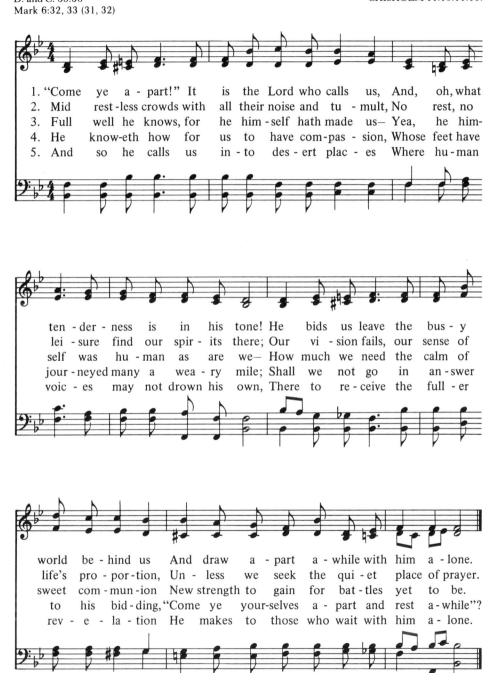

1. "Come ye a - part!" It is the Lord who calls us, And, oh, what ten - der - ness is in his tone! He bids us leave the bus - y world be - hind us And draw a - part a - while with him a - lone.

2. Mid rest - less crowds with all their noise and tu - mult, No rest, no lei - sure find our spir - its there; Our vi - sion fails, our sense of life's pro - por - tion, Un - less we seek the qui - et place of prayer.

3. Full well he knows, for he him - self hath made us— Yea, he him - self was hu - man as are we— How much we need the calm of sweet com - mun - ion New strength to gain for bat - tles yet to be.

4. He know - eth how for us to have com - pas - sion, Whose feet have jour - neyed many a wea - ry mile; Shall we not go in an - swer to his bid - ding, "Come ye your - selves a - part and rest a - while"?

5. And so he calls us in - to des - ert plac - es Where hu - man voic - es may not drown his own, There to re - ceive the full - er rev - e - la - tion He makes to those who wait with him a - lone.

Text: Thomas O. Chisholm, 1866-1960.
Tune: George C. Stebbins, 1846-1945.

80 Our Father, Who in Heaven Doth Dwell

Matthew 6:9-15 (9-13)
II Nephi 14:11, 12

COOLING C.M.

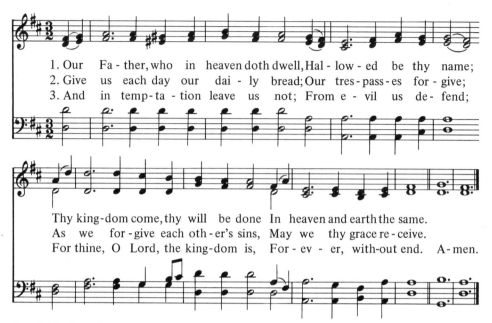

1. Our Fa-ther, who in heaven doth dwell, Hal-low-ed be thy name;
2. Give us each day our dai-ly bread; Our tres-pass-es for-give;
3. And in temp-ta-tion leave us not; From e-vil us de-fend;

Thy king-dom come, thy will be done In heaven and earth the same.
As we for-give each oth-er's sins, May we thy grace re-ceive.
For thine, O Lord, the king-dom is, For-ev-er, with-out end. A-men.

Text: Jubilee Harp; alt.
Tune: Alonzo J. Abbey, 1825-1887.

81 Father Almighty, Grant to Us Thy Blessing

James 1:5
I Nephi 7:56-59

FLEMMING 11.11.11.5.

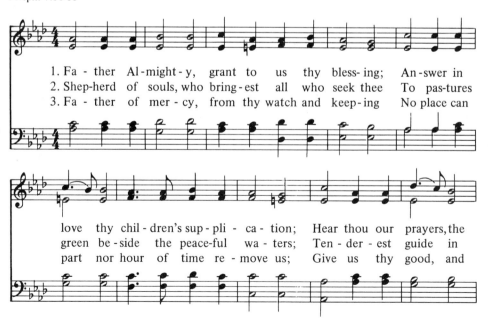

1. Fa-ther Al-might-y, grant to us thy bless-ing; An-swer in
2. Shep-herd of souls, who bring-est all who seek thee To pas-tures
3. Fa-ther of mer-cy, from thy watch and keep-ing No place can

love thy chil-dren's sup-pli-ca-tion; Hear thou our prayers, the
green be-side the peace-ful wa-ters; Ten-der-est guide in
part nor hour of time re-move us; Give us thy good, and

spo - ken and un - spo - ken; Hear us, our Fa - ther.
ways of cheer - ful du - ty, Lead us, Good Shep - herd.
save us from our e - vil, In - fi - nite Spir - it. A-men.

Text: Berwick Hymnal, 1886.
Tune: Friedrich F. Flemming, 1778-1813.

One Hour with Jesus
82

John 4:25, 26
Matthew 11:29, 30 (28-30)

ONE HOUR WITH JESUS 11.11.11.11.

1. One hour with Je-sus, the Shep-herd of the fold, I es-teem of more
2. The world and its fol-ly, I bid them all a-dieu; I find there no
3. One hour with Je-sus, a grand feast to my soul; His bur-dens are

val - ue than sil - ver or gold; The peace-ful com-mun-ion sent
com - fort that's last - ing and true; One hour with Je - sus, that
light and his yoke eas - ily borne; Though hard - ships and tri - als I

down from a - bove Makes clear to my vi - sion his mis - sion of love.
no - ble true friend, Brings peace to my soul that will nev - er - more end.
may have to meet, The Spir - it bears wit - ness the end will be sweet.

Text: William Lewis, 1856-1919.
Tune: John L. Morgan, 1869-1913.

83

Matthew 11:29, 30 (28-30)
Alma 3:57, 58

'Tis the Blessed Hour of Prayer

DOANE II 7.6.7.5.7.6.7.6.

1. 'Tis the bless-ed hour of prayer when our hearts low-ly bend,
2. 'Tis the bless-ed hour of prayer when the Sav-ior draws near
3. 'Tis the bless-ed hour of prayer when the tempt-ed and tried
4. At the bless-ed hour of prayer, trust-ing him, we be-lieve

And we gath-er to Je-sus, our Sav-ior and Friend;
With a ten-der com-pas-sion his chil-dren to hear;
To the Sav-ior who loves them their sor-rows con-fide;
That the bless-ings we're need-ing we'll sure-ly re-ceive;

If we come to him in faith his pro-tec-tion to share,
When he tells us we may cast at his feet ev-ery care,
With a sym-pa-thiz-ing heart he re-moves ev-ery care;
In the full-ness of this trust we shall lose ev-ery care;

What a balm for the wea-ry! Oh, how sweet to be there!

Text: Fanny J. Crosby, 1820-1915.
Tune: W. H. Doane, 1832-1915.

Come Ye Yourselves Apart

84

Mark 6:32-35 (31-34)
Isaiah 40:28, 29, 31

PENITENTIA 10.10.10.10.

1. Come ye your-selves a - part and rest a - while;
2. Come tell me all that ye have said and done,
3. Come ye and rest; the jour - ney is too great,
4. Then, fresh from con - verse with your Lord, re - turn

Wea - ry, I know it, of the press and throng,
Your vic - to - ries and fail - ures, hopes and fears.
And ye will faint be - side the way and sink;
And work till day - light soft - ens in - to even;

Wipe from your brow the sweat and dust of toil,
I know how hard - ly souls are wooed and won;
The bread of life is here for you to eat,
The brief hours are not lost in which ye learn

And in my qui - et strength a - gain be strong.
My choic - est wreaths are al - ways wet with tears.
And here for you the wine of love to drink.
More of your Mas - ter and his peace in heaven.

Text: Edward H. Bickersteth, 1825-1906.
Tune: Edward Dearle, 1806-1891.

85 What a Friend We Have in Jesus

Matthew 21:19, 20 (21, 22)
Moroni 6:5

BLAENWERN 8.7.8.7.D.
Alternate hymn: 86

1. What a friend we have in Je-sus, All our sins and griefs to bear;
2. Have we tri-als and temp-ta-tions? Is there trou-ble an-y-where?
3. Are we weak and heav-y-la-den, Cum-bered with a load of care?

What a priv-i-lege to car-ry Ev-ery-thing to God in prayer!
We should nev-er be dis-cour-aged; Take it to the Lord in prayer!
Still the Sav-ior is our ref-uge; Take it to the Lord in prayer!

Oh, what peace we of-ten for-feit; Oh, what need-less pain we bear
Can we find a friend so faith-ful, Who will all our sor-rows share?
Do thy friends de-spise, for-sake thee? Take it to the Lord in prayer!

All be-cause we do not car-ry Ev-ery-thing to God in prayer.
Je-sus knows our ev-ery weak-ness; Take it to the Lord in prayer!
In his arms he'll take and shield thee; Thou wilt find a sol-ace there.

Text: Joseph Scriven, 1820-1886.
Tune: W. P. Rowlands, 1860-1937; copyright G. A. Gabe, Swansea, S. Wales.

What a Friend We Have in Jesus

86

Matthew 21:19, 20 (21, 22)
Moroni 6:5

ERIE (Converse) 8.7.8.7.D.
Alternate hymn: 85

1. What a friend we have in Je - sus, All our sins and griefs to bear;
2. Have we tri - als and temp- ta - tions? Is there trou-ble an - y - where?
3. Are we weak and heav-y - la - den, Cum - bered with a load of care?

What a priv - i - lege to car - ry Ev - ery-thing to God in prayer!
We should nev - er be dis - cour - aged; Take it to the Lord in prayer!
Still the Sav - ior is our ref - uge; Take it to the Lord in prayer!

Oh, what peace we oft - en for - feit; Oh, what need-less pain we bear
Can we find a friend so faith - ful, Who will all our sor-rows share?
Do thy friends de-spise, for - sake thee? Take it to the Lord in prayer!

All be - cause we do not car - ry Ev - ery-thing to God in prayer.
Je - sus knows our ev - ery weak - ness; Take it to the Lord in prayer!
In his arms he'll take and shield thee; Thou wilt find a sol - ace there.

Text: Joseph Scriven, 1820-1886.
Tune: Charles C. Converse, 1832-1918.

87 Sweet Hour of Prayer

D. and C. 85:36
Psalm 55:16, 17

SWEET HOUR OF PRAYER L.M.D.

1. Sweet hour of prayer, sweet hour of prayer, That calls me from a world of care,
2. Sweet hour of prayer, sweet hour of prayer, Thy wings shall my pe-ti-tion bear

And bids me at my Fa-ther's throne Make all my wants and wish-es known!
To Him, whose truth and faith-ful-ness En-gage the wait-ing soul to bless.

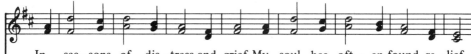

In sea-sons of dis-tress and grief My soul has oft-en found re-lief,
And since he bids me seek his face, Be-lieve his word, and trust his grace,

And oft es-caped the tempt-er's snare By thy re-turn, sweet hour of prayer.
I'll cast on him my ev-ery care And wait for thee, sweet hour of prayer.

Text: William W. Walford, 1772-1850.
Tune: William B. Bradbury, 1816-1868.

Almighty Father, Hear Our Prayer 88

Psalm 52:9
Psalm 97:10-12

INTERCESSION (Refrain) 8.9.

Al - might - y Fa - ther, hear our prayer And

bless all souls that wait be - fore thee. A - men.

Tune: Arr. from Felix Mendelssohn, 1809-1847 by William H. Callcott, 1807-1882.

From Thee All Skill and Science Flow 89

Romans 8:28
II Nephi 3:65

YARRINGTON C.M.

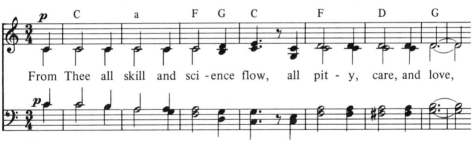

From Thee all skill and sci -ence flow, all pit - y, care, and love,

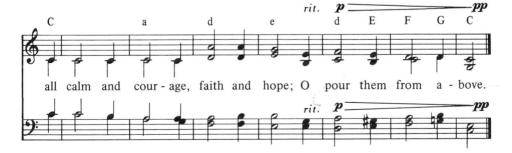

all calm and cour - age, faith and hope; O pour them from a - bove.

Text: Charles Kingsley, 1819-1875.
Tune: From *Responses for the Church Year* by John Yarrington, by permission of Chantry Music Press, Inc.

90   O Help Us, Lord, to Keep This Day

Psalm 118:24
Exodus 20:8

SILVER HILL L.M.

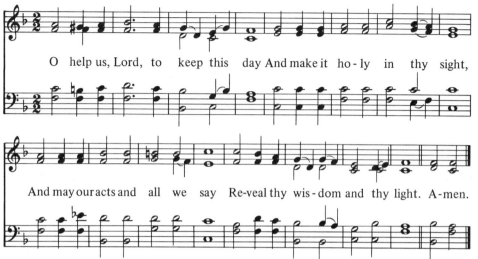

O help us, Lord, to keep this day And make it ho-ly in thy sight,

And may our acts and all we say Re-veal thy wis-dom and thy light. A-men.

Text: Ola Gunsolley Savage, 1895-1976; copyright 1956 Herald Publishing House.
Tune: Frederick C. Maker, 1844-1927.

91   Great God of All the Earth

I Peter 3:8
D. and C. 117:13

OLIVET 6.6.4.6.6.6.4.

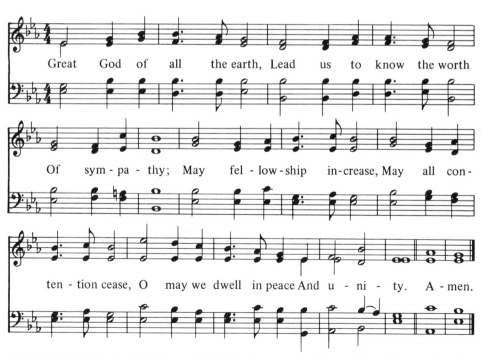

Great God of all the earth, Lead us to know the worth

Of sym-pa-thy; May fel-low-ship in-crease, May all con-

ten-tion cease, O may we dwell in peace And u-ni-ty. A-men.

Text: Leonard B. McWhood, 1870-1939; copyright 1933 by the author. Used by permission of Stuart McWhood.
Tune: Lowell Mason, 1792-1872.

Lord, May Thy Will Be Done 92

SAVAGE 6.2.

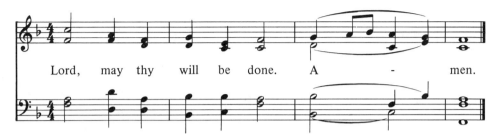

Tune: Ola Gunsolley Savage, 1895-1976; copyright 1956 Herald Publishing House.

Lord, Thank You for This Hour 93

SAVAGE 6.2.

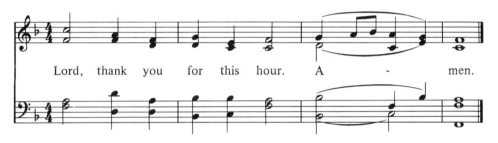

Tune: Ola Gunsolley Savage, 1895-1976; copyright 1956 Herald Publishing House.

Hear Our Prayer, O Lord 94

Psalm 27:7
Enos 1:5

AFTER PRAYER 5.5.6.5.

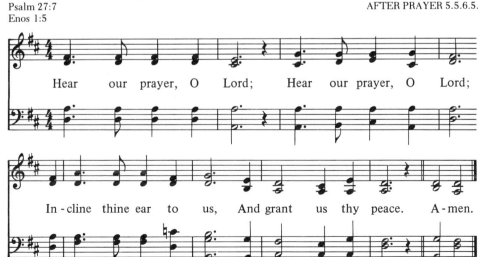

Tune: George Whelpton, 1847-1930.

95 Dresden Amen 96 Threefold Amen

A -men, A - men.

A-men, A-men, A - men.

Tune: Richard Wagner, 1813-1883.

Tune: Danish.

97 Twofold Amen

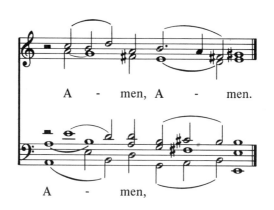

A - men, A - men.

A - men,

Tune: From Thomas Tallis, c. 1505-1585.

98 Fourfold Amen

A - men, A - men, A - men, A-men.

A - men, A - men,

Tune: Franklyn S. Weddle, 1905 - ; copyright 1956 Herald Publishing House.

Sixfold Amen 99

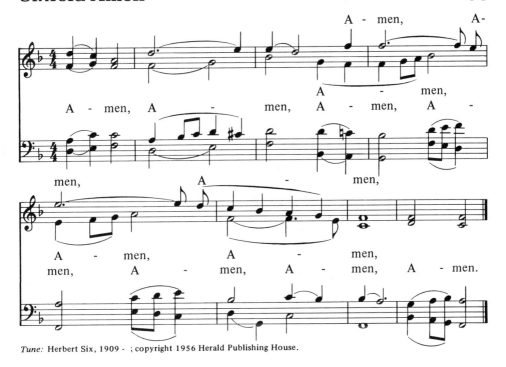

Tune: Herbert Six, 1909 - ; copyright 1956 Herald Publishing House.

Sevenfold Amen 100

Tune: John Stainer, 1840-1901.

101   # Threefold Amen

A - men, A - men, A - men.

Tune: Oliver Houston, Jr., 1928 - ; copyright 1956 Herald Publishing House.

102   # May Thy Presence Be Ours

Jude 24, 25   RUSSIAN MELODY 10.9.10.9.9.
I John 4:7

May thy pres - ence be ours in full meas - ure. Let thy

Spir - it a - bide with - out end. With thy love as our

hearts' great - est treas - ure, We will praise thee, our Lord

and our friend. We will praise thee, our Lord and our friend.

Text: R. Romanov or P. Rogozin; alternate adaptation from the Russian by Don C. Rawson, 1932 - ; alt.; adaptation
   copyright 1979 by Zionic Research Institute, Inc. All rights reserved. Used by permission.
Tune: Russian Melody arr. by Alexander Efimov.

Forgive Us, Lord

103

Micah 6:6, 8
Mosiah 2:28-32

SURSUM CORDA 10.10.10.10.

Unison (or harmony)

1. For - give us, Lord, for shal - low thank - ful - ness,
2. For - give us, Lord, for self - ish thanks and praise,
3. For - give us, Lord, for feast that knows not fast,
4. O - pen our eyes to glimpse thy love's in - tent,

For dull con - tent with warmth and shel - tered care,
For word that speaks at var - i - ance with deed.
For joy in things the while we starve the soul,
Our minds and hearts to plumb its depth and height.

For songs of praise for food and har - vest press,
For - give our thanks for walk - ing pleas - ant ways
For walls and wars that hide thy mer - cies vast
May thank - ful - ness be days in ser - vice spent,

While of thy rich - er gifts we're un - a - ware.
Un - mind - ful of a bro - ken neigh-bor's need.
And mar our vi - sion of the king - dom goal.
Re - flec - tion of Christ's life and love and light. A - men.

Text: William Watkins Reid, Sr., 1890 - ; alt. from *My God Is There, Controlling*; copyright 1965 The Hymn Society of America; used by permission.
Tune: Alfred M. Smith, 1879-1971; copyright by composer. Used by permission of Mrs. Alfred M. Smith.

104

Titus 3:3-7
II Nephi 1:73-77

Amazing Grace

NEW BRITAIN C.M.

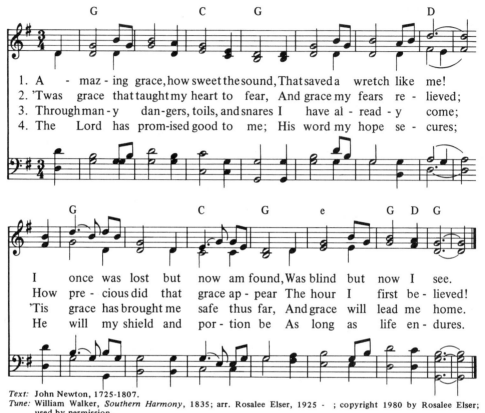

1. A - maz - ing grace, how sweet the sound, That saved a wretch like me!
2. 'Twas grace that taught my heart to fear, And grace my fears re - lieved;
3. Through man - y dan - gers, toils, and snares I have al - read - y come;
4. The Lord has prom-ised good to me; His word my hope se - cures;

I once was lost but now am found, Was blind but now I see.
How pre - cious did that grace ap - pear The hour I first be - lieved!
'Tis grace has brought me safe thus far, And grace will lead me home.
He will my shield and por - tion be As long as life en - dures.

Text: John Newton, 1725-1807.
Tune: William Walker, *Southern Harmony*, 1835; arr. Rosalee Elser, 1925 - ; copyright 1980 by Rosalee Elser; used by permission.

105

D. and C. 16:5d
Alma 16:238

O Thou God, Who Hearest Prayer

FAITHFUL GUIDE 7.7.7.D.

1. O thou God, who hear - est prayer Ev - ery hour and ev - ery-where,
2. Hear and save us, gra - cious Lord, For our trust is in thy word;

For His sake, whose blood we plead, Hear us in our hour of need;
Cleanse us from the stain of sin That thy peace may rule with - in;

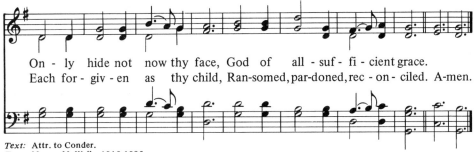

On - ly hide not now thy face, God of all - suf - fi - cient grace.
Each for - giv - en as thy child, Ran-somed, par-doned, rec - on - ciled. A-men.

Text: Attr. to Conder.
Tune: Marcus M. Wells, 1815-1895.

How Shall We Come Before You Now 106

Micah 6:6, 8
Psalm 51:15-17

STRACATHRO C.M.

1. How shall we come be - fore you now In
2. Such mea - ger vir - tues as we claim Are
3. So much re - solved, so lit - tle done; So
4. A bro - ken and a con - trite heart Has

this rich hour of praise? Shall righ - teous - ness or
your own gifts of grace; What can we bring of
quick to judge or blame; En - am - ored with our
brought us to this hour; And from the on - ly

mer - it prompt The joy - ful psalms we raise?
our own strength To of - fer in this place?
fool - ish pride, What mer - it can we claim?
gift we bring, New life springs in - to flower.

Text: Geoffrey F. Spencer, 1927 - ; copyright 1980 Reorganized Church of Jesus Christ of Latter Day Saints.
Tune: Melody from Charles Hutcheson's *Christian Vespers*, Glasgow, 1832; harm. Geoffrey Shaw, 1879-1943; alt.;
from *Songs of Praise*, Enlarged Edition; used by permission of Oxford University Press.

107

Ephesians 2:13-22
D. and C. 122:17

The Love of God

FINLANDIA 11.10.11.10.11.10.
See 315 for a higher setting.

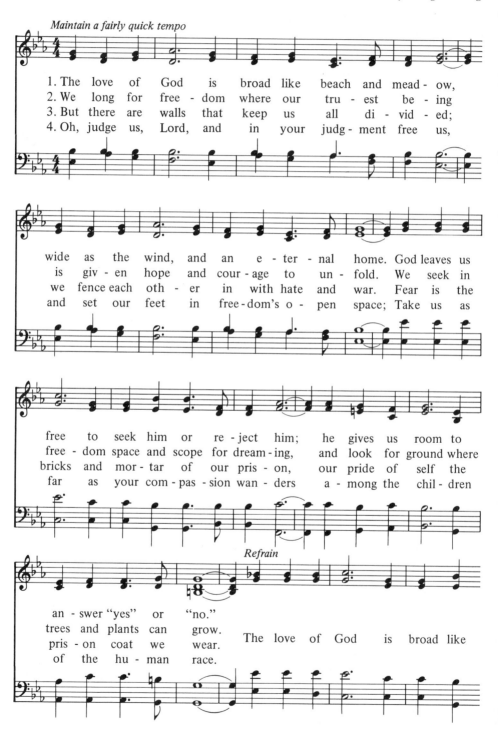

Maintain a fairly quick tempo

1. The love of God is broad like beach and mead-ow,
2. We long for free-dom where our tru-est be-ing
3. But there are walls that keep us all di-vid-ed;
4. Oh, judge us, Lord, and in your judg-ment free us,

wide as the wind, and an e-ter-nal home. God leaves us
is giv-en hope and cour-age to un-fold. We seek in
we fence each oth-er in with hate and war. Fear is the
and set our feet in free-dom's o-pen space; Take us as

free to seek him or re-ject him; he gives us room to
free-dom space and scope for dream-ing, and look for ground where
bricks and mor-tar of our pris-on, our pride of self the
far as your com-pas-sion wan-ders a-mong the chil-dren

Refrain

an-swer "yes" or "no."
trees and plants can grow. The love of God is broad like
pris-on coat we wear.
of the hu-man race.

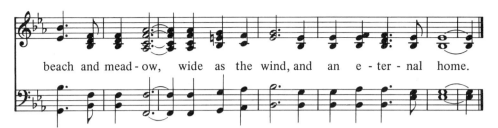

beach and mead-ow, wide as the wind, and an e-ter-nal home.

Text: Anders Frostenson; trans. Fred Kaan, 1929 - ; trans. copyright 1976 Stainer & Bell Ltd. Sole U. S. agent: Galaxy Music Corp., N. Y. Used with permission.
Tune: Jean Sibelius, 1865-1957; arr. copyright, 1933, by Presbyterian Board of Christian Education; renewed, 1961; from *The Hymnbook.* Used by permission of The Westminster Press. Melody is public domain in U.S.A.; outside U.S.A., original melody copyright by Breitkopf & Härtel, Wiesbaden. Used by permission.

Forgive Our Sins as We Forgive 108

I Timothy 1:5
Moroni 7:50-52

DOVE OF PEACE 8.6.8.6.6.

Unison (or harmony)

1. "For - give our sins as we for - give," you taught us,
2. How can your par - don reach and bless the un - for -
3. In blaz - ing light your cross re - veals the truth we
4. Lord, cleanse the depths with - in our souls, and bid re -

Lord, to pray; But you a - lone can grant us grace to
giv - ing heart That broods on wrongs and will not let old
dim - ly know; How small the debts men owe to us; how
sent - ment cease; Then, rec - on - ciled to God and man, our

live the words we say. To live the words we say.
bit - ter - ness de - part? Old bit - ter - ness de - part?
great our debt to you. How great our debt to you.
lives will spread your peace. Our lives will spread your peace.

Text: Rosamond E. Herklots, 1905 - ; used by permission of Oxford University Press.
Tune: American Folk Tune; arr. Austin C. Lovelace, 1919 - ; copyright 1977 by Agape, Carol Stream, IL 60187. International copyright secured. All rights reserved. Used by permission.

109 Here We Have Come, Dear Lord, to Thee

II Timothy 2:19-21

D. and C. 11:4

SILVER HILL L.M.

1. Here we have come, dear Lord, to thee, Of thy trans-
2. We bring to thee no glo - rious gift, No gift that
3. We turn to thee from sin we've served, That we have
4. Ac - cept our true re - pent - ance, Lord. All that we

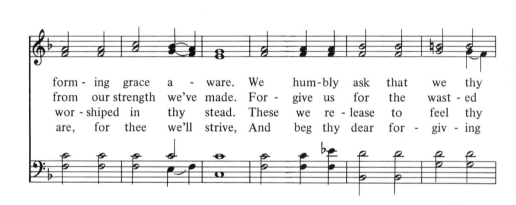

form - ing grace a - ware. We hum-bly ask that we thy
from our strength we've made. For - give us for the wast - ed
wor - shiped in thy stead. These we re - lease to feel thy
are, for thee we'll strive, And beg thy dear for - giv - ing

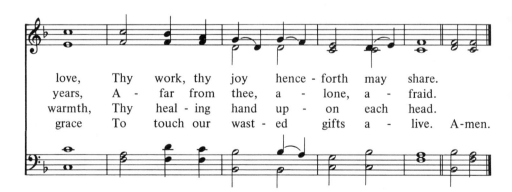

love, Thy work, thy joy hence-forth may share.
years, A - far from thee, a - lone, a - fraid.
warmth, Thy heal - ing hand up - on each head.
grace To touch our wast - ed gifts a - live. A - men.

Text: Cleo Hanthorne Moon, 1904 - ; copyright 1956 Herald Publishing House.
Tune: Frederick C. Maker, 1844-1927.

I Lift My Soul to Thee, Lord

110

Psalm 25:1-7, 20, 21
II Nephi 3:31-34

VIGIL 7.6.7.6.D.*
Alternate tune: HOLY WINGS (1)

1. I lift my soul to thee, Lord; My God, I trust in thee.
2. Re - mem - ber, Lord, thy mer - cies For they have been of old.
3. Turn thou to me; be gra - cious; Bring me from my dis - tress.

May I not be a - sham - ed: Let none ex - ult o'er me.
Re - mem - ber not trans - gres - sions From sin - ful days un - told.
Con - sid - er mine af - flic - tion, My sin which I con - fess.

Let none that wait up - on thee Be put to shame, O Lord,
Ac - cord - ing to thy mer - cy, Re - mem - ber now thy word;
My guilt is great! Oh, par - don For thy name's sake, I pray!

For thou art their sal - va - tion, Their goal and their re - ward.
For thy name's sake, re - mem - ber With stead - fast love, O Lord.
O God, re - deem thy peo - ple: In - struct them in the way.

Text: Arranged from Psalm 25 by Alan D. Tyree, 1929 - ; copyright 1980 Reorganized Church of Jesus Christ of Latter Day Saints.
Tune: Swedish Folk Melody.

*See 210 for a lower setting.

111 Thou Whose Purpose Is to Kindle

Alma 5:38-41
Matthew 5:15-18 (13-16)

LADUE CHAPEL 8.7.8.7.D.
Alternate tune: AUSTRIA (376)

1. Thou whose pur - pose is to kin - dle Now ig - nite____
2. Thou who, in____ thy ho - ly gos - pel, Wills that all____
3. Lord, who still____ a sword de - liv - ers Rath - er than____

____ us with thy fire; While the earth____ a - waits thy
____ should tru - ly live, Help us sense____ our share of
____ a plac - id peace, With thy sharp - ened word dis -

burn - ing, With thy pas - sion us in - spire.
fail - ure, Our tran - quil - li - ty for - give.
turb us, From com - pla - cen - cy re - lease!

Over come our sinful calmness; Rouse us with
Teach us courage as we struggle In all lib-
Save us now from satisfaction, When we pri-

re-demptive shame; Baptize with thy fier-y
erating strife; Lift the smallness of our
vately are free, Yet are un-disturbed in

Spirit; Crown our lives with tongues of flame.
vision By thine own abundant life.
spirit By another's misery.

Text: "Baptism by Fire" in *The Incendiary Fellowship* by David Elton Trueblood, 1900 - ; copyright 1967 by David
Elton Trueblood; used by permission of Harper & Row, Publishers, Inc.
Tune: Ronald Arnatt, 1930 - ; copyright 1971 by Walton Music Corp.; international copyright secured; all rights
reserved; used by permission.

112   Heavenly Father, We Adore Thee

Psalm 86:5, 6
D. and C. 6:15, 16a

OMNI DIE 8.7.8.7.

1. Heaven-ly Fa-ther, we a-dore thee! At thy feet we hum-bly bow,
2. Thou art gra-cious, Lord; for-give us Ev-ery wrong that we have done;
3. In the name of Christ, our Sav-ior, Draw our minds from world-ly care;

Met to wor-ship, Lord, be-fore thee; Grant us each a bless-ing now.
Let no spir-it false de-ceive us; Bid thy Spir-it make us one.
Grant us each thy spe-cial fa-vor; Hear our ear-nest, fer-vent prayer. A-men.

Text: Mark H. Forscutt, 1834-1903.
Tune: Corner's *Gesangbuch*, 1631; arr. by William Smith Rockstro, 1823-1895.

113   Dear Master, in Whose Life I See

II Nephi 3:56, 61
Philippians 4:13

HURSLEY L.M.

1. Dear Mas-ter, in whose life I see All that I
2. Though what I dream and what I do In my weak

would, but fail to be, Let thy clear light for-ev-er
days are al-ways two, Help me, op-pressed by things un-

shine To shame and guide this life of mine.
done, O thou, whose deeds and dreams were one! A - men.

Text: John Hunter, 1848-1917.
Tune: Adapted from *Katholisches Gesangbuch*, Vienna, c. 1774.

Lord, Thy Mercy Now Entreating   114

Psalm 119:57, 58
II Nephi 3:34-36

KINGDOM 8.7.8.7.

1. Lord, thy mer - cy now en - treat - ing, Low be -
2. Sin - ful thoughts and words un - lov - ing Rise a -
3. Hearts that far from thee were stray - ing While in
4. Pre - cious mo - ments i - dly wast - ed, Pre - cious
5. Lord, thy mer - cy still en - treat - ing, We with

fore thy throne we fall; Our mis - deeds to thee con -
gainst us one by one— Acts un - worth - y, deeds un -
prayer we bowed the knee, Lips that while thy prais - es
hours in fol - ly spent, Chris - tian vow and fight un -
shame our sins would own; From hence - forth, the time re -

fess - ing, On thy name we hum - bly call.
think - ing, Good that we have left un - done;
sound - ing Lift - ed not the soul to thee;
heed - ed, Scarce a thought to wis - dom lent—
deem - ing, May we live to thee a - lone. A - men.

Text: Mary A. Sidebotham, 1833-1913.
Tune: V. Earle Copes, 1921 - ; copyright 1959 Abingdon Press. Used by permission.

115 Dear Lord and God of Humankind

Philippians 4:4-7
Matthew 11:29, 30 (28-30)

REST 8.6.8.8.6.

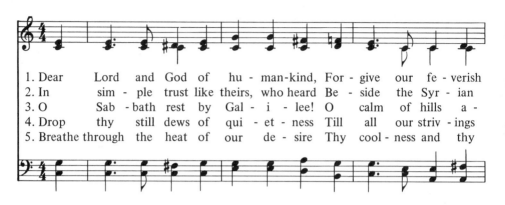

1. Dear Lord and God of hu - man-kind, For - give our fe - verish
2. In sim - ple trust like theirs, who heard Be - side the Syr - ian
3. O Sab -bath rest by Gal - i - lee! O calm of hills a -
4. Drop thy still dews of qui - et - ness Till all our striv -ings
5. Breathe through the heat of our de - sire Thy cool - ness and thy

ways; Re - store to us our right - ful mind, In pur - er
sea The gra - cious call - ing of the Lord, Let us, like
bove! Where Je - sus knelt to share with thee The si - lence
cease; Take from our souls the strain and stress, And let our
balm; Let sense be dumb, let flesh re - tire; Speak through the

lives thy ways to find, In deep - er rev-erence, praise.
them, with - out a word, Rise up and fol - low thee.
of e - ter - ni - ty, In - ter - pret - ed by love.
or - dered lives con - fess The beau - ty of thy peace.
earth - quake, wind, and fire, O still small voice of calm! A - men.

Text: John Greenleaf Whittier, 1807-1892; alt.
Tune: Frederick C. Maker, 1844-1927

Father, When in Love to Thee

116

II Corinthians 7:8-10
D. and C. 64:2d, e

SPANISH CHANT 7.7.7.7.D.

1. Fa - ther, when in love to thee Low we bow the a - dor - ing knee,
2. We re - pent the times we've stood For the things of less - er good,
3. Fa - ther, while we look to thee, Low - ly on the bend - ed knee,

When re - pent - ant to the skies Scarce - ly do we lift our eyes,
And for stew - ard - ship of time We have spent un - linked with thine.
And in pen - i - tence we turn, For thy par - don now we yearn.

Then, O hear us as we plead For thy help in time of need;
In the midst of sin and strife, Teach us how to live a life
Rec - on - cile us by thy love; Lift our souls to things a - bove;

On thy mer - cy we re - ly; Hear, for - give us when we cry.
Marked by grac - es of new birth, Wor - thy of thy saints on earth.
As we hum - bly now draw nigh, Hear, for - give us when we cry. A - men.

Text: Robert Grant, 1785-1838, Alt.
Tune: Arr. by Benjamin Carr, 1769-1831.

117   Oh, for a Closer Walk with God

Alma 30:2
D. and C. 100:7a

NAOMI C.M.

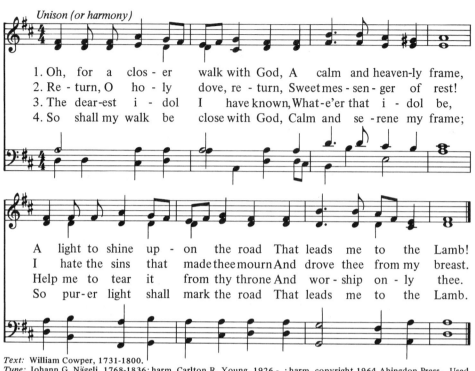

Unison (or harmony)

1. Oh, for a clos-er walk with God, A calm and heaven-ly frame,
2. Re-turn, O ho-ly dove, re-turn, Sweet mes-sen-ger of rest!
3. The dear-est i-dol I have known, What-e'er that i-dol be,
4. So shall my walk be close with God, Calm and se-rene my frame;

A light to shine up-on the road That leads me to the Lamb!
I hate the sins that made thee mourn And drove thee from my breast.
Help me to tear it from thy throne And wor-ship on-ly thee.
So pur-er light shall mark the road That leads me to the Lamb.

Text: William Cowper, 1731-1800.
Tune: Johann G. Nägeli, 1768-1836; harm. Carlton R. Young, 1926 - ; harm. copyright 1964 Abingdon Press. Used by permission.

118   The Weight of Past and Fruitless Guilt

Romans 5:6-11
D. and C. 150:11a

RETREAT L.M.

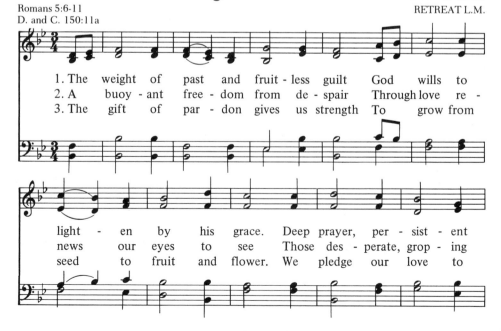

1. The weight of past and fruit-less guilt God wills to
2. A buoy-ant free-dom from de-spair Through love re-
3. The gift of par-don gives us strength To grow from

light-en by his grace. Deep prayer, per-sist-ent
news our eyes to see Those des-perate, grop-ing
seed to fruit and flower. We pledge our love to

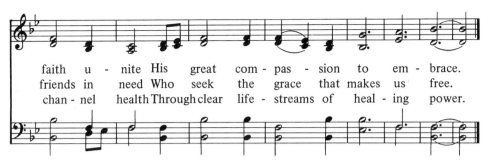

faith u - nite His great com - pas - sion to em - brace.
friends in need Who seek the grace that makes us free.
chan - nel health Through clear life - streams of heal - ing power.

Text: Cleo Hanthorne Moon, 1904 - ; copyright 1980 Reorganized Church of Jesus Christ of Latter Day Saints.
Tune: Thomas Hastings, 1784-1872; harm. Rosalee Elser, 1925 - ; harm. copyright 1980 Rosalee Elser.

Just as I Am, Without One Plea 119

D. and C. 18:6
Mosiah 1:115, 116

WOODWORTH L.M.

1. Just as I am, with - out one plea, But that thy
2. Just as I am, though tossed a - bout With ma - ny a
3. Just as I am, poor, wretch-ed, blind; Sight, rich - es,
4. Just as I am, thou wilt re - ceive, Wilt wel - come,

blood was shed for me, And that thou bid-dest me come to
con - flict, ma - ny a doubt; With strife and fears with - in, with -
heal - ing of the mind, Yea, all I need, in thee to
par - don, cleanse, re - lieve, Be - cause thy prom - ise I be -

thee, O Lamb of God, I come, I come.
out, O Lamb of God, I come, I come.
find, O Lamb of God, I come, I come.
lieve, O Lamb of God, I come, I come. A - men.

Text: Charlotte Elliott, 1789-1871; alt.
Tune: William B. Bradbury, 1816-1868.

120

III Nephi 5:110-112
John 10:4, 9

In Heavenly Love Abiding

AURELIA 7.6.7.6.D

1. In heaven-ly love a-bid-ing, No change my heart shall fear;
2. Wher-ev-er he may guide me, No want shall turn me back;
3. Green pas-tures are be-fore me Which yet I have not seen;

And safe is such con-fid-ing, For noth-ing chang-es here.
My Shep-herd is be-side me, And noth-ing can I lack.
Bright skies will soon be o'er me Where dark-est clouds have been.

The storm may roar with-out me; My heart may low be laid,
His wis-dom ev-er wak-eth; His sight is nev-er dim;
My hope I can-not meas-ure; My path to life is free;

But God is round a-bout me, And I am not dis-mayed.
He knows the way he tak-eth, And I will walk with him.
My Sav-ior has my treas-ure, And he will walk with me.

Text: Anna L. Waring, 1823-1910.
Tune: Samuel S. Wesley, 1810-1876.

Jesus, Priceless Treasure

121

Isaiah 41:10
D. and C. 34:6

JESU, MEINE FREUDE 6.6.5.6.6.5.7.8.6.

1. Je - sus, price-less trea - sure, Source of pur - est plea - sure,
2. In thine arm I rest me; Foes who would mo - lest me
3. Hence, all thoughts of sad - ness! For the Lord of glad - ness,

Tru-est friend to me; Long my heart hath pant - ed Till it well-nigh
Can-not reach me here. Though the earth be shak - ing, Ev - ery heart be
Je - sus, en - ters in; Those who love the Fa - ther, Though the storms may

faint - ed, Thirst-ing af - ter thee. Thine I am, O spot-less Lamb;
quak - ing, God dis-pels our fear; Sin and hell in con-flict fell
gath - er, Still have peace with-in; Yea, what-e'er we here must bear,

I will suf - fer naught to hide thee, Ask for naught be - side thee.
With their heav - iest storms as - sail us: Je - sus will not fail us.
Still in thee lies pur - est plea - sure, Je - sus, price - less trea - sure!

Text: Johann Franck, 1618-1677; trans. Catherine Winkworth, 1827-1878; alt.
Tune: Johann Crüger, 1598-1662; harm. J. S. Bach, 1685-1750.

122

Isaiah 53:4, 5
Jacob 3:16, 17

With Eyes of Faith

CRAIG L.M.

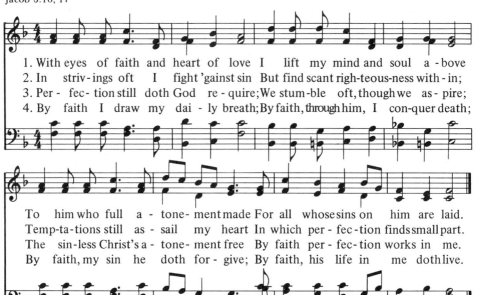

1. With eyes of faith and heart of love I lift my mind and soul a-bove
2. In striv-ings oft I fight 'gainst sin But find scant righ-teous-ness with-in;
3. Per-fec-tion still doth God re-quire; We stum-ble oft, though we as-pire;
4. By faith I draw my dai-ly breath; By faith, through him, I con-quer death;

To him who full a-tone-ment made For all whose sins on him are laid.
Temp-ta-tions still as-sail my heart In which per-fec-tion finds small part.
The sin-less Christ's a-tone-ment free By faith per-fec-tion works in me.
By faith, my sin he doth for-give; By faith, his life in me doth live.

Text: Evan A. Fry, 1902-1959; copyright 1956 Herald Publishing House.
Tune: Franklyn S. Weddle, 1905 - ; copyright 1956 Herald Publishing House.

123

Ether 1:106-108
Isaiah 48:17

He Leadeth Me

HE LEADETH ME L.M. with refrain

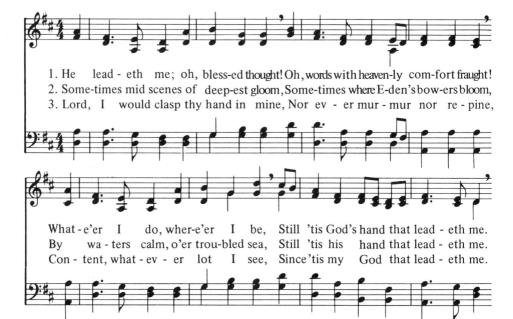

1. He lead-eth me; oh, bless-ed thought! Oh, words with heaven-ly com-fort fraught!
2. Some-times mid scenes of deep-est gloom, Some-times where E-den's bow-ers bloom,
3. Lord, I would clasp thy hand in mine, Nor ev-er mur-mur nor re-pine,

What-e'er I do, wher-e'er I be, Still 'tis God's hand that lead-eth me.
By wa-ters calm, o'er trou-bled sea, Still 'tis his hand that lead-eth me.
Con-tent, what-ev-er lot I see, Since 'tis my God that lead-eth me.

Refrain

He lead-eth me, he lead-eth me, By his own hand he lead-eth me.

His faith-ful fol-lower I would be, For by his hand he lead-eth me.

Text: Joseph H. Gilmore, 1834-1918.
Tune: William B. Bradbury, 1816-1868.

The Lord's My Shepherd 124

Psalm 23
I Nephi 7:56-59

CRIMOND C.M.
Alternate tunes: NEW BRITAIN (104).
*BROTHER JAMES' AIR * (126)*

1. The Lord's my shep-herd; I'll not want. He makes me down to lie
2. My soul he doth re-store a-gain, And me to walk doth make
3. Yea, though I walk in death's dark vale, Yet will I fear no ill,
4. My ta-ble thou hast fur-nish-ed In pres-ence of my foes;
5. Good-ness and mer-cy all my life Shall sure-ly fol-low me;

In pas-tures green. He lead-eth me The qui-et wa-ters by.
With-in the paths of right-teous-ness, E'en for his own name's sake.
For thou art with me; and thy rod And staff me com-fort still.
My head thou dost with oil a-noint, And my cup o-ver-flows.
And in God's house for-ev-er-more My dwell-ing place shall be.

Text: Scottish Psalter, 1650.
Tune: Jessie Seymour Irvine, 1836-1887.

* Repeat last line in each stanza.

125 My Shepherd Will Supply My Need

Psalm 23
Luke 12:29-35 (27-32)

RESIGNATION C.M.D.
Alternate tunes: CRIMOND (124), NEW BRITAIN (104)

Unison (or harmony)

1. My shep-herd will sup-ply my need; Je-ho-vah is his name:
2. When I walk through the shades of death his pres-ence is my stay;
3. The sure pro-vi-sions of my God At-tend me all my days;

In pas-tures fresh he makes me feed, Be-side the liv-ing stream.
One word of his sup-port-ing breath Drives all my fears a-way.
O may his house be my a-bode, And all my work be praise.

He brings my wan-dering spir-it back When I for-sake his ways;
His hand, in sight of all my foes, Doth still my ta-ble spread;
There will I find re-viv-ing rest, And free-ly go and come;

And leads me, for his mer-cy's sake, In paths of truth and grace.
My cup with bless-ings o-ver-flows, His oil a-noints my head.
No more a stran-ger, or a guest, But like a child at home.

Text: Psalm 23, para. by Isaac Watts, 1674-1748; alt.
Tune: Southern Harmony, 1835; harm. Rosalee Elser, 1925 - ; harm. copyright 1980 Rosalee Elser.

I Know Not What the Future Hath 126

Psalm 139:7-14
Isaiah 41:10

BROTHER JAMES' AIR 8.6.8.6.8.6.

1. I know not what the fu-ture hath Of mar-vel or sur-
2. And if my heart and flesh are weak To bear an un-tried
3. I know not where God's is-lands lift Their frond-ed palms in

prise; I on-ly know that life and death God's
pain, The frail-est reed God will not break, But
air; I on-ly know I can-not drift Be-

mer-cy un-der-lies. I on-ly know that
strength-en and sus-tain. The frail-est reed God
yond God's love and care. I on-ly know I

life and death God's mer-cy un-der-lies.
will not break, But strength-en and sus-tain.
can-not drift Be-yond God's love and care.

Text: John Greenleaf Whittier, 1807-1892; alt.
Tune: James Leith Macbeth Bain, c. 1840-1925; harm. Gordon Jacob, 1895- ; adapted by Rosalee Elser, 1925- ,
   by permission of Oxford University Press.

127   I Am Trusting Thee, Lord Jesus

D. and C. 10:6
II Nephi 3:61

BULLINGER 8.5.8.5.

1. I am trust-ing thee, Lord Je - sus; At thy feet I bow;
2. I am trust-ing thee to guide me; Thou a - lone shalt lead,
3. I am trust-ing thee, Lord Je - sus; Nev - er let me fall;

For thy grace and ten - der mer - cy, Lord, we trust thee now.
Ev - ery day and hour sup - ply - ing All that I may need.
I am trust-ing thee for - ev - er, Trust-ing thee for all. A-men.

Text: Frances Ridley Havergal, 1836-1879.
Tune: Ethelbert W. Bullinger, 1837-1913.

128   Abide with Me

Luke 24:28 (29)
Matthew 11:29, 30 (28-30)

EVENTIDE 10.10.10.10.

1. A - bide with me; fast falls the e - ven - tide. The dark-ness
2. Swift to its close ebbs out life's lit - tle day; Earth's joys grow
3. I need thy Spir - it ev - ery pass - ing hour; What but thy
4. I fear no foe with thee at hand to bless; Ills have no

deep - ens; Lord, with me a - bide. When oth - er help - ers fail, and
dim, its glo - ries pass a - way; Change and de - cay in all a -
grace can foil the tempt-er's power? Who like thy - self my guide and
weight, and tears no bit - ter - ness. Where is death's sting? Where, grave, thy

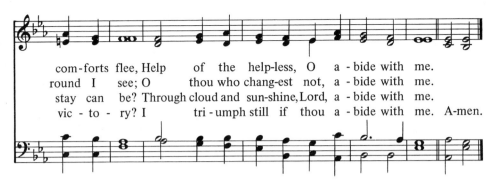

com-forts flee, Help of the help-less, O a - bide with me.
round I see; O thou who chang-est not, a - bide with me.
stay can be? Through cloud and sun-shine, Lord, a - bide with me.
vic - to - ry? I tri - umph still if thou a - bide with me. A-men.

Text: Henry Francis Lyte, 1793-1847.
Tune: William Henry Monk, 1823-1889.

I Need Thee Every Hour 129

Psalm 25:4, 5   NEED 6.4.6.4. with refrain
D. and C. 61:6c-e

1. I need thee ev-ery hour, Most gra - cious Lord; No ten - der voice like
2. I need thee ev-ery hour; Stay thou near - by; Temp-ta - tions lose their
3. I need thee ev-ery hour, In joy or pain; Come quick-ly and a -
4. I need thee ev-ery hour; Teach me thy will, And thy rich prom-is -

Refrain

thine Can peace af - ford.
power When thou art nigh.   I need thee, oh, I need thee; Ev- ery hour I
bide, Or life is vain.
es In me ful - fill.

need thee; Oh, bless me now, my Sav-ior; I come to thee. A - men.

Text: Annie S. Hawks, 1835-1872.
Tune: Robert Lowry, 1826-1899.

130 How Gentle God's Command

I John 5:3
Alma 14:124

JAMES S.M.

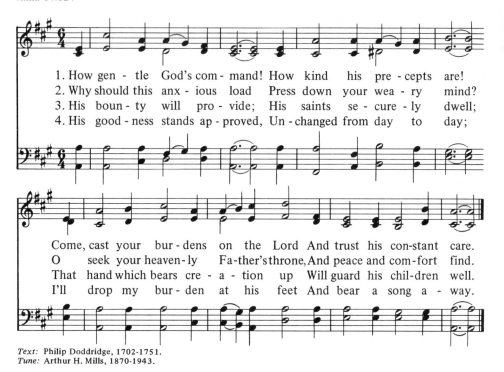

1. How gen - tle God's com - mand! How kind his pre - cepts are!
2. Why should this anx - ious load Press down your wea - ry mind?
3. His boun - ty will pro - vide; His saints se - cure - ly dwell;
4. His good - ness stands ap - proved, Un - changed from day to day;

Come, cast your bur - dens on the Lord And trust his con - stant care.
O seek your heaven - ly Fa - ther's throne, And peace and com - fort find.
That hand which bears cre - a - tion up Will guard his chil - dren well.
I'll drop my bur - den at his feet And bear a song a - way.

Text: Philip Doddridge, 1702-1751.
Tune: Arthur H. Mills, 1870-1943.

131 Unmoved by Fear, My Praise Is Due

I Nephi 5:59
D. and C. 6:15a, b

PARK STREET 8.8.8.8.8.8.

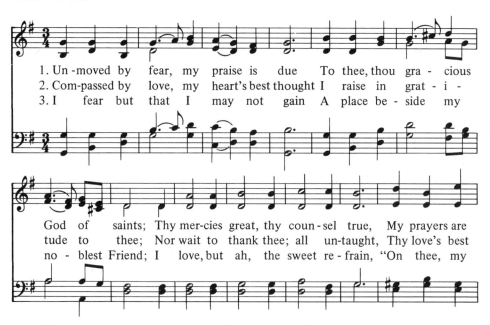

1. Un - moved by fear, my praise is due To thee, thou gra - cious
2. Com - passed by love, my heart's best thought I raise in grat - i -
3. I fear but that I may not gain A place be - side my

God of saints; Thy mer - cies great, thy coun - sel true, My prayers are
tude to thee; Nor wait to thank thee; all un - taught, Thy love's best
no - blest Friend; I love, but ah, the sweet re - frain, "On thee, my

heard and my com-plaints; My prayers are heard and my com-plaints.
gift hath taught it me; Thy love's best gift hath taught it me.
Sav - ior, I de - pend; On thee, my Sav - ior, I de-pend!" A-men.

Text: Joseph Smith III, 1832-1914.
Tune: Frederick M. A. Venua, 1788-1872.

O Love That Wilt Not Let Me Go 132

Ether 5:33, 34
Romans 8:38, 39

ST. MARGARET 8.8.8.8.6.

1. O Love that wilt not let me go, I rest my wea - ry
2. O Light that fol - lowest all my way, I yield my flick -ering
3. O Joy that seek - est me through pain, I can - not close my
4. O Cross that lift - est up my head, I dare not ask to

soul in thee; I give thee back the life I owe That
torch to thee; My heart re - stores its bor - rowed ray That
heart to thee; I trace the rain - bow through the rain And
fly from thee; I lay in dust life's glo - ry dead, And

in thine o - cean depths its flow May rich - er, full - er be.
in thy sun - shine's blaze its day May bright - er, fair - er be.
feel the prom - ise is not vain That morn shall tear - less be.
from the ground there blos - soms red Life that shall end - less be.

Text: George Matheson, 1842-1906.
Tune: Albert Peace, 1844-1912.

133 Cast Thy Burden upon the Lord

Psalm 55:22
Psalm 16:8, 9

BIRMINGHAM 8.6.11.6.6.6.7.5.

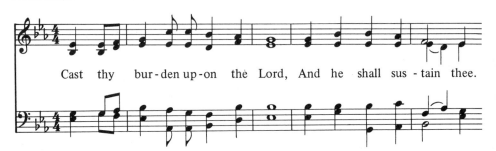

Cast thy bur-den up-on the Lord, And he shall sus-tain thee.

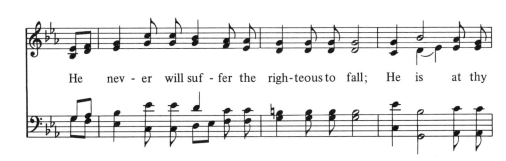

He nev-er will suf-fer the righ-teous to fall; He is at thy

right hand. Thy mer-cy, Lord, is great And far a-bove the heavens;

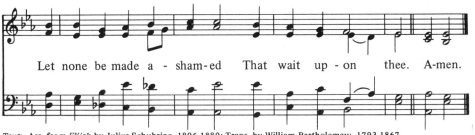

Let none be made a-sham-ed That wait up-on thee. A-men.

Text: Arr. from *Elijah* by Julius Schubring, 1806-1889; Trans. by William Bartholemew, 1793-1867.
Tune: Felix Mendelssohn, 1809-1847.

I Heard the Voice of Jesus Say

Matthew 11:29, 30 (28-30)
D. and C. 63:7

134

VOX DILECTI C.M.D.

1. I heard the voice of Je-sus say, "Come un-to me and rest;
2. I heard the voice of Je-sus say, "Be-hold, I free-ly give
3. I heard the voice of Je-sus say, "I am this dark world's light;

I bring good ti-dings of re-lease To thee who art op-pressed."
The liv-ing wa-ter! Thirst-y one, Stoop down and drink and live."
Look un-to me; thy morn shall rise, And all thy day be bright."

I came to Je-sus as I was, Wea-ry and worn and sad;
I came to Je-sus and I drank Of that life-giv-ing stream;
I looked to Je-sus, and I found In him my star, my sun;

I found in him a rest-ing place, And he has made me glad.
My thirst was quenched, my soul re-vived, And now I live in him.
And in that light of life I'll walk Till trav-eling days are done.

Text: Horatius Bonar, 1808-1889, alt.
Tune: John B. Dykes, 1823-1876.

135 World Around Us, Sky Above Us

II Corinthians 5:16, 17
II Nephi 3:34-36, 42

EBENEZER 8.7.8.7.D.

1. World a - round us, sky a - bove us, Framed our lives from
2. Winds of prom - ise swirl a - round us, Driv - ing us from

in - fan - cy; Lone - ly, we have climbed the moun-tains, Searching
pole to pole; Gold - en i - dols, crim - son al - tars, Lure us

for i - den - ti - ty; Low - ly sta - tions, pain - ful
on, far from our goal. Grant us time to write a

bar - riers, Blur our view and bruise our soul; You, who shape the
chap - ter In our ven - ture on this earth, Teach-ing trust and

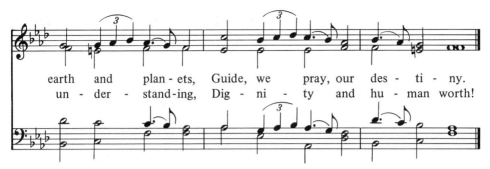

earth   and   plan - ets,   Guide,   we   pray,   our   des - ti - ny.
un - der - stand-ing,   Dig - ni - ty   and   hu - man worth!

Text: Jean E. Garriott, 1918 - ; alt.; copyright 1970 Hymn Society of America; used by permission.
Tune: Thomas J. Williams, 1869-1944; used by permission of Dilys A. Evans and Eluned Crump.

How Firm a Foundation 136

Helaman 2:74, 75
Isaiah 41:10

FOUNDATION 11.11.11.11.

1. How firm a foun - da -tion, ye saints of the Lord Is laid for your
2. In   ev - ery con - di - tion, in sick - ness, in health, In pov - er - ty's
3. Fear not, I am with thee; Oh, be not dis-mayed, For I   am thy
4. The soul that on   Je - sus still leans for re - pose I will not, I

faith in his   ex - cel - lent word; What more   can   he   say   than to
vale or a - bound-ing in wealth, At   home   or   a - broad, on the
God, and will still give thee aid; I'll strength-en thee, help thee, and
can - not de - sert   to his   foes; That soul, though all   hell should en-

you   he hath said, Who un - to the Sav - ior for ref - uge have fled?
land or the sea, As thy days may de - mand so thy suc - cor shall be.
cause thee to stand, Up - held by my righ-teous, om - nip - o - tent hand.
deav - or to shake, I'll nev - er, no, nev - er, no, nev - er for - sake!

Text: "K" in John Rippon's *Selection of Hymns*, 1787.
Tune: Early American Melody; harm. Rosalee Elser, 1925 - ; copyright 1980 Rosalee Elser; used by permission.

137 My Times Are in Thy Hand

Psalm 31:14, 15
D. and C. 98:5g-j

DENNIS S.M.

1. "My times are in thy hand!" My God, I wish them there;
2. "My times are in thy hand," What-ev-er they may be,
3. "My times are in thy hand!" Why should I doubt or fear?

My life, my friends, my soul I leave En-trust-ed to thy care.
If pleas-ing, pain-ful, dark, or bright, As best may seem to thee.
My Fa-ther's hand will nev-er cause His child a need-less tear. A-men.

Text: William Freeman Lloyd, 1791-1853; alt.
Tune: Johann G. Nägeli, 1773-1836; arr. Lowell Mason, 1792-1872.

138 Nearer, My God, to Thee

D. and C. 85:16
Psalm 34:1, 3, 4, 7-9, 22

BETHANY 6.4.6.4.6.6.6.4.
Alternate hymn: 139

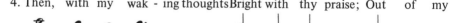

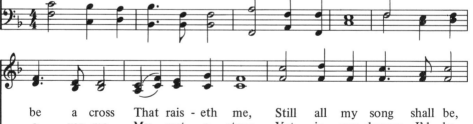

1. Near-er, my God, to thee, Near-er to thee! E'en though it
2. Though like the wan-der-er, The sun gone down, Dark-ness be
3. There let the way ap-pear On-ward to heaven—All that thou
4. Then, with my wak-ing thoughts Bright with thy praise; Out of my

be a cross That rais-eth me, Still all my song shall be,
o-ver me, My rest a stone, Yet in my dreams I'd be
send-est me In mer-cy given— An-gels to beck-on me
ston-y griefs Beth-el I'll raise, So by my woes to be

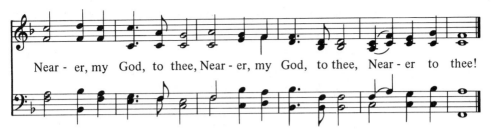

Text: Sarah F. Adams, 1805-1848.
Tune: Lowell Mason, 1792-1872.

Nearer, My God, to Thee

139

D. and C. 85:16
Psalm 34:1, 3, 4, 7-9, 22

WILMINGTON 6.4.6.4.6.6.4.
Alternate hymn: 138

1. Near - er, my God, to thee, Near - er to thee! E'en though it
2. Though like the wan - der - er, The sun gone down, Dark - ness be
3. There let the way ap - pear On - ward to heaven— All that thou
4. Then, with my wak - ing thoughts Bright with thy praise; Out of my

be a cross That rais - eth me, Still all my song shall be,
o - ver me, My rest a stone, Yet in my dreams I'd be
send - est me In mer - cy given— An - gels to beck - on me
ston - y griefs Beth - el I'll raise, So by my woes to be

Near - er, my God, to thee, near - er to thee!

Text: Sarah F. Adams, 1805-1848.
Tune: Erik Routley, 1917 - ; used by permission of the composer.

140 Awake! Ye Saints of God, Awake

Deuteronomy 4:29
Alma 16:219-222

DUKE STREET L.M.

1. A -wake! Ye saints of God, a - wake! Call on the
2. He will re - gard his peo - ple's cry, The wid -ow's
3. Then let your souls be stayed on God; A glo - rious
4. A -wake to un - ion and be one, Or, saith the

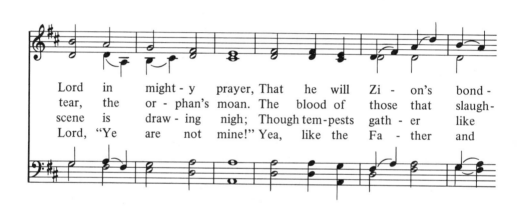

Lord in might - y prayer, That he will Zi - on's bond -
tear, the or - phan's moan. The blood of those that slaugh-
scene is draw - ing nigh; Though tem-pests gath - er like
Lord, "Ye are not mine!" Yea, like the Fa - ther and

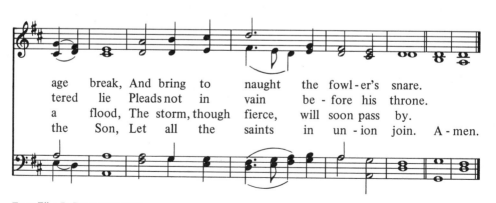

age break, And bring to naught the fowl -er's snare.
tered lie Pleads not in vain be - fore his throne.
a flood, The storm, though fierce, will soon pass by.
the Son, Let all the saints in un - ion join. A - men.

Text: Eliza R. Snow, 1804-1887.
Tune: John C. Hatton, (?)-1793.

Father, in Thy Mysterious Presence 141

I Chronicles 16:28-31
Alma 16:178-182

STRENGTH AND STAY 11.10.11.10.

1. Fa - ther, in thy mys - te - rious pres - ence kneel - ing,
2. Lord, we have wan - dered forth through doubt and sor - row,
3. Now, Fa - ther, now in thy dear pres - ence kneel - ing,

Oh, that our souls feel all thy kin - dling love!
And thou hast made each step an on - ward one;
Our spir - its yearn to feel thy kin - dling love;

For we are weak and need some deep re - veal - ing
So we will ev - er trust each un - known mor - row;
Now make us strong; we need thy deep re - veal - ing

Of trust and strength and calm-ness from a - bove.
Thou wilt sus - tain us till its work is done.
Of trust and strength and calm-ness from a - bove. A - men.

Text: Samuel Johnson, 1822-1882.
Tune: John B. Dykes, 1823-1876. Harm. alt. by Rosalee Elser, 1925 - .

142
A Mighty Fortress Is Our God

Psalm 91:2
D. and C. 18:1a-c

EIN' FESTE BURG 8.7.8.7.6.6.6.6.7.

Descant third stanza

3. That Word a - bove____ all, a - bid - eth;

1. A might-y for-tress is our God, A bul-wark nev-er fail - ing;
2. Did we in our own strength con-fide, Our striv-ing would be los - ing.
3. That Word a - bove all earth - ly powers, No thanks to them, a - bid - eth;

The gifts____ are ours, Who with us sid - eth.

Our help-er He a - mid the flood Of mor-tal ills pre-vail - ing.
Were not the right Man on our side, The Man of God's own choos - ing.
The Spir - it and the gifts are ours Through Him who with us sid - eth.

If all we love and claim—Our loved ones, wealth, and fame— Were from us

We have no foe to fear— Our strength, our help is near. Whose power is man - i -
Such love does Christ re - veal That all our wounds can heal; By his un-bound-ed
If all we love and claim— Our loved ones, wealth, and fame—Were from us stripped a -

stripped a-way, Our God does not be-tray! And is for-ev - er. A-men.

fest To lay our fears to rest. On earth Christ has no e - qual.
grace We stand be-fore God's face; Our Lord has won the bat - tle.
way, Our God does not be-tray! His king-dom is for-ev - er. A-men.

Text: Martin Luther, 1483-1546; tr. Frederick H. Hedge, 1805-1890; rev. Alan Tyree, 1929 - ; copyright 1980 Reorganized Church of Jesus Christ of Latter Day Saints.
Tune: Martin Luther, 1483-1546; descant by Mary E. Caldwell, 1909 - ; descant copyright 1976 by Paragon Associates, Inc.; all rights reserved; used by permission of The Benson Company, Inc., Nashville.

My Faith Looks Up to Thee 143

Moroni 7:47, 48
Hebrews 12:1, 2

OLIVET 6.6.4.6.6.6.4.

1. My faith looks up to thee, Thou Lamb of Cal - va - ry,
2. May thy rich grace im - part Strength to my faint - ing heart,
3. While life's dark maze I tread And griefs a - round me spread,

Sav - ior di - vine! Now hear me while I pray, Take all my
My zeal in - spire; As thou hast died for me, Oh, may my
Be thou my guide; Bid dark-ness turn to day; Wipe sor - row's

guilt a - way; Oh, let me from this day Be whol-ly thine!
love for thee Pure, warm, and change-less be, A liv - ing fire.
tears a - way; Nor let me ev - er stray From thee a - side. A-men.

Text: Ray Palmer, 1808-1887.
Tune: Lowell Mason, 1792-1872.

144

D. and C. 1:8
II Nephi 9:133-137

Standing at the Portal

HERMAS 6.5.6.5.D. with refrain

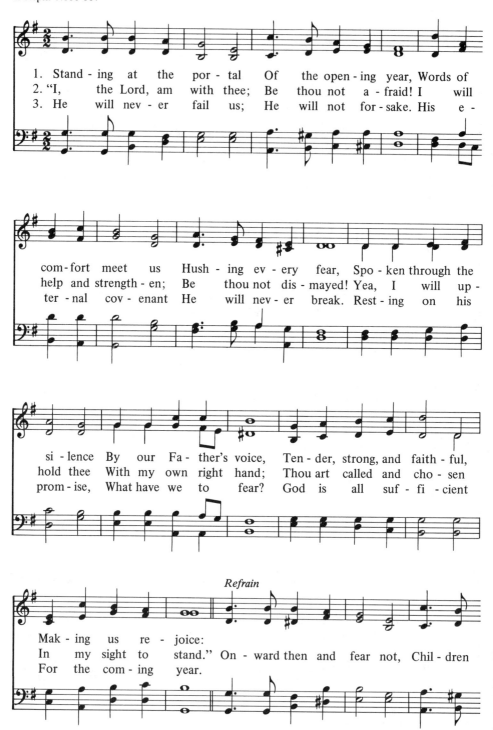

1. Stand-ing at the por-tal Of the open-ing year, Words of com-fort meet us Hush-ing ev-ery fear, Spo-ken through the si-lence By our Fa-ther's voice, Ten-der, strong, and faith-ful, Mak-ing us re-joice:

2. "I, the Lord, am with thee; Be thou not a-fraid! I will help and strength-en; Be thou not dis-mayed! Yea, I will up-hold thee With my own right hand; Thou art called and cho-sen In my sight to stand." On-ward then and fear not, Chil-dren

3. He will nev-er fail us; He will not for-sake. His e-ter-nal cov-enant He will nev-er break. Rest-ing on his prom-ise, What have we to fear? God is all suf-fi-cient For the com-ing year.

Refrain

of the day, For his word shall nev - er, Nev - er pass a - way.

Text and Tune: Frances Ridley Havergal, 1836-1879.

Jesus, Savior, Pilot Me   145

Mark 4:30, 31 (37-39)   PILOT 7.7.7.D.
Psalm 89:8, 9

1. Je - sus, Sav - ior, pi - lot me O - ver life's tem - pes-tuous sea;
2. As a moth - er stills her child, Thou canst hush the o - cean wild;
3. When at last I near the shore, And the fear - ful break-ers roar

Un - known waves be - fore me roll, Hid - ing rock and treacherous shoal;
Bois - terous waves o - bey thy will When thou sayest to them, "Be still."
'Twixt me and the peace-ful rest, Then, while lean - ing on thy breast,

Chart and com - pass come from thee; Je - sus, Sav - ior, pi - lot me.
Won - drous Sov - ereign of the sea, Je - sus, Sav - ior, pi - lot me.
May I hear thee say to me, "Fear not; I will pi-lot thee." A - men.

Text: Edward Hopper, 1818-1888.
Tune: John E. Gould, 1822-1875.

146 Tenderly, Tenderly, Lead Thou Me On

Isaiah 42:16
I Nephi 6:40

TENDERLY LEAD THOU ME ON 10.10.10.10.D.

1. Ten - der - ly, ten - der - ly, lead thou me on, On o'er the way where my
2. Faith-ful - ly, faith - ful - ly, hold-ing my hand, On the rough, slip-pery heights

Sav - ior hath gone; Bright on his path - way the sun - light hath shone;
safe - ly I stand, Look - ing a - way to the heav - en - ly strand;

Ten - der - ly, ten - der - ly, lead thou me on. Close to his hand I so
Ten - der - ly, ten - der - ly, he leads me on. Now has my weak heart grown

trem-bling- ly clung; Faint were the songs I so doubt-ing-ly sung, Bro-ken-ly
trust- ing - ly strong; Ways have grown short that seemed once to be long; Glad-ly I

fall - ing from fal-ter-ing tongue; Ten-der-ly, ten-der-ly, lead thou me on.
join in the tri-um-phant song, Ten-der-ly, ten-der-ly, lead-ing me on. A-men.

Text: Joseph Smith III, 1832-1914.
Tune: Norman W. Smith, 1833-1917.

There Is a Balm in Gilead

147

John 10:11, 13
II Nephi 3:44, 47, 50, 56

BALM IN GILEAD 7.6.7.6. with refrain

There is a balm in Gil - e - ad To make the wound - ed whole;

There is a balm in Gil - e - ad To heal the sin - sick soul.

1. Some-times I feel dis - cour - aged, And think my work's in vain, But
2. If you can't preach like Pe - ter, If you can't pray like Paul, Just

then the Ho - ly Spir - it Re - vives my soul a - gain. There is a
tell the love of Je - sus And say he died for all.

Text: American Folk Hymn.
Tune: American Folk Hymn; arr. Rosalee Elser, 1925 - ; copyright 1980 Rosalee Elser; used by permission.

148 Where Wilt Thou Put Thy Trust?

Psalm 71:5
II Nephi 3:61-66

FERGUSON S.M.

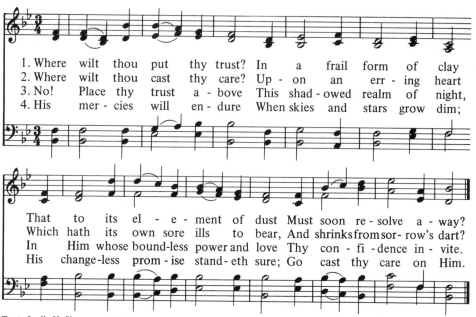

1. Where wilt thou put thy trust? In a frail form of clay
2. Where wilt thou cast thy care? Up-on an err-ing heart
3. No! Place thy trust a-bove This shad-owed realm of night,
4. His mer-cies will en-dure When skies and stars grow dim;

That to its el-e-ment of dust Must soon re-solve a-way?
Which hath its own sore ills to bear, And shrinks from sor-row's dart?
In Him whose bound-less power and love Thy con-fi-dence in-vite.
His change-less prom-ise stand-eth sure; Go cast thy care on Him.

Text: Lydia H. Sigourney, 1793-1865.
Tune: George Kingsley, 1811-1884.

149 Pass Me Not, O Gentle Savior

Alma 13:51
Luke 18:13

PASS ME NOT 8.5.8.5. with refrain

1. Pass me not, O gen-tle Sav-ior; Hear my hum-ble cry; While on
2. Let me at the throne of mer-cy Find a sweet re-lief, Kneel-ing
3. Trust-ing on-ly in thy mer-it I would seek thy face; Heal my
4. Thou, the spring of all my com-fort, More than life to me; Whom have

Refrain

oth-ers thou art call-ing, Do not pass me by.
there in deep con-tri-tion; Help my un-be-lief.
wound-ed, bro-ken spir-it; Save me by thy grace. Sav-ior, Sav-ior,
I on earth be-side thee? Whom in heaven but thee?

hear my hum-ble cry; While on oth-ers thou art call-ing, Do not pass me by.

Text: Fanny J. Crosby, 1820-1915.
Tune: W. H. Doane, 1832-1915.

Lord, in This Hour   150

D. and C. 76:1, 2a, b   WIESBADEN 10.10.10.10.
Romans 11:33, 34, 36

Unison (or harmony)

1. Lord, in this hour en - a - ble us to see   The breadth and
2. Earth-bound, we mark our days from dawn to night;   We know that
3. We count a life from in - fan - cy's first cry   Till death has

depth of thine e - ter - ni - ty.   A   thou - sand years   to
dark - ness ev - er fol - lows light.   Yet, though we can - not
stilled the last un - an - swered "Why?"   But   life and light   go

thee are as a day. Help us to gain this view of time, we pray.
see, we know somewhere Be - yond our shad-owed sphere the sun is there.
on un - end - ing - ly— One bright mo - sa - ic known a - lone to thee.

Text: Naomi Russell, 1921 - ; copyright 1980 Reorganized Church of Jesus Christ of Latter Day Saints.
Tune: Dale G. Rider, 1948 - ; copyright 1974 White Harvest Music Corporation; used by permission.

151 Every Good and Perfect Gift

James 1:17, 18
I Corinthians 13:13

EMERALD 7.6.7.6.7.7.7.7.7.

1. Ev - ery good and per - fect gift Of the Lord's con - fer - ring
2. Bro - ken hearts and dreams a - bound In a world of sor - row;
3. Man - i - fold the gifts of God, For our hu - man need - ing;

Cul - ti - vates the seeds of grace In the soul be - stir - ring.
Still the gift of hope as - sures Vic - tory for to - mor - row.
Char - i - ty, pure love of Christ, Ev - ery gift ex - ceed - ing.

Faith pro - claims a ris - en Lord, Cel - e - brates new
Hope to o - ver - come de - spair, Throw a - side the
In com - pas - sion's ten - der vein, Bread for hun - ger,

life re - stored, Seeks for truth yet un - ex - plored; Faith's foun -
weight of care, And the king - dom's vi - sion share. Free - dom
balm for pain, Love ex - tends its gra - cious reign, Love, the

da - tion nev - er fails, Faith's foun - da - tion nev - er fails.
soars on wings of hope, Free - dom soars on wings of hope.
great - est gift of all, Love, the great - est gift of all.

Text: Geoffrey F. Spencer, 1927 - ; copyright 1980 Reorganized Church of Jesus Christ of Latter Day Saints.
Tune: Mark H. Forscutt, 1834-1903.

Beyond the Mist and Doubt

152

WALHOF 6.6.8.8.6.6.

I John 3:1, 2
Romans 5:8-11

1. Be - yond the mist and doubt Of this un - cer - tain day,
2. Our rest - less in - tel - lect Has all things in its shade,
3. Still in hu - mil - i - ty We know Thee by Thy grace,

accomp.   *accomp.*

I trust in Thine e - ter - nal name, Be - yond all chang - es
But still to Thee my spir - it clings, Ser - ene be - yond all
For sci - en - ce's re - mot - est probe Feels but the fring - es

still the same, And in that name I pray, And in that name I pray.
shak - en things, And I am not a - fraid, And I am not a - fraid.
of Thy robe: Love looks up - on Thy face, Love looks up - on Thy face.

Text: Donald Wynn Hughes, 1911-1967; used by permission of J. D. P. Hughes.
Tune: Frederick F. Jackisch, 1922 - ; alt.; copyright 1978; from *Lutheran Book of Worship*; used by permission of
Augsburg Publishing House.

153

Great Hills May Tremble

Isaiah 54:10
Psalm 46:1, 2, 7, 9, 10

BERGEN MA VIKA 11.10.11.10.

1. Great hills may trem - ble and moun - tains may crum - ble,
2. Though peace be shat - tered by war's ag - i - ta - tion,
3. Strong to pre - serve us in mo - ments of dan - ger,

God's lov - ing - kind - ness con - tin - ues se - cure;
Though change and ten - sion give birth to great fears,
Strong when frus - tra - tion and frail - ty in - crease;

Peace He will give to the con - trite and hum - ble:
God still re - mains an un - shak - en foun - da - tion,
Strong to e - quip us for lov - ing the stran - ger,

Thus saith the Lord— His prom - ise is sure.
Strong to sup - port us through tur - bu - lent years;
Strong where our hu - man re - sourc - es may cease.

Text: Based on Isaiah 54:10 by Lina Sandell, 1832-1903; tr. E. Lincoln Pearson, 1917 - , st. 1, alt.; Bryan Jeffery Leech, 1931 - , st. 2, 3. Copyright 1950, 1973 Covenant Press. All rights reserved. Used by permission.
Tune: Source Unknown.

Sometimes a Light Surprises

154

II Nephi 3:61, 64, 65
D. and C. 10:6

SPRINGTIME 7.6.7.6.D.
Alternate hymn: 155

1. Some - times a light sur - pris - es All Chris-tians while they sing;
2. In ho - ly con - tem - pla - tion We sweet-ly then pur - sue
3. Though vine nor fig tree nei - ther Their prom-ised fruit should bear,

It is the Lord, who ris - es With heal - ing in his wings.
The theme of God's sal - va - tion, And find it ev - er new;
Though all the field should with - er, Nor flocks nor herds be there;

When com - forts are de - clin - ing, He grants the soul a - gain
Set free from pres - ent sor - row, We cheer - ful - ly can say,
Yet God the same a - bid - ing, His praise shall tune my voice;

A sea - son of clear shin - ing To cheer it af - ter rain.
Let the un - known to - mor - row Bring with it what it may,
For, while in him con - fid - ing, I can - not but re - joice.

Text: William Cowper, 1731-1800; alt.
Tune: Swedish Folk Melody; harm. Rosalee Elser, 1925 - ; harm. copyright 1980 by Rosalee Elser. Used by permission.

155

Sometimes a Light Surprises

II Nephi 3:61, 64, 65
D. and C. 10:6

SURPRISE 7.6.7.6.7.6.7.6.6.
Alternate hymn: 154

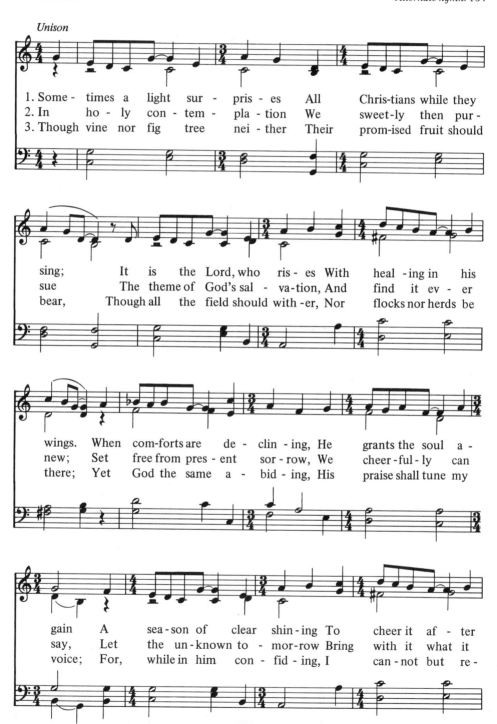

Unison

1. Some - times a light sur - pris - es All Chris-tians while they sing; It is the Lord, who ris - es With heal - ing in his wings. When com-forts are de - clin - ing, He grants the soul a - gain A sea-son of clear shin-ing To cheer it af - ter

2. In ho - ly con - tem - pla - tion We sweet-ly then pur - sue The theme of God's sal - va-tion, And find it ev - er new; Set free from pres - ent sor - row, We cheer-ful - ly can say, Let the un-known to - mor-row Bring with it what it

3. Though vine nor fig tree nei - ther Their prom-ised fruit should bear, Though all the field should with -er, Nor flocks nor herds be there; Yet God the same a - bid - ing, His praise shall tune my voice; For, while in him con - fid - ing, I can - not but re -

rain,   To   cheer it af - ter   rain.
may,   Bring   with it what   it   may.
joice,   I   can - not but   re - joice.

Text: William Cowper, 1731-1800; alt.
Tune: Jane M. Marshall, 1924 - ; copyright 1974 Carl Fischer, Inc., New York; international copyright secured; all rights reserved; used by permission.

Children of the Heavenly Father   156

D. and C. 98:5h-j
John 10:27, 28

TRYGGARE KAN INGEN VARA L.M.

1. Chil - dren of the heaven - ly Fa - ther Safe - ly
2. Nei - ther life nor death shall ev - er From the
3. More se - cure is no one ev - er Than the

in his arms they gath - er; Nest - ling bird nor star in
Lord his chil - dren sev - er; Un - to them his grace he
loved ones of the Sav - ior; Not yon star on high a -

heav - en Such a ref - uge e'er was giv - en.
show - eth, And their sor - rows all he know - eth.
bid - ing Nor the bird in home - nest hid - ing.

Text: Caroline V. Sandell-Berg, 1832-1903; tr. Ernest W. Olson, 1870-1958; alt.; copyright Board of Publication, Lutheran Church in America.
Tune: Traditional Swedish Melody.

157 My Life Flows On in Endless Song

Isaiah 52:7
II Nephi 3:61, 65, 66

HOW CAN I KEEP FROM SINGING 8.7.8.7. with refrain

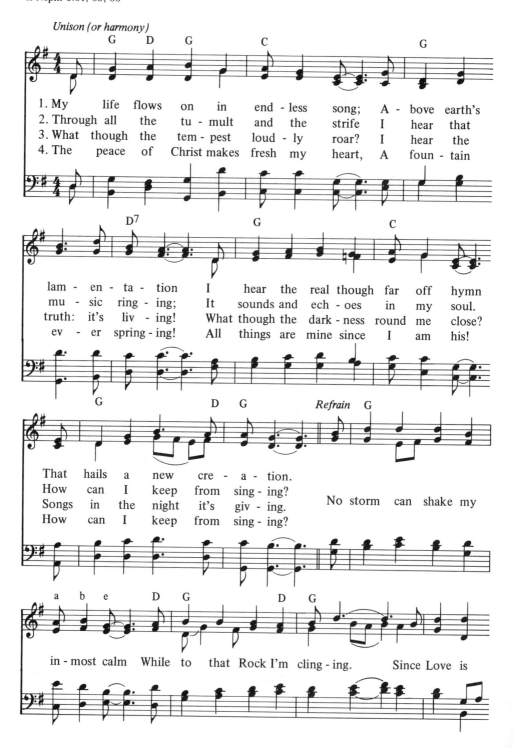

1. My life flows on in end-less song; A-bove earth's lam-en-ta-tion I hear the real though far off hymn That hails a new cre-a-tion.
2. Through all the tu-mult and the strife I hear that mu-sic ring-ing; It sounds and ech-oes in my soul. How can I keep from sing-ing?
3. What though the tem-pest loud-ly roar? I hear the truth: it's liv-ing! What though the dark-ness round me close? Songs in the night it's giv-ing.
4. The peace of Christ makes fresh my heart, A foun-tain ev-er spring-ing! All things are mine since I am his! How can I keep from sing-ing?

No storm can shake my in-most calm While to that Rock I'm cling-ing. Since Love is

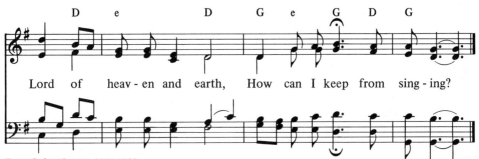

Lord of heav-en and earth, How can I keep from sing-ing?

Text: Robert Lowry, 1826-1899.
Tune: Quaker Hymn; harm. David N. Johnson, 1922 - ; copyright 1977 Praise Publications, Inc.; used by permission.

There's an Old, Old Path 158

Jeremiah 6:16
I Nephi 5:5

THE OLD, OLD PATH 5.5.5.5. with refrain

1. There's an old, old path Where the sun shines through Life's
2. Find the old, old path; 'Twill be ev - er new, For the
3. In this old, old path Are my friends most dear, And I
4. 'Tis an old, old path, Shad-owed vales be - tween, Yet I

Refrain

dark storm clouds From its home of blue,
Sav - ior walks All the way with you,
walk with them, With the an - gels near, In this old, old
fear - less walk With the Naz - a - rene,

path made strange - ly sweet By the touch di - vine of his bless - ed feet.

Text: Vida E. Smith, 1865-1945.
Tune: M. Audentia Anderson, 1872-1963.

159   Oh, for a Faith That Will Not Shrink

II Nephi 13:27-30
D. and C. 5:5b

EVAN C.M.

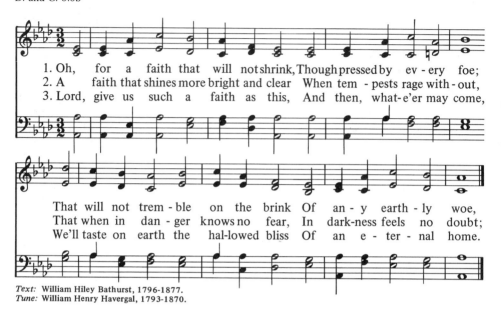

1. Oh, for a faith that will not shrink, Though pressed by ev - ery foe;
2. A faith that shines more bright and clear When tem - pests rage with - out,
3. Lord, give us such a faith as this, And then, what - e'er may come,

That will not trem - ble on the brink Of an - y earth - ly woe,
That when in dan - ger knows no fear, In dark - ness feels no doubt;
We'll taste on earth the hal - lowed bliss Of an e - ter - nal home.

Text: William Hiley Bathurst, 1796-1877.
Tune: William Henry Havergal, 1793-1870.

160   God Is My Strong Salvation

Romans 1:16, 17
Moroni 7:24, 25

AURELIA 7.6.7.6.D.
Alternate hymn: 161

1. God is my strong sal - va - tion; What foe have I to fear?
2. Place on the Lord re - li - ance; My soul, with cour - age wait;

In dark - ness and temp - ta - tion, My light, my help is near.
His truth be thine af - fi - ance When faint and des - o - late.

Though hosts en - camp a - round me, Firm to the fight I stand.
His might thy heart shall strength - en, His love thy joy in - crease.

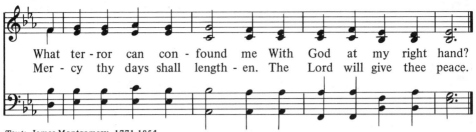

What ter-ror can con-found me With God at my right hand?
Mer-cy thy days shall length-en. The Lord will give thee peace.

Text: James Montgomery, 1771-1854.
Tune: Samuel S. Wesley, 1810-1876.

God Is My Strong Salvation

161

Romans 1:16, 17
Mosiah 3:21

WEDLOCK 7.6.7.6.D.
Alternate Hymn: 160

Unison

1. God is my strong sal - va - tion; What foe have I to fear?
2. Place on the Lord re - li - ance; My soul, with cour - age wait;

In dark - ness and temp - ta - tion, My light, my help is near.
His truth be thine af - fi - ance When faint and des - o - late.

Though hosts en - camp a - round me, Firm to the fight I stand.
His might thy heart shall strength - en, His love thy joy in - crease;

[St. 1.] [St. 2.]

What ter - ror can con - found me With God at my right hand?
Mer - cy thy days shall length - en. The Lord will give thee peace.

Text: James Montgomery, 1771-1854.
Tune: The Sacred Harp, 1844; arr. by Rosalee Elser, 1925 - ; copyright 1980 Rosalee Elser. Used by permission.

162 Savior, Like a Shepherd Lead Us

John 10:27, 29
I Nephi 7:56-59

BRADBURY 8.7.8.7.D.

1. Sav - ior, like a shep-herd lead us; Much we need thy ten - der care;
2. We are thine, do thou be - friend us; Be the guard-ian of our way;
3. Ear - ly let us seek thy fa - vor; Ear - ly let us do thy will;

In thy pleas- ant pas-tures feed us; For our use thy folds pre - pare.
Keep thy flock, from sin de - fend us; Seek us when we go a - stray.
Bless - ed Lord and on - ly Sav - ior, With thy love our bos-oms fill.

Bless - ed Je - sus, bless - ed Je - sus, Thou hast bought us, thine we are;
Bless - ed Je - sus, bless - ed Je - sus, Hear thy chil-dren when they pray:
Bless - ed Je - sus, bless - ed Je - sus, Thou hast loved us, love us still;

Bless - ed Je - sus, bless - ed Je - sus, Thou hast bought us, thine we are.
Bless - ed Je - sus, bless - ed Je - sus, Hear thy chil-dren when they pray.
Bless - ed Je - sus, bless - ed Je - sus, Thou hast loved us, love us still.

Text: From *Hymns for the Young,* 1836. Attr. to Dorothy A. Thrupp, 1779-1847.
Tune: William B. Bradbury, 1816-1868. Harm. alt. by Rosalee Elser, 1925 - .

Thy Love, O God

Romans 12:1, 2
Hebrews 13:20, 21

MORA PROCTOR 11.10.11.10.

Unison

1. Thy love, O God, has all the world cre - at - ed, And led thy
2. We bring thee, Lord, in fer - vent in - ter - ces - sion The chil - dren
3. From out the dark - ness of our hope's frus - tra - tion, From all the
4. In pit - y look up - on thy chil - dren's striv - ing For life and
5. In - spire thy church, mid earth's dis - cord - ant voic - es, To preach the

peo - ple to this pres - ent hour; In Christ we see life's glo - ry
of thy world-wide fam - i - ly: With con - trite hearts we of - fer
bro - ken i - dols of our pride, We turn to seek thy truth's il -
free-dom, peace, com - mu - ni - ty, Till at the full - ness of thy
gos - pel of our Lord a - bove, Un - til the day this war - ring

con - sum - mat - ed; Thy Spir - it man - i - fests his liv - ing power.
our con - fes - sion, For we have sinned a - gainst thy char - i - ty.
lu - mi - na - tion, And find thy mer - cy wait - ing at our side.
truth ar - riv - ing, We reach in Christ the goal of u - ni - ty.
world re - joic - es To hear the might - y har - mo - nies of love.

Text: Albert F. Bayly, 1901 - ; alt.; used by permission of the author.
Tune: William J. Reynolds, 1920 - ; copyright 1975 Broadman Press; all rights reserved; used by permission.

164 God of Smallness, God of Greatness

Philippians 3:12-14
II Timothy 1:6, 7

HYMN OF PRAISE 8.7.8.7.

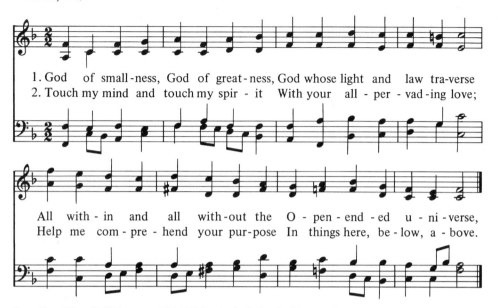

1. God of small-ness, God of great-ness, God whose light and law tra-verse
2. Touch my mind and touch my spir - it With your all - per - vad-ing love;

All with - in and all with-out the O - pen-end - ed u - ni-verse,
Help me com-pre - hend your pur-pose In things here, be - low, a - bove.

Text: Naomi Russell, 1921 - ; copyright 1980 Reorganized Church of Jesus Christ of Latter Day Saints.
Tune: William Graves, 1915 - ; alt.; copyright 1956 Herald Publishing House.

165 Pour Down Thy Spirit from Above

D. and C. 64:2d, e
Mosiah 11:139, 140

HAMBURG L.M.

1. Pour down thy Spir - it from a - bove And bid all
2. If in the souls where love should be, A - rise the
3. When-e'er in this wide world we meet Un - kind - ly
4. In ev - ery land, in ev - ery home, In ev - ery

strife and dis - cord cease; Join heart to heart in mu -
storm of fierce self - will, Calm thou the trou - bled, an -
deeds that an - ger move, Teach us for - give - ness; tri -
heart let love in - crease; Let love pro - claim thy king -

tual   love;   O   reign a - mong   us,   Prince   of   Peace.
gry   sea;   Speak   to   the   tem - pest, "Peace,   be   still."
umph sweet   To   con -quer e - vil   will   with   love!
dom   come;   O   reign a - mong   us,   Prince   of   Peace. A - men.

Text: William Romanis, 1824-1899.
Tune: Gregorian Chant, arr. Lowell Mason, 1792-1872.

Come, Ye Disconsolate 166

II Nephi 3:42, 47, 50
Colossians 3:1-4

CONSOLATOR 11.10.11.10.

1. Come,   ye   dis - con - so - late,   wher - e'er ye   lan - guish, Come   to   the
2. Joy   of   the   des - o - late,   light   of   the   stray - ing, Hope   of   the
3. Here   take   the   Bread   of   Life;   drink wa - ters   flow - ing   Forth from the

mer - cy   seat,   fer - vent - ly   kneel;   Here   bring your   wound - ed hearts,
pen - i - tent,   fade - less   and   pure!   Here speaks the   Com - fort - er,
throne   of   God,   pure   from   a - bove: Come to   the   feast   of love;

here   tell   your   an - guish: Earth has   no   sor - row that God can-not   heal.
ten - der - ly   say - ing, "Earth has   no   sor - row that God can-not   cure."
come, ev - er   know -ing   Earth has   no   sor - row God can -not re - move.

Text: Thomas Moore, 1779-1852, sts. 1, 2, alt.; Thomas Hastings, 1784-1872, st. 3, alt.
Tune: Samuel Webbe, 1740-1816.

167 Jesus, the Very Thought of Thee

Acts 2:28
D. and C. 6:16

ST. AGNES C.M.

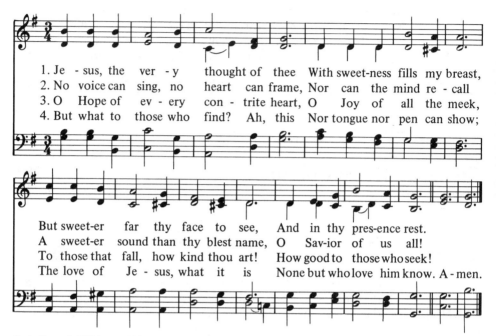

1. Je - sus, the ver - y thought of thee With sweet-ness fills my breast,
2. No voice can sing, no heart can frame, Nor can the mind re - call
3. O Hope of ev - ery con - trite heart, O Joy of all the meek,
4. But what to those who find? Ah, this Nor tongue nor pen can show;

But sweet-er far thy face to see, And in thy pres-ence rest.
A sweet-er sound than thy blest name, O Sav-ior of us all!
To those that fall, how kind thou art! How good to those who seek!
The love of Je - sus, what it is None but who love him know. A - men.

Text: Bernard of Clairvaux, 1091-1153; trans. Edward Caswall, 1814-1878; alt.
Tune: John B. Dykes, 1823-1876.

168 Draw Thou My Soul, O Christ

Hebrews 10:22-24
D. and C. 85:16

ST. EDMUND 6.4.6.4.6.6.6.4.

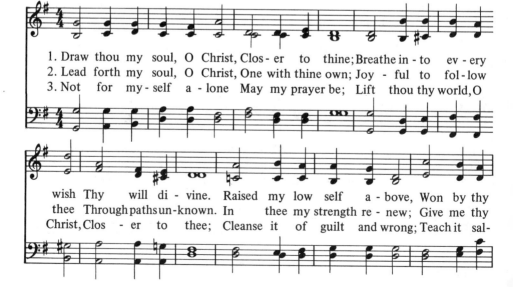

1. Draw thou my soul, O Christ, Clos - er to thine; Breathe in - to ev - ery
2. Lead forth my soul, O Christ, One with thine own; Joy - ful to fol - low
3. Not for my - self a - lone May my prayer be; Lift thou thy world, O

wish Thy will di - vine. Raised my low self a - bove, Won by thy
thee Through paths un-known. In thee my strength re - new; Give me thy
Christ, Clos - er to thee; Cleanse it of guilt and wrong; Teach it sal-

Text: Lucy Larcom, 1826-1893.
Tune: Arthur S. Sullivan, 1842-1900.

Mysterious Presence, Source of All 169

II Nephi 6:103, 104
Deuteronomy 30:14-16, 19, 20

ADON OLOM L.M.

Moderato

1. Mys - te - rious Pres - ence, source of all— The world with -
2. Your breath is in the rush - ing wind; Your spir - it
3. Your hand un - seen to ac - cents clear A - woke the
4. That touch di - vine still, Lord, im - part; Still give the

out, the soul with - in— O fount of life, now
stirs in leaf and flower; Nor will you from the
psalm - ist's trem - bling lyre, And touched the lips of
proph - et's burn - ing word; And vo - cal in each

hear our call, And pour your liv - ing wa - ters in.
ea - ger mind With - hold your love and light and power.
ho - ly seer With flame from your own al - tar fire.
wait - ing heart Let liv - ing psalms of praise be heard.

Text: Seth Curtis Beach, 1837-1932, alt.
Tune: Eliezer Gerovitch, 1844-1914.

170 Love Divine, All Loves Excelling

I John 3:1-3
D. and C. 34:6

BLAENWERN 8.7.8.7.D.

1. Love di - vine, all loves ex - cel - ling, Joy of heaven to earth come down,
2. Breathe, O breathe thy lov - ing Spir - it In - to ev - ery trou - bled breast;
3. Come, Al - might - y to de - liv - er, Let us all thy grace re - ceive!
4. Fin - ish then thy new cre - a - tion; Pure and spot - less may we be.

Fix in us thy hum - ble dwell - ing; All thy faith - ful mer - cies crown.
Let us all in thee in - her - it; Let us find the prom - ised rest.
Sud - den - ly re - turn and nev - er, Nev - er more thy tem - ples leave.
Let us see thy great sal - va - tion Per - fect - ly re - stored in thee;

Je - sus, thou art all com - pas - sion; Pure, un - bound - ed love thou art.
Take a - way the love of sin - ning; Al - pha and O - me - ga be;
Thee we would be al - ways bless - ing, Serv - ing thee like those a - bove;
Changed from glo - ry in - to glo - ry Till in heaven we take our place,

Vis - it us with thy sal - va - tion; En - ter ev - ery trem - bling heart.
End of faith, as its be - gin - ning, Set our hearts at lib - er - ty.
We would praise thee with - out ceas - ing, Glo - ry in thy per - fect love.
Till we cast our crowns be - fore thee, Lost in won - der, love, and praise. A - men.

Text: Charles Wesley, 1707-1788.
Tune: W. P. Rowlands, 1860-1937; copyright G. A. Gabe, Swansea, S. Wales.

Help Us Accept Each Other

171

II Nephi 13:29
I John 4:16, 19

AURELIA 7.6.7.6.D.
Alternate tune: THAXTED (375)

1. Help us ac - cept each oth - er as Christ ac - cept - ed us;
2. Teach us, O Lord, your les - sons, as in our dai - ly life
3. Let your ac - cept - ance change us, so that we may be moved
4. Lord, for to - day's en - coun - ters with all who are in need,

Teach us as sis - ter, bro - ther each per - son to em - brace.
We strug - gle to be hu - man and search for hope and faith.
In liv - ing sit - u - a - tions to do the truth in love;
Who hun - ger for ac - cept - ance, for righ - teous - ness and bread,

Be pres - ent, Lord, a - mong us and bring us to be - lieve
Teach us to care for peo - ple, for all— not just for some,
To prac - tice your ac - cept - ance un - til we know by heart
We need new eyes for see - ing, new hands for hold - ing on:

We are our - selves ac - cept - ed and meant to love and live.
To love them as we find them and as they may be - come.
The ta - ble of for - give - ness and laugh - ter's heal - ing art.
Re - new us with your Spir - it; Lord free us, make us one!

Text: Fred Kaan, 1929 - ; copyright 1975 by Agape, Carol Stream, IL 60187. International copyright secured. All rights reserved. Used by permission.
Tune: Samuel S. Wesley, 1810-1876.

172   God, Who Touchest Earth with Beauty

Psalm 51:10-12
Daniel 12:3

SACRED REST 8.5.8.5.

1. God, who touch-est earth with beau-ty, Make my heart a - new;
2. Like thy springs and run - ning wa - ters Make me crys - tal pure;
3. Like thy danc - ing waves in sun - light Make me glad and free;
4. Like the arch - ing of the heav - ens Lift my thoughts a - bove;
5. God, who touch-est earth with beau-ty, Make my heart a - new;

With thy Spir - it re - cre - ate me, Pure and strong and true.
Like thy rocks of tower-ing gran-deur Make me strong and sure.
Like the straight-ness of the pine trees Let me up - right be.
Turn my dreams to no - ble ac - tion—Min - is - tries of love.
Keep me ev - er, by thy Spir - it, Pure and strong and true. A - men.

Text: Mary S. Edgar, 1889-1973; from *Under Open Skies*, copyright 1955 by Clarke, Irwin and Co. Ltd. Used
by permission.
Tune: J. B. Birkbeck, 1831-1917.

173   Break Thou the Bread of Life

John 6:47-49
D. and C. 32:3a, d, e

BREAD OF LIFE 6.4.6.4.D.

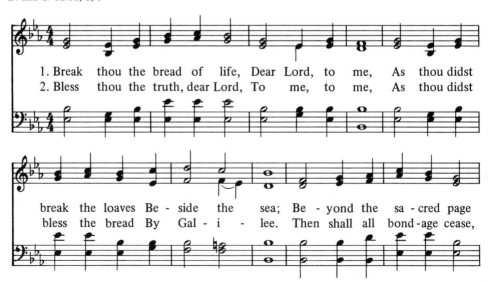

1. Break thou the bread of life, Dear Lord, to me, As thou didst
2. Bless thou the truth, dear Lord, To me, to me, As thou didst

break the loaves Be - side the sea; Be - yond the sa - cred page
bless the bread By Gal - i - lee. Then shall all bond-age cease,

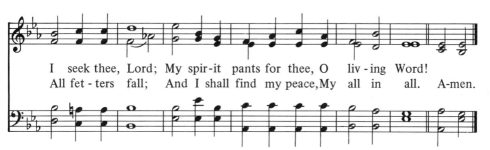

I seek thee, Lord; My spir-it pants for thee, O liv-ing Word!
All fet-ters fall; And I shall find my peace, My all in all. A-men.

Text: Mary A. Lathbury, 1841-1913.
Tune: William F. Sherwin, 1826-1888.

O Christ, My Lord, Create in Me 174

Matthew 6:10, 11 (9, 10)
II Nephi 8:18, 20

RETREAT L.M.

1. O Christ, my Lord, cre-ate in me The per-son
2. O Lord, may ev-ery soul em-brace The won-ders
3. O Christ, make vis-i-ble your Church, As all for
4. Em-man-u-el, O Prince of Peace, To ev-ery

I am meant to be. My soul es-tranged, I'm prone to
of your match-less grace. From guilt and fear each one set
life and mean-ing search. Your will be done! O set a-
na-tion bring re-lease. Beat from each sword a plow-share

sin; Re-deem my life, with-out, with-in.
free; Cre-ate a new hu-man-i-ty.
flame That fel-low-ship which bears your name.
strong; Your king-dom come: my prayer, my song. A-men.

Text: Chester E. Custer, 1920 - ; alt.; copyright 1972 by the author; used by permission.
Tune: Thomas Hastings, 1784-1872; arr. Rosalee Elser, 1925 - ; copyright 1980 Rosalee Elser; used by permission.

175

I Nephi 7:56-59
Colossians 3:11-14

O God of Every Nation

ST. THEODULPH 7.6.7.6.D.

1. O God of ev-ery na - tion, of ev - ery race and land,
2. From lust for wealth and pow - er, from scorn of truth and right,
3. When hope and cour-age fal - ter, let thy still voice be heard;

Re - deem thy whole cre - a - tion with thine al - might-y hand.
From trust in bombs that show - er de - struc-tion through the night,
With faith that none can al - ter, thy ser - vants un - der-gird.

Where hate and fear di - vide us and bit - ter threats are hurled,
From pride of race and sta - tion and blind-ness to thy way,
Keep bright in us the vi - sion of days when war shall cease,

In love and mer - cy guide us, and heal our strife-torn world.
De - liv - er ev - ery na - tion, E - ter - nal God, we pray.
When ha - tred and di - vi - sion give way to love and peace.

Text: William Watkins Reid, Jr., 1923 - ; alt.; copyright 1958 The Hymn Society of America; used by permission.
Tune: Melchior Teschner, 1584-1635.

Teach Me, God, to Wonder

176

Alma 17:69
John 17:3

TEACH ME GOD 6.5.9. with refrain

Unison (or harmony)

1. Teach me God to won - der. Teach me God to see.
2. Let me God be o - pen, Let me lov - ing be.
3. Let me God be read - y, Let me be a - wake—
4. Teach me God to know you, Hear you when you speak—

Let your world of beau - ty cap - ture me.
Let your world of peo - ple speak to me.
In your pres - ent king - dom my place take.
See you in my neigh - bor when we meet.

Refrain

Praise to you be giv - en; Love for you be lived.

Life be cel - e - brat - ed; Joy you give.

Text: Walter Farquharson, 1936 - ; copyright 1977 The Frederick Harris Music Company; used by permission.
Tune: Ron Klusmeier; copyright 1977 The Frederick Harris Music Company; harm. 1980 Rosalee Elser, 1925 - ;
used by permission.

177 O God, in Restless Living

John 14:27
Moroni 7:3

NYLAND 7.6.7.6.D.

1. O God, in rest-less liv-ing We lose our spir-its' peace.
2. Teach us, be-yond our striv-ing, The rich re-wards of rest.
3. Re-cep-tive make our spir-its, Our need is to be still;

Calm our un-wise con-fu-sion, Bid thou our clam-or cease.
Who does not live se-rene-ly Is nev-er deep-ly blest.
As dawn fades flick-ering can-dle So dim our anx-ious will.

Let anx-ious hearts grow qui-et, Like pools at eve-ning still,
O tran-quil, ra-diant Sun-light, Bring thou our lives to flower,
Re-veal thy ra-diance through us, Thine am-ple strength re-lease.

Till thy re-flect-ed heav-ens All our spir-its fill.
Less wear-ied with our ef-fort, More a-ware of power.
Not ours but thine the tri-umph In the power of peace.

Text: Harry Emerson Fosdick, 1878-1969; used by permission of Elinor F. Downs.
Tune: Traditional Finnish Melody; harm. David Evans, 1874-1948; from the *Revised Church Hymnary 1927* by permission of Oxford University Press.

Lord, I Was Blind: I Could Not See

178

John 9:25
Alma 16:198-200

SOLOTHURN L.M.

Unison (or harmony)

1. Lord, I was blind: I could not see In Thy marred
2. Lord, I was deaf: I could not hear The thrill - ing
3. Lord, I was mute: I could not speak The grace and
4. Lord, I was dead: I could not stir My life - less
5. Lord, Thou hast made the blind to see, The deaf to

vis - age an - y grace; But now the beau - ty
mu - sic of Thy voice; But now I hear Thee
glo - ry of Thy name; But now, as touched with
soul to come to Thee; But now, since Thou hast
hear, the mute to speak, The dead to live; and

of Thy face In ra - diant vi - sion dawns on me.
and re - joice, And all Thine ut - tered words are dear.
liv - ing flame, My lips Thine ea - ger prais - es wake.
quick - ened me, I rise from sin's dark sep - ul - cher.
lo, I break The chains of my cap - tiv - i - ty.

Text: William Todd Matson, 1833-1899.
Tune: Swiss Traditional Melody; arr. Ralph Vaughan Williams, 1872-1958; used by permission of Oxford University Press.

179

Breathe on Me, Breath of God

John 20:21, 22
D. and C. 10:6, 7

TRENTHAM S.M.

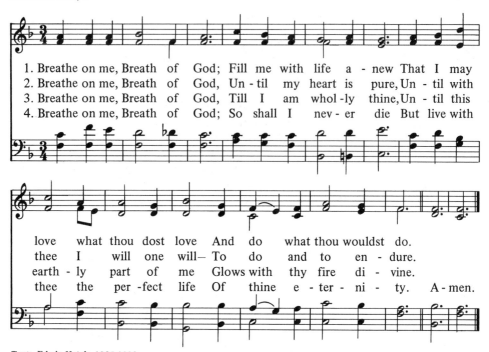

1. Breathe on me, Breath of God; Fill me with life a - new That I may
2. Breathe on me, Breath of God, Un - til my heart is pure, Un - til with
3. Breathe on me, Breath of God, Till I am whol -ly thine, Un - til this
4. Breathe on me, Breath of God; So shall I nev - er die But live with

love what thou dost love And do what thou wouldst do.
thee I will one will— To do and to en - dure.
earth - ly part of me Glows with thy fire di - vine.
thee the per -fect life Of thine e - ter - ni - ty. A - men.

Text: Edwin Hatch, 1835-1889.
Tune: Robert Jackson, 1842-1914.

180

Take Time to Be Holy

Leviticus 20:7, 8
II Nephi 3:30

HOLINESS 11.11.11.11.

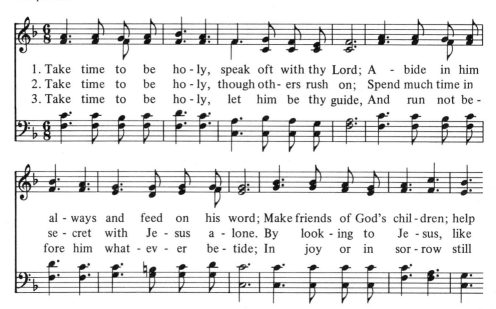

1. Take time to be ho - ly, speak oft with thy Lord; A - bide in him
2. Take time to be ho - ly, though oth- ers rush on; Spend much time in
3. Take time to be ho - ly, let him be thy guide, And run not be -

al - ways and feed on his word; Make friends of God's chil -dren; help
se - cret with Je - sus a - lone. By look - ing to Je - sus, like
fore him what - ev - er be - tide; In joy or in sor - row still

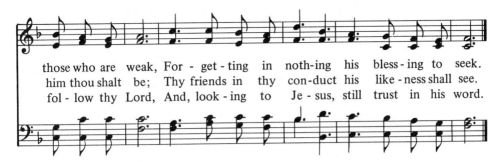

those who are weak, For - get - ting in noth-ing his bless-ing to seek.
him thou shalt be; Thy friends in thy con-duct his like-ness shall see.
fol - low thy Lord, And, look - ing to Je - sus, still trust in his word.

Text: William D. Longstaff, 1822-1894, alt.
Tune: George Coles Stebbins, 1846-1945.

Spirit of God, Descend upon My Heart 181

Mosiah 2:20-23
D. and C. 12:4a

MORECAMBE 10.10.10.10.

1. Spir - it of God, de - scend up - on my heart; Wean it from earth,
2. I ask no dream, no proph - et ec - sta - sies, No sud - den rend-
3. Teach me to feel that thou art al - ways nigh; Teach me the strug-
4. Teach me to love thee as thine an - gels love, One ho - ly pas-

through all its pul - ses move; Stoop to my weak-ness, might - y
ing of the veil of clay, No an - gel vis - it - ant, no
gles of the soul to bear, To check the ris - ing doubt, the
sion fill - ing all my frame, Bap - tis - m of the heaven-de-

as thou art, And make me love thee as I ought to love.
o - pening skies, But take the dim-ness of my soul a - way.
reb - el sigh; Teach me the pa - tience of un - an-swered prayer.
scend-ed Dove, My heart an al - tar, and thy love the flame. A-men.

Text: George Croly, 1780-1860.
Tune: Frederick Cook Atkinson, 1841-1897.

182

Make Room Within My Heart, O God

Philippians 2:5-11
Psalm 51:1, 10-12

KINGSFOLD C.M.D.
Alternate tune: MASSACHUSETTS (300)

1. Make room with-in my heart, O God, That you may form in me
2. Di - rect my will, O King of kings; Sub - ject it to your own,

The im - age you have shown in Christ, My ver - y life to be.
That ev - er - y im - pulse, ac - tion, word May make your king-dom known.

In - spire my thought, O loft - y One, To reach the high - est plane,
Ef - fect my prayer, great Trin - i - ty, E - ter - nal Three-in - One;

That I may know the mind of Christ, And him as great-est gain.
Com - bine each part of me to praise The Fa - ther, Spir - it, Son.

Text: Bryan Jeffery Leech, 1931 - ; copyright 1973 by Fred Bock Music Company. All rights reserved. Used by permission.
Tune: Melody coll. Lucy Broadwood, 1858-1929; harm. and arr. Ralph Vaughan Williams, 1872-1958; from the *English Hymnal* by permission of Oxford University Press.

Lord, Lead Me by Your Spirit

183

D. and C. 83:7a-d
Ether 5:28

HOLY WINGS 7.6.7.6.D.

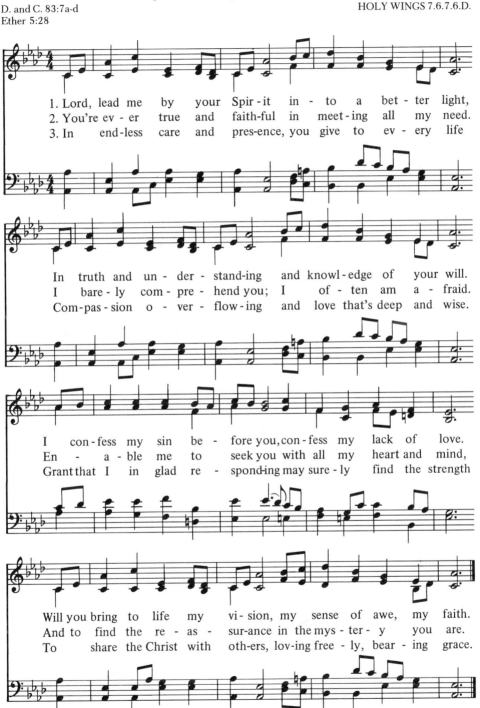

1. Lord, lead me by your Spir-it in-to a bet-ter light,
In truth and un-der-stand-ing and knowl-edge of your will.
I con-fess my sin be - fore you, con-fess my lack of love.
Will you bring to life my vi-sion, my sense of awe, my faith.

2. You're ev - er true and faith-ful in meet-ing all my need.
I bare-ly com-pre-hend you; I of-ten am a - fraid.
En - a - ble me to seek you with all my heart and mind,
And to find the re - as - sur-ance in the mys-ter-y you are.

3. In end-less care and pres-ence, you give to ev - ery life
Com-pas-sion o - ver - flow-ing and love that's deep and wise.
Grant that I in glad re - spond-ing may sure-ly find the strength
To share the Christ with oth-ers, lov-ing free - ly, bear - ing grace.

Text: Eric L. Selden, 1925 -   ; alt.; copyright 1980 Reorganized Church of Jesus Christ of Latter Day Saints.
Tune: Swedish Folk Melody; harm. Mark S. Dickey, 1885- 1961; alt.

184 God Who Gives to Life Its Goodness

Psalm 96:1, 11-13
D. and C. 81:4c

ABBOT'S LEIGH 8.7.8.7.D.

1. God who gives to life its good-ness, God, cre-a-tor of all joy,
2. God who fills the earth with beau-ty, God who binds each friend to friend,

God who gives to us our free-dom, God who bless-es tool and toy:
God who names us co-cre-a-tors, God who wills that cha-os end:

Teach us how to laugh and praise you, deep with-in, your prais-es sing,
Grant us now cre-a-tive spir-its, minds re-spon-sive to your mind,

Till the whole cre-a-tion dan-ces for the good-ness of its King.
Hearts and wills your rule ex-tend-ing, all our acts by love re-fined.

Text: Walter Henry Farquharson, 1936 - ; alt.; used by permission of the author.
Tune: Cyril Vincent Taylor, 1907 - ; from *The BBC Hymn Book*; used by permission of Oxford University Press.

Lord of All Hopefulness

185

Exodus 13:21
II Nephi 3:61

SLANE 10.11.11.12.

1. Lord of all hope-ful-ness, Lord of all joy,
2. Lord of all ea-ger-ness, Lord of all faith,
3. Lord of all kind-li-ness, Lord of all grace,
4. Lord of all gen-tle-ness, Lord of all calm,

Whose trust, ev-er child-like, no cares could de-stroy,
Whose strong hands were skilled at the plane and the lathe,
Your hands swift to wel-come, your arms to em-brace,
Whose voice is con-tent-ment, whose pre-sence is balm,

Be there at our wak-ing, and give us, we pray, Your
Be there at our la-bors, and give us, we pray, Your
Be there at our hom-ing, and give us, we pray, Your
Be there at our sleep-ing, and give us, we pray, Your

bliss in our hearts, Lord, at the break of the day.
strength in our hearts, Lord, at the noon of the day.
love in our hearts, Lord, at the eve of the day.
peace in our hearts, Lord, at the end of the day. A-men.

Text: Jan Struther, 1901-1953; from *Enlarged Songs of Praise* by permission of Oxford University Press.
Tune: Irish Traditional Melody; harm. Erik Routley, 1917 - ; used by permission of Erik Routley.

God's Word for Us

Creator of Sunrises

John 15:1, 2, 4, 7
Ephesians 3:14-19

I LOVE THEE 11.11.11.11.

1. Cre - a - tor of sun - ri - ses, com - ets, and trees
2. For - give us the will - ful ex - ces - ses of greed
3. For - give us the wreck - age of ha - tred and war

Whose sam - pler of love is much grand - er than these,
That screen from un - car - ing eyes those who have need.
That sad - den our souls and the in - no - cent scar.

Call forth from thy chil - dren the col - ors of life
Though shar - ing be knowl - edge or serv - ice or bread,
Re - store us to or - der of sun - rise and trees

That free us for laugh - ter, that free us from strife.
E - quip us with faith as in truth we are led.
And love that can make the earth grand - er than these.

Text: Evelyn Maples, 1919 - ; copyright 1980 Reorganized Church of Jesus Christ of Latter Day Saints.
Tune: Christian Harmony, 1805, alt.; harm. David N. Johnson, 1922 - . Harm. copyright 1977 Praise Publications, Inc. Used by permission.

187 Great Is Thy Faithfulness

D. and C. 17:4a, b
D. and C. 34:1

FAITHFULNESS 11.10.11.10. with refrain

1. Great is thy faith-ful-ness, O God my Fa-ther; There is no
2. Sum-mer and win-ter and spring-time and har-vest, Sun, moon, and
3. Par-don for sin and a peace that en-dur-eth, Thy own dear

shad-ow of turn-ing with thee; Thou chang-est not, thy com-
stars in their cours-es a-bove Join with all na-ture in
pres-ence to cheer and to guide; Strength for to-day and bright

pas-sions, they fail not; As thou hast been thou for-ev-er wilt be.
man-i-fold wit-ness To thy great faith-ful-ness, mer-cy, and love.
hope for to-mor-row, Bless-ings all mine, with ten thou-sand be-side!

Refrain

Great is thy faith-ful-ness! Great is thy faith-ful-ness! Morn-ing by

morn-ing new mer-cies I see; All of my bless-ings thy

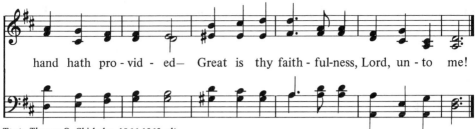

hand hath pro - vid - ed— Great is thy faith - ful-ness, Lord, un - to me!

Text: Thomas O. Chisholm, 1866-1960, alt.
Tune: William M. Runyan, 1870-1957.
Text and tune copyright 1923; renewal 1951 extended by Hope Publishing Company, Carol Stream, IL 60187; all rights reserved; used by permission.

O Love of God, How Strong and True 188

II Nephi 1:72-75
Ephesians 3:8-12

DEDICARE L.M.
Alternate hymn: 189

1. O love of God, how strong and true, E - ter - nal
2. O wide em - brac - ing, won - drous love, We read thee
3. We read thee best in Christ who came To bear for
4. We read thy power to bless and save In dark - ness

and yet ev - er new; Un - com - pre - hend - ed
in the sky a - bove; We read thee in the
us the cross of shame, Sent by the Fa - ther
e - ven of the grave; Still more in res - ur -

and un - bought, Be - yond all knowl-edge and all thought.
earth be - low, In seas that swell and streams that flow.
from on high Our life to live, our death to die.
rec - tion light We read the full - ness of thy might.

Text: Horatius Bonar, 1808-1889.
Tune: Franklyn S. Weddle, 1905 - ; harm. Evan A. Fry, 1902-1959; copyright 1956 Herald Publishing House.

189
O Love of God, How Strong and True

Romans 11:33-36
Alma 5:21, 22

DE TAR L.M.
Alternate hymn: 188

* (obligato)

1. O love of God, how strong and true,
    love,
    came
    save

E - ter - nal
We read thee
To bear for
E - ven in the

and yet ev - er new;
in the sky a - bove;
us the cross of shame,
dark-ness of the grave;

Un - com-pre-hend-ed and un -
We read thee in the earth be -
Sent by the Fa - ther from on
Still more in res - ur - rec - tion

bought,
low,
high
light

Be - yond all knowledge and all
In seas that swell and streams that
Our life to live, our death to
We read the full - ness of thy

* Options: (a) Using the text, the obligato may be sung by high voices.
  (b) Melody and obligato lines may be sung *a cappella*.
  (c) Once the melody is familiar, the accompanist need not play the melody and obligato
      parts with the singers.

thought.
flow.
die.
might,

2. O wide em-brac-ing, wondrous
3. We read thee best in Christ who
4. We read thy power to bless and

thy   might.

Text: Horatius Bonar, 1808-1889.
Tune: Calvin Hampton, 1938 - ; copyright 1973 Concordia Publishing House; used by permission.

Creator God, Creating Still   190

D. and C. 22:23
D. and C. 90:1e-g

MORNING SONG C.M.

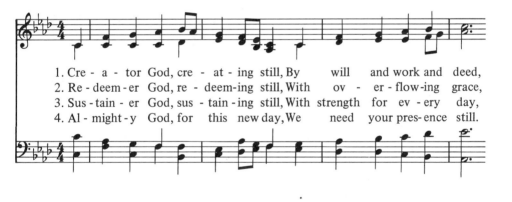

1. Cre - a - tor God, cre - at - ing still, By   will   and work and deed,
2. Re - deem - er God, re - deem-ing still, With   ov - er - flow-ing grace,
3. Sus - tain - er God, sus - tain-ing still, With strength for ev - ery day,
4. Al - might-y God, for   this new day, We   need   your pres-ence still.

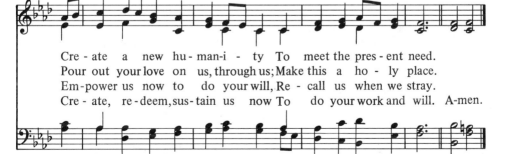

Cre - ate   a   new hu - man-i - ty To meet the pres - ent need.
Pour out your love on us, through us; Make this a ho - ly place.
Em-power us now to   do your will, Re - call us when we stray.
Cre - ate, re - deem, sus-tain us now To   do your work and will. A-men.

Text: Jane Parker Huber; copyright 1977 by the author; alt. 1980; used by permission.
Tune: Wyeth's *Repository of Sacred Music, Part Second*, 1813; harm. Rosalee Elser, 1925 - ; copyright 1980 by
Rosalee Elser; used by permission.

191

Proverbs 3:5, 6
D. and C. 22:23

God of Our Fathers

NATIONAL HYMN 10.10.10.10.

Fanfare optional

1. God of our fa-thers, whose al-might-y hand
2. Thy love di-vine hath led us in the past;
3. From war's a-larms, from dead-ly pes-ti-lence,
4. Re-fresh thy peo-ple on their toil-some way;

Leads forth in beau-ty all the star-ry band
In this free land by thee our lot is cast;
Be thy strong arm our ev-er sure de-fense;
Lead us from night to nev-er-end-ing day;

Of shin-ing worlds in splen-dor through the skies,
Be thou our Rul-er, Guard-ian, Guide, and Stay,
Thy true re-li-gion in our hearts in-crease;
Fill all our lives with love and grace di-vine,

Our grate-ful songs be-fore thy throne a-rise.
Thy word our law, thy paths our cho-sen way.
Thy boun-teous good-ness nour-ish us in peace.
And glo-ry, laud, and praise be ev-er thine. A-men.

Text: Daniel C. Roberts, 1841-1907.
Tune: George William Warren, 1828-1902.

God of Eternity

192

I Chronicles 29:11-13
Alma 14:124, 125

GOD OF ETERNITY 6.4.6.4.6.6.6.4.

1. God of e - ter - ni - ty, Sav - ior and King,
2. God of e - ter - ni - ty, An - cient of Days,
3. God of e - ter - ni - ty, Rul - er di - vine,
4. God of e - ter - ni - ty, Love is Thy name;

Help us to hon - or Thee, Help while we sing;
Glo - rious in maj - es - ty, Au - thor of Praise;
Strength of the might - y hills, All power is Thine;
God of the earth and sea, Thee we pro - claim;

Now may the clouds of night Break in - to splen - dor bright,
Hear Thou our ear - nest call, While at thy feet we fall,
Bound - less Thy reign shall be, Won - drous Thy vic - to - ry,
Love through Thine on - ly Son Thy work of grace hath done;

Je - sus, our life and light, Our Lord and King!
Je - sus, our all in all, Our Lord and King!
Earth shall be fill'd with Thee, Our Lord and King!
O bless - ed Three in One, Our Lord and King! A - men.

Text: Fanny J. Crosby, 1820-1915.
Tune: Ira Allan Sankey, 1874-1915.

193 · My God, How Wonderful Thou Art

Psalm 145:8-12
Jeremiah 31:3

COOLING C.M.

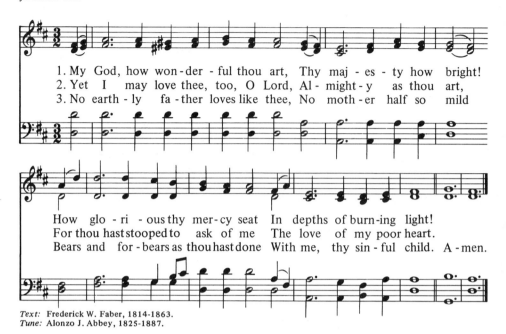

1. My God, how won-der-ful thou art, Thy maj-es-ty how bright!
2. Yet I may love thee, too, O Lord, Al-might-y as thou art,
3. No earth-ly fa-ther loves like thee, No moth-er half so mild

How glo-ri-ous thy mer-cy seat In depths of burn-ing light!
For thou hast stooped to ask of me The love of my poor heart.
Bears and for-bears as thou hast done With me, thy sin-ful child. A-men.

Text: Frederick W. Faber, 1814-1863.
Tune: Alonzo J. Abbey, 1825-1887.

194 · Earth with Her Ten Thousand Flowers

Ephesians 3:14-19
Ether 5:33, 34

TOPLADY 7.7.7.D.

1. Earth with her ten thou-sand flowers, Air with all its beams and showers,
2. Sounds a-mong the vales and hills, In the woods, and by the rills,
3. Na-ture speaks of joy and pain; Floods may come from spring-time rain.

Heav-en's in-fi-nite ex-panse, O-cean's lus-trous coun-te-nance—
Of the breeze and of the bird, Of the gen-tle mur-mur stirred—
While we know de-light and strife, Christ is hope for all our life.

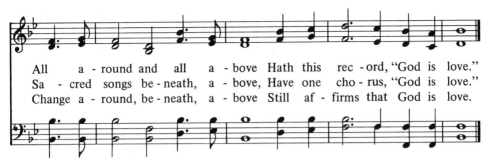

All a - round and all a - bove Hath this rec - ord, "God is love."
Sa - cred songs be - neath, a - bove, Have one cho - rus, "God is love."
Change a - round, be - neath, a - bove Still af - firms that God is love.

Text: W. W. Phelps, 1792-1872, Sts. 1, 2; Barbara Howard, 1930 - , St. 3, copyright 1980 Reorganized Church of Jesus Christ of Latter Day Saints.
Tune: Thomas Hastings 1784-1872.

The Lord Almighty Spoke the Word 195

John 1:1-4
Hebrews 1:1-3

SYDENHAM STREET 8.8.8.6.
Alternate tune: JUST AS I AM (421)

1. The Lord al - might - y spoke the Word, the
2. The Lord al - might - y gave the Word that
3. O Lord al - might - y, liv - ing Word, and

morn - ing stars to - geth - er sang; the Word he spoke through
came to us in flesh to dwell; the Word he gave broke
Spir - it blest, we wor - ship thee: thy Word pro-claim, and

cha - os broke, and worlds in or - der sprang.
through the grave, and van - quished sin and hell.
in thy name the king - dom that shall be.

Text: Charles E. Watson, 1869-1942; copyright Rodborough Tabernacle Church; used by permission.
Tune: Frederick R. C. Clarke, 1931 - ; copyright by the composer; used by permission.

196 The Lord Our God Alone Is Strong

Ecclesiastes 3:14
D. and C. 85:36

TALLIS' CANON L.M.

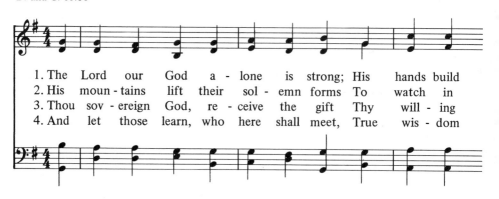

1. The Lord our God a - lone is strong; His hands build
2. His moun - tains lift their sol - emn forms To watch in
3. Thou sov - ereign God, re - ceive the gift Thy will - ing
4. And let those learn, who here shall meet, True wis - dom

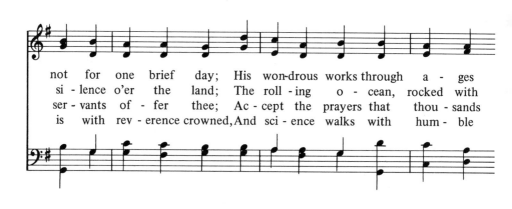

not for one brief day; His won-drous works through a - ges
si - lence o'er the land; The roll - ing o - cean, rocked with
ser - vants of - fer thee; Ac - cept the prayers that thou - sands
is with rev - erence crowned, And sci - ence walks with hum - ble

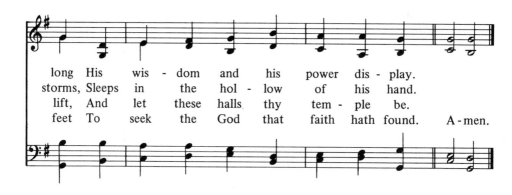

long His wis - dom and his power dis - play.
storms, Sleeps in the hol - low of his hand.
lift, And let these halls thy tem - ple be.
feet To seek the God that faith hath found. A - men.

Alternate Setting: to be sung as a canon (round).

The four-part setting can be used to accompany this canon by repeating the last four chords before the Amen.

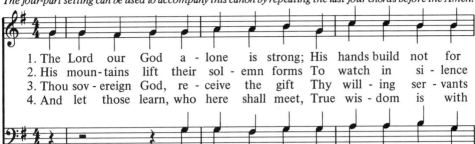

1. The Lord our God a - lone is strong; His hands build not for
2. His moun - tains lift their sol - emn forms To watch in si - lence
3. Thou sov - ereign God, re - ceive the gift Thy will - ing ser - vants
4. And let those learn, who here shall meet, True wis - dom is with

1. The Lord our God a - lone is strong; His
2. His moun - tains lift their sol - emn forms To
3. Thou sov - ereign God, re - ceive the gift Thy
4. And let those learn, who here shall meet, True

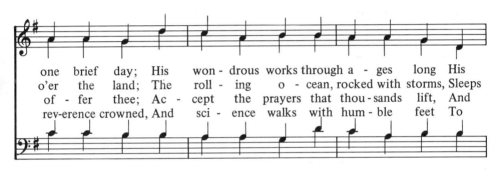

one brief day; His won - drous works through a - ges long His
o'er the land; The roll - ing o - cean, rocked with storms, Sleeps
of - fer thee; Ac - cept the prayers that thou - sands lift, And
rev - erence crowned, And sci - ence walks with hum - ble feet To

hands build not for one brief day; His won - drous works through
watch in si - lence o'er the land; The roll - ing o - cean,
will - ing ser - vants of - fer thee; Ac - cept the prayers that
wis - dom is with rev - erence crowned, And sci - ence walks with

wis - dom and his power dis - play.
in the hol - low of his hand.
let these halls thy tem - ple be.
seek the God that faith hath found. A - men.

a - ges long His wis - dom and his power dis - play.
rocked with storms, Sleeps in the hol - low of his hand.
thou - sands lift, And let these halls thy tem - ple be.
hum - ble feet To seek the God that faith hath found. A - men.

Text: Caleb T. Winchester, 1847-1920.
Tune: Thomas Tallis, c. 1505-1585.

197

Mosiah 3:16, 21
D. and C. 1:3

Let God Be God

LET GOD BE GOD 11.10.11.10. with refrain

Unison (or harmony)

1. Let God be God, in this our pres-ent mo-ment, Let God be
2. Let God be God, or we shall nev-er fin-ish The task to
3. Let Christ be Lord, in all His ris-en pow-er; His gra-cious

Mas-ter, hold-ing in con-trol All parts of life as
which He calls us ev-'ry day; Lest err-ing, we in
Spir-it, un-sup-pressed and free; Our Fa-ther, re-cre-

gifts of His be-stow-ment, For mak-ing us now bro-ken,
un-be-lief di-min-ish The force, the pow'r He wish-es
ate us for this hour In-to the ones you wish for

strong and whole.
to dis-play. Let God be God, let Christ be Lord!
us to be.

Text: Bryan Jeffery Leech, 1931 - ; alt.; copyright 1972 by Fred Bock Music Company; all rights reserved; used
by permission.
Tune: Gordon H. Carlson; copyright 1973 by the composer; used by permission.

God of Earth and Planets

Proverbs 3:5, 6
Isaiah 26:3, 4

HERMAS 6.5.6.5.D.

1. God of earth and plan - ets Rang - ing out - er space:
2. God of flower and o - cean— Fra - grance, beau - ty, power:

We in si - lent won - der Glimpse thy might and grace.
Of thy love and boun - ty Share we ev - ery hour.

God of worlds and a - toms, Each a mas - ter - piece:
God who sent us Je - sus— Teach - er, Friend, and Guide:

Deep - est probes of sci - ence Awe and faith in - crease.
We who are thy chil - dren In thy care a - bide.

Text: William Watkins Reid, Jr., 1923 - ; alt.; copyright 1965 Hymn Society of America; used by permission.
Tune: Frances Ridley Havergal, 1836-1879.

199

II Corinthians 13:4
Galatians 2:20

He Lives in Us! Immortal King!

HURST C.M.

1. He lives in us! Im-mor-tal King! Cre-a-tion bows to Him.
2. He lives for us! What joy is ours! He light-ens ev-ery mind.
3. He lives through us! How great our task! What prom-ise we ful-fill!

He breathed in us the breath of life To make us one with Him.
He quick-ens us to know our worth; We sense His grand de-sign.
O-be-dient to His Spir-it's call, We im-ple-ment His will.

Text: Linda E. Coffman, 1945 - ; copyright 1980 Reorganized Church of Jesus Christ of Latter Day Saints.
Tune: Frances H. Booth, 1923 - ; harm. alt. by Rosalee Elser, 1925 - ; copyright 1956 Herald Publishing House.

200

Jacob 3:9-14
Psalm 90:1, 2

O God, Our Help in Ages Past

ST. ANNE C.M.

Descant

1. O God, our help in a-ges past, Our hope for years to come,
2. Be-fore the hills in or-der stood, Or earth re-ceived her frame,
3. A thou-sand a-ges in thy sight Are like an eve-ning gone,
4. Time, like an ev-er-roll-ing stream, Bears all its sons a-way;
5. O God, our help in a-ges past, Our hope for years to come,

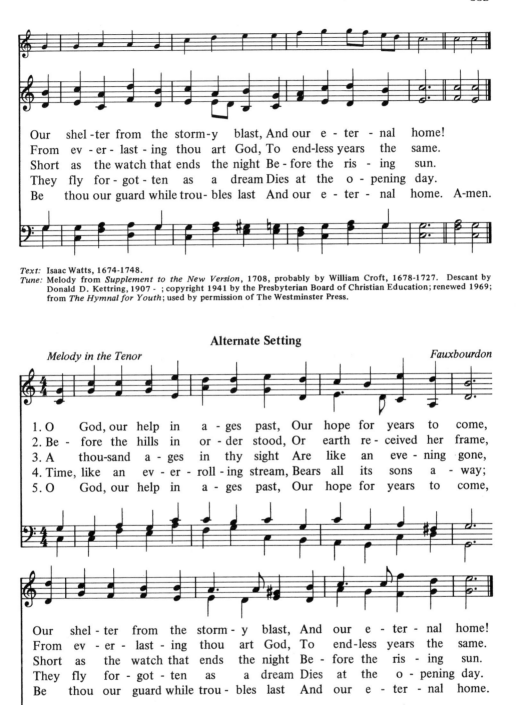

Text: Isaac Watts, 1674-1748.

Tune: Melody from *Supplement to the New Version*, 1708, probably by William Croft, 1678-1727. Descant by Donald D. Kettring, 1907 - ; copyright 1941 by the Presbyterian Board of Christian Education; renewed 1969; from *The Hymnal for Youth*; used by permission of The Westminster Press.

Alternate Setting

Melody in the Tenor

Fauxbourdon

1. O God, our help in a - ges past, Our hope for years to come,
2. Be - fore the hills in or - der stood, Or earth re - ceived her frame,
3. A thou-sand a - ges in thy sight Are like an eve - ning gone,
4. Time, like an ev - er - roll - ing stream, Bears all its sons a - way;
5. O God, our help in a - ges past, Our hope for years to come,

Our shel - ter from the storm - y blast, And our e - ter - nal home!
From ev - er - last - ing thou art God, To end-less years the same.
Short as the watch that ends the night Be - fore the ris - ing sun.
They fly for - got - ten as a dream Dies at the o - pening day.
Be thou our guard while trou - bles last And our e - ter - nal home.

Text: Isaac Watts, 1674-1748.

Tune: Arr. by Martin Shaw, 1875-1958; copyright J. Curwen & Sons, Ltd.; used by permission of G. Schirmer, Inc.

201 Come, Thou Long-expected Jesus

Luke 2:25-31
Ephesians 3:8-12

HYFRYDOL 8.7.8.7.D.

1. Come, thou long-ex-pect-ed Je-sus, Born to set all peo-ple free;
2. Born all peo-ple to de-liv-er, Born a child and yet a King,

From our fears and sins re-lease us; Let us find our rest in thee.
Born to reign in us for-ev-er, Now thy gra-cious king-dom bring.

Be our strength and con-so-la-tion; Hope of all the earth thou art;
By thine own e-ter-nal Spir-it Rule in all our hearts a-lone;

Dear de-sire of ev-ery na-tion, Joy of ev-ery long-ing heart.
By thine all-suf-fi-cient mer-it Raise us to thy glo-ri-ous throne. A-men.

Text: Charles Wesley, 1707-1788.
Tune: Rowland Hugh Prichard, 1811-1887.

My Song Is Love Unknown

202

Romans 5:6-11
Titus 3:3-7

LOVE UNKNOWN 6.6.6.6.4.4.4.4.

remains constant

1. My song is love un - known, My Sav - ior's love to me, Love
2. He came from His blest throne Sal - va - tion to be - stow, But
3. Some - times they strew His way, And His sweet prais - es sing, Re -
4. They rise, and needs will have My dear Lord made a - way; A
5. Here might I stay and sing, No sto - ry so di - vine: Nev -

to the love - less shown That they might love - ly be.
we made strange, and none The longed-for Christ would know.
sound - ing all the day Ho - san - nas to their King.
mur - der - er they save— The Prince of Life they slay.
er was love, dear King, Nev - er was grief like thine.

O who am I That for my sake
But O my Friend, My Friend in - deed,
Then "Cru - ci - fy!" Is all their breath,
Yet stead - fast He To suff - 'ring goes,
This is my Friend In whose sweet praise

My Lord should take Frail flesh, and die?
Who at my need His life did spend.
And for His death They thirst and cry.
That He His foes From thence might free.
I all my days Could glad - ly spend.

Text: Samuel Crossman, 1624-1683
Tune: John Ireland, 1879-1962; copyright and reprinted by permission of Mrs. Norah Kirby, successor to the late
Dr. John Ireland. Duplication is prohibited without written permission of the copyright owner.

203 In the Cross of Christ I Glory

D. and C. 17:5a-d
Galatians 6:14

RATHBUN 8.7.8.7.

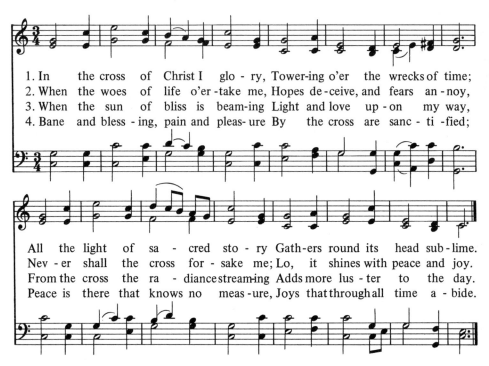

1. In the cross of Christ I glo - ry, Tower-ing o'er the wrecks of time;
2. When the woes of life o'er -take me, Hopes de -ceive, and fears an -noy,
3. When the sun of bliss is beam-ing Light and love up - on my way,
4. Bane and bless - ing, pain and pleas- ure By the cross are sanc - ti -fied;

All the light of sa - cred sto - ry Gath-ers round its head sub -lime.
Nev - er shall the cross for - sake me; Lo, it shines with peace and joy.
From the cross the ra - diance stream-ing Adds more lus - ter to the day.
Peace is there that knows no meas -ure, Joys that through all time a - bide.

Text: John Bowring, 1792-1872.
Tune: Ithamar Conkey, 1815-1867.

204 My Jesus, I Love Thee

Moroni 7:11
I Peter 1:8

GORDON 11.11.11.11.

My Je - sus, I love thee; I know thou art mine; For thee all the

fol - lies of sin I re - sign; My gra -cious Re - deem - er, my Sav-

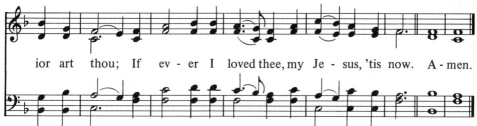

ior art thou; If ev - er I loved thee, my Je - sus, 'tis now. A - men.

Text: William R. Featherstone, 1842-1878.
Tune: Adoniram J. Gordon, 1836-1895.

My Children, "Hear Ye Him," My Word — 205

D. and C. 76:4g
John 1:14

ROCKINGHAM L.M.

1. My chil - dren, "hear ye him," my Word: In Je - sus
2. All words are to - kens, sym - bols still, With - out the
3. For rev - e - la - tion's light is dim Un - less in
4. The gos - pel was in Christ him - self, A liv - ing

is the gos - pel found; The gos - pel is the Life
mean - ing I in - tend Un - til it comes through life -
life it is re - vealed; Ex - pe - rience on - ly can
mes - sage all could see; That Life is light for all

ex - pressed; The Life is light and can't be bound.
e - vent: By liv - ing it you com - pre - hend.
re - lease My clear - est mes - sage, till then sealed.
the world: "My grace in your life, full and free."

Text: Alan D. Tyree, 1929 - ; copyright 1980 Reorganized Church of Jesus Christ of Latter Day Saints.
Tune: Edward Miller, 1731-1807.

206 Come, Thou, O King of Kings

Isaiah 61:1-3
D. and C. 42:3a, b

LENOX 6.6.6.6.8.8.8.8.

1. Come, Thou, O King of kings! We've wait-ed long for thee,
2. Ho - san - nas now shall sound From all the ran-somed throng,
3. Hail! Prince of life and peace! Thrice wel-come to thy throne!

With heal-ing in thy wings, To set thy peo-ple free.
And glo-ry ech-o round A new tri-um-phal song.
While saints of ev-'ry race Their Lord and Sav-ior own.

Come, thou de-sire of na-tions, come; Come, thou de-sire of
With songs of joy, a hap-pier strain, With songs of joy, a
The thank-ful na-tions bow the knee; The thank-ful na-tions

na-tions, come; Let Is-rael now be gath-ered home.
hap-pier strain, We wel-come in thy peace-ful reign.
bow the knee, And ev-ery tongue gives praise to thee. A-men.

Text: Parley P. Pratt, 1807-1857; alt. Alan D. Tyree, 1929 - .
Tune: Lewis Edson, 1748-1820.

O Thou, Whose Youthful Years Were Spent 207

Matthew 20:26-28
Luke 2:51, 52

O JESU 8.6.8.6.8.8.8.

1. O thou, whose youth-ful years were spent In Naz-a-reth's
2. Thou hon-ored guest at Ca-na's feast, For thee were
3. The friend-ly home of Laz-a-rus Shared love and
4. Thou, who didst walk Em-ma-us road And talk with

qui-et ways Where home and shop were tem-ples blest
ta-bles spread; O wel-come, wel-come to our house,
peace with thee; Make now our home thy dwel-ling place
anx-ious men, Whose pre-sence graced their cot-tage board,

With sim-ple faith and praise, Grant, Lord, that mid the
Par-take of love and bread; May we thy ben-e-
And us thy fam-i-ly; Give ear to Ma-ry's
Made dull hearts glow a-gain: Lo, here's our path, and

world's mad press Our homes re-flect thy ho-li-ness.
dic-tion know As hearth-side joys and friend-ships grow.
eag-er quest; May Mar-tha's house-hold skills be blest.
here's our gate; Come, sup with us; the night grows late.

Text: William Watkins Reid, Sr., 1890 - . Copyright 1961 by The Hymn Society of America; used by permission.
Tune: Hirschberg Gesangbuch, 1741; attr. to Johann Balthasar Reimann, 1702-1749; alt.

208

Hope of the World

John 16:33
D. and C. 10:12

ANCIENT OF DAYS 11.10.11.10.
Alternate hymn: 209

1. Hope of the world, thou Christ of great com - pas - sion,
2. Hope of the world, God's gift from high - est heav - en,
3. Hope of the world, a - foot on dust - y high - ways,
4. Hope of the world, who by thy cross didst save us

Speak to our fear - ful hearts by con - flict rent.
Bring - ing to hun - gry souls the bread of life,
Show - ing to wan - dering souls the path of light,
From death and dark de - spair, from sin and guilt,

Save us, thy peo - ple, from con - sum - ing pas - sion,
Still let thy spir - it un - to us be giv - en
Walk thou be - side us lest the tempt - ing by - ways
We ren - der back the love thy mer - cy gave us;

Who by our own false hopes and aims are spent.
To heal earth's wounds and end her bit - ter strife.
Lure us a - way from thee to end - less night.
Take thou our lives and use them as thou wilt. A - men.

Text: Georgia Harkness, 1891-1974. From *Eleven Ecumenical Hymns*, copyright 1954 by The Hymn Society of America. Used by permission.
Tune: J. Albert Jeffery, 1854-1929.

Hope of the World

D. and C. 153:9
Romans 12:1, 2

VICAR 11.10.11.10.
Alternate hymn: 208

Unison (or Harmony) The small notes are for the accompanist.

1. Hope of the world, thou Christ of great com- pas- sion,
2. Hope of the world, God's gift from high- est heav- en,
3. Hope of the world, a - foot on dust - y high- ways,
4. Hope of the world, who by thy cross didst save us

Speak to our fear - ful hearts by con - flict rent.
Bring - ing to hun - gry souls the bread of life,
Show - ing to wan - dering souls the path of light,
From death and dark de - spair, from sin and guilt,

Save us, thy peo - ple, from con - sum - ing pas - sion,
Still let thy spir - it un - to us be giv - en,
Walk thou be - side us lest the tempt - ing by - ways
We ren - der back the love thy mer - cy gave us;

Who by our own false hopes and aims are spent.
To heal earth's wounds and end her bit - ter strife.
Lure us a - way from thee to end - less night.
Take thou our lives, and use them as thou wilt. A - men.

Text: Georgia Harkness, 1891-1974. From *Eleven Ecumenical Hymns*, copyright 1954 by The Hymn Society of America. Used by permission.
Tune: V. Earle Copes, 1921 - ; copyright 1963 Abingdon Press; altered by Rosalee Elser, 1925 - . Used by permission.

210
O Young and Fearless Prophet

D. and C. 4:1
II Nephi 13:29, 30

VIGIL 7.6.7.6.D.
See 110 for a higher setting.

1. O young and fear-less Proph-et of an-cient Gal-i-lee,
2. We mar-vel at the pur-pose that held thee to thy course
3. Cre-ate in us the splen-dor that dawns when hearts are kind,
4. O young and fear-less Proph-et, we need thy pres-ence here,

Thy life is still a sum-mons to serve hu-man-i-ty,
While ev-er on the hill-top be-fore thee loomed the cross,
That knows not race nor sta-tion as bound-aries of the mind,
A-mid our pride and glo-ry to see thy face ap-pear,

To make our thoughts and ac-tions less prone to please the crowd,
Thy stead-fast face set for-ward where love and du-ty shone,
That learns to val-ue beau-ty in heart or brain or soul,
Once more to hear thy chal-lenge a-bove our noi-sy day,

To stand with hum-ble cour-age for truth with strength en-dowed.
While we be-tray so quick-ly and leave thee there a-lone.
And longs to bind God's chil-dren in-to one per-fect whole.
A-gain to lead us for-ward a-long God's ho-ly way.

Text: S. Ralph Harlow, 1885-1972; alt.
Tune: Swedish Folk Melody.

O Come, O Come, Emmanuel

211

Zechariah 9:9, 10
Alma 5:17, 18

VENI EMMANUEL L.M. with refrain

Unison (or harmony)

1. O come, O come, Emmanuel, And ransom captive
2. O come, thou Wisdom from on high, And order all things
3. O come, Desire of nations, bind All peoples in one

Israel, That mourns in lonely exile
far and nigh; To us the path of knowledge
heart and mind; Bid envy, strife, and quarrels

Refrain

here, Until the Son of God appear.
show, And cause us in its ways to go. Rejoice! Re-
cease, Fill the whole world with heaven's peace.

joice! Emmanuel Shall come to thee, O Israel!

Text: Latin, c. 9th century; tr. John M. Neale, 1818-1866, St. 1, alt.; tr. Henry S. Coffin, 1877-1954, Sts. 2, 3, alt.
Tune: Adapted from Plainsong, Mode I, by Thomas Helmore, 1811-1890; alt.

212 — I Know That My Redeemer Lives

Job 19:25
I Peter 1:3-5

BRADFORD C.M.

1. I know that my Re-deem-er lives And ev - er prays for me;
2. I find him lift - ing up my head; He brings sal - va - tion near;
3. He wills that I should ho - ly be; What can with-stand his will?
4. Je - sus, I hang up - on thy word; I stead-fast-ly be-lieve

A to - ken of his love he gives, A pledge of lib - er - ty.
His pres - ence makes me free in - deed, And he will soon ap-pear.
The coun - sel of his grace in me He sure - ly shall ful-fill.
Thou wilt re - turn and claim me, Lord, And to thy - self re -ceive.

Text: Charles Wesley, 1707-1788.
Tune: George F. Handel, 1685-1759.

213 — I Sought the Lord

John 15:16
Romans 5:1, 2

PEACE 10.10.10.6.

1. I sought the Lord, and af - ter - ward I knew He
2. Thou didst reach forth thy hand and mine en - fold; I
3. I find, I walk, I love, but oh, the whole Of

moved my soul to seek him, seek - ing me; It was not
walked and sank not on the storm-vexed sea; 'Twas not so
love is but my an-swer, Lord, to thee! For thou were

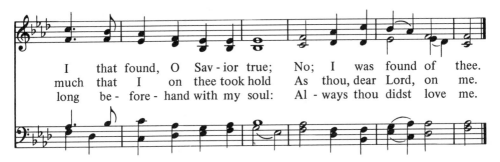

I that found, O Sav-ior true; No; I was found of thee.
much that I on thee took hold As thou, dear Lord, on me.
long be-fore-hand with my soul: Al-ways thou didst love me.

Text: Anonymous, 1880; rev. in *The Pilgrim Hymnal,* 1904.
Tune: The Revivalist, 1868; adapt. by Rosalee Elser, 1925 - ; copyright 1980 by Rosalee Elser; used by permission.

There's a Spirit in the Air

214

D. and C. 1:4b-e
Acts 2:41-43, 46, 47

LAUDS 7.7.7.7.

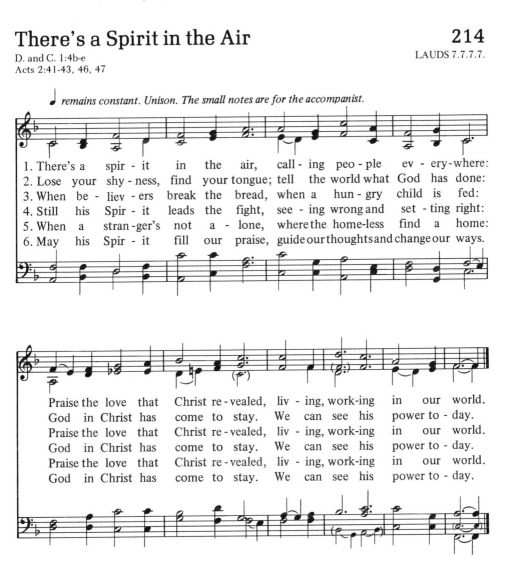

♩ *remains constant. Unison. The small notes are for the accompanist.*

1. There's a spir-it in the air, call-ing peo-ple ev-ery-where:
2. Lose your shy-ness, find your tongue; tell the world what God has done:
3. When be-liev-ers break the bread, when a hun-gry child is fed:
4. Still his Spir-it leads the fight, see-ing wrong and set-ting right:
5. When a stran-ger's not a-lone, where the home-less find a home:
6. May his Spir-it fill our praise, guide our thoughts and change our ways.

Praise the love that Christ re-vealed, liv-ing, work-ing in our world.
God in Christ has come to stay. We can see his power to-day.
Praise the love that Christ re-vealed, liv-ing, work-ing in our world.
God in Christ has come to stay. We can see his power to-day.
Praise the love that Christ re-vealed, liv-ing, work-ing in our world.
God in Christ has come to stay. We can see his power to-day.

Text: Brian Wren, 1936 - ; copyright Oxford University Press; used by permission.
Tune: John Wilson, 1905 - ; copyright Oxford University Press; used by permission.

215

Tell Me the Story of Jesus

Romans 10:13-16 (13-17)
D. and C. 65:1a, d

STORY OF JESUS 8.7.8.7.D. with refrain

1. Tell me the sto - ry of Je - sus, Write on my heart ev - ery word,
2. Fast - ing a - lone in the des - ert, Tell of the days that he passed,
3. Tell of the cross where they nailed him, Writh - ing in an - guish and pain;

Refrain: Tell me the sto - ry of Je - sus, Write on my heart ev - ery word,

Fine

Tell me the sto - ry most pre - cious, Sweet-est that ev - er was heard;
How for our sins he was tempt - ed, Yet was tri - um - phant at last;
Tell of the grave where they laid him; Tell how he liv - eth a - gain;

Tell me the sto - ry most pre - cious, Sweet-est that ev - er was heard.

Tell how the an - gels, in cho - rus, Sang as they wel-comed his birth,
Tell of the years of his la - bor, Tell of the sor - row he bore;
Love in that sto - ry so ten - der, Clear - er than ev - er I see;

D. C.

"Glo - ry to God in the high - est! Peace and good ti - dings to earth."
He was de-spised and af - flict - ed, Home-less, re - ject - ed and poor.
Stay, let me weep while you whis - per, Love paid the ran-som for me.

Text: Fanny J. Crosby, 1820-1915.
Tune: John R. Sweney, 1837-1899.

What Wondrous Love Is This
216

I Nephi 3:70, 86, 87
John 1:29

WONDROUS LOVE 12.9.12.12.9.

Unison (or harmony)

1. What won-drous love is this, O my soul, O my soul,
2. What won-drous love is this, O my soul, O my soul,

What won-drous love is this, O my soul! What won-drous love is
What won-drous love is this, O my soul! What won-drous love is

this That caused the Lord of life To bear the pain-ful cross For my
this That caused the Lord of all To lay a-side his crown For my

soul, for my soul, To bear the pain-ful cross For my soul.
soul, for my soul, To lay a-side his crown For my soul.

Text: John Newton, 1725-1807.
Tune: From *Southern Harmony*, 1835. Harm. by Louita Clothier, 1936 - ; copyright 1974 Herald Publishing House.

217

We Would See Jesus

John 12:21-23
D. and C. 17:5a-d

CUSHMAN 11.10.11.10.
Alternate hymn: 218

1. We would see Jesus! Lo, his star is shin-ing
2. We would see Jesus on the moun-tain teach-ing,
3. We would see Jesus in his work of heal-ing
4. We would see Jesus; in the ear-ly morn-ing

A - bove the sta - ble while the an - gels sing;
With all the lis - tening peo - ple gath -ered round,
At e - ven - tide be - fore the sun was set;
Still as of old he calls us, "Fol - low me;"

There in a man - ger on the hay re - clin - ing;
While birds and flowers and sky a - bove are preach - ing
Di - vine and hu - man, in his deep re - veal - ing
Let us a - rise, all less - er serv -ice scorn - ing.

Haste, let us lay our gifts be - fore the King.
The bless - ed - ness which sim - ple trust has found.
Of God and hu - man -kind in serv - ice met.
Lord, we are thine, we give our - selves to thee!

Text: J. Edgar Park, 1879-1956.
Tune: Herbert B. Turner, 1852-1927.

We Would See Jesus

218

John 12:21-23
D. and C. 38:2

MORA PROCTOR 11.10.11.10.
Alternate hymn: 217

Unison

1. We would see Je - sus! Lo, his star is shin - ing
2. We would see Je - sus on the moun-tain teach - ing,
3. We would see Je - sus in his work of heal - ing
4. We would see Je - sus; in the ear - ly morn - ing

A - bove the sta - ble while the an - gels sing;
With all the lis - tening peo - ple gath - ered round,
At e - ven - tide be - fore the sun was set;
Still as of old he calls us, "Fol - low me;"

There in a man - ger on the hay re - clin - ing;
While birds and flow-ers and sky a - bove are preach - ing
Di - vine and hu - man, in his deep re - veal - ing
Let us a - rise, all less - er ser - vice scorn - ing.

Haste, let us lay our gifts be - fore the King.
The bless - ed - ness which sim - ple trust has found.
Of God and hu - man-kind in ser - vice met.
Lord, we are thine, we give our - selves to thee!

Text: J. Edgar Park, 1879-1956.
Tune: William J. Reynolds, 1920 - ; copyright 1975 Broadman Press. All rights reserved. Used by permission.

219   O Master Workman of the Race

D. and C. 22:23b
Luke 2:46-49

MATERNA C.M.D.

1. O Mas - ter Work-man of the race, Thou man of Gal - li - lee
2. O Car - pen - ter of Naz - a - reth, Build-er of life di - vine,
3. O thou who dost the vi - sion send And gives to each a task,

Who with the eyes of ear - ly youth E - ter - nal things did see,
Who shap - est us to God's own law, Thy-self the fair de - sign,
And with the task suf - fi-cient strength, Show us thy will, we ask;

We thank thee for thy boy - hood faith That shone thy whole life through:
Build us a tower of Christ - like height That we the land may view,
Give us a con-science bold and good, Give us a pur - pose true,

"Did ye not know it is my work My Fa - ther's work to do?"
And see like thee our no - blest work Our Fa - ther's work to do.
That it may be our high - est joy Our Fa - ther's work to do.

Text: Jay T. Stocking, 1870-1936.
Tune: Samuel A. Ward, 1847-1903.

Of the Father's Love Begotten

220

Revelation 1:7, 8
Mosiah 8:28-35

DIVINUM MYSTERIUM 8.7.8.7.8.7.7.

Unison

1. Of the Fa-ther's love be-got-ten, Ere the worlds be-gan to be,
2. This is he whom seers in old time Chant-ed of with one ac-cord;
3. O ye heights of heaven, a-dore him; An-gel hosts, his prais-es sing;

He is Al-pha and O-me-ga, He the source, the end-ing he,
Whom the voic-es of the proph-ets Prom-ised in their faith-ful word;
Powers, do-min-ions, bow be-fore him, And ex-tol our God and King;

Of the things that are, that have been, And that fu-ture
Now he shines, the long ex-pect - ed; Let cre-a-tion
Let no tongue on earth be si - lent, Ev-ery voice in

years shall see, Ev-er-more and ev-er-more!
praise its Lord, Ev-er-more and ev-er-more!
con-cert ring, Ev-er-more and ev-er-more! A - men.

Text: Aurelius Clemens Prudentius, 348-413; tr. John M. Neale, 1818-1866, and Henry W. Baker, 1821-1877.
Tune: 13th Century Plainsong, Mode V, published in *Piae Cantiones*, 1582.

221 For the Book of Mormon's Witness

D. and C. 42:5
II Nephi 12:37

KINGDOM 8.7.8.7.

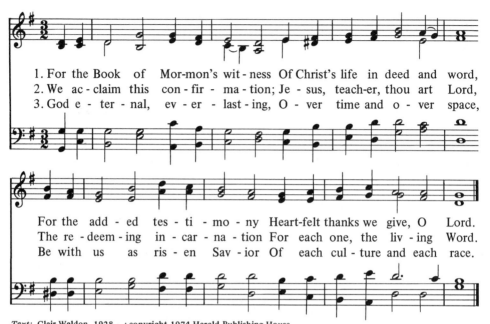

1. For the Book of Mor-mon's wit-ness Of Christ's life in deed and word,
2. We ac-claim this con-fir-ma-tion; Je-sus, teach-er, thou art Lord,
3. God e-ter-nal, ev-er-last-ing, O-ver time and o-ver space,

For the add-ed tes-ti-mo-ny Heart-felt thanks we give, O Lord.
The re-deem-ing in-car-na-tion For each one, the liv-ing Word.
Be with us as ris-en Sav-ior Of each cul-ture and each race.

Text: Clair Weldon, 1928 - ; copyright 1974 Herald Publishing House.
Tune: V. Earle Copes, 1921 - ; copyright 1959 Abingdon Press; used by permission.

222 O Son of God, Thou Madest Known

D. and C. 4:1
Psalm 90:16, 17

BROOKFIELD L.M.

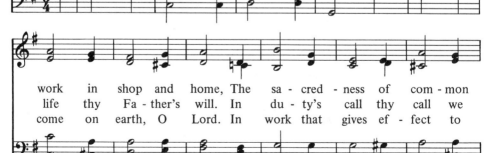

1. O Son of God, thou mad-est known, Through qui-et
2. O Work-man true, may we ful-fill In dai-ly
3. And thus we pray in deed and word, Thy king-dom

work in shop and home, The sa-cred-ness of com-mon
life thy Fa-ther's will. In du-ty's call thy call we
come on earth, O Lord. In work that gives ef-fect to

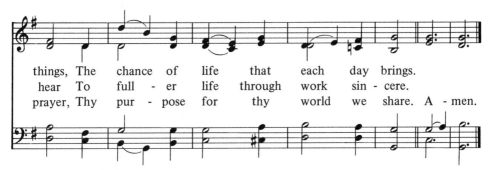

things, The chance of life that each day brings.
hear To full - er life through work sin - cere.
prayer, Thy pur - pose for thy world we share. A - men.

Text: Milton S. Littlefield, 1864-1934.
Tune: Thomas B. Southgate, 1814-1868.

Jesus Loves the Little Children 223

Mark 10:11-14 (13-16)
Moroni 8:18

CHILDREN 8.7.7.7.11.

1. Je - sus loves the lit - tle chil - dren, All the chil - dren of the
2. Je - sus died for all the chil - dren, All the chil - dren of the
3. Je - sus rose to save the chil - dren, All the chil - dren of the

world; Red and yel - low, black and white, They are pre - cious in his
world; Red and yel - low, black and white, All are pre - cious in his
world; Broth - ers, sis - ters of each land, Just reach out and take his

sight. Je - sus loves the lit - tle chil - dren of the world.
sight. Je - sus died for all the chil - dren of the world.
hand. Je - sus rose to save the chil - dren of the world.

Text: Anonymous, sts. 1 & 2; Rosalee Elser, 1925 - , st. 3.
Tune: George F. Root, 1820-1895; arr. John Obetz, 1933 - ; copyright 1980 Reorganized Church of Jesus Christ of
    Latter Day Saints.

224 O Jesus Christ, to Thee May Hymns Be Rising

Luke 13:34, 35
I Nephi 3:187

CITY OF GOD 11.10.11.10

1. O Je - sus Christ, to thee may hymns be ris - ing
2. Grant us new cour - age, sac - ri - fi - cial, hum - ble,
3. Show us thy Spir - it, brood - ing o'er each cit - y,

In ev - 'ry cit - y for thy love and care;
Strong in thy strength to ven - ture and to dare;
As thou didst weep a - bove Je - ru - sa - lem.

In - spire our wor - ship; grant the glad sur - pris - ing
To lift the fall - en, guide the feet that stum - ble,
Seek - ing to gath - er all in love and pit - y,

That thy blest Spir - it brings us ev - 'ry - where.
Seek out the lone - ly and God's mer - cy share.
And heal - ing those who touch thy gar - ment's hem.

The hymn may be concluded by repeating the first stanza.

Text: Bradford Gray Webster, 1898 - ; alt.; from *Five New Hymns on the City*, copyright 1954 The Hymn Society of America; used by permission.
Tune: Daniel Moe, 1926 - ; copyright 1957 Augsburg Publishing House; reprinted by permission.

When, His Salvation Bringing

225

Matthew 21:5-7 (6-9)
D. and C. 110:23a-c

SPRINGTIME 7.6.7.6.D.

1. When, his salvation bringing, To Zion Jesus came,
2. And since the Lord retaineth His love for children still,
3. For should we fail proclaiming Our great Redeemer's praise,

The children all stood singing Hosanna to his name;
Though now as King he reigneth On Zion's heavenly hill,
The stones, our silence shaming, Would their hosannas raise.

Nor did their zeal offend him, But as he rode along
We'll flock around his banner Who sits upon his throne,
But shall we only render The tribute of our words?

He let them still attend him, And smiled to hear their song.
And cry aloud, "Hosanna To David's royal Son!"
No, while our hearts are tender, They, too, shall be the Lord's.

Text: John King, 1789-1858.
Tune: Swedish Folk Melody; harm. Rosalee Elser, 1925 - ; harm. copyright 1980 by Rosalee Elser. Used by permission.

226

III Nephi 4:44, 45, 48
Hebrews 1:1-3

Fairest Lord Jesus

SCHÖNSTER HERR JESU 5.6.8.5.5.8.

Descant

2. Fair are the wood-lands,
3. Fair is the moon-light

1. Fair-est Lord Je-sus, Rul-er of all na-ture, O thou of
2. Fair are the mead-ows, Fair-er still the wood-lands, Robed in the
3. Fair is the sun-shine, Fair-er still the moon-light, And all the

Robed   in the bloom-ing garb of spring.   Je-sus is fair-er, Je-sus is
And   all the twin-kling star-ry host.   Jesus shines brighter, Jesus shines

God and man the Son, Thee will I cher-ish, Thee will I
bloom-ing garb of spring. Je-sus is fair-er, Je-sus is
twin-kling, star-ry host. Je-sus shines bright-er, Je-sus shines

pur - er,   Who makes the woe-ful heart to   sing.
pur - er   Than all the an-gels heaven can boast. A-men.

hon-or, Thou, my soul's glo-ry, joy, and crown.
pur-er, Who makes the woe-ful heart to sing.
pur-er Than all the an-gels heaven can boast. A-men.

Text: Münster Gesangbuch, 1677; *Schlesische Volkslieder,* 1842; tr. *Church Chorals and Choir Studies,* 1850.
Tune: Silesian Folk Melody in *Schlesische Volkslieder,* 1842; descant by W. Frederic Miller, copyright 1941 the Presbyterian Board of Christian Education; renewed 1969; from *The Hymnal for Youth;* used by permission of The Westminster Press.

Word of God, Come Down on Earth

227

John 16:13, 14
John 1:17

LIEBSTER JESU 7.8.7.8.8.8.

1. Word of God, come down on earth, Living rain from heav'n descending; Touch our hearts and bring to birth Faith and hope and love unending. Word almighty, we revere you; Word made flesh, we long to hear you.

2. Word eternal, throned on high, Word that brought to life creation, Word that came from heav'n to die, Crucified for our salvation, Saving Word, the world restoring, Speak to us, your love outpouring.

3. Word that caused blind eyes to see, Speak and heal our mortal blindness; Deaf we are: our healer be; Loose our tongues to tell your kindness. Be our Word in pity spoken; Heal the world, by our sin broken.

4. Word that speaks your Father's love, One with him beyond all telling, Word that sends us from above God the Spirit, with us dwelling, Word of truth, to all truth lead us, Word of life, with one Bread feed us. A-men.

Text: James Quinn, copyright © 1969 Geoffrey Chapman, a division of Cassell Ltd., London; used by permission.
Tune: Johann Rudolph Ahle, 1625-1673; arr. Johann Sebastian Bach, 1685-1750.

228 Crown Him with Many Crowns

D. and C. 85:2
II Nephi 1:71-73

DIADEMATA S.M.D.

Descant (stanza 4 only)

4. Crown him Lord, The Po-ten-tate of time;

1. Crown him with man-y crowns, The Lamb up-on his throne:
2. Crown him the Lord of love: Be-hold his hands and side,
3. Crown him the Lord of life: Who tri-umphed o'er the grave,
4. Crown him the Lord of years: The po-ten-tate of time,

Crown him Lord, In-ef-fa-bly sub-lime.

Hark! how the heav'n-ly an-them drowns All mu-sic but its own!
Rich wounds, yet vis-i-ble a-bove, In beau-ty glo-ri-fied;
And rose vic-to-rious in the strife For those he came to save;
Cre-a-tor of the roll-ing spheres, In-ef-fa-bly sub-lime.

Crown him Lord, Crown him Lord,

A-wake, my soul, and sing Of him who died for thee;
His reign shall know no end, And 'round his pierc-ed feet
His glo-ries now we sing, Who died and rose on high,
All hail, Re-deem-er, hail! For thou hast died for me;

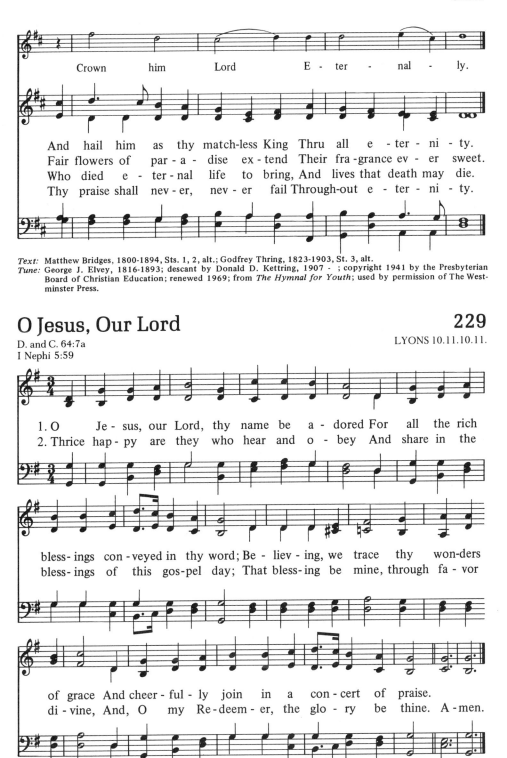

Crown him Lord E - ter - nal - ly.

And hail him as thy match-less King Thru all e - ter - ni - ty.
Fair flowers of par - a - dise ex - tend Their fra-grance ev - er sweet.
Who died e - ter - nal life to bring, And lives that death may die.
Thy praise shall nev - er, nev - er fail Through-out e - ter - ni - ty.

Text: Matthew Bridges, 1800-1894, Sts. 1, 2, alt.; Godfrey Thring, 1823-1903, St. 3, alt.
Tune: George J. Elvey, 1816-1893; descant by Donald D. Kettring, 1907 - ; copyright 1941 by the Presbyterian
Board of Christian Education; renewed 1969; from *The Hymnal for Youth*; used by permission of The West-
minster Press.

O Jesus, Our Lord

229
LYONS 10.11.10.11.

D. and C. 64:7a
I Nephi 5:59

1. O Je - sus, our Lord, thy name be a - dored For all the rich
2. Thrice hap - py are they who hear and o - bey And share in the

bless- ings con - veyed in thy word; Be - liev - ing, we trace thy won-ders
bless- ings of this gos-pel day; That bless-ing be mine, through fa - vor

of grace And cheer-ful - ly join in a con - cert of praise.
di - vine, And, O my Re-deem - er, the glo - ry be thine. A - men.

Text: European Edition, 1840.
Tune: Adapted from Johann Michael Haydn, 1737-1806.

230
Look at This Man, Born of God

Philippians 2:5-11
Luke 4:16-21

MABUNE 7.6.7.6.D

1. Look at this man, born of God In a low-ly man-ger.
2. Look at this man, born of God One with the af-flict-ed.
3. Look at this man, born of God, To-tal-ly self-giv-ing;

Man of sor-row and tra-vail, Nor to grief a stran-ger.
Nev-er such a-maz-ing grace In our race de-pict-ed.
No re-ward but cru-el death, E-ven then for-giv-ing.

Bro-ken-heart-ed for the poor, His own good un-heed-ing;
Bear-ing hu-man pain and sin, Poor and sick be-friend-ing;
Lift-ed up up-on the cross, End-less love in him re-vealed;

Look at this man, love of God, All our loves ex-ceed-ing.
Look at this man, sent of God; God's own life ex-tend-ing.
Look at this man, Son of God, By whose suff'-ring we are healed.

Text: Ko Yuki, 1896 - ; by permission of the Hymnal Committee, United Church of Christ in Japan. Trans. Hiroshi Yamada, 1935 - ; arr. Geoffrey F. Spencer, 1927 - ; copyright 1980 Reorganized Church of Jesus Christ of Latter Day Saints.
Tune: Seigi Abe; used by permission of the Hymnal Committee, United Church of Christ in Japan.

Angels from the Realms of Glory 231

Matthew 3:1, 2, 10, 11 (2:1, 2, 10, 11)
Luke 2:8-14

REGENT SQUARE 8.7.8.7. with refrain

1. An - gels from the realms of glo - ry, Wing your flight o'er
2. Shep -herds in the fields a - bid - ing, Watch - ing o'er your
3. Sag - es, leave your con - tem - pla - tions, Bright - er vi - sions
4. Saints be - fore the al - tar bend - ing, Watch - ing long in

all the earth; Ye who sang cre - a - tion's sto - ry
flocks by night, God with us is now re - sid - ing,
beam a - far. Seek the great De - sire of na - tions—
hope and fear. Sud - den - ly the Lord, de - scend - ing,

Refrain

Now pro - claim Mes - si - ah's birth:
Yon - der shines the in - fant light;
Ye have seen his na - tal star;   Come and wor - ship,
In his tem - ple shall ap - pear;

Come and wor - ship, Wor - ship Christ, the new - born King.

Text: James Montgomery, 1771-1854.
Tune: Henry Smart, 1813-1879.

232

Away in a Manger

Luke 2:11, 12
Alma 5:19

MUELLER 11.11.11.11.
Alternate hymn: 233

1. A - way in a man - ger, no crib for his bed,
2. The cat - tle are low - ing; the poor ba - by wakes,
3. Be near me, Lord Je - sus; I ask thee to stay

The lit - tle Lord Je - sus laid down his sweet head;
But lit - tle Lord Je - sus, no cry - ing he makes.
Close by me for - ev - er, and love me, I pray.

The stars in the sky looked down where he lay,
I love thee, Lord Je - sus; look down from the sky
Bless all the dear chil - dren in thy ten - der care,

The lit - tle Lord Je - sus, a - sleep on the hay.
And stay by my cra - dle till morn - ing is nigh.
And fit us for heav - en to live with thee there.

Text: Anonymous.
Tune: James R. Murray, 1841-1905.

Away in a Manger

Luke 2:6, 7
Alma 5:19

CRADLE SONG 11.11.11.11.
Alternate hymn: 232

1. A - way in a man - ger, no crib for his bed,
2. The cat - tle are low - ing, the poor ba - by wakes,
3. Be near me, Lord Je - sus; I ask thee to stay

The lit - tle Lord Je - sus laid down his sweet head;
But lit - tle Lord Je - sus, no cry - ing he makes.
Close by me for - ev - er, and love me, I pray.

The stars in the bright sky looked down where he lay,
I love thee, Lord Je - sus; look down from the sky
Bless all the dear chil - dren in thy ten - der care,

The lit - tle Lord Je - sus, a - sleep on the hay.
And stay by my cra - dle till morn - ing is nigh.
And fit us for heav - en to live with thee there.

Text: Anonymous.
Tune: Melody by W. J. Kirkpatrick, 1838-1921; harm. by Rosalee Elser, 1925 - . Copyright 1980 by Rosalee Elser.
Used by permission.

234

Luke 1:26-30
Matthew 2:3, 4 (1:20, 21)

Joseph, Kind Joseph

STAR IN THE EAST 11.10.11.10.D.

1. Jo - seph, kind Jo - seph, look down in the man - ger; look on this
2. Ma - ry, brave Ma - ry, look down at your first - born; cra - dle him
3. Je - sus, dear Je - sus, look out at the hill - side; see how the

child to be known as your son. Care for him ten - der - ly
close to you now while you may. Treas - ure these mo - ments so
night is made bright by your star. On - ly the faith - ful will

un - til his Fa - ther calls him to do what no oth - er has done.
they will sus - tain you when he must go to show oth - ers the way.
fol - low its guid - ing; on - ly the wise see the Light that you are.

Refrain

An - gels in cho - rus sing glad hal - le - lu - jahs; hills ech - o

back the good news of the birth. Beth - le - hem sleeps but all

heav - en re - joic - es; God's gift of in - fi - nite love bless-es earth.

Text: Naomi Russell, 1921 - ; copyright 1980 Reorganized Church of Jesus Christ of Latter Day Saints.
Tune: Appalachian Folk Hymn attr. to R. Herron; harm. John Obetz, 1933 - ; copyright 1980 Reorganized Church of Jesus Christ of Latter Day Saints.

O Thou Joyful, O Thou Wonderful 235

Matthew 2:1-6 (1:18-23)
Luke 2:4-11

O SANCTISSIMA 4.5.7.6.6.7.

1. O thou joy - ful, O thou won-der - ful Grace re - veal - ing
2. O thou joy - ful, O thou won-der - ful Love re - veal - ing
3. O thou joy - ful, O thou won-der - ful Peace re - veal - ing

Christ-mas - tide! Je - sus came to win us From all sin with-
Christ-mas - tide! Loud ho - san - nas sing - ing And all prais - es
Christ-mas - tide! Dark - ness dis - ap - pear - eth, God's own light now

in us: Glo - ri - fy the ho - ly child!
bring - ing: May thy love with us a - bide.
near - eth: Peace and joy to all be - tide.

Text: Johannes D. Falk, 1768-1826, St. 1; Anonymous, Sts. 2, 3; trans. Henry Katterjohn, 1869-1931.
Tune: Tattersall's Psalmody, 1794.

236

While Humble Shepherds

Hebrews 1:6
I Nephi 3:58, 62

CHRISTMAS 8.6.8.6.6.

1. While hum-ble shep-herds watched their flocks In Beth-lehem's
2. "Fear not," he said, for sud - den dread Had seized each
3. "To you, in Beth - le - hem this day Is born of
4. Thus spake the an - gel; and forth-with Ap - peared a
5. "All glo - ry be to God on high, And to the

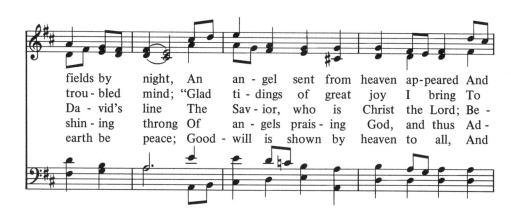

fields by night, An an - gel sent from heaven ap-peared And
trou - bled mind; "Glad ti - dings of great joy I bring To
Da - vid's line The Sav - ior, who is Christ the Lord; Be -
shin - ing throng Of an - gels prais - ing God, and thus Ad -
earth be peace; Good - will is shown by heaven to all, And

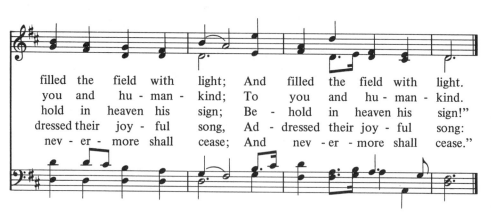

filled the field with light; And filled the field with light.
you and hu - man - kind; To you and hu - man - kind.
hold in heaven his sign; Be - hold in heaven his sign!"
dressed their joy - ful song, Ad - dressed their joy - ful song:
nev - er - more shall cease; And nev - er - more shall cease."

Text: Nahum Tate, 1652-1715.
Tune: George F. Handel, 1685-1759.

Angels We Have Heard on High

237

Luke 2:8-14
D. and C. 76:4g

GLORIA 7.7.7.7. with refrain

1. An - gels we have heard on high Sweet - ly sing - ing o'er the plains,
2. Shep-herds, why this ju - bi - lee? Why your joy - ous songs pro - long?
3. Come to Beth - le - hem and see Him whose birth the an - gels sing;

And the moun - tains in re - ply Ech - o - ing their joy - ous strains.
What the glad - some ti - dings be Which in - spire your heaven - ly song?
Come a - dore, on bend - ed knee, Christ the Lord, our new - born King.

Refrain

Glo - - - ri - a in ex - cel-sis De - o,

Glo - - - ri - a in ex-cel-sis De - o.

Text: Traditional French Carol.
Tune: Traditional French Carol.

238

D. and C. 108:7c
I Nephi 3:66, 67

O Come, All Ye Faithful

ADESTE FIDELES 12.10.11. with refrain

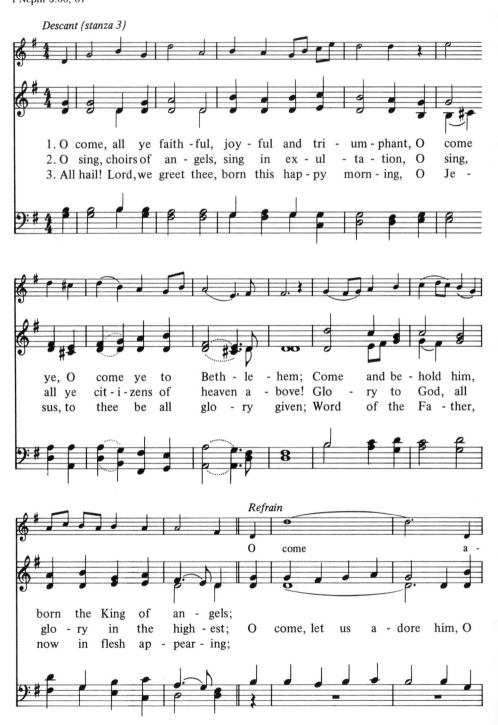

Descant (stanza 3)

1. O come, all ye faith-ful, joy-ful and tri-um-phant, O come
2. O sing, choirs of an-gels, sing in ex-ul-ta-tion, O sing,
3. All hail! Lord, we greet thee, born this hap-py morn-ing, O Je-

ye, O come ye to Beth-le-hem; Come and be-hold him,
all ye cit-i-zens of heaven a-bove! Glo-ry to God, all
sus, to thee be all glo-ry given; Word of the Fa-ther,

Refrain

O come a-

born the King of an-gels;
glo-ry in the high-est; O come, let us a-dore him, O
now in flesh ap-pear-ing;

dore

come, let us a - dore him, O come, let us a - dore him, Christ, the Lord!

Text: Anonymous, Latin, 18th Century; trans. Frederick Oakeley, 1802-1880, and others.
Tune: John F. Wade, c. 1710-1786; descant by Lawrence Curry, 1906 - ; copyright 1941 by the Presbyterian Board of Christian Education; renewed 1969; from *The Hymnal for Youth*; used by permission of The Westminster Press.

Alternate Setting: Stanza 2

Melody in the Tenor   *Fauxbourdon*

2. O sing, choirs of an - gels, sing in ex - ul - ta - tion, Sing,

all ye cit - i - zens of heaven a - bove! Glo - ry to God, all

O come, let us a - dore him, O

glo - ry in the high - est; O come, let us a -

O come, let us a - dore him, O

come, let us a - dore him,

dore him, a dore him, O come, let us a - dore him, Christ, the Lord!

come, let us a - dore him,

Setting: Arr. by Martin Shaw, 1875-1958; copyright 1924 Martin Shaw; used by permission of G. Schirmer, Inc.

239
Silvery Star, Precious Star

Luke 2:8-16
Helaman 5:59, 66

STARLIGHT AND SONG 7.7.7.7. with refrain

1. Sil - ver - y star, pre - cious star, Shin - ing o - ver Beth - le - hem,
2. Beau - ti - ful song, won - drous song Kneel - ing shep - herds wept to hear,
3. Ba - by Sa - vior, born at night In the a - ges long a - go,
4. Lo, we hear the song o'er - head! Lo, we see the star a - rise!

Guid - ing Wise Men from a - far, In the still night lead - ing them.
Chant - ed by God's ho - ly throng, Sing - ing peace and joy and cheer.
An - gels sang and stars gave light For thy hum - ble home be - low.
Like the Wise Men we are led In the still night un - to Christ.

Refrain

Star - light and song All the night long,

Her - alds of morn; Je - sus is born.

Text: Elbert A. Smith, 1871-1959.
Tune: Audentia Anderson, 1872-1963. Text and tune copyright 1950 Herald Publishing House.

Once in Royal David's City

240

Luke 2:52
I John 3:2

IRBY 8.7.8.7.8.7.

1. Once in roy - al Da - vid's cit - y Stood a low - ly
2. He came down to earth from heav - en Who is God and
3. For he is our child - hood's pat - tern; Day by day like
4. And our eyes at last shall see him, Through his own re -

cat - tle shed, Where a moth - er laid her ba - by
Lord of all, And his shel - ter was a sta - ble,
us he grew; He was lit - tle, weak, and help - less;
deem - ing love; For that child so dear and gen - tle

In a man - ger for his bed: Mar - y was that
And his cra - dle was a stall: With the poor, and
Tears and smiles like us he knew: And he feel - eth
Is our Lord in heaven a - bove, And he leads his

moth - er mild, Je - sus Christ her lit - tle child.
mean, and low - ly Lived on earth our Sav - ior ho - ly.
for our sad - ness, And he shar - eth all our glad - ness.
chil - dren on To the place where he is gone.

Text: Cecil Frances Alexander, 1818-1895; alt.
Tune: Henry J. Gauntlett, 1805-1876

241
Sing Songs of Joy

Matthew 3:1, 2 (2:1, 2)
Luke 1:26-33

SONGS OF JOY 4.5.4.4.5.

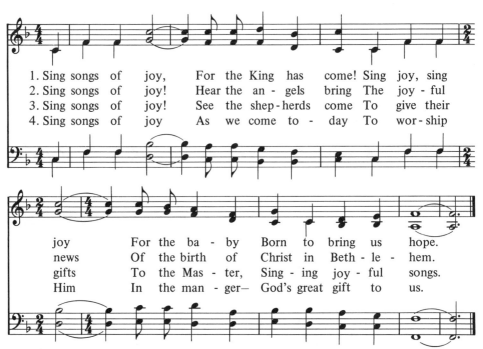

1. Sing songs of joy, For the King has come! Sing joy, sing joy For the ba - by Born to bring us hope.
2. Sing songs of joy! Hear the an - gels bring The joy - ful news Of the birth of Christ in Beth - le - hem.
3. Sing songs of joy! See the shep - herds come To give their gifts To the Mas - ter, Sing - ing joy - ful songs.
4. Sing songs of joy As we come to - day To wor - ship Him In the man - ger— God's great gift to us.

Text and Tune: Pamela Robison, 1947 - ; copyright 1980 Reorganized Church of Jesus Christ of Latter Day Saints.

242
Infant Holy, Infant Lowly

Luke 2:7-20
Matthew 3:10, 11, (2:10, 11)

W ZLOBIE LEZY 8.7.8.7.8.8.7.

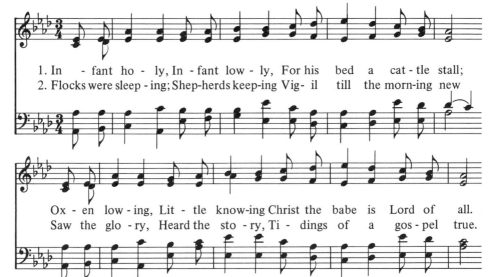

1. In - fant ho - ly, In - fant low - ly, For his bed a cat - tle stall; Ox - en low - ing, Lit - tle know - ing Christ the babe is Lord of all.
2. Flocks were sleep - ing; Shep-herds keep-ing Vig- il till the morn-ing new Saw the glo - ry, Heard the sto - ry, Ti - dings of a gos - pel true.

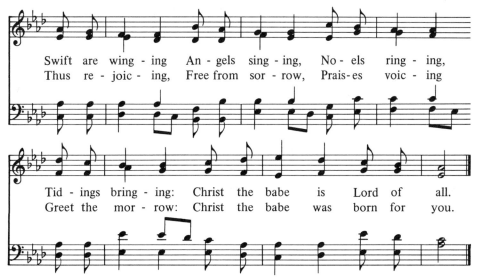

Swift are wing - ing An - gels sing - ing, No - els ring - ing,
Thus re - joic - ing, Free from sor - row, Prais - es voic - ing

Tid - ings bring - ing: Christ the babe is Lord of all.
Greet the mor - row: Christ the babe was born for you.

Text: From the Polish; paraphrase by Edith M. G. Reed, 1885-1933; from *Kingsway Carol Book*; used by permission of Evans Bros. Ltd.
Tune: Polish Carol; harm. David H. Jones, 1900 - ; copyright 1955 by John Ribble, from *The Hymnbook*, used by permission of the Westminster Press.

Good News! Great Joy to All the Earth 243

Luke 2:7-20
Matthew 3:10, 11 (2:10, 11)

DETROIT C.M.

Unison (or harmony)

1. Good news! Great joy to all the earth—The Prince of Peace is born!
2. Re - joice in hope! Cast out all fear! God's love in - cludes us all.
3. Rise up for peace! Let ev - ery life Re - spond with heart and hand:
4. Re - joice! Give thanks! The Christ has come: Re - ceive his life; be free!

God's peace he brings to hu - man hearts By fear and con - flict torn.
In Christ God calls us all to peace: Now heed that trum - pet call!
Cast out the bit - ter - ness and strife In ours and ev - ery land.
Let all the world be whole in him Who brings God's lib - er - ty!

Text: Frank von Christierson, 1900 - ; copyright 1976 The Hymn Society of America; used by permission.
Tune: Supplement to Kentucky Harmony, 1820; harm. Rosalee Elser, 1925 - ; copyright 1980 Rosalee Elser; used by permission.

244

Silent Night! Holy Night!

Luke 2:8, 13, 14, 16
D. and C. 17:5a-d

STILLE NACHT 6.6.8.9.6.6.

1. Si - lent night! Ho - ly night! All is calm, all is bright Round yon
2. Si - lent night! Ho - ly night! Shep-herds quake at the sight! Glo - ries
3. Si - lent night! Ho - ly night! Son of God, love's pure light Ra - diant

vir - gin moth - er and child! Ho - ly In - fant, so ten - der and mild,
stream from heav - en a - far, Heaven - ly hosts sing Al - le - lu - ia,
beams from thy ho - ly face With the dawn of re - deem - ing grace,

Sleep in heav - en - ly peace;___ Sleep in heav - en - ly peace.
Christ, the Sav - ior, is born; ___ Christ, the Sav - ior, is born!
Je - sus, Lord, at thy birth;___ Je - sus, Lord, at thy birth.

Text: Joseph Mohr, 1792-1848; tr. John Freeman Young, 1820-1885.
Tune: Franz Gruber, 1787-1863.

On This Day Earth Shall Ring

245

Luke 2:15-20
Matthew 3:1-11 (2:1-11)

PERSONENT HODIE
6.6.6.6.6. with refrain

Unison (or harmony)

1. On this day earth shall ring With the song chil-dren sing
2. God's bright star o'er his head, Wise men three to him led;
3. On this day an-gels sing; With their song earth shall ring,

To the Lord, Christ our King, Born on earth to save us;
Kneel they low by his bed, Lay their gifts be-fore him,
Prais-ing Christ, Heav-en's King, Born on earth to save us;

Refrain

Him the Fa-ther gave us.
Praise him and a-dore him. *Id-e-o - o-o, Id-e-o -
Peace and love he gave us.

o - o, Id-e-o glo-ri-a in ex-cel-sis De-o!

* Ideo is pronounced Ē - dā - o. The refrain means "Therefore give glory to God in the highest."

Special stanza for Easter:

4. For our kind he was slain,
Deep in grave he hath lain;
And he rose yet again
Swift to reign in glory.
This the Easter Story.

Special stanza for Pentecost:

5. Now at God's Pentecost,
Thee we praise, Holy Ghost;
Losing thee, we are lost.
May thy grace amending
Give us peace unending.

Text: *Piae Cantiones*, 1582; tr. Jane M. Joseph, c. 1894-1929; copyright 1924 J. Curwen & Sons, Ltd.; used by permission of G. Schirmer, Inc.
Tune: *Piae Cantiones*, 1582; harm. Rosalee Elser, 1925 - ; copyright 1980 Rosalee Elser; used by permission.

246

The First Nowell

Matthew 3:1, 9-11 (2:1, 9-11)
Alma 10:19, 26

THE FIRST NOWELL   Irregular with refrain

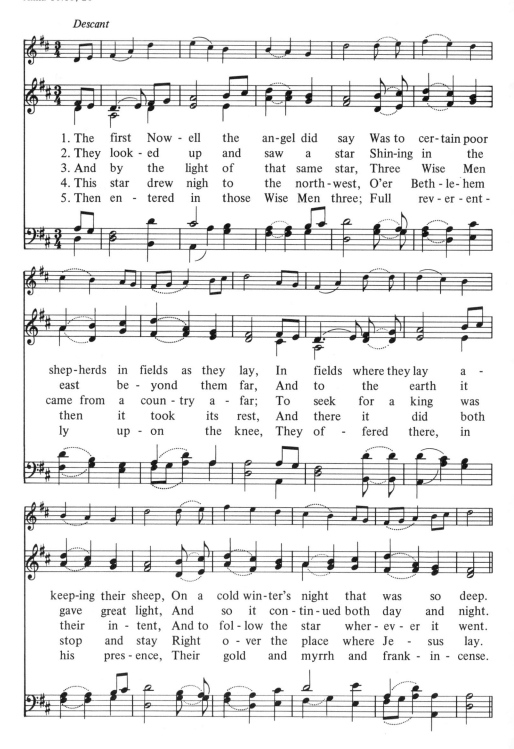

Descant

1. The first Now - ell the an-gel did say Was to cer-tain poor
2. They look - ed up and saw a star Shin-ing in the
3. And by the light of that same star, Three Wise Men
4. This star drew nigh to the north-west, O'er Beth - le-hem
5. Then en - tered in those Wise Men three; Full rev - er - ent -

shep-herds in fields as they lay, In fields where they lay a -
east be - yond them far, And to the earth it
came from a coun - try a - far; To seek for a king was
then it took its rest, And there it did both
ly up - on the knee, They of - fered there, in

keep-ing their sheep, On a cold win-ter's night that was so deep.
gave great light, And so it con - tin - ued both day and night.
their in - tent, And to fol - low the star wher - ev - er it went.
stop and stay Right o - ver the place where Je - sus lay.
his pres - ence, Their gold and myrrh and frank - in - cense.

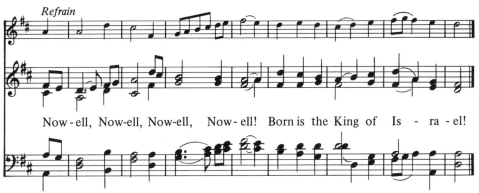

Refrain

Now-ell, Now-ell, Now-ell, Now-ell! Born is the King of Is-ra-el!

Text: Traditional English Carol.
Tune: Traditional English Melody in W. Sandys' *Christmas Carols*, 1833; descant by Kathryn Reese O'Boyle, copyright 1941 by the Presbyterian Board of Christian Education; renewed 1969; from *The Hymnal for Youth*; used by permission of The Westminster Press.

Newborn of God 247

Mosiah 1:97-102
Luke 2:16-19

TOULON 10.10.10.10.

1. New - born of God, his glo - ry man - i - fest, God's gift of love so won - drous - ly ex - pressed! The Ho - ly Child who brought his gift to earth At Christ - mas time in true hearts finds re - birth.
2. The fresh - ness of God's life was in this child. He grew in youth, in man - hood, ho - ly, mild. A no - bler life this world shall nev - er see; By him we know what God with us can be.
3. If one bright day can bring such love and peace, What glo - ry when his king - dom shall in - crease! Then Christ - mas joy will hal - low all our days, And thoughts of him en - light - en all our ways!

Text: Frank W. Mills, 1876-1963; alt.; copyright 1956 Herald Publishing House.
Tune: Louis Bourgeois, c. 1510-c. 1561.

248 O Little Town of Bethlehem

Alma 5:19
Micah 5:2

ST. LOUIS 8.6.8.6.7.6.8.6.
Alternate tune: FOREST GREEN (484)

1. O lit - tle town of Beth- le -hem, How still we see thee lie!
2. For Christ is born of Mar - y, And gath - ered all a - bove,
3. How si - lent- ly, how si - lent -ly The won - drous gift is given!
4. O Ho - ly Child of Beth - le - hem, De -scend to us, we pray;

A - bove thy deep and dream -less sleep The si - lent stars go by;
While mor - tals sleep, the an - gels keep Their watch of won -dering love.
So God im - parts to hu - man hearts The bless - ings of his heaven.
Cast out our sin and en - ter in; Be born in us to - day.

Yet in thy dark streets shin - eth The ev - er -last - ing Light;
O morn - ing stars, to - geth - er Pro - claim the ho - ly birth,
No ear may hear his com - ing, But in this world of sin,
We hear the Christ - mas an - gels The great glad ti -dings tell;

The hopes and fears of all the years Are met in thee to - night.
And prais - es sing to God the King, And peace, good -will on earth!
Where meek souls will re -ceive him, still The dear Christ en - ters in.
O come to us, a - bide with us, Our Lord Im - man - u - el!

Text: Phillips Brooks, 1835-1893.
Tune: Lewis H. Redner, 1831-1908.

Go, Tell It on the Mountain

249

Luke 1:30-33
Luke 2:7-11

GO TELL IT 7.6.7.6. with refrain

Unison

Go, tell it on the moun - tain, O-ver the hills and ev - 'ry-where;

Go, tell it on the moun - tain That Je - sus Christ is born!

Fine

Harmony

1. While shep - herds kept their watch - ing O'er si - lent flocks by night,
2. The shep - herds feared and trem - bled When lo! a - bove the earth
3. Down in a low - ly man - ger The hum - ble Christ was born,

D. C.

Be - hold through-out the heav - ens There shone a ho - ly light.
Rang out the an - gel cho - rus That hailed our Sav - ior's birth.
And God sent us sal - va - tion That bless - ed Christ-mas morn.

Text: American Folk Hymn; stanzas by John W. Work, Jr., 1872-1925.
Tune: American Folk Melody, harm. by John W. Work, III, 1901-1967.
Text and tune from *American Negro Songs and Spirituals.* Used by permission of Mrs. John W. Work, III.

250   I Heard the Bells on Christmas Day

Luke 2:14
Isaiah 12:2

WALTHAM L.M.

```
1. I    heard  the   bells  on    Christ - mas  Day  Their
2. I    thought how,  as    the   day    had  come, The
3. And  in     de - spair  I     bowed  my   head; "There
4. Then pealed the   bells  more  loud   and  deep: "God
5. Till, ring - ing, sing - ing   on     its  way,  The
```

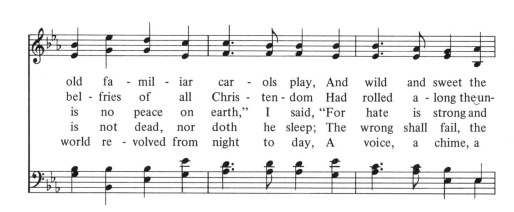

```
old   fa - mil - iar  car - ols  play,  And   wild and sweet the
bel - fries of   all   Chris - ten - dom  Had   rolled a - long the un-
is    no  peace on    earth," I    said, "For   hate  is  strong and
is    not dead,  nor   doth  he   sleep; The   wrong shall fail, the
world re - volved from night to   day,  A     voice, a   chime, a
```

```
words re - peat  Of   peace on   earth, good - will to   men.
bro - ken song    Of   peace on   earth, good - will to   men,
mocks the song    Of   peace on   earth, good - will to   men."
right pre - vail,  With peace on   earth, good - will to   men."
chant sub - lime   Of   peace on   earth, good - will to   men!
```

Text: Henry W. Longfellow, 1807-1882.
Tune: J. Baptiste Calkin, 1827-1905.

I Wonder as I Wander

251

Romans 5:6-8
I Peter 2:21-24

I WONDER AS I WANDER 12.11.11.12.

Unison

1. I won-der as I wan-der, out un-der the sky, How
2. When Ma-ry birthed Je-sus, 'twas in a cow's stall, With
3. If Je-sus had want-ed for an-y wee thing, A
4. I won-der as I wan-der, out un-der the sky, How

Je - sus the Sav - ior did come for to die For
wise men and farm-ers and shep-herds and all; But
star in the sky or a bird on the wing, Or
Je - sus the Sav - ior did come for to die For

poor or - nery peo - ple like you and like I; I
high from God's heav-en a star's light did fall, And the
all of God's an-gels in heav'n for to sing, He
poor or - nery peo - ple like you and like I; I

won - der as I wan - der, out un - der the sky.
prom - ise of a - ges it then did re - call.
sure - ly could have had it, 'cause he was the King.
won - der as I wan - der, out un - der the sky.

Text and Tune: Appalachian Folk Carol collected and adapted by John Jacob Niles, 1892 - ; copyright 1934, 1944
G. Schirmer, Inc. Arr. 1980 Rosalee Elser, 1925 - ; used by permission.

252   Hark, the Herald Angels Sing

Mosiah 1:102, 103
II Corinthians 5:17, 18, 21

MENDELSSOHN 7.7.7.7.D. with repeat

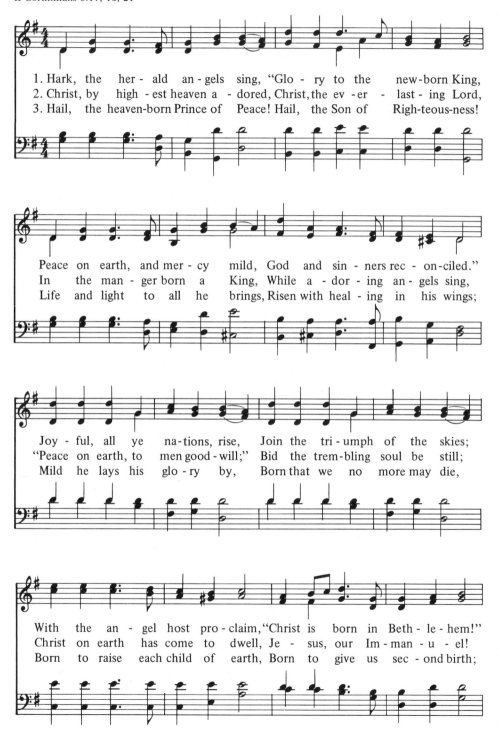

1. Hark, the her - ald an - gels sing, "Glo - ry to the new-born King,
2. Christ, by high - est heaven a - dored, Christ, the ev - er - last - ing Lord,
3. Hail, the heaven-born Prince of Peace! Hail, the Son of Right-teous-ness!

Peace on earth, and mer - cy mild, God and sin - ners rec - on-ciled."
In the man - ger born a King, While a - dor - ing an - gels sing,
Life and light to all he brings, Risen with heal - ing in his wings;

Joy - ful, all ye na-tions, rise, Join the tri - umph of the skies;
"Peace on earth, to men good - will;" Bid the trem-bling soul be still;
Mild he lays his glo - ry by, Born that we no more may die,

With the an - gel host pro - claim, "Christ is born in Beth - le - hem!"
Christ on earth has come to dwell, Je - sus, our Im - man - u - el!
Born to raise each child of earth, Born to give us sec - ond birth;

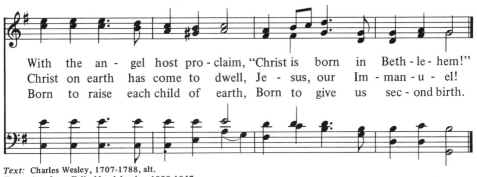

With the an - gel host pro - claim, "Christ is born in Beth - le - hem!"
Christ on earth has come to dwell, Je - sus, our Im - man - u - el!
Born to raise each child of earth, Born to give us sec - ond birth.

Text: Charles Wesley, 1707-1788, alt.
Tune: Arr. from Felix Mendelssohn, 1809-1847.

Heir of All the Waiting Ages 253

Matthew 2:3-6 (1:20-23) PICARDY 8.7.8.7.8.7.
Luke 2:25-32

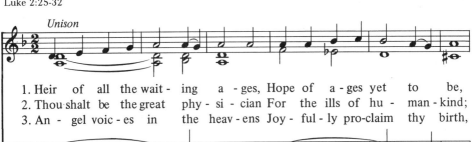

1. Heir of all the wait - ing a - ges, Hope of a - ges yet to be,
2. Thou shalt be the great phy - si - cian For the ills of hu - man - kind;
3. An - gel voic - es in the heav - ens Joy - ful - ly pro-claim thy birth,

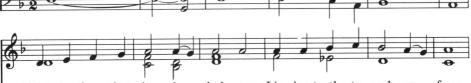

Light to those that sit in dark - ness, Liv - ing truth to make us free:
Thou shalt heal the wound-ed spir - it, And give vi - sion to the blind—
Sing - ing of a prom - ised king - dom, Reign of righ-teous- ness and worth—

Strick- en souls shall know the com - fort Of thy gra - cious min-is - try.
Larg - er life for all who seek it In the child - like heart and mind.
Songs of proph-e - cy and prom - ise, Peace, good-will have come to earth.

Text: Marion Franklin Ham, 1867-1956; alt.; copyright Beacon Press. Used by permission.
Tune: Traditional French Carol.

254

As with Gladness Men of Old

Matthew 3:9, 10 (2:9, 10)
D. and C. 17:5a-g

DIX 7.7.7.D.

1. As with glad - ness men of old Did the guid - ing
2. As with joy - ful steps they sped To that low - ly
3. As they of - fered gifts most rare At that man - ger
4. Ho - ly Je - sus, ev - ery day Keep us in the

star be - hold, As with joy they hailed its light
man - ger bed, There to bend the knee be - fore
rude and bare, So may we with ho - ly joy,
nar - row way; And when earth - ly things are past,

Lead - ing on - ward, beam - ing bright, So, most gra - cious
Him whom heaven and earth a - dore, So may we with
Pure and free from sin's al - loy, All our cost - liest
Bring our ran - somed souls at last Where they need no

Lord, may we Ev - er - more be led to thee.
will - ing feet Ev - er seek thy mer - cy seat.
treas - ures bring, Christ, to thee, our heaven - ly King.
star to guide, Where no clouds thy glo - ry hide.

Text: William C. Dix, 1837-1898.
Tune: Arr. from Conrad Kocher, 1786-1872, by W. H. Monk, 1823-1889.

Lo, How a Rose E'er Blooming

255

Isaiah 11:1, 2
I Nephi 3:58-62

ES IST EIN ROS' 7.6.7.6.6.7.6.

♩ *remains constant*

1. Lo, how a rose e'er bloom - ing From ten - der stem hath
2. I - sai - ah 'twas fore - told it, The rose I have in
3. This flower, whose fra - grance ten - der With sweet-ness fills the

sprung! Of Jes - se's lin - eage com - ing As those of old have
mind; With Ma - ry we be - hold it, The vir - gin moth - er
air, Dis - pels with glo - rious splen - dor The dark - ness ev - ery -

sung. It came a flow - er bright, A - mid the
kind. To show God's love a - right Of her was
where. True man, yet ver - y God, From sin and

cold of win - ter, When half - spent was the night.
born a Sav - ior, When half - spent was the night.
death He saves us And light - ens ev - ery load.

Text: German, 16th century, tr. Theodore Baker, 1851-1934, Sts. 1, 2, alt.; tr. Harriet Krauth Spaeth, 1845-1925, St. 3.
Tune: Geistliche Kirchengesäng, Cologne, 1599; harm. Michael Praetorius, 1571-1621.

256 It Came Upon the Midnight Clear

Helaman 2:111, 112
Luke 2:8-14

CAROL C.M.D.

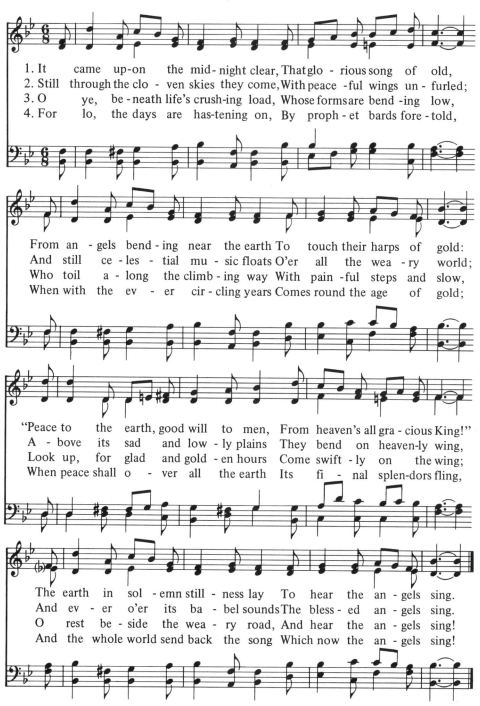

1. It came up-on the mid-night clear, That glo-rious song of old,
2. Still through the clo-ven skies they come, With peace-ful wings un-furled;
3. O ye, be-neath life's crush-ing load, Whose forms are bend-ing low,
4. For lo, the days are has-tening on, By proph-et bards fore-told,

From an-gels bend-ing near the earth To touch their harps of gold:
And still ce-les-tial mu-sic floats O'er all the wea-ry world;
Who toil a-long the climb-ing way With pain-ful steps and slow,
When with the ev-er cir-cling years Comes round the age of gold;

"Peace to the earth, good will to men, From heaven's all gra-cious King!"
A-bove its sad and low-ly plains They bend on heaven-ly wing,
Look up, for glad and gold-en hours Come swift-ly on the wing;
When peace shall o-ver all the earth Its fi-nal splen-dors fling,

The earth in sol-emn still-ness lay To hear the an-gels sing.
And ev-er o'er its ba-bel sounds The bless-ed an-gels sing.
O rest be-side the wea-ry road, And hear the an-gels sing!
And the whole world send back the song Which now the an-gels sing!

Text: Edmund H. Sears, 1810-1876.
Tune: Richard S. Willis, 1819-1900.

What Child Is This

257

Matthew 3:9-11 (2:9-11)
Luke 2:6-18

GREENSLEEVES 8.7.8.7. with refrain

Unison (or harmony)

1. What Child is this who, laid to rest, On Ma-ry's lap is sleep-ing?
2. Why lies he in such mean es-tate Where ox and ass are feed-ing?
3. So bring him in-cense, gold, and myrrh; Come, peas-ant, king, to own him.

Whom an-gels greet with an-thems sweet, While shep-herds watch are keep-ing?
Good Chris-tian, fear; for sin-ners here The si-lent Word is plead-ing.
The King of kings sal-va-tion brings; Let lov-ing hearts en-throne him.

Refrain

This, this is Christ the King, Whom shep-herds guard and an-gels sing:

Haste, haste to bring him praise, The Babe, the Son of Ma-ry.

Text: William Chatterton Dix, 1837-1898.
Tune: 16th Century English Tune.

258

Joy to the World!

Alma 3:87, 88
Psalm 98:1-9

ANTIOCH 8.6.8.6.6.8.

1. Joy to the world! The Lord is come; Let earth re - ceive its King;
2. Joy to the world; The Sav - ior reigns; Let all their songs em - ploy
3. No more let sin and sor - row grow, Nor thorns in - fest the ground;
4. He rules the world with truth and grace, And makes the na - tions prove

Let ev - ery heart pre - pare him room,
While fields and floods, rocks, hills, and plains
He comes to make his bless - ings flow
The glo - ries of his righ - teous - ness

And heaven and na - ture sing, And heaven and na - ture sing,
Re - peat the sound-ing joy, Re - peat the sound-ing joy,
Far as the curse is found, Far as the curse is found,
And won - ders of his love, And won - ders of his love,

And heaven and na-ture sing,

And heaven and na-ture sing, And heaven and na-

And heaven, and heaven and na - ture sing.
Re - peat, re - peat the sound - ing joy.
Far as, far as the curse is found.
And won - ders, won - ders of his love.

ture sing.

Text: Based on Psalm 98, by Isaac Watts, 1674-1748.
Tune: George F. Handel, 1685-1759; arr. by Lowell Mason, 1792-1872.

Jesus, Good Above All Other

259

Isaiah 9:6, 7
John 6:37-40

QUEM PASTORES 8.8.8.7.

1. Je - sus, good a - bove all oth - er,
2. Je - sus, cra - dled in a man - ger,
3. Je - sus, for thy peo - ple dy - ing,
4. Lord, in all our do - ings guide us;

Gen - tle child of gen - tle moth - er,
For us fac - ing ev - ery dan - ger,
Ris - en Mas - ter, death de - fy - ing,
Pride and hate shall ne'er di - vide us;

In a sta - ble born our broth - er,
Liv - ing as a home - less stran - ger,
Lord, in heaven thy grace sup - ply - ing,
We'll go on with thee be - side us,

Give us grace to per - se - vere.
Make we thee our King most dear.
Keep us to thy pres - ence near.
And with joy we'll per - se - vere!

Text: Percy Dearmer, 1867-1936; sts. 1 & 2 borrowed from 12th century Latin, tr. John Mason Neale, 1818-1866; from *The English Hymnal* by permission of Oxford University Press.
Tune: 14th Century German Carol Melody; arr. Ralph Vaughan Williams, 1872-1958; from *The English Hymnal*; used by permission of Oxford University Press.

260 Good Christian Friends, Rejoice

Matthew 2:3, 4 (1:20, 21)
II Nephi 1:73, 74

IN DULCI JUBILO 6.6.7.7.7.8.5.5.

1. Good Chris - tian friends, re - joice With heart and soul and voice;
2. Good Chris - tian friends, re - joice With heart and soul and voice;
3. Good Chris - tian friends, re - joice With heart and soul and voice;

Give ye heed to what we say: Je - sus Christ is born to - day;
Now ye hear of end - less bliss: Je - sus Christ was born for this!
Now ye need not fear the grave; Je - sus Christ was born to save!

Ox and ass be - fore him bow, And he is in the man - ger now.
He has o - pened heav - en's door, And we are blest for - ev - er - more.
Calls you one and calls you all To gain his ev - er - last - ing hall.

Christ is born to - day! Christ is born to - day!
Christ was born for this! Christ was born for this!
Christ was born to save! Christ was born to save!

Text: Medieval Latin Carol; tr. John M. Neale, 1818-1866, alt.
Tune: German carol, 14th century.

Sound over All Waters

261

Isaiah 52:6, 7
I Nephi 3:197, 198

ST. DENIO 11.11.11.11.

1. Sound o-ver all wa-ters, reach out from all lands,
   The chor-us of voic-es, the clasp-ing of hands;
   Sing hymns that were sung by the stars of the morn;
   Sing songs of the an-gels when Je-sus was born.

2. Blow, bu-gles of bat-tle, the march-es of peace,
   East, west, north and south, let the long quar-rel cease;
   O sing ye the song an-gels sang at the birth;
   Sing glo-ry to God and good-will on the earth.

3. With glad ju-bi-la-tions, bring hope to the world;
   The dark night is end-ing, and dawn has un-furled;
   Rise, hope of the a-ges, a-rise like the sun;
   All speech flow to mu-sic; all hearts beat as one!

Text: John Greenleaf Whittier, 1807-1892; alt.
Tune: Welsh Hymn Melody; John Robert's *Canaidau y Cyssegr*, 1839.

262 O Sacred Head, Now Wounded

Isaiah 53:5-7
Titus 3:3-7

PASSION CHORALE 7.6.7.6.D.

1. O sa-cred Head, now wound-ed, With grief and shame weighed down;
2. What thou, my Lord, hast suf-fered Was all for sin-ners' gain;
3. What lan-guage shall I bor-row To thank thee, dear-est Friend,

Now scorn-ful-ly sur-round-ed With thorns, thine on-ly crown;
Mine, mine was the trans-gres-sion, But thine the dead-ly pain.
For this thy dy-ing sor-row, Thy pit-y with-out end?

O sa-cred Head, what glo-ry, What bliss till now was thine!
Lo, here I fall, my Sav-ior; 'Tis I de-serve thy place.
O make me thine for-ev-er; And should I faint-ing be,

Yet though de-spised and go-ry, I joy to call thee mine.
Look on me with thy fa-vor; Vouch-safe to me thy grace.
Lord, let me nev-er, nev-er Out-live my love to thee. A-men.

Text: Attr. to Bernard of Clairvaux, 1091 - 1153; tr. (German) by Paul Gerhardt, 1607 - 1676; tr. (English) by James
W. Alexander, 1804 - 1859.
Tune: Hans Leo Hassler, 1564 - 1612; harm. by J. S. Bach, 1685 - 1750.

Lift High the Cross

John 3:14, 15
John 12:23, 24

CRUCIFIER 10.10.10.10.

Unison

Lift high the cross, the love of Christ pro - claim

Fine

till all the world a - dore his sa - cred name.

Harmony

1. Come, Chris - tian, fol - low where our Sav - ior trod,
2. O Lord, once lift - ed high on Cal - va - ry,
3. O may our song of tri - umph ev - er be

D. C.

accomp.

O love vic - to - rious, Christ the Son of God.
As thou hast prom - ised, draw us un - to thee.
Praise to the Cru - ci - fied for vic - to - ry.

Text: George William Kitchin, 1827-1912; Michael Robert Newbolt, 1874-1956; alt.; used by permission of the proprietors of *Hymns Ancient and Modern.*
Tune: Sydney Hugo Nicholson, 1875-1947; used by permission of the proprietors of *Hymns Ancient and Modern.*

264 'Tis Midnight, and on Olive's Brow

D. and C. 36:11b

Mark 14:35-40 (31-36)

OLIVE'S BROW L.M.

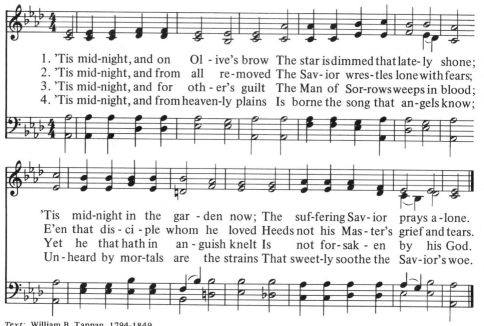

1. 'Tis mid-night, and on Ol - ive's brow The star is dimmed that late-ly shone;
2. 'Tis mid-night, and from all re-moved The Sav-ior wres-tles lone with fears;
3. 'Tis mid-night, and for oth - er's guilt The Man of Sor-rows weeps in blood;
4. 'Tis mid-night, and from heaven-ly plains Is borne the song that an-gels know;

'Tis mid-night in the gar - den now; The suf-fering Sav-ior prays a-lone.
E'en that dis - ci - ple whom he loved Heeds not his Mas-ter's grief and tears.
Yet he that hath in an - guish knelt Is not for-sak - en by his God.
Un-heard by mor-tals are the strains That sweet-ly soothe the Sav-ior's woe.

Text: William B. Tappan, 1794-1849.
Tune: William B. Bradbury, 1816-1868.

265 When I Survey the Wondrous Cross

D. and C. 19:3a

Galatians 6:14

ROCKINGHAM L.M.

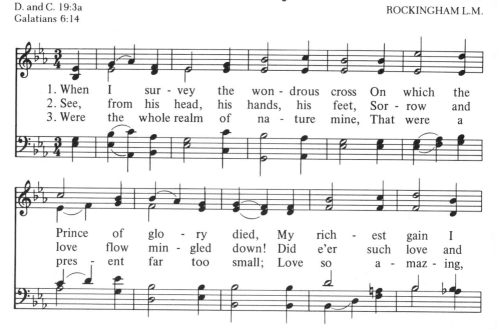

1. When I sur - vey the won - drous cross On which the
2. See, from his head, his hands, his feet, Sor - row and
3. Were the whole realm of na - ture mine, That were a

Prince of glo - ry died, My rich - est gain I
love flow min - gled down! Did e'er such love and
pres - ent far too small; Love so a - maz - ing,

count but loss And pour con - tempt on all my pride.
sor - row meet, Or thorns com - pose so rich a crown?
so di - vine, De - mands my soul, my life, my all.

Text: Isaac Watts, 1674-1748.
Tune: Edward Miller, 1731-1807.

Alternate Setting

Melody in the Tenor   *Fauxbourdon*

1. When I sur - vey the won - drous cross On which the
2. See, from his head, his hands, his feet, Sor - row and
3. Were the whole realm of na - ture mine, That were a

Prince of glo - ry died, My rich - est gain I
love flow min - gled down! Did e'er such love and
pres - ent far too small; Love so a - maz - ing,

count but loss And pour con - tempt on all my pride.
sor - row meet, Or thorns com - pose so rich a crown?
so di - vine, De - mands my soul, my life, my all.

Setting: Geoffrey Shaw, 1879-1943; used by permission of Faith Press Ltd.

266

Go to Dark Gethsemane

Matthew 26:35, 36 (38, 39)
D. and C. 36:11b

GETHSEMANE 7.7.7.D.

1. Go to dark Geth - sem - a - ne, Ye who feel the
2. See him at the judg - ment hall, Beat - en, bound, re -
3. Cal - vary's mourn - ful moun - tain climb; There a - dor - ing
4. Ear - ly has - ten to the tomb Where they laid his

tempt - er's power; Your Re - deem - er's con - flict see;
viled, ar - raigned; See him meek - ly bear - ing all;
at his feet, Mark that mir - a - cle of time,
breath - less clay; All is sol - i - tude and gloom.

Watch with him one bit - ter hour; Turn not from his
Love for us his soul sus - tained. Shun not suf - fering,
God's own sac - ri - fice com - plete. "It is fin - ished!"
Who has tak - en him a - way? Christ is ris'n! He

griefs a - way; Learn of Je - sus Christ to pray.
shame, nor loss; Learn of Christ to bear the cross.
hear him cry; Learn of Je - sus Christ to die.
meets our eyes. Sav - ior, cause us so to rise.

Text: James Montgomery, 1771-1854.
Tune: Richard Redhead, 1820-1901.

Were You There

267

I Corinthians 15:3, 4
D. and C. 17:5a-d

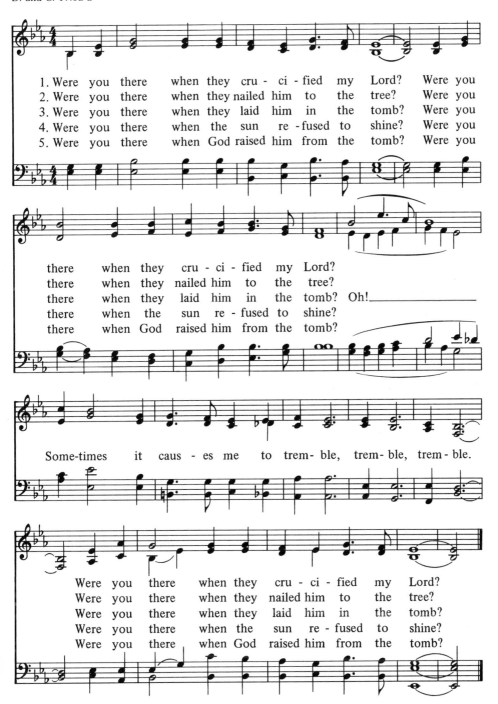

1. Were you there when they cru - ci - fied my Lord? Were you
2. Were you there when they nailed him to the tree? Were you
3. Were you there when they laid him in the tomb? Were you
4. Were you there when the sun re - fused to shine? Were you
5. Were you there when God raised him from the tomb? Were you

there when they cru - ci - fied my Lord?
there when they nailed him to the tree?
there when they laid him in the tomb? Oh!_____
there when the sun re - fused to shine?
there when God raised him from the tomb?

Some-times it caus - es me to trem - ble, trem - ble, trem - ble.

Were you there when they cru - ci - fied my Lord?
Were you there when they nailed him to the tree?
Were you there when they laid him in the tomb?
Were you there when the sun re - fused to shine?
Were you there when God raised him from the tomb?

Text: American Folk Hymn.
Tune: American Folk Hymn.

268 Ride On, Ride On in Majesty

Luke 19:36, 37 (37, 38)
I Nephi 3:82-86

DEUS TUORUM MILITUM L.M.

Unison (or harmony)

1. Ride on, ride on in maj - es - ty! Hark, all the
2. Ride on, ride on in maj - es - ty! In low - ly
3. Ride on, ride on in maj - es - ty! As all the
4. Ride on, ride on in maj - es - ty! In low - ly

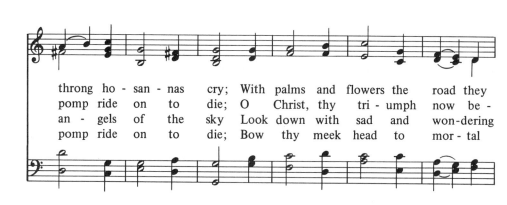

throng ho - san - nas cry; With palms and flowers the road they
pomp ride on to die; O Christ, thy tri - umph now be -
an - gels of the sky Look down with sad and won - dering
pomp ride on to die; Bow thy meek head to mor - tal

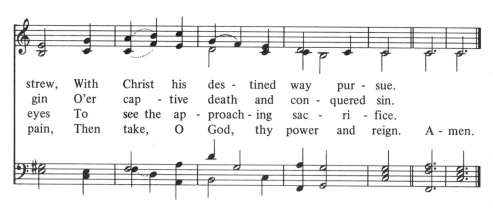

strew, With Christ his des - tined way pur - sue.
gin O'er cap - tive death and con - quered sin.
eyes To see the ap - proach - ing sac - ri - fice.
pain, Then take, O God, thy power and reign. A - men.

Text: Henry H. Milman, 1791-1868, alt.
Tune: From *Grenoble Antiphoner,* 1753.

Deep Were His Wounds

269

II Nephi 1:71-75
Acts 5:30-32

MARLEE 6.6.6.6.8.8.

1. Deep were his wounds, and red, On cru - el
2. He suf - fered shame and scorn, And wretch - ed,
3. His life, his all, he gave When he was

Cal - va - ry, As on the cross he bled In
dire dis - grace; For - sak - en and for - lorn, He
cru - ci - fied; Our bur - dened souls to save, What

bit - ter ag - o - ny. But they, whom sin has
hung there in our place. But all who would from
fear - ful death he died! But each of us, though

wound - ed sore, Find heal - ing in the wounds he bore.
sin be free Look to his cross for vic - to - ry.
dead in sin, Through him e - ter - nal life may win.

Text: William Johnson, 1906 - .
Tune: Leland B. Sateren, 1913 - .
Text and tune copyright 1958 the Lutheran *Service Book and Hymnal*; used by permission.

270

John 16:32, 33
Luke 22:41, 42

When Jesus Wept

WHEN JESUS WEPT L.M.

Unison

(1)* When Je - sus wept, the fall - ing tear

(2) In mer - cy flowed be - yond all bound;

(3) When Je - sus groaned, a trem - bling fear

(4) Seized all the guilt - y world a - round.

* May be used as a four part canon unaccompanied.

Text: William Billings, 1746-1800.
Tune: William Billings, 1746-1800; harm. by Richard D. Wetzel, 1935 - ; copyright 1972 by The Westminster Press.
Used by permission.

271

John 11:25, 26
I Corinthians 15:54-57

Lift Your Glad Voices

TRUMPET 10.11.11.11.12.11.10.11.

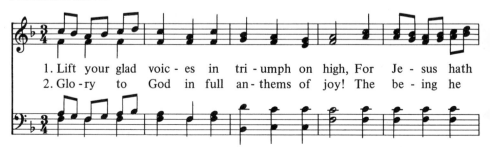

1. Lift your glad voic - es in tri - umph on high, For Je - sus hath

2. Glo - ry to God in full an - thems of joy! The be - ing he

ris - en, and we can - not die. Vain were the ter - rors that
gave us death can - not de - stroy. Sad were the life we must

gath - ered a - round him, And short the do - min - ion of death and the
part with to - mor - row If tears were our birth - right and death were our

grave; He burst from the fet - ters of dark - ness that bound him, Re -
end; But Je - sus hath cheered the dark val - ley of sor - row; We'll

splen - dent in glo - ry, to live and to save. Loud was the cho - rus of
rise from the dead and im - mor - tal as - cend. Lift then your voic - es in

an - gels on high; The Sav - ior hath ris - en, and we shall not die.
tri - umph on high, For Je - sus hath ris - en, and we shall not die.

Text: Henry Ware, Jr., 1794-1843, alt.
Tune: Isaac B. Woodbury, 1819-1858.

272   Christ Is Alive

D. and C. 76:4g   WHITEFIELD L.M. with alleluias
Galatians 2:20

1. Christ is a-live! Let Christians sing! His cross stands emp-ty to the
2. Christ is a-live! No long-er bound To dis-tant years in Pal-es-
3. Not throned a-bove, re-mote-ly high, Un-touched, un-moved by hu-man
4. In ev-ery in-sult, rift, and war Where col-or, scorn, or wealth di-
5. Christ is a-live! His spir-it burns Through this and ev-ery fu-ture

sky.
tine,
pains,   Al-le-lu-ia, al-le-lu-ia, al-le-lu - ia!
vide,
age,

Let streets and homes with prais-es ring; His love in death shall nev-er die.
He comes to claim the here and now And con-quer ev-ery place and time.
But dai-ly in the midst of life Our Sav-ior with the Fa-ther reigns.
He suf-fers still, yet loves the more, And lives though ev - er cru-ci-fied.
Till all cre-a-tion lives and learns His joy, his jus-tice, love and praise.

Al-le-lu-ia, al-le-lu-ia, al-le-lu - ia!

Text: Brian Wren, 1936 - . Used by permission of Oxford University Press.
Tune: Keith Landis, 1922 - ; harm. Jeffrey Rickard; copyright 1977 Praise Publications, Inc. Used by permission.

I Know That My Redeemer Lives 273

D. and C. 76:3a, f, h
III Nephi 5:11-17

LASST UNS ERFREUEN L.M. with alleluias
Alternate hymn: 274

1. I know that my Re-deem-er lives; What joy the blest as-sur-ance gives.
2. He lives to bless me with his love; He lives to plead for me a - bove;
3. He lives and grants me dai - ly breath; He lives, and I shall con-quer death.
4. He lives, all glo - ry to his name; He lives, my Sav-ior still the same;

He lives, he lives, who once was dead;
He lives my hun- gry soul to feed;
He lives my man-sion to pre- pare;
What joy the blest as - sur-ance gives—

Al-le - lu - ia! Al-le - lu - ia!

He lives, my ev - er - last - ing Head!
He lives to help in time of need.
He lives to bring me safe - ly there.
I know that my Re - deem-er lives!

Al-le - lu - ia! Al-le - lu - ia!

Al-le - lu - ia! Al - le - lu - ia! Al - le lu - ia!

Text: Samuel Medley, 1738-1799.
Tune: Melody from *Geistliche Kirchengesäng*, Cologne, 1623; arr. & harm. Ralph Vaughan Williams, 1872-1958.
From *The English Hymnal* by permission of Oxford University Press.

274   I Know That My Redeemer Lives

D. and C. 76:3a, f, h
III Nephi 5:11-17

TRURO L.M.
Alternate hymn: 273

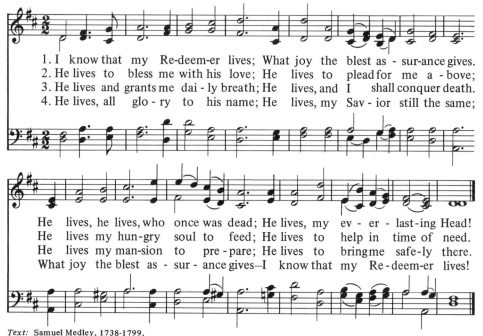

1. I know that my Re-deem-er lives; What joy the blest as-sur-ance gives.
2. He lives to bless me with his love; He lives to plead for me a-bove;
3. He lives and grants me dai-ly breath; He lives, and I shall conquer death.
4. He lives, all glo-ry to his name; He lives, my Sav-ior still the same;

He lives, he lives, who once was dead; He lives, my ev-er-last-ing Head!
He lives my hun-gry soul to feed; He lives to help in time of need.
He lives my man-sion to pre-pare; He lives to bring me safe-ly there.
What joy the blest as-sur-ance gives—I know that my Re-deem-er lives!

Text: Samuel Medley, 1738-1799.
Tune: Charles Burney, 1726-1814.

275   Good Christian Friends, Rejoice and Sing

I Corinthians 15:20-22
D. and C. 76:3f, g

VULPIUS (Gelobt Sei Gott) 8.8.8. with refrain

1. Good Chris-tian friends, re-joice and sing! Now is the
2. The Lord of life is risen to-day; Bring flowers of
3. Praise we in songs of vic-to-ry That love, that
4. Thy name we bless, O ris-en Lord, And sing to-

tri-umph of our King! To all the world glad news we bring:
song to strew his way; Let all the world re-joice and say:
life which can-not die, And sing with hearts up-lift-ed high:
day with one ac-cord The life laid down, the life re-stored:

Text: Cyril A. Alington, 1872-1955, alt.; used by permission of Hymns Ancient and Modern Ltd.
Tune: Melchior Vulpius, c. 1570-1615.

The Strife Is O'er 276

Ether 5:7-9
I Timothy 2:4-6

VICTORY 8.8.8. with alleluias

Al - le - lu - ia! Al - le - lu - ia! Al - le - lu - ia!

1. The strife is o'er, the bat - tle done; Now is the vic - tor's
2. Death's might - iest pow'rs have done their worst, And Je - sus has his
3. On the third morn, he rose a - gain, Glo - rious in maj - es -
4. Lord, by the stripes that wounded thee From death's dread sting thy

tri - umph won; O let the song of praise be sung:
foes dis - persed; Let shouts of praise and joy out - burst:
ty to reign; O let us swell the joy - ful strain: Al - le - lu - ia!
serv - ants free That we may live and sing to thee:

Text: From 17th Century Latin, trans. Francis Pott, 1832-1909.
Tune: Giovanni P. da Palestrina, 1525-1594; arr. William H. Monk, 1823-1889.

277

Angels, Roll the Rock Away

I Corinthians 15:18-22
Psalm 71:22, 23

EASTER HYMN 7.7.7.7. with alleluias
Alternate tune: LLANFAIR (278)

1. An - gels, roll the rock a - way!
2. 'Tis the Sav - ior! Ser - aphs, raise, Al - le - lu - ia!
3. Praise him, all ye heaven-ly choirs!

Death, yield up thy might - y prey!
Your tri - um - phant shout of praise, Al - le - lu - ia!
Praise him, sweep your gold - en lyres!

See, he ris - es from the tomb,
Let the earth's re - mot - est bound, Al - le - lu - ia!
Praise him in the no - blest songs,

Ris - es with im - mor - tal bloom,
Hear the joy - in - spir - ing sound, Al - le - lu - ia!
Praise him with ten thou - sand tongues!

Text: Thomas Scott, 1705-1775.
Tune: Lyra Davidica, 1708.

Jesus Christ Is Risen Today

278

John 20:19, 20
Matthew 28:2-5 (2-7)

LLANFAIR 7.7.7.7. with alleluias
Alternate tune: EASTER HYMN (277)

1. Je - sus Christ is risen to - day,
2. Hymns of praise then let us sing, Al - le - lu - ia!
3. Sing we to our God a - bove,

Our tri - um -phant ho - ly day,
Un - to Christ, our heaven - ly King, Al - le - lu - ia!
Praise e - ter - nal as His love;

Who did once, up - on the cross,
Who en - dured the cross and grave, Al - le - lu - ia!
Praise Him, all ye heaven-ly host,

Suf - fer to re - deem our loss.
Sin - ners to re - deem and save. Al - le - lu - ia!
Fa - ther, Son, and Ho - ly Ghost.

Text: Latin, 14th Century; trans. in *Lyra Davidica*, 1708; stanza 2, John Arnold's *Compleat Psalmodist*, 1749;
stanza 3, Charles Wesley, 1707-1788.
Tune: Robert Williams, c. 1781-1821; harm. David Evans, 1874-1948. From *The Revised Church Hymnary* by
permission of Oxford University Press.

279 Let Us Sing of Easter Gladness

Acts 4:31-33
Romans 6:4-8

HOLY MANNA 8.7.8.7.D.

1. Let us sing of Eas-ter glad-ness That re-joic-es ev-ery day,
2. When we touch Truth's heal-ing gar-ment And be-hold life's pu-ri-ty,
3. Liv-ing meek-ly as the Mas-ter, Who of God was glo-ri-fied,

Sing of hope and faith up-lift-ed; Love has rolled the stone a-way.
When we find in Love the ref-uge That is man's se-cu-ri-ty,
Look-ing ev-er to the ra-diance Of his won-drous Eas-ter-tide;

Lo, the prom-ise and ful-fill-ment, Lo, the Man whom God hath made,
When we turn from earth to Spir-it, And from self have won re-lease,
Freed of fear, of pain, and sor-row, Giv-ing God the hon-or due,

Seen in glo-ry of an Eas-ter Crowned with light that can-not fade.
Then we see the ris-en Sav-ior, Then we know his prom-ised peace.
Ev-ery day will be an Eas-ter Filled with ben-e-dic-tions new.

Now the Green Blade Rises

280

Ezekiel 37:3-5
John 1:11, 12

NOËL NOUVELET 11.10.10.11.

1. Now the green blade ris - es from the bur - ied grain,
2. In the grave they laid him, Love whom sin had slain,
3. Forth he came at Eas - ter, like the ris - en grain,
4. When our hearts are win - try, griev - ing, or in pain,

Wheat that in dark earth man - y days has lain;
Think - ing that he would nev - er wake a - gain,
He that for three days in the grave had lain;
Your touch can call us back to life a - gain,

Love lives a - gain, that with the dead has been:
Laid in the earth like grain that sleeps un - seen:
Raised from the dead my liv - ing Lord is seen:
Fields of our hearts that dead and bare have been:

Love is come a - gain like wheat a - ris - ing green.

Text: J. M. C. Crum, 1872-1958; from *The Oxford Book of Carols* by permission of Oxford University Press.
Tune: Traditional French Carol.

281

Romans 5:5
I Peter 5:6, 7

Holy Spirit, Truth Divine

HOLY SPIRIT, TRUTH DIVINE 7.7.7.7.

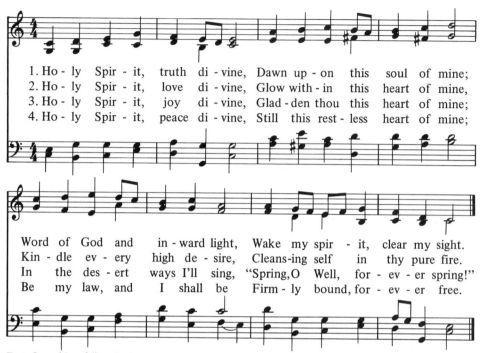

1. Ho - ly Spir - it, truth di - vine, Dawn up - on this soul of mine;
2. Ho - ly Spir - it, love di - vine, Glow with - in this heart of mine,
3. Ho - ly Spir - it, joy di - vine, Glad - den thou this heart of mine;
4. Ho - ly Spir - it, peace di - vine, Still this rest - less heart of mine;

Word of God and in - ward light, Wake my spir - it, clear my sight.
Kin - dle ev - ery high de - sire, Cleans - ing self in thy pure fire.
In the des - ert ways I'll sing, "Spring, O Well, for - ev - er spring!"
Be my law, and I shall be Firm - ly bound, for - ev - er free.

Text: Samuel Longfellow, 1819-1892.
Tune: R. Walker Robson, copyright 1936 Paterson's Publications, Ltd.; used by permission.

282

James 1:17
D. and C. 10:7a

When Kindled by Thy Spirit's Light

MARYTON L.M.

When kin - dled by Thy Spir - it's light, Our minds, il -

lumed, more clear - ly see That ev - ery good which in us

is De - rives, E - ter - nal One, from Thee. A - men.

Text: E. Y. Hunker, 1899-1966; copyright 1980 Reorganized Church of Jesus Christ of Latter Day Saints.
Tune: H Percy Smith, 1825-1898.

Come, O Creator Spirit 283

John 14:6, 10, 16, 17
D. and C. 18:6

VENI CREATOR L.M.

Unison — ♪ remains constant

1. Come, O Cre - a - tor Spir - it, come, And make with - in our
2. O Com - fort - er, that name is thine, Of God most high the
3. Our sens - es with thy light in - flame, Our hearts to heaven - ly
4. May we by thee the Fa - ther learn, And know the Son, and

hearts thy home; To us thy grace ce - les - tial give,
gift di - vine; The well of life, the fire of love,
love re - claim; Our bod - ies' poor in - fir - mi - ty
thee dis - cern, Who art of both; and so a - dore

Who of thy breath - ing move and live.
Our souls' a - noint - ing from a - bove.
With strength per - pet - ual for - ti - fy.
In per - fect faith for - ev - er - more. A - men.

Text: *Veni Creator Spiritus* attr. Hrabanus Maurus, 776-856; trans. Robert Bridges, 1844-1930.
Tune: Sarum plainsong Mode VIII; harm. Winfred Douglas, 1867-1944.

284 Gracious Spirit, Dwell with Me

Galatians 5:22-25
D. and C. 10:6, 7

ASHBURTON 7.7.7.D.

1. Gra - cious Spir - it, dwell with me, I my - self would
2. Truth - ful Spir - it, dwell with me, I my - self would
3. Ho - ly Spir - it, dwell with me, I my - self would

gra - cious be; And with words that help and heal
truth - ful be; And with wis - dom kind and clear
ho - ly be; Cleansed and freed from sin, I would

Would thy life in mine re - veal; And with ac - tions
Let thy life in mine ap - pear; And with ac - tions
Choose and cher - ish all things good; And what - ev - er

bold but meek Would for Christ, my Sav - ior, speak.
neigh - bor - ly Speak my Lord's sin - cer - i - ty.
I can be, Give to God who gave me thee. A - men.

Text: Thomas T. Lynch, 1818-1871, alt.
Tune: Robert Jackson, 1842-1914.

O Holy Dove of God Descending

285

Luke 3:28, 29
Moroni 10:5-7

LOIS 9.9.9.6.

1. O ho-ly Dove of God de-scend-ing, You are the love that knows no end-ing. All of our shat-tered dreams You're mend-ing: Spir-it, now live in me.

2. O ho-ly Wind of God now blow-ing, You are the seed that God is sow-ing. You are the life that starts us grow-ing: Spir-it, now live in me.

3. O ho-ly Rain of God now fall-ing, You make the Word of God en-thrall-ing, You are that in-ner voice now call-ing: Spir-it, now live in me.

4. O ho-ly Flame of God now burn-ing, You are the power of Christ re-turn-ing. You are the an-swer to our yearn-ing: Spir-it, now live in me. A-men.

Text and Tune: Bryan Jeffery Leech, 1931 - ; copyright 1976 by Fred Bock Music Company; all rights reserved; used by permission.

286 Come, Holy Ghost, Our Hearts Inspire

John 14:16-18
II Nephi 13:26

LLOYD C.M.

1. Come, Ho - ly Ghost, our hearts in - spire; Let us thine in - fluence prove;
2. Come, Ho - ly Ghost, for moved by thee The proph - ets wrote and spoke;
3. Ex - pand thy wings, ce - les - tial dove; Brood o'er our na - tures' night;
4. God, through thine aid we then shall know If thou with - in us shine,

Source of the old pro - phet - ic fire, Fountain of light and love!
Un - lock the truth, thy - self the key; Un - seal the sa - cred book.
On our dis - or - dered spir - its move, And let there now be light.
And sound with all thy saints be - low The depth of love di - vine. A - men.

Text: Charles Wesley, 1707-1788.
Tune: Cuthbert Howard, 1856-1927.

287 Holy Spirit, Come with Power

Ephesians 4:30
D. and C. 85:1

BEACH SPRING 8.7.8.7.D.

1. Ho-ly Spir - it, come with pow-er: Breathe in - to our ach-ing night.
2. Ho-ly Spir - it, come with fire. Burn us with your pres-ence new.
3. Ho-ly Spir - it, bring your mes-sage; Burn and breathe each word a - new

We ex - pect you this glad hour, Wait-ing for your strength and light.
Let us as one might-y choir Sing our hymn of praise to you.
Deep in - to our tir - ed liv - ing Till we strive your work to do.

We are joy - ful, we are ea - ger, Yearn-ing for your gra - cious deed;
Burn a - way our wast-ed sad - ness And en - flame us with your love;
Teach us love and trust-ing kind-ness; Bare our arms to those who hurt;

Rest up - on your con-gre - ga - tion; Give us power of God, we plead.
Burst up - on our con-gre - ga - tion. Give us glad - ness from a - bove.
Breathe up - on our con-gre - ga - tion And in - spire us with your Word.

Text: Ann Neufeld Rupp, 1932 - .
Tune: The Sacred Harp, 1844; harm. Rosalee Elser, 1925 - ; copyright 1980 Rosalee Elser; used by permission.

Spirit Divine, Attend Our Prayer   **288**

Luke 11:14 (13)   ST. AGNES C.M.
Romans 8:26, 27   *Alternate tune: Richmond (346)*

1. Spir - it di - vine, at - tend our prayer, And make our hearts thy home;
2. Come as the light! To us re - veal The truth we long to know.
3. Come as the fire, and purge our hearts Like sac - ri - fi - cial flame
4. Come as the wind, O breath of God! O pen - te - cos - tal grace!

De - scend with all thy gra-cious power; Come, Ho - ly Spir - it, come.
Re - veal the nar - row path of right, The way of du - ty show.
Till our whole souls an of-fering be In love's re - deem-ing name.
Come, make thy great sal - va-tion known Wide as the hu - man race.

Text: Andrew Reed, 1787-1862; adapted by Samuel Longfellow, 1819-1892.
Tune: John B. Dykes, 1823-1876.

289

Alma 3:27-29
Romans 8:14-16

Come Down, O Love Divine

DOWN AMPNEY 6.6.11.D.

♩ remains constant

1. Come down, O Love di - vine; Seek thou this soul of mine,
2. O let it free - ly burn, Till earth - ly pas - sions turn
3. And so the yearn - ing strong, With which the soul will long,

And vis - it it with thine own ar - dor glow - ing;
To dust and ash - es in its heat con - sum - ing;
Shall far sur - pass the power of hu - man tell - ing;

O Com-fort - er, draw near; With - in my heart ap - pear
And let thy glo - rious light Shine ev - er on my sight,
For none can guess Love's grace, Till each be - comes the place

And kin - dle it, thy ho - ly flame be - stow - ing.
And clothe me round the while my path il - lum - ing.
Where - in the Ho - ly Spir - it makes his dwell - ing. A-men.

Text: Bianco da Siena, d. 1434; trans. Richard F. Littledale, 1833-1890.
Tune: Ralph Vaughan Williams, 1872-1958. From *The English Hymnal* by permission of Oxford University Press.

There's a Church Within Us

290

Ephesians 4:11-16
D. and C. 150:12

THE CHURCH WITHIN US 8.8.7.7.8.

1. There's a church with-in us, O Lord,
2. There's po-ten-tial with-in us, O Lord,
3. There's some build-ing to be done, O Lord,
4. There's the church with-in us, O Lord,

There's a church with-in us, O Lord.
Some-thing's stir-ring with-in us, O Lord.
There's some build-ing to be done, O Lord.
There's the church with-in us, O Lord.

Not a build-ing but a soul, Not a por-tion but a whole,
Some-thing's strain-ing to have birth, To be vis-i-ble on earth;
Not with steel, not with stone, But with lives which are our own
Not a build-ing but one soul, Not a por-tion but one whole,

There's a church with-in us, O Lord.
There's po-ten-tial with-in us, O Lord.
There's the church to be built, O Lord.
We are your Church in the world.

Text and Tune: Kent E. Schneider, 1946 - ; copyright 1967 Hope Publishing Co., Carol Stream, IL 60187. Harm. alt. by Rosalee Elser, 1925 - ; copyright 1981 Hope Publishing Co. All rights reserved. Used by permission.

291 Church of Christ, in Latter Days

D. and C. 3:15e, 16, 17
I Corinthians 12:27

ELSWORTH 7.7.7.7.

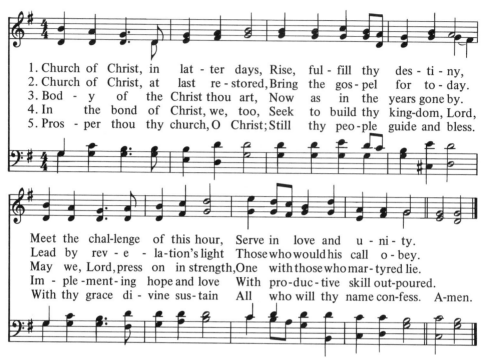

1. Church of Christ, in lat-ter days, Rise, ful-fill thy des-ti-ny,
2. Church of Christ, at last re-stored, Bring the gos-pel for to-day.
3. Bod-y of the Christ thou art, Now as in the years gone by.
4. In the bond of Christ, we, too, Seek to build thy king-dom, Lord,
5. Pros-per thou thy church, O Christ; Still thy peo-ple guide and bless.

Meet the chal-lenge of this hour, Serve in love and u-ni-ty.
Lead by rev-e-la-tion's light Those who would his call o-bey.
May we, Lord, press on in strength, One with those who mar-tyred lie.
Im-ple-ment-ing hope and love With pro-duc-tive skill out-poured.
With thy grace di-vine sus-tain All who will thy name con-fess. A-men.

Text and Tune: Franklyn S. Weddle, 1905 - ; copyright 1956 Herald Publishing House.

292 By Thy Redeeming Cross, O Lord

I Corinthians 1:18
D. and C. 150:12

BELMONT C.M.

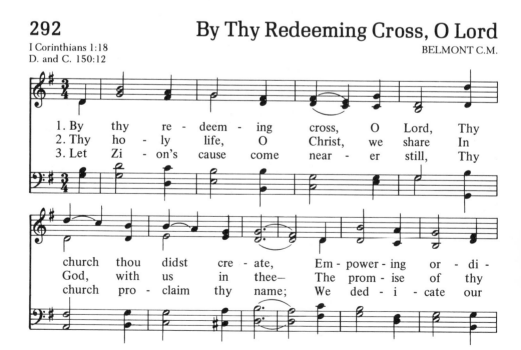

1. By thy re-deem-ing cross, O Lord, Thy
2. Thy ho-ly life, O Christ, we share In
3. Let Zi-on's cause come near-er still, Thy

church thou didst cre-ate, Em-pow-er-ing or-di-
God, with us in thee— The prom-ise of thy
church pro-claim thy name; We ded-i-cate our

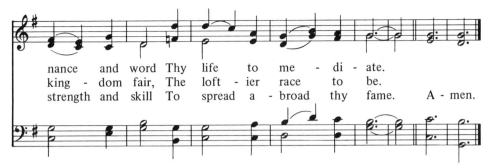

nance and word Thy life to me - di - ate.
king - dom fair, The loft - ier race to be.
strength and skill To spread a - broad thy fame. A - men.

Text: Arthur A. Oakman, 1905-1975; copyright 1956 Herald Publishing House.
Tune: William Gardiner's *Sacred Melodies*, 1812.

Prophetic Church, the Future Waits 293

Alma 5:38-41
D. and C. 138:3a, b

DEUS TUORUM MILITUM (Grenoble) L.M.

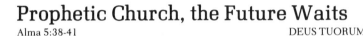

1. Pro - phet - ic Church, the fu - ture waits Thy li - ber -
2. Free from the bonds that bind the mind To nar - row
3. A free - dom that re - veres the past, But trusts the

at - ing min - is - try; Go for - ward in the
thought and life - less creed; Free from a so - cial
dawn - ing fu - ture more; And bids the soul, in

power of love, Pro - claim the truth that makes us free.
code that fails To serve the cause of hu - man need;
search of truth, Ad - ven - ture bold - ly and ex - plore.

Text: Marion Franklin Ham, 1867-1956, alt.; copyright Beacon Press; used by permission.
Tune: Melody from the *Grenoble Antiphoner*, 1753.

294 The Church's One Foundation

D. and C. 140:5c, d
I Corinthians 3:10, 11

AURELIA 7.6.7.6.D.

1. The Church's one foun-da - tion Is Je - sus Christ, her Lord;
2. E - lect from ev - ery na - tion, Yet one o'er all the earth,
3. 'Mid toil and trib-u - la - tion And tu-mult of her war,
4. Yet she on earth hath un - ion With God, the Three in One,

She is his new cre - a - tion By wa - ter and the word;
Her char - ter of sal - va - tion—One Lord, one faith, one birth;
She waits the con-sum-ma - tion Of peace for - ev - er - more,
And mys - tic sweet com-mun - ion With those whose rest is won.

From heaven he came and sought her To be his ho - ly bride;
One ho - ly name she bless - es, Par - takes one ho - ly food,
Till with the vi - sion glo - rious Her long - ing eyes are blest,
Oh, hap - py ones and ho - ly! Lord, give us grace that we,

With his own blood he bought her, And for her life he died.
And to one hope she press - es With ev - ery grace en - dued,
And the great church vic - to - rious Shall be the church at rest.
Like them, the meek and low - ly, On high may dwell with thee.

Text: Samuel J. Stone, 1839-1900.
Tune: Samuel S. Wesley, 1810-1876.

Christ Is the Foundation

Ephesians 2:19-21
I Corinthians 3:10, 11

PENITENCE 6.5.6.5.D.

1. Christ is the foun - da - tion Of the house we raise;
2. Here may vows be seal - ed By thy Spir - it, Lord;
3. Here may ev - ery to - ken Of thy pres - ence be;
4. Here may God the Fa - ther, Christ the Sav - ior, Son,

Be its walls sal - va - tion, And its gate - ways praise;
Here the sick be heal - ed, And the lost re - stored;
Here may chains be bro - ken, Pris - oners here set free;
With the Ho - ly Spir - it, Be a - dored as one

May its thresh - old low - ly To the Lord be dear;
Here the bro - ken - heart - ed Thy for - give - ness prove;
Here may light il - lu - mine Ev - ery soul of thine,
Till the whole cre - a - tion At thy foot - stool fall,

May the hearts be ho - ly That shall wor - ship here.
Here the friends long part - ed Be re - stored to love.
Lift - ing up the hu - man In - to the di - vine.
And in ad - o - ra - tion Own thee Lord of all.

Text: John Samuel Bewley Monsell, 1811-1875.
Tune: Spencer Lane, 1843-1903.

296

Afar in Old Judea

Matthew 17:4 (5)

D. and C. 4:1a-c

EWING 7.6.7.6.D.

1. A - far in old Ju - de - a, A - bove the Jor - dan stream,
2. In an - cient Za - ra - hem - la, A - bove the tem - ple towers
3. Then in a time of search-ing, A youth who sought God's way
4. To - day the heavens are o - pen To souls pre - pared to hear

A heaven - ly light de - scend - ed On a bap - tis - mal scene.
Ap - peared the Christ of Ju - dah To crown the watch - ful hours.
Saw in Pal - my - ra's wood-land A light be - yond his day,
The won-drous rev - e - la - tion Of Christ, who's ev - er near.

Then came the con - fir - ma - tion Of Je - sus, from a - bove,
A voice, se - rene yet pierc - ing Be - yond our words to tell,
And when the vi - sion o - pened To him whose sight was dim,
The Sav - ior of the a - ges Still lives with us to - day;

The sac - ra - men - tal sig - net: The Spir - it as a dove,
Pro - claimed him as the Sav - ior Whom proph-ets did fore - tell.
He heard the Fa - ther say - ing, "This is my Son, hear him!"
He seeks to help us know him And leads us in his way.

Text: Roy A. Cheville, 1897 - , alt. Copyright 1956 Herald Publishing House.
Tune: Alexander Ewing, 1830-1895.

The Church's Life

297

D. and C. 83:7b-e
Romans 12:3-8

RICHMOND BEACH 8.7.8.7.8.8.7.

Unison (or harmony*) ♩ *remains constant*

1. The church's life is built up - on The rock of rev - e -
la - tion. Our joy - ful hearts are nur-tured by Pro - phet-ic in - spi-
ra - tion. No pri - vate creed shall dull our mind Nor sel - fish
pride un - du - ly bind The Spir - it's val - i - da - tion.

2. A church which seeks the king -dom's goal Re - sponds with con-se-
cra - tion. God's light is not our own do - main— His word is for the
na - tions. Pro - phet-ic fire con-sumes the whole: All mem-bers
share pro-phet- ic role; God's will is our sal - va - tion.

3. We do not dare to rest con - tent In face of our con-
di - tion; Through com-mon mind, our full con - sent Will bet - ter serve our
mis - sion. To those who seek to know His mind, Ex - pand-ing
gift of truth to find, The Lord grants his com - mis - sion.

* Tenors should read the treble clef when necessary.

Text: Geoffrey F. Spencer, 1927 -   , and Alan D. Tyree, 1929 - . Copyright 1980 Reorganized Church of Jesus
Christ of Latter Day Saints.
Tune: A. Royce Eckhardt, 1937 - ; copyright 1973 Covenant Press; used by permission.

298

Fountain of All Revelation

D. and C. 10:11b, c, 12
I Corinthians 2:9-13

LESLIE 8.7.8.7.D.

1. Foun-tain of all rev - e - la -tion, Grant us thy life - giv - ing power;
2. God, our rock of rev - e - la -tion, We would build our lives on thee;

With - out thee no sure sal - va -tion Will de - liv - er us this hour.
For with-out thy sure foun - da - tion None can find sta - bil - i - ty.

May no veil of our tra - di - tion Mask the light that comes from thee!
We will or - der not thy wis-dom To some cher-ished form or mold,

Let not pride nor low am - bi -tion Waste the strength that sets us free.
But will search for truths now hid-den As we live by those we hold. A-men.

Text: Deam Ferris, 1912 - . Copyright 1956 by Herald Publishing House.
Tune: Franklyn S. Weddle, 1905 - . Alt. by Evan A. Fry, 1902-1959. Copyright 1956 by Herald Publishing House.

The Living Word of Scripture

299

John 5:40 (39)
Hebrews 12:1

VIGIL 7.6.7.6.D.
See 210 for a lower setting.

1. The liv - ing Word of scrip - ture Pro - vides the guide and source
2. A proph - et on the moun - tain, A child with - in the womb,
3. De - liv - erance in the des - ert, A pil - lar's guid - ing ray,
4. Our bro - thers and our sis - ters, True saints of ev - ery age

For saints in search of wis - dom And light to chart their course.
A youth in ear - nest search - ing, The wo - men at the tomb;
The grove's re - stor - ing vi - sion, Pro - phet - ic power to - day;
Who share with us their sto - ry, Speak out from ev - ery page.

The stran - gers and the pil - grims Who owned the cause sub - lime
How glo - ri - ous a com - pany Reach out their hands to ours;
In all the gen - er - a - tions Of his - tory's broad ex - panse,
That sto - ry is not end - ed, For still God's voice is heard

Have glimpsed the rev - e - la - tion, And an - swered in their time.
Their faith a vi - brant wit - ness To God's re - deem - ing powers.
The Word has proved suf - fi - cient For ev - ery cir - cum - stance.
Through all who bear the call - ing To be the liv - ing Word.

Text: Geoffrey F. Spencer, 1927 - ; copyright 1980 Reorganized Church of Jesus Christ of Latter Day Saints.
Tune: Swedish Folk Melody.

300

How Can Creation's Voice Be Still

Hebrews 11:13-16
James 1:2-4

MASSACHUSETTS C.M.D.
Alternate tune: RESIGNATION (125)

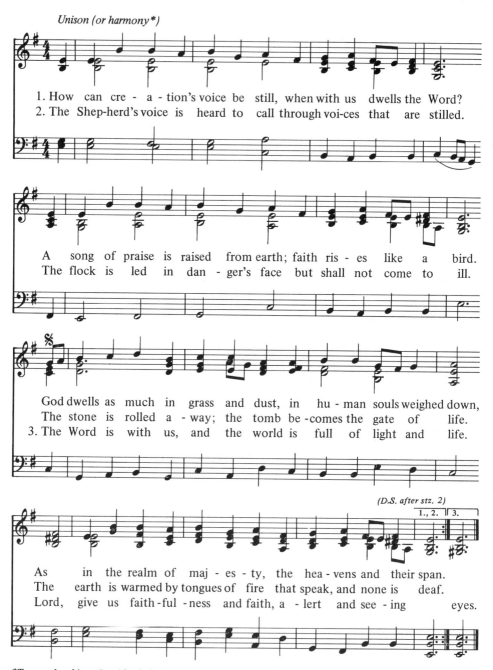

Unison (or harmony*)

1. How can cre - a - tion's voice be still, when with us dwells the Word?
2. The Shep-herd's voice is heard to call through voi-ces that are stilled.

A song of praise is raised from earth; faith ris - es like a bird.
The flock is led in dan - ger's face but shall not come to ill.

God dwells as much in grass and dust, in hu - man souls weighed down,
The stone is rolled a - way; the tomb be -comes the gate of life.
3. The Word is with us, and the world is full of light and life.

(D.S. after stz. 2)

As in the realm of maj - es - ty, the hea - vens and their span.
The earth is warmed by tongues of fire that speak, and none is deaf.
Lord, give us faith-ful - ness and faith, a - lert and see - ing eyes.

*Tenors should read treble clef when necessary.

Text: Anders Frostenson, trans. Fred Kaan, 1929 - ; trans. copyright 1976 Stainer & Bell Ltd. Sole U. S. agent: Galaxy Music Corp., N. Y. Used with permission.
Tune: Katherine K. Davis, 1892-1980; copyright 1964 Abingdon Press. Used with permission.

O God, Our Source of Truth

301

I Corinthians 13:8-12
D. and C. 95:3a

VINEYARD HAVEN S.M. with refrain
Alternate hymn: 302

1. O God, our Source of truth By whom we find our way,
2. We trea-sure what we have Of truth, an am - ple ray;
3. At best, we know in part, Which lim - its what we say.
4. When as a child we spoke And un - der-stood and thought,
5. For a - dult days, the truth Through dark-ened glass is shown.

Re - veal the knowl-edge that we seek Suf - fi - cient for our day.
We brief - ly hold that cher-ished light—It van - ish - es a - way.
But when the per - fect light is come, The part is done a - way.
A child - ish faith and sim - ple joy Were all we craved or sought.
Still yearn we for the prom-ised day: To know as we are known.

Refrain

Lord, guide us, di - rect us, Shine light up - on our way.

> = marcato accent — marked, stressed.
— = tenuto — held; sustained to full value.

Text: Alan D. Tyree, 1929 - ; copyright 1980 Reorganized Church of Jesus Christ of Latter Day Saints.
Tune: Richard Dirksen, 1921 - ; © copyright 1974 Harold Flammer, Inc.; sole selling agent; Shawnee Press, Inc.,
Delaware Water Gap PA 18327; international copyright secured; all rights reserved; reprinted with permission.

302

O God, Our Source of Truth

I Corinthians 13:8-12
D. and C. 95:3a

FESTAL SONG S.M.
See 378 for a higher setting
Alternate hymn: 301

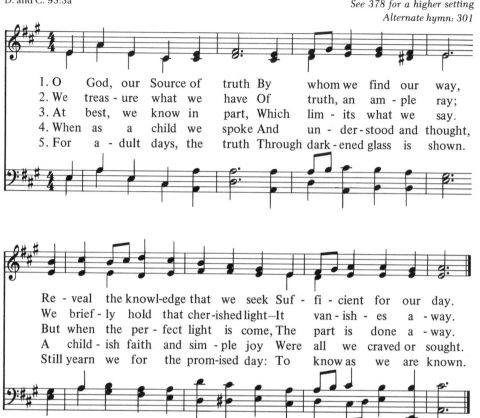

1. O God, our Source of truth By whom we find our way,
2. We treas-ure what we have Of truth, an am-ple ray;
3. At best, we know in part, Which lim-its what we say.
4. When as a child we spoke And un-der-stood and thought,
5. For a-dult days, the truth Through dark-ened glass is shown.

Re - veal the knowl-edge that we seek Suf - fi - cient for our day.
We brief - ly hold that cher-ished light—It van - ish - es a - way.
But when the per - fect light is come, The part is done a - way.
A child-ish faith and sim - ple joy Were all we craved or sought.
Still yearn we for the prom-ised day: To know as we are known.

Text: Alan D. Tyree, 1929 - ; copyright 1980 Reorganized Church of Jesus Christ of Latter Day Saints.
Tune: William H. Walter, 1825-1893.

303

Walk in the Light

Ephesians 5:8
II Nephi 15:10

MANOAH C.M.

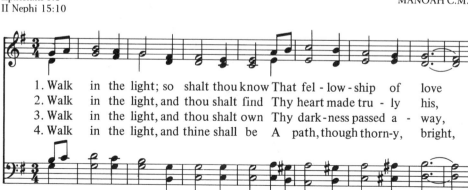

1. Walk in the light; so shalt thou know That fel - low - ship of love
2. Walk in the light, and thou shalt find Thy heart made tru - ly his,
3. Walk in the light, and thou shalt own Thy dark-ness passed a - way,
4. Walk in the light, and thine shall be A path, though thorn-y, bright,

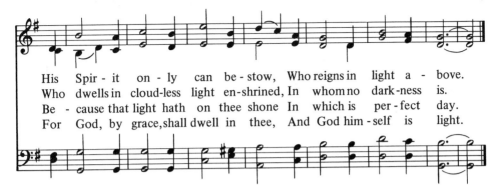

His Spir-it on-ly can be-stow, Who reigns in light a - bove.
Who dwells in cloud-less light en-shrined, In whom no dark-ness is.
Be - cause that light hath on thee shone In which is per-fect day.
For God, by grace, shall dwell in thee, And God him-self is light.

Text: Bernard Barton, 1784-1849.
Tune: Arr. from Gioacchino A. Rossini, 1792-1868.

Life of Ages, Richly Poured

304

II Nephi 1:117-120
Acts 10:34, 35

HARTS 7.7.7.7.

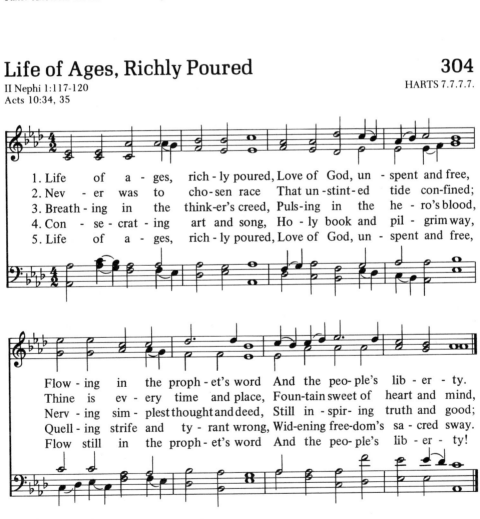

1. Life of a - ges, rich - ly poured, Love of God, un - spent and free,
2. Nev - er was to cho-sen race That un-stint-ed tide con-fined;
3. Breath-ing in the think-er's creed, Puls-ing in the he - ro's blood,
4. Con - se-crat-ing art and song, Ho - ly book and pil - grim way,
5. Life of a - ges, rich - ly poured, Love of God, un - spent and free,

Flow - ing in the proph-et's word And the peo- ple's lib - er - ty.
Thine is ev - er y time and place, Foun-tain sweet of heart and mind,
Nerv - ing sim - plest thought and deed, Still in-spir- ing truth and good;
Quell - ing strife and ty - rant wrong, Wid-ening free-dom's sa - cred sway.
Flow still in the proph- et's word And the peo- ple's lib - er - ty!

Text: Samuel Johnson, 1822-1882.
Tune: Benjamin Milgrove, 1731-1810; harm. Eric Thiman, 1900-1959; used by permission of the United Reformed
Church, London.

305

O Word of God Incarnate

D. and C. 90:1
John 1:1, 14

MUNICH 7.6.7.6.D.

1. O Word of God in - car - nate, O wis - dom from on high,
2. The Church from her dear Mas - ter Re - ceived the gift di - vine,

O truth un - changed, un-chang - ing, O light of our dark sky,
And still that light she lift - eth O'er all the earth to shine.

We praise thee for the ra - diance That from the hal - lowed page,
It is the chart and com - pass That o'er life's surg - ing sea,

A lan - tern to our foot - steps, Shines on from age to age.
'Mid mists and rocks and dark - ness, Still guides, O Christ to thee.

Text: William Walsham How, 1823-1897.
Tune: Meiningen Gesangbuch, 1693.

God Has Spoken Through the Ages

306

John 16:12-14
II Timothy 3:14-17

VAN FLEET 8.7.8.7.D.

1. God has spo-ken through the a - ges, Giv - ing light and truth for all.
2. Through the pag - es of the Scrip-tures, God's e - ter - nal truths are shown,
3. While we thank thee for thy Scrip-tures, For thy word re -vealed of old,
4. Speed the day of Zi - on's wit - ness, When all peo-ples of the earth

If our minds are tuned to hear him, Can we not dis - cern his call?
But in fi - nite words and phras-es God him-self can - not be known;
Lead us, Lord, to new re - veal-ment; Still to us new truths un - fold.
Who have writ - ten sa - cred Scrip-tures Shall per-ceive each Scrip - ture's worth.

God, whose works are nev - er end - ed, And whose words shall nev - er cease,
For the In - fi - nite is broad-er Than our minds can ev - er know;
As our in - tel - lect in - creas-es, As our spir - its grow toward thee,
Then all na - tions which have writ-ten Shall each oth - er's Scrip-tures know.

Of those words will give his chil-dren, And his Scrip-tures still in-crease.
God's un-bound-ed store of wis - dom Waits our read-i - ness to grow.
Lord, with Ho - ly Spir - it quick - en; Make us know and hear and see.
Give one wit - ness of the Sav - ior, Which to ev - ery tribe shall go. A-men.

307 We Thank Thee, O God, for a Prophet

Mosiah 8:67-69
Amos 3:7

PROPHET 9.8.9.8.D.

1. We thank thee, O God, for a proph-et To guide us in
2. When dark clouds of trou-ble hang o'er us And threat-en our

these lat-ter days; We thank thee for send-ing the gos-pel To
peace to de-stroy, There is hope smil-ing bright-ly be-fore us, And we

light-en our minds with its rays; We thank thee for ev-er-y
know that de-liv-erance is nigh. We doubt not the Lord nor his

bless-ing Be-stowed by thy boun-te-ous hands; We feel it a
good-ness; We've proved him in days that are past; The Saints who will

pleas-ure to serve thee, And love to o-bey thy com-mands.
la-bor for Zi-on Will sure-ly be bless-ed at last. A-men.

Text: William Fowler, 1830-1865, alt.
Tune: Caroline E. S. Norton, 1808-1877; alt.

God Who Spoke in the Beginning

308

John 1:1-4, 14
Hebrews 1:1-3

UNSER HERRSCHER
(Neander) 8.7.8.7.8.7.

1. God who spoke in the be - gin - ning, Form - ing rock and
2. God who spoke through peo - ple, na - tions, Through e - vents long
3. God whose speech be - comes in - car - nate— Christ is ser - vant,

shap - ing spar, Set all life and growth in mo - tion,
past and gone, Show - ing still to - day his pur - pose,
Christ is Lord!— Calls us to a life of ser - vice,

Earth - ly world and dis - tant star; He who calls the
Speaks su - preme - ly through his Son; He who calls the
Heart and will to ac - tion stirred; He who us - es

earth to or - der Is the ground of what we are.
earth to or - der Gives his word and it is done.
our o - be - dience, Has the first and fi - nal word.

Text: Fred Kaan, 1929 - ; alt. by permission; copyright 1968 by Galliard Ltd. Sole U. S. agent: Galaxy Music Corp., N. Y. Used by permission.
Tune: Joachim Neander, 1650-1680.

309

We Limit Not the Truth of God

John 16:12-14
D. and C. 147:7

HILLS C.M.D.

1. We lim - it not the truth of God To our poor reach of mind
2. Who dares to bind to their dull sense The or - a - cles of heaven
3. O Fa - ther, Son and Spir - it, send Us in - crease from a - bove;

By no - tions of our day and sect, Crude, par - tial, and con - fined.
For all the na - tions, tongues, and climes, And all the a - ges given?
En - large, ex - pand all Chris - tian souls To com - pre - hend thy love,

No, let a new and bet - ter hope With - in our hearts be stirred—
That u - ni - verse, how much un - known! That o - cean un - ex - plored!
And make us all go on to know, With no - bler powers con - ferred,

The Lord hath yet more light and truth To break forth from his word.

Text: George Rawson, 1807-1889.
Tune: Louise Hills Lewis, 1887-1948.

Lord, Save Your World

John 3:16, 17
I Nephi 1:23

310

KEDRON L.M.

1. Lord, save your world; in bit - ter need To
2. Lord, save your world; our souls are bound In
3. Lord, save your world; we strive in vain To
4. Lord, save your world, since you have sent The
5. Then save us now, by Je - sus' power, And

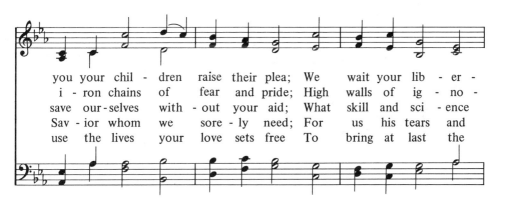

you your chil - dren raise their plea; We wait your lib - er -
i - ron chains of fear and pride; High walls of ig - no -
save our - selves with - out your aid; What skill and sci - ence
Sav - ior whom we sore - ly need; For us his tears and
use the lives your love sets free To bring at last the

at - ing deed To sig - nal hope and set us free.
rance a - bound And fac - es from each oth - er hide.
slow - ly gain Is seen to e - vil ends be - trayed.
blood were spent That from our bonds we might be freed.
glo - rious hour When all shall find your lib - er - ty.

Text: Albert F. Bayly, 1901 - ; used by permission of the author.
Tune: William Walker's *Southern Harmony*, 1835; arr. Rosalee Elser, 1925 - ; copyright 1980 Rosalee Elser; used by permission.

311

Guide Us, O Thou Great Jehovah

D. and C. 98:4d-f
II Nephi 13:27-30

SIBERIA 8.7.8.7.8.7.
Alternate tune: CWM RHONDDA (419)

1. Guide us, O thou great Je - ho - vah, Saints un - to the
2. O - pen, Je - sus, Zi - on's foun - tains; Let her rich - est
3. When the earth be - gins to trem - ble, Bid our fear - ful

prom - ised land; We are weak, but thou art a - ble;
bless - ings come; Let the fi - er - y, cloud - y pil - lar
thoughts be still; When thy judg - ments spread de - struc - tion,

Hold us with thy power - ful hand. Ho - ly Spir - it,
Guard us to that ho - ly home. Great Re - deem - er,
Keep us safe on Zi - on's hill, Sing - ing prais - es,

Ho - ly Spir - it, Feed us till the Sav - ior comes.
Great Re - deem - er, Bring, O bring the wel - come day!
Sing - ing prais - es, Songs of glo - ry un - to thee. A - men.

Text: William Williams, 1717-1791; tr. by Peter Williams, 1722-1796; rev. by Robert Robinson, 1735-1790.
Tune: German Melody, attr. to S. B. Pond, 1792-1871.

Let Us Pray for One Another

312

Colossians 1:9, 10
D. and C. 18:6a

DECATUR 8.7.8.7.D.

1. Let us pray for one an-oth-er That our minds and hearts may blend
2. We are walk-ing down time's vis-ta; Zi - on's ban-ner now un-furled
3. O'er the world the day is dawn-ing Through the Spir-it's light and power

As we grow in love and mer-cy, Day by day, till life shall end.
Calls to stew-ard-ship of car-ing And re-demp-tion of the world.
When the peo-ple of all na-tions Sense the chal-lenge of this hour.

We can see how oth-ers need us; May we al - so dare to say
Let us pray that we may ev - er Sense God's guid-ance in the way;
That our lives may now be giv-en To each oth - er in His way,

That in love we'll share to-geth - er; For each oth - er let us pray.
As we try to live for oth-ers, For each oth - er let us pray.
In the name of Christ the Sav-ior, For each oth - er let us pray.

313

Jacob 4:3-6
Exodus 13:21

Redeemer of Israel

MEDITATION (Beloved) 11.8.11.8.

1. Re - deem - er of Is - rael, our on - ly de - light,
2. We know he is com - ing to gath - er his sheep
3. How long we have wan - dered as stran - gers in sin
4. As chil - dren of Zi - on, good ti - dings for us,

On whom for a bless - ing we call,
And plant them in Zi - on in love;
And cried in the des - ert for thee!
The to - kens al - read - y ap - pear;

Our shad - ow by day, and our pil - lar by night,
For why in the val - ley of death should they weep
Our foes have re - joiced when our sor - rows they've seen,
Fear not and be just, for the king - dom is ours,

Our King, our Com - pan - ion, our All!
Or a - lone in the wil - der - ness rove?
But Is - rael will short - ly be free.
And the hour of re - demp - tion is near.

Text: W. W. Phelps, 1792-1872; arr. from Joseph Swain, 1761-1796.
Tune: Freeman Lewis, 1780-1859.

The Cause of Zion Summons Us 314

D. and C. 140:5c, d
D. and C. 137:6a

ST. MATTHEW C.M.D.
Alternate tune: ELLACOMBE (471)

1. The cause of Zi - on sum - mons us To claim a dis - tant dream:
2. The cause of Zi - on cel - e - brates The vic - tory o - ver fear,
3. The cause of Zi - on proph - e - sies The fu - ture yet to be,

The love of God in ev - ery place, The will of God su - preme.
The wit - ness of the king - dom's pow-er, New life al - read - y here.
When men and wom - en ev - ery - where Shall walk in dig - ni - ty.

The vi - sion calls us to our task. For - sak - ing self and pride,
Al - though ful - fill - ment seems re - mote, The jour - ney just be - gun,
We now an - ti - ci - pate the day When pain and tears shall cease,

We love and re - con - cile with Christ The world for which he died.
The King-dom has al - read - y come; The vic - tor - y is won.
When hu - man-kind shall live as one In righ-teous - ness and peace.

Text: Geoffrey F. Spencer, 1927 - . Copyright 1980 Reorganized Church of Jesus Christ of Latter Day Saints.
Tune: William Croft, 1678-1727.

315

Acts 10:34, 35
Alma 14:127, 128

This Is My Song

FINLANDIA 11.10.11.10.11.10.
See 107 for a lower setting.

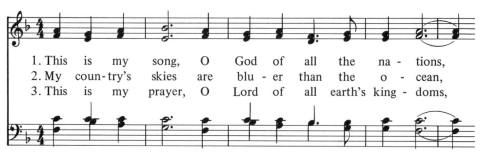

1. This is my song, O God of all the na - tions,
2. My coun-try's skies are blu - er than the o - cean,
3. This is my prayer, O Lord of all earth's king - doms,

A song of peace for lands a - far and mine. My land is
And sun - light beams on clo - ver - leaf and pine. But oth - er
Thy king-dom come; on earth thy will be done. Let Christ be

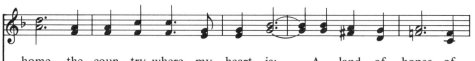

home, the coun - try where my heart is: A land of hopes, of
lands have sun - light too, and clo - ver, And skies are ev - 'ry -
lift - ed up till all shall serve him, And hearts u - nit - ed

dreams, of grand de - sign; But oth - er hearts in oth - er lands are
where as blue as mine. Oh, hear my song, thou God of all the
learn to live as one. Oh, hear my prayer, thou God of all the

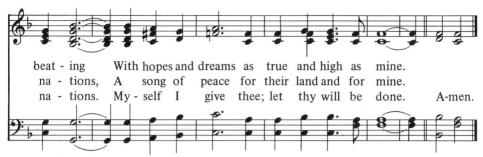

beat - ing   With hopes and dreams as   true and high as   mine.
na - tions,   A   song of   peace for their land and for   mine.
na - tions.   My - self   I   give thee; let   thy will be   done.   A - men.

Onward to Zion   316

D. and C. 81:4c   ZION 9.10.9.10.
Psalm 50:1-5

1. On - ward to   Zi - on, faith - ful and strong, Zi - on the
2. On - ward to   Zi - on, to Christ we be - long, Serv - ice the
3. We have the   prom - ise that Je - sus will come, Zi - on the
4. Je - sus the   Sav - ior, meet - ing the throng, Oh, may his

beau - ti - ful   beck - ons us   on,   On - ward and   up - ward
watch - word we   fight a - gainst wrong!   On - ward to   Zi - on,
beau - ti - ful   beck - ons us   on,   Let us be   faith - ful,
com - ing be   not de - layed long;   To God the   glo - ry,

bat - tle   a - long,
march with   a   song,
his will   be   done,   Zi - on the beau - ti - ful beck - ons us   on.
to him   the   song,

317

Send Forth Thy Light, O Zion

Psalm 43:3, 4
D. and C. 16:3c, 4e

LANCASHIRE 7.6.7.6.D.

1. Send forth thy light, O Zi - on! Out from thy towers shall go
2. Send forth thy love, O Zi - on! Thy call is from a - bove,
3. Send forth thy life, O Zi - on! Not for thy - self a - lone

The ra - diant beams a peo - ple In tune with God can know.
To make on earth in - car - nate Christ's sac - ri - fi - cial love.
Have come life - giv - ing pow - ers By which the soul has grown.

Up - borne by high - er con - cepts Of God's e - ter - nal call,
For by the saints out - reach - ing To those their lives can bless
Thy prom - ise builds a peo - ple Well-skilled in mind and hand.

Let shine a - far the guide-lights, Re - veal - ing God to all.
Shall come Zi - on - ic wit - ness To heal earth's bro - ken - ness.
Thy life is like a leav - en Of hope in ev - ery land.

Text: Roy A. Cheville, 1897 - , alt.; copyright 1956 Herald Publishing House.
Tune: Henry Smart, 1813-1879.

Hail to the Brightness

318

Isaiah 40:9-11
D. and C. 34:6

WESLEY 11.10.11.10.

1. Hail to the bright - ness of Zi - on's glad morn - ing!
2. Hail to the bright - ness of Zi - on's glad morn - ing,
3. See, from all lands, from the isles of the o - cean,

Joy to the lands that in dark - ness have lain!
Long by the proph - ets of Is - rael fore - told;
Praise to Je - ho - vah as - cend - ing on high;

Hushed be the ac - cents of sor - row and mourn - ing;
Hail to the mil - lions from bond - age re - turn - ing;
Fall - en the en - gines of war and com - mo - tion;

Zi - on in tri - umph be - gins her mild reign.
Gen - tiles and Jews the blest vi - sion be - hold.
Shouts of sal - va - tion are rend - ing the sky.

Text: Thomas Hastings, 1784-1872.
Tune: Lowell Mason, 1792-1872.

319

O Day of God, Draw Nigh

Psalm 145:17-19
I Nephi 1:23

FESTAL SONG S.M.
See 378 for a higher setting.

1. O day of God, draw nigh In beau-ty and in power;
2. Bring to our trou-bled minds, Un-cer-tain and a-fraid,
3. Bring jus-tice to our land That all may dwell se-cure,
4. Bring to our world of strife Thy sov-ereign word of peace,
5. O day of God, draw nigh As at cre-a-tion's birth.

Come with thy time-less judg-ment now To match our pres-ent hour.
The qui-et of a stead-fast faith, Calm of a call o-beyed.
And fine-ly build for days to come Foun-da-tions that en-dure.
That war may haunt the earth no more And des-o-la-tions cease.
Let there be light a-gain, and set Thy judg-ments on the earth.

Text: R. B. Y. Scott, 1899 - ; used by permission of the author.
Tune: William H. Walter, 1825-1893.

320

Thy Kingdom Come, O Lord

Matthew 6:11
Isaiah 1:26, 27

ST. CECILIA 6.6.6.6.

1. Thy king-dom come, O Lord, Wide-cir-cling as the sun;
2. One in the bond of peace, Of ser-vice glad and free,
3. Speed, speed the longed-for time Fore-told by rap-tured seers-
4. Till rise at last, to span Its firm foun-da-tions broad,

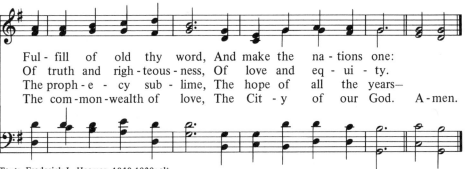

Ful - fill of old thy word, And make the na - tions one:
Of truth and righ - teous - ness, Of love and eq - ui - ty.
The proph - e - cy sub - lime, The hope of all the years—
The com - mon - wealth of love, The Cit - y of our God. A - men.

Text: Frederick L. Hosmer, 1840-1929; alt.
Tune: Leighton G. Hayne, 1836-1883.

Where Beauty, Truth, and Love Make One 321

Alma 14:96, 97
Joel 3:16, 17

ALSTONE L.M.

1. Where beau - ty, truth, and love make one, The heaven - ly
2. For beau - ty is the smile di - vine That in the
3. Truth is his thought that makes us free, Un - veil - ing
4. Love is the Fa - ther's heart that knows His chil - dren's

king - dom is be - gun; Shine, light of God, that
Fa - ther's face doth shine, And na - ture an - swering
life's re - al - i - ty, As age by age to
joys, his chil - dren's woes; This was the way the

we may see On earth this no - ble trin - i - ty.
tells a - broad The ver - y glo - ry of the Lord.
ea - ger hearts More of his pur - pose God im - parts.
Mas - ter trod Who gave the world a Sav - ior God.

Text: Ernest Dodgshun, 1876-1944, alt.
Tune: Christopher E. Willing, 1830-1904.

322 O How Blessed Are the Poor in Spirit

Matthew 5:2-11
Romans 14:17-19

THE BEATITUDES 9.8.9.6. with refrain

Unison (or harmony)

1. O how blessed are the poor in spir - it; Theirs is the
2. O how blessed are the meek and hum - ble; They will in -
3. O how blessed are the mer - cy giv - ers; Such mer - cy
4. O how blessed are the true peace-mak - ers; They will be

king - dom of heav - en. And how blessed are the sad and mournful;
her - it the earth. And how blessed those who hunger for goodness;
they will re - ceive. And how blessed are the pure in heart;
known as God's chil - dren. And how blessed those who suffer for jus-tice;

They'll be con-soled by God.
They all will feast with God.
They sure - ly will see God.   Blessed and hap-py we shall be.
They will be honored by God.

Lis - ten to the Mas - ter's word!   Soon the King-dom's

com - ing— watch and see: the King-dom of the Lord!

Text and Tune: Richard K. Avery, 1934 - , and Donald S. Marsh, 1923 - ; alt. by Rosalee Elser, 1925 - ; copyright 1979 Hope Publishing Co., Carol Stream, IL; used by permission.

These Things Shall Be: A Loftier Race   323

D. and C. 49:5a, b   TRURO L.M.
Isaiah 2:2, 3

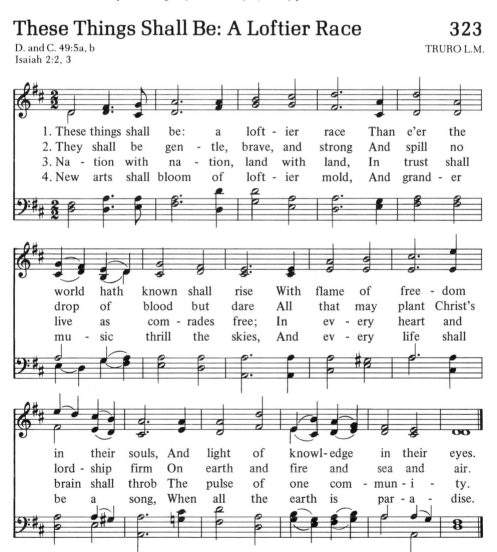

1. These things shall be: a loft - ier race Than e'er the
2. They shall be gen - tle, brave, and strong And spill no
3. Na - tion with na - tion, land with land, In trust shall
4. New arts shall bloom of loft - ier mold, And grand - er

world hath known shall rise With flame of free - dom
drop of blood but dare All that may plant Christ's
live as com - rades free; In ev - ery heart and
mu - sic thrill the skies, And ev - ery life shall

in their souls, And light of knowl-edge in their eyes.
lord - ship firm On earth and fire and sea and air.
brain shall throb The pulse of one com - mun - i - ty.
be a song, When all the earth is par - a - dise.

Text: John A. Symonds, 1840-1893, alt.
Tune: Charles Burney, 1726-1814.

324

God Is Working His Purpose Out

D. and C. 2:1a-c
II Nephi 9:133-137

PURPOSE Irregular

Unison

1. God is work-ing his pur-pose out As year suc-
2. From ut-most east to ut-most west, Where hu-man
3. All we can do is noth-ing worth Un-less God

2nd stz.

Octaves to the end

ceeds to year; God is work-ing his
feet have trod, By the mouth of man-y
bless-es the deed; Vain-ly we hope for the

pur-pose out, And the time is draw-ing near; What can we
mes-sen-gers Goes forth the voice of God: "Fight ye the
har-vest-tide Till God gives life to the seed; Yet near-er and

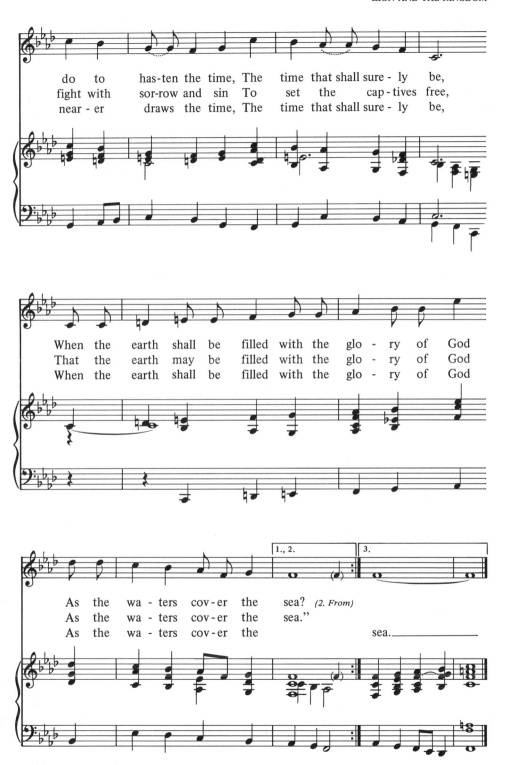

do to has-ten the time, The time that shall sure - ly be,
fight with sor-row and sin To set the cap - tives free,
near - er draws the time, The time that shall sure - ly be,

When the earth shall be filled with the glo - ry of God
That the earth may be filled with the glo - ry of God
When the earth shall be filled with the glo - ry of God

As the wa - ters cov - er the sea? *(2. From)*
As the wa - ters cov - er the sea."
As the wa - ters cov - er the sea._____

Text: Arthur C. Ainger, 1841-1919.
Tune: Martin Shaw, 1875-1958; from *Enlarged Songs of Praise* by permission of Oxford University Press.

325 According to Thy Gracious Word

Luke 22:17-20
III Nephi 8:33-36

MARTYRDOM C.M.

1. Ac - cord - ing to thy gra-cious word, In meek hu - mil - i - ty,
2. Thy bod - y, bro-ken for my sake, My bread from heaven shall be;
3. Geth-sem - a - ne, can I for - get? Or there thy con-flict see,
4. When to the cross I turn mine eyes, And rest on Cal - va - ry,

This will I do, my dy - ing Lord, I will re - mem-ber thee.
The cup, thy pre-cious blood I take, And thus re - mem-ber thee.
Thine ag - o - ny and blood-y sweat, And not re - mem-ber thee?
O Lamb of God, my sac - ri - fice, I must re-mem-ber thee. A - men.

Text: James Montgomery, 1771-1854.
Tune: Hugh Wilson, 1764-1825.

326 Leave We Now the Table of Our Lord

Matthew 26:25-27 (29, 30)
John 15:15, 16

GOD BE WITH YOU 9.8.8.9.
Alternate tune: Randolph (489)

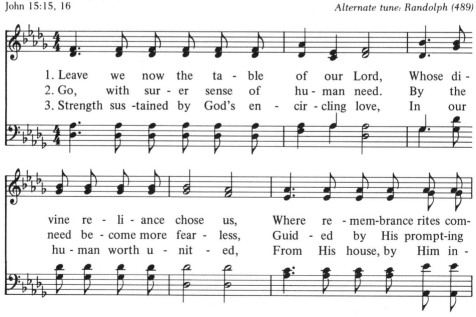

1. Leave we now the ta - ble of our Lord, Whose di -
2. Go, with sur - er sense of hu - man need. By the
3. Strength sus -tained by God's en - cir - cling love, In our

vine re - li - ance chose us, Where re - mem-brance rites com-
need be - come more fear - less, Guid - ed by His prompt-ing
hu - man worth u - nit - ed, From His house, by Him in -

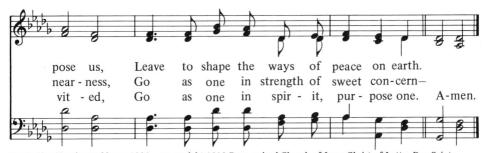

pose us, Leave to shape the ways of peace on earth.
near - ness, Go as one in strength of sweet con-cern—
vit - ed, Go as one in spir - it, pur - pose one. A-men.

Text: Cleo Hanthorne Moon, 1904 - ; copyright 1980 Reorganized Church of Jesus Christ of Latter Day Saints.
Tune: W. G. Tomer, 1832-1896.

Now Let Us from This Table Rise 327

I Corinthians 11:26
John 6:35

WAREHAM L.M.

1. Now let us from this ta - ble rise Re - newed in
2. With minds a - lert up - held by grace, To spread the
3. To fill each hu - man house with love, It is the
4. Then give us cour - age, Fa - ther - God, To choose a -

bod - y, mind, and soul; With Christ we die and
Word in speech and deed, We fol - low in the
sac - ra - ment of care; The work that Christ be -
gain the pil - grim way, And help us to ac -

live a - gain, His self - less love has made us whole.
steps of Christ At one with man in hope and need.
gan to do We hum - bly pledge our - selves to share.
cept with joy The chal - lenge of to - mor - row's day.

Text: Fred Kaan, 1929 - ; copyright 1968 by Galliard Ltd. Sole U. S. agent: Galaxy Music Corp., N. Y. Used
by permission.
Tune: William Knapp, 1698-1768.

328

Here, O My Lord

John 6:56, 57
D. and C. 17:22a

LANGRAN 10.10.10.10.

1. Here, O my Lord, I see thee face to face;
Here would I touch and han - dle things un - seen;
Here grasp with firm - er hand the e - ter - nal grace,
And all my wea - ri - ness up - on thee lean.

2. Here would I feed up - on the bread of God,
Here drink with thee the roy - al wine of heaven;
Here would I lay a - side each earth - ly load,
Here taste a - fresh the calm of sin for - given.

3. This is the hour of ban - quet and of song;
This is the heaven - ly ta - ble spread for me.
Here let me feast, and feast - ing still pro - long
The brief, bright hour of fel - low - ship with thee. A - men.

Text: Horatius Bonar, 1808-1889.
Tune: James Langran, 1835-1909.

Bread of the World

329

John 6:47-51
Galatians 2:20

RENDEZ A DIEU 9.8.9.8.D.

Bread of the world, in mer-cy bro-ken, Wine of the
soul, in mer-cy shed, By whom the words of life are spo-ken,
And in whose death our sins are dead, Look on the heart by sor-row
bro-ken, Look on the tears by sin-ners shed, And be Thy
feast to us the to-ken That by Thy grace our souls are fed.

Text: Reginald Heber, 1783-1826.
Tune: Attr. to Louis Bourgeois, c. 1510-c. 1561.

330 In Memory of the Savior's Love

Moroni 6: 5, 6
Mark 14:20-24 (22-24)

ST. PETER C.M.

1. In mem - ory of the Sav - ior's love We keep the sa - cred feast,
2. By faith we take the bread of life With which our souls are fed,
3. Be - neath his ban - ner thus we sing The won - ders of his love,

Where each who bears the Sav - ior's name Is made a wel-come guest.
The cup in to - ken of his blood That was for sin - ners shed.
And thus an - tic - i - pate by faith The heaven - ly feast a - bove.

Text: Thomas Cotterill, 1779-1823.
Tune: Alexander R. Reinagle, 1799-1877.

331 Father, Who in Jesus Found Us

D. and C. 11:4, 5
Colossians 3:11-17

QUEM PASTORES 8.8.8.7.

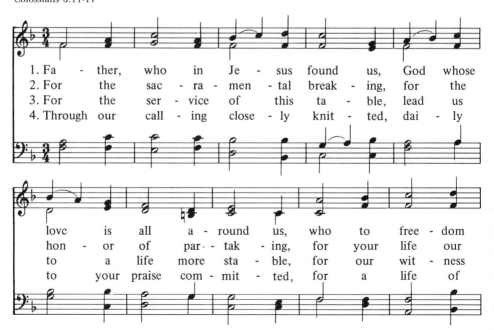

1. Fa - ther, who in Je - sus found us, God whose
2. For the sac - ra - men - tal break - ing, for the
3. For the ser - vice of this ta - ble, lead us
4. Through our call - ing close - ly knit - ted, dai - ly

love is all a - round us, who to free - dom
hon - or of par - tak - ing, for your life our
to a life more sta - ble, for our wit - ness
to your praise com - mit - ted, for a life of

new   un - bound us,   keep   our   hearts with joy   a - flame.
lives   re - mak - ing, young and   old,   we   praise your name.
make   us   a - ble;   bless - ing on   our   work we   claim.
ser - vice fit - ted, let   us   now   your   love pro - claim.

Text: Fred Kaan, 1929 -   ; copyright 1968 by Galliard Ltd. Sole U. S. agent: Galaxy Music Corp., N. Y. Used
by permission.
Tune: 14th Century German Carol Melody; arr. Ralph Vaughan Williams, 1872-1958; from *The English Hymnal*;
used by permission of Oxford University Press.

O Lord, How Can It Be   332

Psalm 116:12, 13   KIRTLAND 6.8.6.
III Nephi 8:33-39

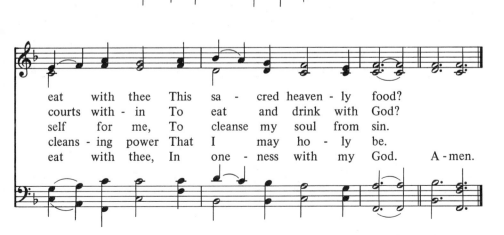

1. O   Lord, how   can   it   be   That   I   may   come   to
2. My   robe   is   marked with sin;   How can   I   come   thy
3. O   Lord, by   faith   I   see   That thou didst give   thy -
4. In   this   sweet morn - ing hour, O   seal   on   me   thy
5. And then   with heart full free   I   reach my   hand   to

eat   with   thee   This   sa - cred heaven - ly   food?
courts with - in   To   eat   and   drink with God?
self   for   me,   To   cleanse my   soul from sin.
cleans - ing power That   I   may   ho - ly   be.
eat   with   thee, In   one - ness with my   God.   A - men.

Text and Tune: Charles Fry, 1872-1969.

333 Here at Thy Table, Lord

III Nephi 9:40-45
D. and C. 135:3

BREAD OF LIFE 6.4.6.4.D.

1. Here at thy ta - ble, Lord, This sa - cred hour,
O let us feel thee near In lov - ing power,
Call - ing our thoughts a - way From self and sin
As to thy ban - quet hall We en - ter in.

2. Sit at our feast, dear Lord; Break thou the bread;
Fill thou the cup that brings Life to the dead,
That we may find in thee Par - don and peace,
And from all bond - age win A full re - lease.

3. So shall our life of faith Be full, be sweet,
And we shall find our strength For each day meet.
Fed by thy liv - ing bread, All hun - ger past,
We shall be sat - is - fied And saved at last.

4. Come then, O ho - ly Christ; Feed us, we pray;
Touch with thy pierc - ed hand Each com - mon day,
Mak - ing this earth - ly life Full of thy grace
Till in the home of heaven We find our place. A - men.

Text: May P. Hoyt.
Tune: William F. Sherwin, 1826-1888.

We Come, Aware of Sin

334

Alma 14:124, 128
Matthew 11:29, 30

NUN DANKET ALLE GOTT 6.7.6.7.6.6.6.6.

1. We come, a-ware of sin with-in us and a-round us,
2. You give us, in your stead, this bread that we may eat it
3. Your rec-on-cil-ing love has freed us in this hour.

To seek for-give-ness, Lord, for wrongs that long have bound us.
And have your Spir-it near to guide us as we need it.
We go re-newed, re-stored, through your re-deeming pow-er.

Help us to find re-lease through your per-vad-ing peace
Through this sym-bol-ic wine, you grant us strength di-vine;
As dark-ness leaves with dawn, our bur-dens now are gone,

And fill our com-ing days with grat-i-tude and praise.
We drink and feel our souls a-gain be-com-ing whole.
Each crush-ing care e-rased by mir-a-cle of grace.

Text: Naomi Russell, 1921 - ; copyright 1980 Reorganized Church of Jesus Christ of Latter Day Saints.
Tune: Johann Cruger, 1598-1662; harm. Felix Mendelssohn, 1809-1847.

335

O God, the Eternal Father

Matthew 26:24, 26 (28, 29)
III Nephi 8:33, 36

ST. ALPHEGE 7.6.7.6.

1. O God, the e - ter - nal Fa - ther, Bless to our souls this bread
2. We eat in true re - mem-brance Of sa - cred blood once shed,
3. The name of Christ our Sav - ior We take on us a - new,
4. As we keep his com-mand-ments, Re - mem-bering him each hour,

As we par - take in mem - ory Of Christ, our liv - ing head.
Of Je - sus' bro - ken bod - y, His ris - ing from the dead.
And cov - e - nant be - fore him His will in all to do.
His Spir - it will be with us In guid - ing love and power.

Text: Evan A. Fry 1902-1959; copyright 1956 Herald Publishing House.
Tune: H J. Gauntlett, 1805-1876.

336

Be Present at Our Table, Lord

Luke 24:29, 30 (30, 31)
D. and C. 59:3

UXBRIDGE L.M.

Be pres - ent at our ta - ble, Lord; Be here and

ev - ery-where a - dored; Thy chil - dren bless; and grant that

we May find com - mun - ion here with thee. A - men.

Text: John Cennick, 1718-1755; alt. Margaret Athey, 1936 - .
Tune: Lowell Mason, 1792-1872.

'Twas on That Dark, That Solemn Night 337

III Nephi 8:33, 36
Luke 22:19-21

HAMBURG L.M.

1. 'Twas on that dark, that sol - emn night, When powers of
2. Be - fore the mourn - ful scene be - gan, He took the
3. "This is my bod - y bro - ken for sin; Re - ceive and
4. "Do this," he said, "till time shall end, In mem - ory

earth and hell a - rose A - gainst the Son, e'en
bread and blessed and broke; What love through all his
eat the liv - ing food." He took the cup, and
of your dy - ing friend; Meet at my ta - ble

God's de - light, His friends be - trayed him to his foes.
ac - tions ran! What won-drous words of grace he spoke!
blessed the wine, "'Tis the new cov - 'nant in my blood."
and re - cord The love of your de - part - ed Lord."

Text: Isaac Watts, 1674-1748.
Tune: Gregorian Chant, arr. Lowell Mason, 1792-1872.

338

Luke 22:19, 20
D. and C. 26:1a-c

Here at Thy Table, Lord, We Meet

COMMUNION C.M.

1. Here at thy ta - ble, Lord, we meet To feed on
2. He who pre - pares this rich re - past Him - self comes
3. Here peace and par - don sweet - ly flow, Oh, what de -
4. Deep was the suf - fering he en - dured Up - on the ac -
5. Sure there was nev - er love so free, Dear Sav - ior,

food di - vine. Thy bod - y is the bread we
down and dies, And then in - vites us thus to
light - ful food! We eat the bread and drink the
curs - ed tree, For me, each wel - come guest may
so di - vine! Well thou mayest claim this heart of

eat, Thy pre - cious blood the wine.
feast Up - on the sac - ri - fice.
wine But think on no - bler good.
say, 'Twas all en - dured for me.
me, Which owes so much to thine. A - men.

Text: Samuel Stennett, 1727-1795.
Tune: Charles Fry, 1872-1969.

Beneath the Forms of Outward Rite

339

John 6:33, 34
I Corinthians 10:16, 17

ST. COLUMBA C.M.

1. Be - neath the forms of out - ward rite Thy sup - per, Lord, is spread In ev - ery qui - et up - per room Where faint - ing souls are fed.

2. The bread is al - ways sa - cred bread Which feeds our com - mon need, And when we bear each oth - er's pain We feast with thee in - deed.

3. The bless - ed cup is on - ly passed In mem - o - ry of Thee, For life a - new pours out its wine In love that sets us free.

4. Oh, Mas - ter, through these sym - bols shared, Re - store us, in this hour, To be Thy bod - y here on earth With sac - ra - men - tal power.

Text: James A. Blaisdell, 1867-1957; alt. by Barbara Howard, 1930 - ; copyright 1980 Reorganized Church of Jesus Christ of Latter Day Saints.
Tune: Traditional Irish Melody.

340

For Bread Before Us Broken

I Corinthians 10:16, 17
III Nephi 8:33-39

EWING 7.6.7.6.D.

1. For bread be-fore us bro-ken, For wine be-fore us poured,
2. We join in sol-emn prom-ise Here at this ho-ly board

For words which thou hast spo-ken, We give thee thanks, O Lord.
That we may be more wor-thy To have thy Spir-it, Lord.

In prayer that we'll be strength-ened, And be a-gain re-stored,
For serv-ice now en-dow us, As-sured of watch and ward,

In faith that thou wilt aid us, We seek thy ta-ble, Lord.
And send us forth u-nit-ed To build thy king-dom, Lord. A-men.

Text: Roy A. Cheville, 1897 - . Copyright 1956 by Herald Publishing House.
Tune: Alexander Ewing, 1830-1895.

Remembering Thy Son, O God

341

I John 1:7-9
Mosiah 2:3

MARNIE 12.10.12.10.

1. Re - mem - ber - ing thy Son, O God, to thee we come
2. Christ gives us in his stead this blest me - mo - rial bread
3. Di - rect us in thy way; be with us ev - 'ry day.

A - ware of sins from which we seek re - lease.
That we may eat of it, and drink the wine;
Lord, touch our eyes that we may clear - ly see

For - give our er - ring ways on this thy ho - ly day;
As we par - take, dear Lord, in keep - ing with thy word,
The plan thou hast de - signed for us and hu - man - kind;

For - give us, Lord, we pray, and grant thy peace.
Touch ev - 'ry heart and make it tru - ly thine.
O may we ev - er find our faith in thee.

Text: Naomi Russell, 1921 - ; copyright 1980 Reorganized Church of Jesus Christ of Latter Day Saints.
Tune: Harold Neal, 1916 - ; arr. Rosalee Elser, 1925 - ; copyright 1980 Reorganized Church of Latter
Day Saints.

342

Let Us Break Bread Together

D. and C. 17:22a
I Corinthians 11:26-29

LET US BREAK BREAD 10.10. with refrain

Unison (or harmony)

1. Let us break bread to-geth-er on our knees; Let us
2. Let us drink wine to-geth-er on our knees; Let us

break bread to-geth-er on our knees.
drink wine to-geth-er on our knees. When I fall on my

knees, with my face to the ris-ing sun, O Lord, have mer-cy on me.

3. Let us praise God to-geth-er on our knees. Let us praise God to-

geth-er on our knees. When I fall on my knees with my

Text: American Folk Hymn.
Tune: American Folk Hymn; harm. by Rosalee Elser, 1925 - ; copyright 1980 Rosalee Elser; used by permission.

An Upper Room Did Our Lord Prepare   343

D. and C. 17:22a
I Corinthians 11:23-26

FOLKSONG 9.8.9.8.

Unison

1. An Up-per Room did our Lord pre-pare for those he loved un-til the end: and his dis-ci-ples still gath-er there, to cel-e-brate their Ris-en Friend.
2. A last-ing gift Je-sus gave his own: to share his bread, his lov-ing cup. What-ev-er bur-dens may bow us down, he by his Cross shall lift us up.
3. And af-ter Sup-per he washed their feet, for ser-vice, too, is sac-ra-ment. In him our joy shall be made com-plete— sent out to serve, as he was sent.
4. No end there is! We de-part in peace. He loves be-yond our ut-ter-most: in ev-ery room in our Fa-ther's house he will be there, as Lord and Host.

Text: F. Pratt Green, 1903 - ; used by permission of Oxford University Press.
Tune: English Traditional Melody; arr. John Wilson, 1905 - ; by permission of Oxford University Press.

344

Come, Risen Lord

Luke 24:29-31 (30-32)
Acts 2:46, 47

SURSUM CORDA 10.10.10.10.

Unison (or harmony)

1. Come, ris - en Lord, and deign to be our guest;
2. We meet, as in that up - per room they met,
3. One bod - y we, one bod - y who par - take,
4. One with each oth - er, Lord, for one in thee,

Nay, let us be thy guests— the feast is thine;
Thou at the ta - ble, bless - ing, yet dost stand;
One church u - nit - ed in com - mun - ion blest;
Who art one Sav - ior and one liv - ing Head;

Thy - self at thine own board make man - i - fest
"This is my bod - y;" so thou giv - est yet:
One name we bear, one bread of life we break,
Then o - pen thou our eyes, that we may see;

In this our sac - ra - ment of bread and wine.
Faith still re - ceives the cup as from thy hand.
With all thy saints on earth and saints at rest.
Be known to us in break - ing of the bread. A - men.

Text: George Wallace Briggs, 1875-1959; from *Enlarged Songs of Praise* by permission of Oxford University Press.
Tune: Alfred M. Smith, 1879-1971; copyright by composer. Used by permission of Mrs. Alfred M. Smith.

You Satisfy the Hungry Heart

345

John 6:32-34
I Corinthians 10:16, 17

GIFT OF FINEST WHEAT
C.M. with refrain

Unison (or harmony)

Refrain

You sat-is-fy the hun-gry heart With gift of fin-est wheat;

Come give to us, O sav-ing Lord, The bread of life to eat.

Fine

Manuals only

Pedal

1. As when the shep-herd calls his sheep, They know and heed his voice,
2. With joy-ful lips we sing to you Our praise and grat-i-tude,
3. Here is the cup we bless and share The blood of Christ out-poured;
4. The mys-t'ry of your pres-ence, Lord, No mor-tal tongue can tell:
5. You give your-self to us, O Lord; Then self-less let us be,

Manuals only

Pedal

Repeat Refrain

So when you call your fam-'ly, Lord, We fol-low and re-joice.
That you should count us wor-thy, Lord, To share this heav'n-ly food.
And here one cup, one loaf, de-clare Our one-ness in the Lord.
Whom all the world can-not con-tain Comes in our hearts to dwell.
To serve each oth-er in your name In truth and char-i-ty.

Text: Omer Westendorf, 1916 - .
Tune: Robert E. Kreutz, 1922 - .

346 Lord, Let Thy Holy Spirit Come

Romans 9:14-16
D. and C. 68:4a-c

RICHMOND C.M.

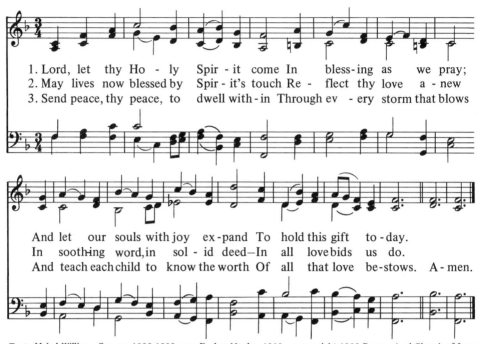

1. Lord, let thy Ho - ly Spir - it come In bless-ing as we pray;
2. May lives now blessed by Spir - it's touch Re - flect thy love a - new
3. Send peace, thy peace, to dwell with-in Through ev - ery storm that blows

And let our souls with joy ex -pand To hold this gift to - day.
In sooth-ing word, in sol - id deed—In all love bids us do.
And teach each child to know the worth Of all that love be-stows. A - men.

Text: Mabel Williams Crayne, 1880-1980; rev. Evelyn Maples, 1919 - ; copyright 1980 Reorganized Church of Jesus Christ of Latter Day Saints.
Tune: Thomas Haweis, 1734-1820; abr. by Samuel Webbe, Jr., 1770-1843.

347 O Master to All Children Dear

Moroni 8:18
D. and C. 17:19

MARYTON L.M.

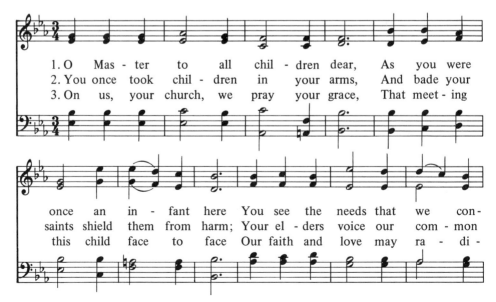

1. O Mas - ter to all chil - dren dear, As you were
2. You once took chil - dren in your arms, And bade your
3. On us, your church, we pray your grace, That meet - ing

once an in - fant here You see the needs that we con-
saints shield them from harm; Your el - ders voice our com - mon
this child face to face Our faith and love may ra - di-

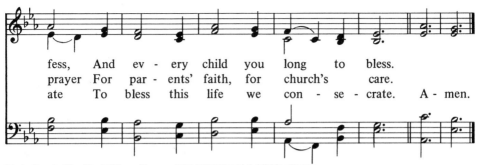

fess, And ev - ery child you long to bless.
prayer For par - ents' faith, for church's care.
ate To bless this life we con - se - crate. A - men.

Text: Roy A. Cheville, 1897 - ; alt.; copyright 1956 Herald Publishing House.
Tune: H. Percy Smith, 1825-1898.

We Bring Our Children, Lord, to Thee 348

Mark 10:11-14 (13-16)
D. and C. 68:4a-c

HESPERUS L.M.

1. We bring our chil - dren, Lord, to thee Be - fore this
2. Teach us to know our chil - dren's worth, To cel - e -
3. We thank thee for each pre - cious life Born in - to

loved com - mu - ni - ty, Con - firm - ing pres - ence
brate their gifts from birth. Let each be par - ent,
beau - ty, in - to strife. Let each child feel thy

of thy grace As lit - tle ones en - rich this place.
lov - ing all, Re - spond - ing gent - ly to each call.
time - less care, Un - ceas - ing, lov - ing, ev - ery - where.

Text: Evelyn Maples, 1919 - ; copyright 1980 Reorganized Church of Jesus Christ of Latter Day Saints.
Tune: Henry Baker, 1835-1910.

349
The Vision of a Life to Be

Mosiah 2:25, 27
Matthew 19:13-15

GRATEFULNESS L.M.

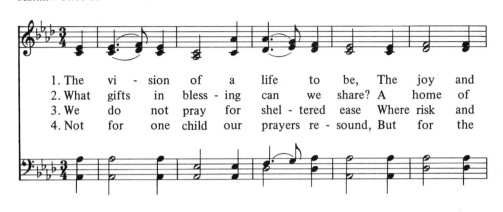

1. The vi - sion of a life to be, The joy and
2. What gifts in bless - ing can we share? A home of
3. We do not pray for shel - tered ease Where risk and
4. Not for one child our prayers re - sound, But for the

hope of all the race, The price - less gift of
true com - mu - ni - ty, A con - gre - ga - tion's
strug - gle have no part, But for - ti - tude for
chil - dren of the earth May joy in - crease and

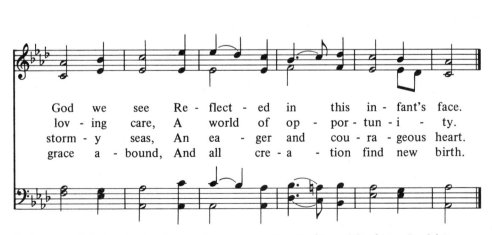

God we see Re - flect - ed in this in - fant's face.
lov - ing care, A world of op - por - tun - i - ty.
storm - y seas, An ea - ger and cou - ra - geous heart.
grace a - bound, And all cre - a - tion find new birth.

Text: Geoffrey F. Spencer, 1927 - ; copyright 1980 Reorganized Church of Jesus Christ of Latter Day Saints.
Tune: Mary A. Bradford, 1821-1902.

Baptized in Water

350

Moroni 6:3-5
Matthew 3:40-43 (13-15)

BROTHER JAMES' AIR 8.6.8.6.8.6.

1. Bap - tized in wa - ter, you be - came a per - son born
2. To some it comes as burst - ing light in this, your spe -
3. You now share mem - ber - ship with - in a larg - er fam -

a - new. You made a cov - e - nant, and now God
cial hour; It may come slow - ly, and in time, as
i - ly. Each time you take the bread and wine, you'll

adds his prom - ise, too: His Ho - ly Spir - it
an un - fold - ing flower. How - ev - er it may
know that you will be A - mong the man - y

can be yours to - day and all life through.
come to you, you'll feel God's love and power.
car - ing Saints in world com - mu - ni - ty.

Text: Naomi Russell, 1921 - ; alt. by Alan D. Tyree, 1929 - ; copyright 1980 Reorganized Church of Jesus Christ of Latter Day Saints.
Tune: James Leith Macbeth Bain, c. 1840-1925; harm. Gordon Jacob, 1895 - ; adapted by Rosalee Elser, 1925 - ; by permission of Oxford University Press.

351   Redeeming Grace Has Touched Our Lives

Romans 6:3, 4
D. and C. 39:2

DOMINUS REGIT ME 8.7.8.7.

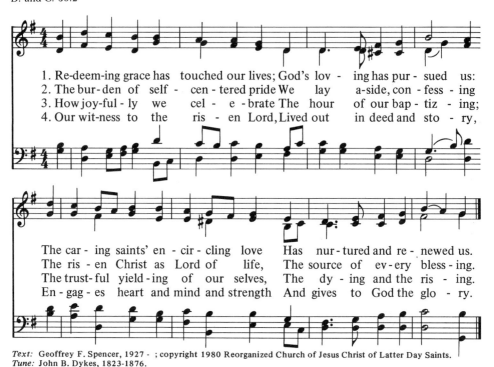

1. Re-deem-ing grace has touched our lives; God's lov - ing has pur - sued us:
2. The bur- den of self - cen - tered pride We lay a-side, con - fess - ing
3. How joy-ful - ly we cel - e -brate The hour of our bap - tiz - ing;
4. Our wit-ness to the ris - en Lord, Lived out in deed and sto - ry,

The car - ing saints' en - cir - cling love Has nur-tured and re - newed us.
The ris - en Christ as Lord of life, The source of ev - ery bless - ing.
The trust-ful yield - ing of our selves, The dy - ing and the ris - ing.
En - gag - es heart and mind and strength And gives to God the glo - ry.

Text: Geoffrey F. Spencer, 1927 - ; copyright 1980 Reorganized Church of Jesus Christ of Latter Day Saints.
Tune: John B. Dykes, 1823-1876.

352   O Lord, Thy People Gathered Here

Romans 8:16-17
II Nephi 13:22-26

HURSLEY L.M.

1. O Lord, thy peo - ple gath - ered here Lift up their
2. Thy peo - ple's joy is born of prayer That all may
3. We o - pen doors of fel - low-ship To these who

joy - ful hearts as one In thanks for these who find to -
com - pre - hend some - day The mu - tual love of Saints, and
make the life - long vow To walk in cov - e - nant with

day New life in thee, with thine be - gun.
more— Thy love which is the light, the way.
thee, And in bap - ti - sm seal it now. A - men.

Text: Roy A. Cheville, 1897 - ; copyright 1956 Herald Publishing House.
Tune: Adapted from *Katholisches Gesangbuch*, Vienna, c. 1774.

Jesus, Mighty King in Zion

353

II Nephi 13:7-10
Matthew 28:17-19 (18-20)

STUTTGART 8.7.8.7.

1. Je - sus, might - y King in Zi - on, Thou a -
2. As an em - blem of thy pas - sion, And thy
3. Fear - less of the world's de - spis - ing, We the
4. We will fol - low none but Je - sus, Je - sus

lone our Guide shalt be; Thy com - mis - sion we re -
vic - tory o'er the grave, We who seek the great sal -
an - cient path pur - sue, Bur - ied with our Lord, and
is the Life, the Way; This the path in which he

ly on, We will fol - low none but thee.
va - tion Are bap - tized be - neath the wave.
ris - ing To a life di - vine - ly new.
leads us, This the gate to end - less day. A - men.

Text: John Fellows, ?-1785.
Tune: Christian F. Witt, 1660-1716, *Psalmodia Sacra*, 1715; adapt. by Henry J. Gauntlett, 1805-1876.

354 Here at the Water's Brink We Stand

Matthew 3:45 (16)
D. and C. 17:21

CONFIRMATION C.M.

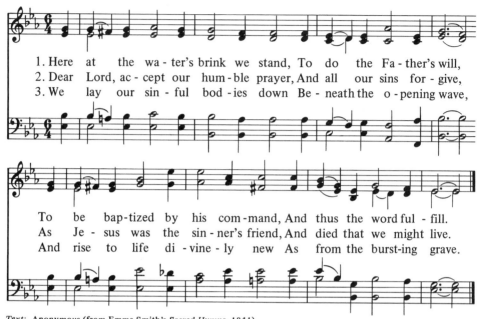

1. Here at the wa - ter's brink we stand, To do the Fa - ther's will,
2. Dear Lord, ac - cept our hum - ble prayer, And all our sins for - give,
3. We lay our sin - ful bod - ies down Be - neath the o - pening wave,

To be bap-tized by his com -mand, And thus the word ful - fill.
As Je - sus was the sin - ner's friend, And died that we might live.
And rise to life di - vine - ly new As from the burst-ing grave.

Text: Anonymous (from Emma Smith's *Sacred Hymns*, 1841).
Tune: Louise Hills Lewis, 1887-1948.

355 Descend, O Spirit, Purging Flame

Ephesians 2:18-22
Titus 3:5-7

MENDON L.M.

1. De - scend, O Spir - it, purg - ing flame, Mark us this
2. Wash us with wa - ter, make us pure; Thrust us in
3. For - bid us not this sec - ond birth; Grant un - to

day with Je - sus' name! Con - firm our faith, con - sume our
mis - sion to en - dure. Let now your heal - ing wa - ters
us the great - er worth! Con -script us in your ser - vice,

doubt; Seal us as Christ's, with - in, with - out.
win New life, new hope, re - lease from sin.
Lord; Bap - tize all na - tions with your Word. A - men.

Text: Scott Francis Brenner, 1903 - ; copyright 1972 The Westminster Press; from *The Worshipbook—Services and Hymns*; used and altered by permission.
Tune: Traditional German Melody, arr. by Samuel Dyer, 1785-1835.

O God in Heaven, We Believe

356

D. and C. 3:16-18
Leviticus 20:7, 8

DOVE OF PEACE 8.6.8.6.6.

Unison

1. O God in heav - en, we be - lieve The prom - ise
2. When we re - pent of all our sins And come with
3. As we are bur - ied in the stream, In Je - sus'
4. O Lord, ac - cept our hum - ble prayer, And all our

we have read; Thy word with meek - ness we re - ceive, And
bro - ken heart, We to thy cov - e - nant en - ter in And
bless - ed name, Oh, may thy light up - on us beam, The
sins for - give; New life im - part from this good hour And

fol - low Christ, our head, And fol - low Christ, our head.
choose the bet - ter part, And choose the bet - ter part.
Spir - it's heav-en - ly flame, The Spir - it's heav -en - ly flame.
grant that we may live, And grant that we may live. A-men.

Text: Parley P. Pratt, 1807-1857.
Tune: American Folk Tune; arr. Austin C. Lovelace, 1919 - ; copyright 1977 by Agape, Carol Stream, IL 60187; international copyright secured; all rights reserved; used by permission.

357

My Lord, I Come This Hour to Make

Mosiah 3:8, 9
Acts 2:37-39

NORSE AIR (No Other Plea, or Landas) C.M.D.
See 405 for a lower setting.

1. My Lord, I come this hour to make My cov - e - nant with thee.
2. A life - long prom - ise I would make: Thee on - ly will I serve.

Re - veal - ing truth and bound-less grace, Thy love has won my heart.
I seek for - give - ness now of thee; I come to be re - born.

I have no oth - er gift for thee Ex - cept the life I bring.
En - dow my life with love and power To grow and live for thee.

I give my - self, so let me be A hum - ble child of thine.
Help me re - flect thy won-drous love As oth - ers have for me.

Text: William F. Webb, 1928 - . Copyright 1980 Reorganized Church of Jesus Christ of Latter Day Saints.
Tune: Norse Folk Melody; arr. William J. Kirkpatrick, 1838-1921.

O God, to Us Be Present Here

358

D. and C. 17:18b, c
Romans 8:14-16

ST. MATTHEW C.M.D.

1. O God, to us be pres-ent here, In lay-ing on of hands,
2. We claim the blest re-la-tion-ship, Em-pow-ered by your Son,
3. We do not claim the Spir-it's gifts For priv-i-lege or gain;

Sym-bol-ic of the Spir-it's pow-er That ser-vant-hood de-mands.
That shat-ters ev-ery bar-ri-er And makes of man-y one.
Who-ev-er knows the ser-vant's joy Must bear the ser-vant's pain.

This sac-ra-men-tal act con-firms Bap-ti-sm's call to life,
The new com-mu-ni-ty in Christ Is giv-en from a-bove;
Yet we would ask for strength to share The suf-fering Lord's tra-vail,

That fash-ions pur-pose from de-spair And har-mo-ny from strife.
The Spir-it bonds the Saints of God In u-ni-ty and love.
For grace to keep the faith un-til Your king-dom shall pre-vail.

Text: Geoffrey F. Spencer, 1927 - ; copyright 1980 Reorganized Church of Jesus Christ of Latter Day Saints.
Tune: William Croft, 1678-1727.

359 Obedient, Lord, to Thy Command

Acts 8:14-17
D. and C. 53:2a, b

EISENACH L.M.

1. O - be - dient, Lord, to thy com - mand,
2. Bap - tize them with the Ho - ly Ghost,
3. May Spir - it's light and truth and power,

Bap - tized in wa - ter in thy name,
That Spir - it which is teach - er, guide,
Its knowl - edge, wis - dom, joy, and peace,

These now thy prom - ised bless - ing seek,
That in their hearts pre - pared by faith
Its tes - ti - mo - ny of thy Son

The seal of their a - dop - tion claim.
The Com - fort - er may now a - bide.
Bring life that nev - er - more shall cease. A - men.

Text: Evan A. Fry, 1902-1959; copyright 1956 Herald Publishing House.
Tune: Johann H. Schein, 1586-1630; harm. Johann Sebastian Bach, 1685-1750.

O Lord, We Come As Children All

360

Romans 6:3-5
Mosiah 2:18-22

MASSACHUSETTS C.M.D.

Unison (or harmony *)

1. O Lord, we come as chil-dren all Be - fore thy gra - cious face,
2. In con - fir - ma - tion's sac - ra - ment, We can per - ceive thy hand
3. The sym - bol of this sa - cred rite Has mean-ing for us all

And pray thy Ho - ly Spir - it now May per - me - ate this place.
Placed there with those that now con-firm—Oh, lead us by that hand!
As new - born Saints join el - der ones In an - swer to God's call.

While in bap - ti - sm's cleans-ing stream, We con - se - crat - ed there
As we em - brace thy prom-ised grace, A - like both young and old,
Lord Je - sus Christ, em - pow'r us now With Ho - ly Spir - it's might

Our heart, our soul, our mind's in - tent To serve with lov - ing care.
We pray thy Spir - it to sus - tain Our lives, with love en - fold.
To serve thy cause un - flinch-ing - ly, Find fa - vor in thy sight.

* Tenors should read treble clef when necessary.

Text: Alan D. Tyree, 1929 - ; copyright 1980 Reorganized Church of Jesus Christ of Latter Day Saints.
Tune: Katherine K. Davis, 1892-1980; copyright 1964 Abingdon Press. Used with permission.

361 Behold Thy Sons and Daughters, Lord

John 14:26
II Nephi 13:10, 15-17

CONFIRMATION C.M.

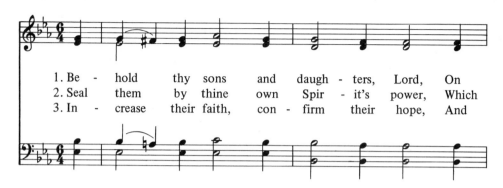

1. Be - hold thy sons and daugh - ters, Lord, On
2. Seal them by thine own Spir - it's power, Which
3. In - crease their faith, con - firm their hope, And

whom we lay our hands; They have ful - filled the
pu - ri - fies from sin, And may they find from
guide them in the way; With com - fort bear their

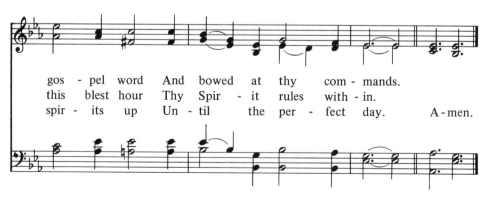

gos - pel word And bowed at thy com - mands.
this blest hour Thy Spir - it rules with - in.
spir - its up Un - til the per - fect day. A - men.

Text: Parley P. Pratt, 1807-1857; alt.
Tune: Louise Hills Lewis, 1887-1948.

A Diligent and Grateful Heart

362

D. and C. 97:4c, d
D. and C. 153:9b

ST. COLUMBA C.M.

1. A dil - i - gent and grate - ful heart Prompts me to sing thy praise. Thy love and mer - cies from the start Have blessed me all my days.

2. I thank Thee for the means to serve With tal - ents and with tithes, For shar - ing brings the ut - most joy When lift - ing oth - er lives.

3. My thanks I give for stew - ard - ship To min - is - ter through deeds, To serve and share with pa - tient care Thy peo - ple in their needs.

4. O Lord, I ded - i - cate my all In this re - sponse to thee. Help me to mag - ni - fy this call In deep hu - mil - i - ty.

Text: Raymond Gunn, 1925 - ; copyright 1980 Reorganized Church of Jesus Christ of Latter Day Saints.
Tune: Traditional Irish Melody.

363 According to the Gifts That God

D. and C. 119:8b
I Peter 2:9

EVAN C.M.

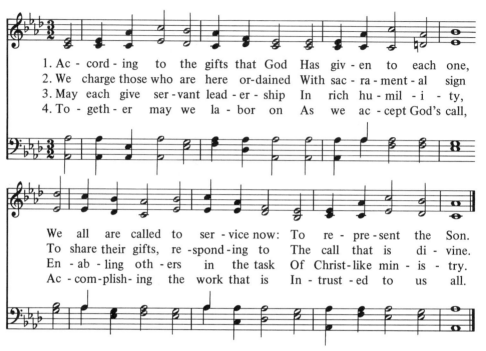

1. Ac - cord - ing to the gifts that God Has giv - en to each one,
2. We charge those who are here or-dained With sac - ra - ment - al sign
3. May each give ser -vant lead - er - ship In rich hu - mil - i - ty,
4. To - geth - er may we la - bor on As we ac - cept God's call,

We all are called to ser - vice now: To re - pre - sent the Son.
To share their gifts, re -spond-ing to The call that is di - vine.
En - ab - ling oth - ers in the task Of Christ-like min - is - try.
Ac - com-plish- ing the work that is In - trust - ed to us all.

Text: Peter A. Judd, 1943 - ; copyright 1980 Reorganized Church of Jesus Christ of Latter Day Saints.
Tune: William H. Havergal, 1793-1870.

364 Lord, Pour Thy Spirit from on High

Mosiah 9:51-55
I Peter 5:1-3

HAMBURG L.M.

1. Lord, pour thy Spir - it from on high, And thine or -
2. Wis - dom and zeal and faith im - part, Firm - ness and

dain - ed ser - vants bless; Grac - es and gifts to each sup -
meek - ness from a - bove, To bear thy peo - ple in their

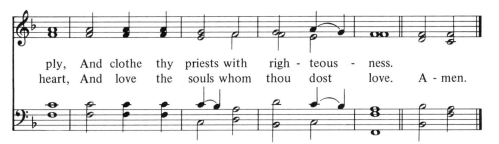

ply, And clothe thy priests with righ - teous - ness.
heart, And love the souls whom thou dost love. A - men.

Text: James Montgomery, 1771-1854.
Tune: Plainsong, Mode I, arr. Lowell Mason, 1792-1872.

Lord God, We Meet in Jesus' Name 365

John 15:15, 16
Moroni 3:1-3

HICKS L.M.

1. Lord God, we meet in Je - sus' name And praise you for your dai - ly care. Christ's ser - vant min - is - try we claim As mod - el for the work we share.
2. Through or - di - na - tion we af - firm Your gifts of love and dig - ni - ty. May your great Spir - it now con - firm This call to serve hu - man - i - ty.
3. By grace are priest - hood gifts re - ceived— Di - verse, u - nique, sus - tained by skill— To help us all meet hu - man need, As Zi - on's cause comes near - er still.

Text: Kenneth L. McLaughlin, 1951 - ; copyright 1980 Reorganized Church of Jesus Christ of Latter Day Saints.
Tune: Arthur H. Mills, 1870-1943.

366 By Revelation Called of God

Alma 12:2-5
Ephesians 4:11-13

MANOAH C.M.

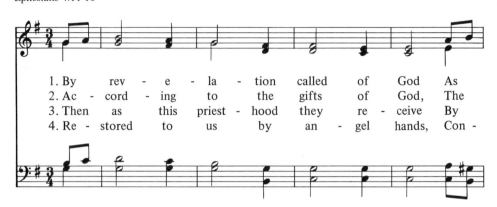

1. By rev - e - la - tion called of God As
2. Ac - cord - ing to the gifts of God, The
3. Then as this priest - hood they re - ceive By
4. Re - stored to us by an - gel hands, Con -

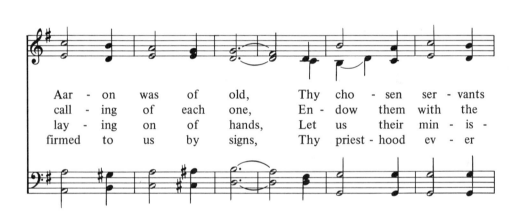

Aar - on was of old, Thy cho - sen ser - vants
call - ing of each one, En - dow them with the
lay - ing on of hands, Let us their min - is -
firmed to us by signs, Thy priest - hood ev - er

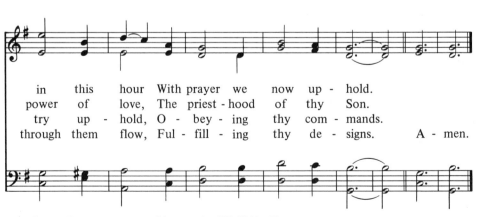

in this hour With prayer we now up - hold.
power of love, The priest - hood of thy Son.
try up - hold, O - bey - ing thy com - mands.
through them flow, Ful - fill - ing thy de - signs. A - men.

Text: Evan A. Fry, 1902-1959; copyright 1956 Herald Publishing House.
Tune: Arr. from Gioacchino A. Rossini, 1792-1868, in Henry W. Greatorex's *Collection of Church Music*, 1851.

O God, from Whom Mankind Derives Its Name 367

D. and C. 111:2
I Corinthians 13:1-7

CARPENTER 10.10.10.10.
See 494 for a lower setting.

1. O God, from whom man - kind de - rives its name,
2. May through their un - ion oth - er lives be blessed,
3. Pre - serve their days from in - ward - ness of heart;
4. From stage to stage on life's un - fold - ing way
5. Lord, bless us all to whom this day brings joy.

Whose cov - e - nant of grace re - mains the same,
Their door be wide to stran - ger and to guest.
To each the gift of truth - ful speech im - part.
Bring to their minds the vows they make this day.
Let no e - vents our u - ni - ty de - stroy,

Be with these two who now be - fore you wait;
Give them the un - der - stand - ing that is kind;
Their bond be strong a - gainst all strain and strife
Your Spir - it be their guide in ev - ery move,
And help us, till all sense of time is lost,

Grant them the bless - ing of an o - pen mind.
En - large the love they come to con - se - crate.
A - mid the chang - es of this earth - ly life.
Their faith in Christ the ba - sis of their love.
To live in love and not to count the cost. A - men.

Text: Fred Kaan, 1929 - ; copyright © 1968 by Galliard Ltd. Sole U. S. agent: Galaxy Music Corp., N. Y. Used by permission.
Tune: Keith Landis, 1922 - ; harm. Erik Routley, 1917 - ; copyright 1977 Praise Publications, Inc.; used by permission.

368

Matthew 19:4-6
Ephesians 5:25-28

O Perfect Love

O PERFECT LOVE 11.10.11.10.

1. O per - fect Love, all hu - man thought tran-scend - ing,
2. O per - fect Life, be thou their full as - sur - ance
3. Grant them the joy which bright- ens earth - ly sor - row;

Low - ly we kneel in prayer be - fore thy throne,
Of ten - der char - i - ty and stead - fast faith,
Grant them the peace which calms all earth - ly strife,

That theirs may be the love which knows no end - ing
Of pa - tient hope and qui - et, brave en - dur - ance,
And to life's day the glo - rious un - known mor - row

Whom thou for - ev - er - more dost join in one.
With child -like trust that fears nor pain nor death.
That dawns up - on e - ter - nal love and life. A-men.

Text: Dorothy Frances Blomfield Gurney, 1858-1932. Used by permission of Oxford University Press.
Tune: Arr. from Joseph Barnby, 1838-1896.

Commission and Commitment

Bear Each Other's Burdens

369

Galatians 6:2
D. and C. 150:7

OLWEN (Poverty)
6.6.8.D. with repeat

1. Bear each oth - er's bur - dens, Share each oth - er's suf - f'ring,
2. God calls us to heal - ing, Di - vine love re - veal - ing,

And love as the Sav - ior has shown. The strength of our
Wher - ev - er we meet hu - man need. In times so mo -

car - ing Heals pain souls are bear - ing And we are no
men - tous, Ex - pect - ant, por - ten - tous, The world suf - fers

long - er a - lone. Bear each oth - er's bur - dens, Share
an - guish and greed. God calls us to heal - ing, Di -

each oth - er's suf - f'ring, And love as the Sav - ior has shown.
vine love re - veal - ing, Wher - ev - er we meet hu - man need.

Text: Barbara Howard, 1930 - ; copyright 1980 Reorganized Church of Jesus Christ of Latter Day Saints.
Tune: Welsh Carol; arr. Caradog Roberts, 1879-1935; used by permission of the Union of Welsh Independents, Swansea, Wales.

370   Eternal God, Whose Power Upholds

II Nephi 9:133-137
Romans 11:33, 34, 36

FOREST GREEN C.M.D.

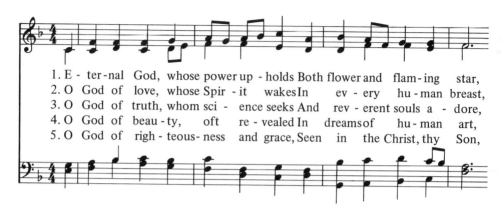

1. E - ter - nal God, whose power up - holds Both flower and flam - ing star,
2. O God of love, whose Spir - it wakes In ev - ery hu - man breast,
3. O God of truth, whom sci - ence seeks And rev - erent souls a - dore,
4. O God of beau - ty, oft re - vealed In dreams of hu - man art,
5. O God of righ - teous - ness and grace, Seen in the Christ, thy Son,

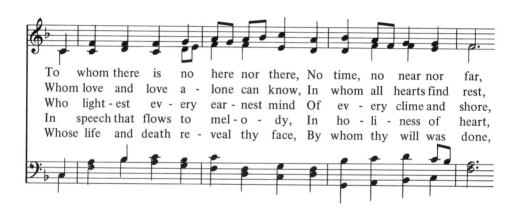

To whom there is no here nor there, No time, no near nor far,
Whom love and love a - lone can know, In whom all hearts find rest,
Who light - est ev - ery ear - nest mind Of ev - ery clime and shore,
In speech that flows to mel - o - dy, In ho - li - ness of heart,
Whose life and death re - veal thy face, By whom thy will was done,

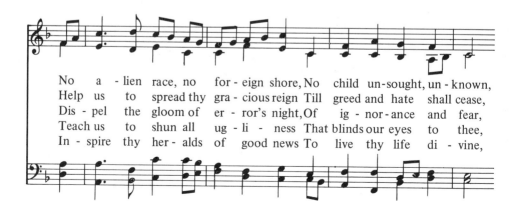

No a - lien race, no for - eign shore, No child un - sought, un - known,
Help us to spread thy gra - cious reign Till greed and hate shall cease,
Dis - pel the gloom of er - ror's night, Of ig - nor - ance and fear,
Teach us to shun all ug - li - ness That blinds our eyes to thee,
In - spire thy her - alds of good news To live thy life di - vine,

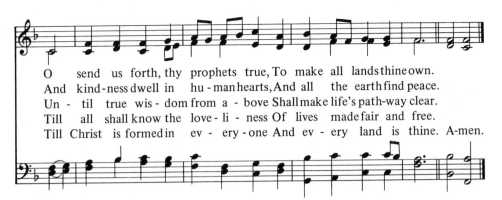

O send us forth, thy prophets true, To make all lands thine own.
And kindness dwell in human hearts, And all the earth find peace.
Until true wisdom from above Shall make life's pathway clear.
Till all shall know the loveliness Of lives made fair and free.
Till Christ is formed in everyone And every land is thine. A-men.

Text: Henry H. Tweedy, 1868-1953.
Tune: English Traditional Melody; coll., adapt. and arr. by Ralph Vaughan Williams, 1872-1958; from *The English Hymnal* by permission of Oxford University Press.

Jesus Calls Us O'er the Tumult 371

Matthew 4:19 (20)
Mosiah 3:16, 17

GALILEE 8.7.8.7.

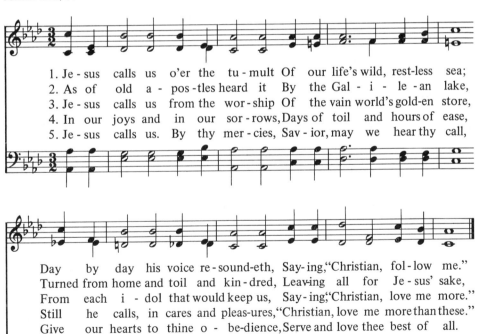

1. Je-sus calls us o'er the tu-mult Of our life's wild, rest-less sea;
2. As of old a-pos-tles heard it By the Gal-i-le-an lake,
3. Je-sus calls us from the wor-ship Of the vain world's gold-en store,
4. In our joys and in our sor-rows, Days of toil and hours of ease,
5. Je-sus calls us. By thy mer-cies, Sav-ior, may we hear thy call,

Day by day his voice re-sound-eth, Say-ing, "Christian, fol-low me."
Turned from home and toil and kin-dred, Leav-ing all for Je-sus' sake,
From each i-dol that would keep us, Say-ing, "Christian, love me more."
Still he calls, in cares and pleas-ures, "Christian, love me more than these."
Give our hearts to thine o-be-dience, Serve and love thee best of all.

Text: Cecil F. Alexander, 1818-1895, alt.
Tune: William H. Jude, 1851-1922.

372

Behold the Savior at Your Door

Revelation 3:20
D. and C. 63:1a

THE SAVIOR AT THE DOOR C.M. with refrain

1. Be-hold the Sav-ior at your door, Your kind - est, tru-est friend,
2. Oh, yes, the bless-ed Son of God, Though Lord of all a - bove,
3. "If an - y -one will hear my voice And o - pen un - to me,

Is seek - ing en-trance to your heart, Your life with his to blend.
Now paus - es at your low - ly door And speaks in tones of love.
I'll sup with him and he with me, And friends we'll al - ways be."

Refrain

The Sav - ior's knock-ing at your door, And ask - ing en - trance in;

He's knock - ing, ask - ing o'er and o'er; O o - pen un - to him!

Text: W. H. Bagby, 19th century, U. S.
Tune: James H. Rosecrans, 19th century, U. S.

Where Restless Crowds Are Thronging 373

Luke 4:18, 19
Mark 6:33-37 (32-37)

CRAIGMILLAR 7.6.7.6.D.

1. Where rest-less crowds are throng - ing A - long the cit - y ways,
2. In scenes of want and sor - row And haunts of fla - grant wrong,
3. O Christ, be - hold thy peo - ple—They press on ev - 'ry hand!

Where pride and greed and tur - moil Con - sume the fe - vered days,
In homes where kind-ness fal - ters And strife and fear are strong,
Bring light to all the cit - ies Of our be - lov - ed land.

Where vain am - bi - tions ban - ish All thoughts of praise and prayer,
In bus - y street of bar - ter, In lone - ly thor - ough-fare,
May all our bit - ter striv - ing Give way to vi - sions fair

The peo - ple's spir - its wa - ver: But thou, O Christ, art there.
The peo - ple's spir - its lan - guish: But thou, O Christ, art there.
Of right-eous - ness and jus - tice: For thou, O Christ, art there.

Text: Thomas Curtis Clark, 1877-1953; alt.; from *Five City Hymns*, copyright 1954 The Hymn Society of America; used by permission.
Tune: Erik Routley, 1917 - ; from *Eternal Light* by Erik Routley; copyright 1971 Carl Fischer, Inc., New York. International copyright secured. All rights reserved. Used by permission.

374

Lead On, O King Eternal

Psalm 31:1-3, 5
I Nephi 6:38-41

LANCASHIRE 7.6.7.6.D.

1. Lead on, O King E - ter - nal. The day of march has come;
2. Lead on, O King E - ter - nal, Till sin's fierce war shall cease,
3. Lead on, O King E - ter - nal. We fol - low, not with fears,

Hence-forth in fields of con - quest Thy tents shall be our home.
And ho - li - ness shall whis - per The sweet a - men of peace;
For glad-ness breaks like morn - ing Wher- e'er thy face ap - pears.

Through days of prep - a - ra - tion Thy grace has made us strong,
For not with swords' loud clash - ing Nor roll of stir - ring drums—
Thy cross is lift - ed o'er us, We jour - ney in its light;

And now, O King E - ter - nal, We lift our bat - tle song.
With deeds of love and mer - cy The heaven- ly king-dom comes.
The crown a - waits the con -quest; Lead on, O God of might. A-men.

Text: Ernest W. Shurtleff, 1862-1917.
Tune: Henry Smart, 1813-1879.

The City Is Alive, O God

John 3:16, 17
Matthew 23:37

THAXTED C.M.D. with repeat

Unison

1. The cit-y is a-live, O God, With sound of rush-ing feet,
2. O God, in-spire your church to-day To take Christ's ser-vant role,

With flash-ing lights and ra-pid change That pulse through ev-ery street.
To love the world, to hear its claims, To sense its yearn-ing soul;

But oft there's in-hu-man-i-ty Be-hind the bright fa-cade,
To live with-in the mar-ket-place, To serve both weak and strong,

And emp-ty souls with hun-gry hearts Cry out for help, O God.
To lose her-self, to share her dream, To give the world her song!

And emp-ty souls with hun-gry hearts Cry out for help, O God.
To lose her-self, to share her dream, To give the world her song.

Text: William Watkins Reid, Jr., 1923 - ; alt.; copyright 1969 The Hymn Society of America; used by permission.
Tune: Gustav Holst, 1874-1934, adapted from *The Planets*; copyright 1921 Goodwin & Tabb; used by permission
of G. Schirmer, Inc.

376   We Are Living, We Are Dwelling

Joel 2:27-29
Joshua 24:14-16

AUSTRIA 8.7.8.7.D.

1. We are liv-ing, we are dwell-ing In a grand and awe-ful time
2. Worlds are chang-ing, old forms crum-bling; Souls of cour-age times de-mand;

When each hour some fate is tell-ing: To be liv-ing is sub-lime.
Those who see the way as proph-ets Lead on toward the prom-ised land.

Rise, O saints, in all thy vig-or; Stand e-rect on ho-ly sod;
Rise, O saints, in all thy vi-sion, Let thy voice be heard a-broad.

Turn from aim-less in-de-ci-sion, Rise up in the strength of God.
Speak! let all thy faith and wis-dom Count for Zi-on, count for God.

Text: A. Cleveland Coxe, 1818-1896, alt.
Tune: Franz Joseph Haydn, 1732-1809.

Let Your Heart Be Broken

377

D. and C. 153:9
Jacob 2:22-24

BJORKLUND MAJOR 6.5.6.5.D.

Unison

1. Let your heart be bro - ken For a world in need:
2. Blest to be a bless - ing, Priv - i - leged to care,
3. Add to your be - liev - ing Deeds that prove it true.
4. Let your heart be ten - der And your vi - sion clear;

Feed the mouths that hun - ger, Soothe the wounds that bleed,
Chal - lenged by the need— Ap - par - ent ev - ery - where.
Know - ing Christ as Sav - ior, Make Him Mas - ter, too.
See the world as God sees, Serve all far and near.

Give the cup of wa - ter And the loaf of bread—
Where the world is want - ing, Fill the va - cant place.
Fol - low in His foot - steps, Go where He has trod;
Let your heart be bro - ken By an - oth - er's pain;

Be the hands of Je - sus, Serv - ing in His stead.
Be the means through which the Lord re - veals His grace.
In the world's great trou - ble Risk your - self for God.
Share your rich re - sourc - es, Give and give a - gain.

378   Rise Up, O Saints of God

D. and C. 4:1   FESTAL SONG S.M.
Alma 14:92-96   *See 319 for a lower setting.*

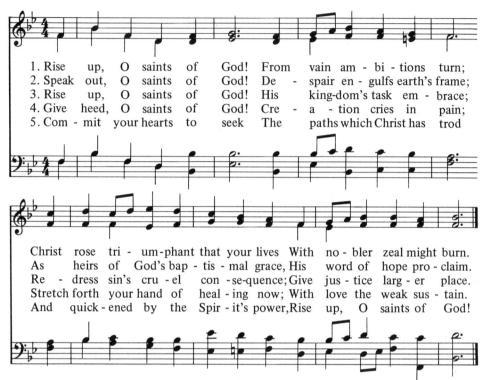

1. Rise up, O saints of God! From vain am-bi-tions turn;
2. Speak out, O saints of God! De - spair en-gulfs earth's frame;
3. Rise up, O saints of God! His king-dom's task em - brace;
4. Give heed, O saints of God! Cre - a - tion cries in pain;
5. Com - mit your hearts to seek The paths which Christ has trod

Christ rose tri - um-phant that your lives With no - bler zeal might burn.
As heirs of God's bap - tis - mal grace, His word of hope pro - claim.
Re - dress sin's cru - el con - se-quence; Give jus - tice larg - er place.
Stretch forth your hand of heal - ing now; With love the weak sus - tain.
And quick - ened by the Spir - it's power, Rise up, O saints of God!

Text: Norman O. Forness, 1936 - ; copyright 1978 from *Lutheran Book of Worship*; used by permission of Augsburg Publishing House representing the publishers and copyright holders.
Tune: William H. Walter, 1825-1893.

379   Thou Must Be True Thyself

James 1:25-27   LOYALTY 6.6.8.6.8.6.
I John 2:4-10

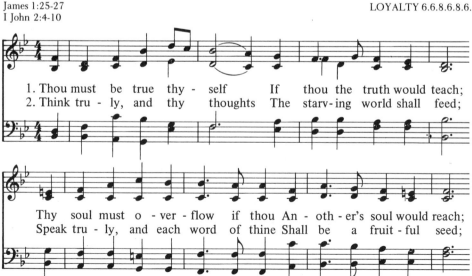

1. Thou must be true thy - self If thou the truth would teach;
2. Think tru - ly, and thy thoughts The starv - ing world shall feed;

Thy soul must o - ver - flow if thou An - oth - er's soul would reach;
Speak tru - ly, and each word of thine Shall be a fruit - ful seed;

It needs the o-ver-flow of heart To give the lips full speech.
Live tru-ly, and thy life shall be A great and no-ble creed.

Text: Horatius Bonar, 1808-1889, alt.
Tune: Attr. to Benjamin Franklin, 1706-1790.

Though Anxious and Disheartened 380

D. and C. 68:1d
II Nephi 13:29

RUTHERFORD 7.6.7.6.7.6.7.5.

Though anx-ious and dis-heart-ened, Be peo-ple of good cheer.

Move out in faith em-pow-ered, My Spir-it will be there.

In love sup-port each oth-er With un-der-stand-ing hearts.

Move out, pro-claim my gos-pel; I have gone be-fore.

Text: Arr. from *D. and C.* 154 by Barbara Howard, 1930 - , and Rosalee Elser, 1925 - ; copyright 1980 Reorganized Church of Jesus Christ of Latter Day Saints.
Tune: Adapted from Chrétien Urhan, 1790-1845, by Edward F. Rimbault, 1816-1876.

381 Hark! The Voice of Jesus Calling

D. and C. 6:2
Isaiah 6:8

ELLESDIE 8.7.8.7.D.
See 390 for a higher setting.

1. Hark! The voice of Je-sus call-ing, "Who will go and work to-day?
2. If you can-not cross the o-cean And far mis-sion lands ex-plore,
3. Let none hear you i-dly say-ing, "There is noth-ing I can do,"

Fields are white and har-vests wait-ing; Who will bear the sheaves a-way?"
You can find the need-y near-er; You can help them at your door.
While so ma-ny souls are dy-ing, And the Mas-ter calls for you.

Ear-nest-ly the Mas-ter call-eth; Rich re-ward he of-fers free;
If you can-not give your thou-sands, You can serve with will-ing might,
Take the task he gives you glad-ly; Let his work your pleas-ure be;

Who will an-swer, glad-ly say-ing, "Here am I, O Lord, send me."
And what-e'er you do for Je-sus Will be pre-cious in his sight.
An-swer quick-ly when he call-eth, "Here am I, O Lord, send me."

Text: Daniel March, 1816-1909, alt.
Tune: Wolfgang Amadeus Mozart, 1756-1791; arr. by Hubert P. Main, 1839-1926.

God Forgave My Sin in Jesus' Name

382

Alma 15:60, 61
I Corinthians 2:9-12

FREELY, FREELY
9.9.9.9. with refrain

1. God for-gave my sin in Je-sus' name; I've been born a-gain in Je-sus' name; And in Je-sus' name I come to you To share his love as he told me to.

2. All power is given in Je-sus' name, In earth and heaven in Je-sus' name; And in Je-sus' name I come to you To share his power as he told me to.

Refrain

He said, "Free-ly, free-ly you have re-ceived: Free-ly, free-ly give. Go in my name, and, be-cause you be-lieve, Oth-ers will know that I live."

383 Where Cross the Crowded Ways of Life

Matthew 10:38 (42)
Hebrews 13:14, 16

GERMANY (Gardiner) L.M.

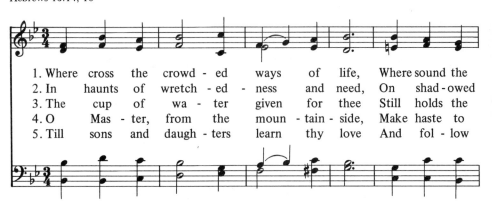

1. Where cross the crowd - ed ways of life, Where sound the
2. In haunts of wretch - ed - ness and need, On shad - owed
3. The cup of wa - ter given for thee Still holds the
4. O Mas - ter, from the moun - tain - side, Make haste to
5. Till sons and daugh - ters learn thy love And fol - low

cries of race and clan, A - bove the noise of
thresh - olds dark with fears, From paths where hide the
fresh - ness of thy grace; Yet long these mul - ti -
heal these hearts of pain; A - mong these rest - less
where thy feet have trod; Till glo - rious from thy

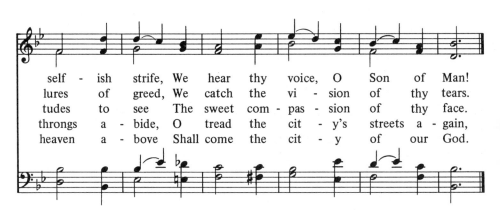

self - ish strife, We hear thy voice, O Son of Man!
lures of greed, We catch the vi - sion of thy tears.
tudes to see The sweet com - pas - sion of thy face.
throngs a - bide, O tread the cit - y's streets a - gain,
heaven a - bove Shall come the cit - y of our God.

Text: Frank Mason North, 1850-1935, alt.
Tune: William Gardiner's *Sacred Melodies*, 1815.

Come, Labor On

384

II Nephi 13:28-30
Hebrews 12:1-2

ORA LABORA 4.10.10.10.4.

Unison (or harmony)

1. Come, la-bor on. Who dares stand i-dle on the har-vest plain, While all a-round us waves the gold-en grain? And to each ser-vant does the Mas-ter say, "Go work to-day."

2. Come, la-bor on. Claim the high call-ing an-gels can-not share— To young and old the gos-pel glad-ness bear; Re-deem the time; its hours too swift-ly fly. The night draws nigh.

3. Come, la-bor on. A-way with gloom-y doubts and faith-less fear! No arm so weak but may do serv-ice here: By fee-blest a-gents may our God ful-fill His righ-teous will.

4. Come, la-bor on. No time for rest till glows the west-ern sky, Till the long shad-ows o'er our path-way lie, And a glad sound comes with the set-ting sun, "Well done, well done!"

Text: Jane Laurie Borthwick, 1813-1897.
Tune: T. Tertius Noble, 1867-1953; arr. Rosalee Elser, 1925 - ; copyright 1980 Rosalee Elser; used by permission.

385

O Jesus, Thou Art Standing

Revelation 3:20
II Nephi 14:4, 5

ST. HILDA 7.6.7.6.D.

1. O Je - sus, thou art stand - ing Out - side the fast-closed door,
2. O Je - sus, thou art knock - ing, And, lo, thy hand is scarred,
3. O Je - sus, thou art plead - ing In ac - cents meek and low,

In low - ly pa - tience wait - ing To pass the thresh-old o'er.
And thorns thy brow en - cir - cle, And tears thy face have marred.
"I died for you, my chil - dren, And will ye treat me so?"

We bear the name of Chris - tians, His name and sign we bear;
O love that pass - eth knowl - edge, So pa - tient - ly to wait!
O Lord, with shame and sor - row, We o - pen now the door;

O shame, thrice shame up - on us To keep him stand-ing there!
O sin that hath no e - qual, So fast to bar the gate!
Dear Sav - ior, en - ter, en - ter, And leave us nev -er -more! A-men.

Text: William Walsham How, 1823-1897.
Tune: Justin H. Knecht, 1752-1817, and Edward Husband, 1843-1908.

Come Now, Sound the Call of Zion

386

D. and C. 136:3c
D. and C. 6:3

PITTSFIELD 8.7.8.7.D.

1. Come now, sound the call of Zi - on! Share with peo - ple of the earth.
2. Saints with vi - sion of the fu - ture Need foun - da - tions strong and true;

All are called to be dis - ci - ples; Now's the time for world re - birth.
As they seek new rev - e - la - tion, God's in - tent is born a - new.

Dare we search for new hor - i - zons? Is our faith a hope - less dream?
Jour - ney forth to high ad - ven - ture, Bring - ing faith and hope to all.

Or by faith shall we be build - ers And with God the world re - deem?
Each in - vest - ment made in oth - ers Is re - sponse to Zi - on's call.

Text: Eric L. Selden, 1925 - ; copyright 1980 Reorganized Church of Jesus Christ of Latter Day Saints.
Tune: H. R. Mills, 1844-1933.

387   O My People, Saith the Spirit

D. and C. 153:9
D. and C. 81:4c

MY REDEEMER (Admonition) 8.7.8.7.D.

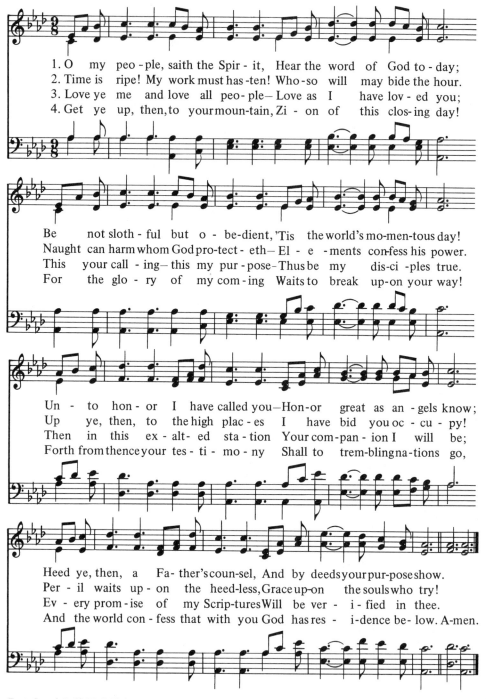

1. O my peo-ple, saith the Spir-it, Hear the word of God to-day;
2. Time is ripe! My work must has-ten! Who-so will may bide the hour.
3. Love ye me and love all peo-ple— Love as I have lov-ed you;
4. Get ye up, then, to your moun-tain, Zi - on of this clos-ing day!

Be not sloth-ful but o - be-dient, 'Tis the world's mo-men-tous day!
Naught can harm whom God pro-tect - eth— El - e -ments con-fess his power.
This your call - ing— this my pur - pose— Thus be my dis-ci -ples true.
For the glo - ry of my com-ing Waits to break up-on your way!

Un - to hon - or I have called you—Hon-or great as an - gels know;
Up ye, then, to the high plac - es I have bid you oc - cu - py!
Then in this ex - alt - ed sta - tion Your com-pan - ion I will be;
Forth from thence your tes - ti - mo - ny Shall to trem-bling na-tions go,

Heed ye, then, a Fa- ther's coun-sel, And by deeds your pur-pose show.
Per - il waits up - on the heed-less, Grace up-on the souls who try!
Ev - ery prom - ise of my Scrip-tures Will be ver - i -fied in thee.
And the world con - fess that with you God has res - i-dence be- low. A-men.

Text: Joseph Luff, 1852-1948.
Tune: James McGranahan, 1840-1907, alt.

Brothers and Sisters of Mine

388

Luke 6:36-38
Mosiah 2:22, 24, 28

MINE ARE THE HUNGRY 11.11.11.11.

1. Broth - ers and sis - ters of mine are the hun - gry Who
2. Stran - gers and neigh - bors, they claim my at - ten - tion; They
3. Peo - ple are they, men and wom - en and chil - dren; And
4. God of all liv - ing, we make our con - fes - sion: Too

sigh in their sor - row and weep in their pain.
sleep by my door - step, they sit by my bed.
each has a heart keep - ing time with my own.
long we have wast - ed the wealth of our lands.

Sis - ters and broth - ers of mine are the home-less Who
Neigh - bors and stran - gers, their an - guish con - cerns me, And
Peo - ple are they, per - sons made in God's im - age; So
God of all lov - ing, re - new our com - pas - sion And

wait with - out shel - ter from wind and from rain.
I must not feast till the hun - gry are fed.
what shall I of - fer them, bread or a stone?
o - pen our hearts while we reach out our hands.

Text: Kenneth I. Morse, 1913 - .
Tune: Wilbur E. Brumbaugh, 1931-1977.
   Text and tune copyright 1974 by The Brethren Press, Elgin, IL; harm. alt. by Rosalee Elser, 1925 - ; used
   by permission.

389

If Suddenly upon the Street

John 14:21
D. and C. 11:4, 5

MOZART 8.8.8.D.

1. If sud-den-ly up-on the street My gra-cious Sav-ior
2. His eye would pierce my out-ward show; His thought my in-most
3. If on the day or in the place Where-in he met me

I should meet, And he should say, "As I love thee,
thought would know; And if I said, "I love thee, Lord,"
face to face My life could show some kind-ness done,

What love hast thou to of-fer me?" Then what could this poor
He would not heed my spo-ken word Un-less my dai-ly
Some pur-pose formed, some work be-gun For his dear sake, then

heart of mine Dare of-fer to that heart di-vine?
life should tell That ver-i-ly I loved him well.
were it meet Love's gift to lay at Je-sus' feet.

Text: Clarence F. Richardson, 1879 - ?
Tune: Wolfgang Amadeus Mozart, 1756-1791.

Hast Thou Heard It, O My Brother 390

D. and C. 65:1a
Psalm 37:3-4

ELLESDIE 8.7.8.7.D.
See 381 for a lower setting.

1. Hast thou heard it, O my broth-er, God's e - ter - nal voice to thee,
2. Wilt thou an - swer, O my sis - ter, Doubt-ing not the beck-oning star
3. Hast thou heard it, O my neigh-bor, Like pro-phet - ic souls of yore?

Soft - ly call - ing toward the out-land Where his Zi - on yet shall be?
Like a bea - con guid - ing for-ward Where the fron - tier coun-tries are?
When the com-mon mind was list-less, They God's vi - tal mes - sage bore.

"Some-thing for you; go and find it. Brave the broad un-chart-ed sea,
Hear God's whis-per in the still-ness,"Go, my child, I bid you go.
Search the stores of earth and heav-en; Watch the skies for guid -ing ray;

Where be - yond the seen ho - ri - zon Lies the land of prom-ise free."
When you move in faith, my Spir - it Shall with-in your spir - it glow."
Trust in God and in each oth - er For the light of each newday.

Text: Roy A. Cheville, 1897 - , alt. Copyright 1950 Herald Publishing House.
Tune: Wolfgang Amadeus Mozart, 1756-1791, arr. by Hubert P. Main, 1839-1926.

391

Joshua 24:15
Alma 3:57, 58

Jesus Is Calling

JESUS IS CALLING TODAY 10.8.10.7. with refrain

1. Je-sus is call-ing! O hear him to-day, Call-ing for you,
2. Je-sus is call-ing! Your ser-vice he needs, Call-ing for you,
3. Je-sus is call-ing! He stands at the door, Call-ing for you,

Call-ing for you. Will you not quick-ly the sum-mons o-bey?
Call-ing for you. Ten-der-ly, pa-tient-ly with you he pleads;
Call-ing for you. O-pen your heart, and his mer-cy im-plore;

Refrain

Je-sus is call-ing for you! Call-ing for you; Call-ing for you! Hear him to-day; do not turn him a-way! Je-sus is call-ing for you!

Text: Charles H. Gabriel, 1856-1932.
Tune: Luther O. Emerson, 1820-1915, alt. by Rosalee Elser, 1925 - .

Go, Make of All Disciples

392

Matthew 28:17-19 (18-20)
Alma 14:82, 96

LANCASHIRE 7.6.7.6.D.

1. "Go, make of all dis - ci - ples." We hear the call, O Lord,
2. "Go, make of all dis - ci - ples," bap - tiz - ing in the name
3. "Go, make of all dis - ci - ples." We at thy feet would stay
4. "Go, make of all dis - ci - ples." We wel - come thy com - mand.

That comes from thee, our Fa - ther, In thine e - ter - nal Word.
Of Fa - ther, Son, and Spir - it, From age to age the same.
Un - til each life's vo - ca - tion Ac - cents thy ho - ly way.
"Lo, I am with you al - way." We take thy guid - ing hand.

In - spire our ways of learn - ing Through ear - nest, fer - vent prayer,
We call each new dis - ci - ple To fol - low thee, O Lord,
We cul - ti - vate the na - ture God plants in ev - ery heart,
The task looms large be - fore us; We fol - low with - out fear,

And let our dai - ly liv - ing Re - veal thee ev - ery - where.
Re - deem - ing soul and bod - y By wa - ter and the Word.
Re - veal - ing in our wit - ness The Mas - ter Teach - er's art.
In heaven and earth thy pow - er Shall bring God's king - dom here.

Text: Leon M. Adkins, 1896 - ; copyright 1955, 1964 Abingdon Press; used by permission.
Tune: Henry Smart, 1813-1879.

393

Soldiers of Christ, Arise

II Nephi 1:36-38
D. and C. 26:3d-g

DIADEMATA S.M.D.

1. Sol - diers of Christ, a - rise And put your ar - mor on,
2. Stand then in His great might, With all His strength en - dued,
3. Leave no un - guard - ed place, No weak - ness of the soul;

Strong in the strength which God sup - plies Through His e - ter - nal Son;
And take, to arm you for the fight, The pan - o - ply of God;
Take ev - ery vir - tue, ev - ery grace, And for - ti - fy the whole,

Strong in the Lord of hosts, And in His might - y power,
From strength to strength go on, Wres - tle and fight and pray;
That hav - ing all things done, And all your con - flicts past,

Who in the strength of Je - sus trusts Is more than con - quer - or.
Tread all the powers of dark - ness down, And win the well-fought day.
You may o'er - come through Christ a - lone, And stand com - plete at last.

Text: Charles Wesley, 1707-1788, alt.
Tune: George J. Elvey, 1816-1893.

The Voice of God Is Calling

394

Alma 3:57-59
Isaiah 6:8

WEBB 7.6.7.6.D.

1. The voice of God is call - ing Its sum - mons un - to men
2. I hear my peo - ple cry - ing In cot and mine and slum;
3. We heed, O Lord, thy sum - mons, And an - swer, "Here are we!"

As once he spoke in Zi - on, So now he speaks a - gain:
No field or mart is si - lent; No cit - y street is dumb.
Send us up - on thine er - rand; Let us thy serv -ants be.

Whom shall I send to suc - cor My peo - ple in their need?
I see my peo - ple fall - ing In dark - ness and de - spair;
Our strength is dust and ash - es, Our years a pass - ing hour—

Whom shall I send to loos -en The bonds of lust and greed?
Whom shall I send to shat-ter The fet - ters which they bear?
But thou canst use our weak-ness To mag - ni - fy thy power. A-men.

Text: John Haynes Holmes, 1879-1964; used by permission of Roger W. Holmes.
Tune: George J. Webb, 1803-1887.

395

D. and C. 59:4, 5a, b
D. and C. 101:2b-f

God of Creation

JUDAS MACCABEUS
5.7.8.5.8.5.8.5. with refrain

1. God of cre - a - tion, help us each to un - der - stand
2. Earth's stores of rich - es, like life - giv - ing rain and sun
3. Grant us di - rec - tion as we seek for bet - ter ways

How to use the vast re - sourc - es of both sea and land.
Are your gen - er - ous pro - vi - sions meant for ev - ery - one.
To pro - vide for our well - be - ing and pro - long our days.

Teach us how to plant and har - vest— not for graft or greed
May we use them as in - tend - ed— nev - er waste - ful - ly—
Field and for - est, air and wa - ter— may we ev - er share

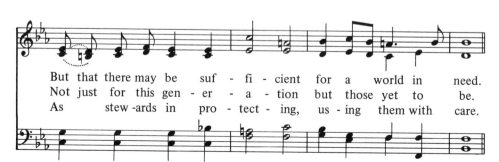

But that there may be suf - fi - cient for a world in need.
Not just for this gen - er - a - tion but those yet to be.
As stew - ards in pro - tect - ing, us - ing them with care.

Refrain

God of cre - a - tion, we would be cre - a - tors too,

Bless our ef - forts us - ing wise - ly all that comes from you. A - men.

Text: Naomi Russell, 1921 - ; copyright 1980 Reorganized Church of Jesus Christ of Latter Day Saints.
Tune: George Friedrich Handel, 1685-1759.

O Lord of Heaven and Earth and Sea 396

Mosiah 2:36
Psalm 95:3-6

ALMSGIVING 8.8.8.4.

1. O Lord of heaven and earth and sea, To thee all praise and glo - ry
2. We lose what on our - selves we spend; We have as treas - ure with - out
3. What-ev - er, Lord, we yield to thee Re - paid a thou - sand-fold will
4. To thee from whom we all de - rive Our life, our gifts, our power to

be! How shall we show our love to thee, Who giv-est all?
end What-ev - er, Lord, to thee we lend, Who giv-est all.
be; Then glad-ly will we give to thee, Who giv-est all—
give. Oh, may we ev - er with thee live, Who giv-est all! A - men.

Text: Christopher Wordsworth, 1807-1885.
Tune: John B. Dykes, 1823-1876.

397

D. and C. 101:2b-e
Mosiah 2:19-23

All Things Are Thine

GERMANY (Gardiner) L.M.

1. All things are thine, O Lord of life! Thou hast or-
2. Thou hast e - nough for all thy saints, In field, in
3. To work to - geth - er, Lord, with thee, We own to
4. Yet word a - lone will not suf - fice For stew - ard-

dained these gifts a - bove That we may build on earth with
mine, in sea, in air, If we shall learn to dwell as
be our com - mon call, To build a blest com - mu - ni -
ship of farm or mart; This mind, this hand must im - ple -

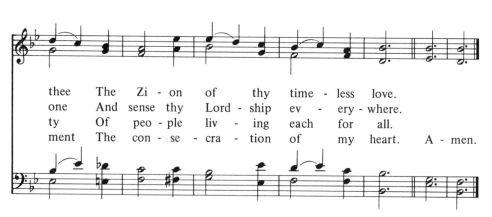

thee The Zi - on of thy time - less love.
one And sense thy Lord - ship ev - ery - where.
ty Of peo - ple liv - ing each for all.
ment The con - se - cra - tion of my heart. A - men.

Text: Roy A. Cheville, 1897 - ; alt.; copyright 1950 Herald Publishing House.
Tune: William Gardiner's *Sacred Melodies*, 1815.

Let Us Give Praise to the God of Creation 398

D. and C. 137:6
D. and C. 140:5c, d

WESLEY 11.10.11.10.

1. Let us give praise to the God of cre - a - tion,
2. Per - sons are a - gents by God's gra - cious will - ing,
3. All things are sa - cred, for use with thanks - giv - ing,
4. Gift - ed - ness flows from the fount of cre - a - tion;
5. Now let the saints hail so rich a foun - da - tion,

Lord of all his - tory and source of all power,
Blessed with as - sur - ance of ul - ti - mate worth.
Bound - less re - sour - ces for each to em - ploy;
Truth from all sour - ces de - mands dis - ci - pline;
Forged in our her - i - tage, liv - ing to - day;

Call - ing us now to the world's re - stor - a - tion;
Power is with - in us for his - tory's ful - fill - ing,
Strength for the bod - y and soul's ful - ler liv - ing;
Wom - en and men shar - ing skill's ded - i - ca - tion,
God who per - sists in the prom - ised sal - va - tion

Grant - ing us strength for the needs of this hour.
Stew - ards of all the re - sour - ces of earth.
Spir - it and el - e - ment bond - ed in joy.
Bear - ing the bur - dens of sor - row and sin.
Goes on be - fore us and shows us the way.

Text: Geoffrey F. Spencer, 1927 - . Copyright 1980 Reorganized Church of Jesus Christ of Latter Day Saints.
Tune: Lowell Mason, 1792-1872.

399

I Timothy 6:11-14
II Corinthians 5:16-18

A Charge to Keep I Have

BOYLSTON S.M.

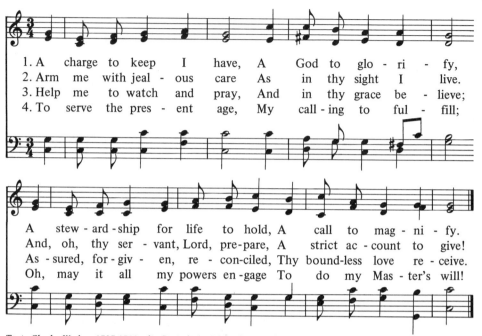

1. A charge to keep I have, A God to glo - ri - fy,
2. Arm me with jeal - ous care As in thy sight I live.
3. Help me to watch and pray, And in thy grace be - lieve;
4. To serve the pres - ent age, My call - ing to ful - fill;

A stew - ard - ship for life to hold, A call to mag - ni - fy.
And, oh, thy ser - vant, Lord, pre-pare, A strict ac - count to give!
As - sured, for - giv - en, re - con-ciled, Thy bound-less love re - ceive.
Oh, may it all my powers en -gage To do my Mas - ter's will!

Text: Charles Wesley, 1707-1788, alt.; St. 3 alt. by Richard Howard, 1929 - .
Tune: Lowell Mason, 1792-1872.

400

II Corinthians 9:7, 8
Proverbs 3:9

Source of All Gifts

MENDON L.M.

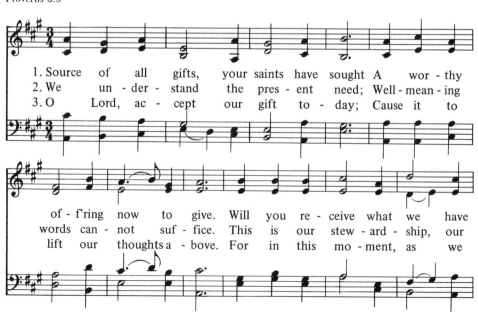

1. Source of all gifts, your saints have sought A wor - thy
2. We un - der - stand the pres - ent need; Well - mean - ing
3. O Lord, ac - cept our gift to - day; Cause it to

of - f'ring now to give. Will you re - ceive what we have
words can - not suf - fice. This is our stew - ard - ship, our
lift our thoughts a - bove. For in this mo - ment, as we

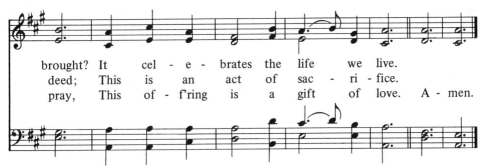

brought? It cel - e - brates the life we live.
deed; This is an act of sac - ri - fice.
pray, This of - f'ring is a gift of love. A - men.

Text: Margaret Athey, 1936 - ; copyright 1980 Reorganized Church of Jesus Christ of Latter Day Saints.
Tune: Traditional German Melody; arr. by Samuel Dyer, 1785-1835.

We Give Thee But Thine Own

401

ST. ANDREW S.M.

Matthew 25:41 (40)
I Chronicles 29:14

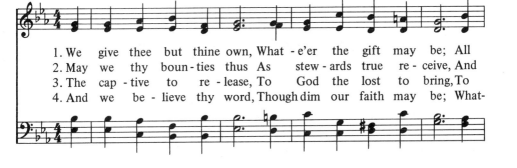

1. We give thee but thine own, What - e'er the gift may be; All
2. May we thy boun - ties thus As stew - ards true re - ceive, And
3. The cap - tive to re - lease, To God the lost to bring, To
4. And we be - lieve thy word, Though dim our faith may be; What-

that we have is thine a - lone, A trust, O Lord, from thee.
glad - ly as thou bless - est us To thee our first - fruits give.
teach the way of life and peace It is a Christ - like thing.
e'er for thine we do, O Lord, We do it un - to thee. A - men.

Text: William Walsham How, 1823-1897.
Tune: Joseph Barnby, 1838-1896.

402

D. and C. 150:7
D. and C. 59:4, 5a, b

God in His Love for Us

ECOLOGY 11.10.11.10.

Unison (or harmony)

1. God in his love for us lent us this plan - et,
2. Thanks be to God for its boun - ty and beau - ty,
3. Long have our tra - gic wars ruined our har - vest;
4. Cas - ual de - spoil - ers, or high priests of Mam - mon

Gave it a pur - pose in time and in space;
Life that sus - tains us in bod - y and mind:
Long has Earth bowed to the ter - ror of force.
Sell - ing the fu - ture for pre - sent re - wards,

Small as a spark from the fire of cre - a - tion,
Plen - ty for all, if we learn how to share it,
Now we pol - lute it, in cyn - i - cal si - lence:
Care - less of life and con - temp - tuous of beau - ty:

Cra - dle of life and the home of our race.
Rich - es un - dreamed of to fath - om and find.
Poi - son the foun - tain of life at its source.
Bid us re - mem - ber, the Earth is the Lord's!

F♯ on last stanza only.

Text: F. Pratt Green, 1903 - ; alt.; from *Sixteen Stewardship Hymns of the Environment*, copyright 1973 by the Hymn Society of America. Used by permission.
Tune: Austin C. Lovelace, 1919 - ; copyright 1974 Augsburg Publishing House. Used by permission.

Brothers, Sisters, Let Us Gladly

403

D. and C. 4:1
Romans 12:1

GENEVA 8.7.8.7.D.
Alternate tune: HYMN TO JOY (20)

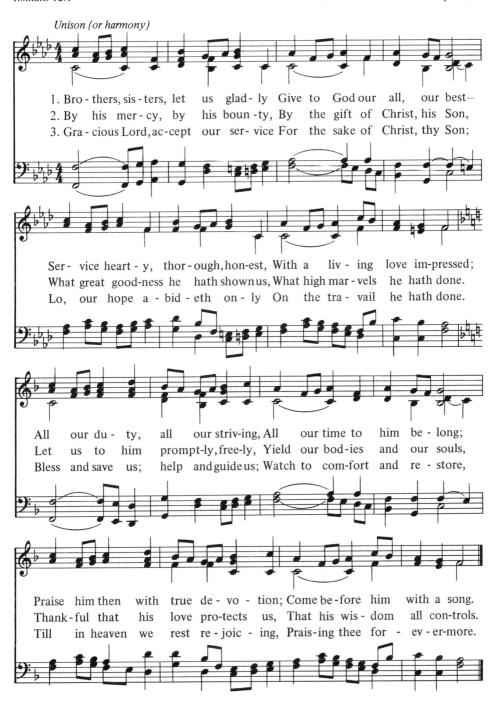

1. Bro-thers, sis-ters, let us glad-ly Give to God our all, our best—
2. By his mer-cy, by his boun-ty, By the gift of Christ, his Son,
3. Gra-cious Lord, ac-cept our ser-vice For the sake of Christ, thy Son;

Ser-vice heart-y, thor-ough, hon-est, With a liv-ing love im-pressed;
What great good-ness he hath shown us, What high mar-vels he hath done.
Lo, our hope a-bid-eth on-ly On the tra-vail he hath done.

All our du-ty, all our striv-ing, All our time to him be-long;
Let us to him prompt-ly, free-ly, Yield our bod-ies and our souls,
Bless and save us; help and guide us; Watch to com-fort and re-store,

Praise him then with true de-vo-tion; Come be-fore him with a song.
Thank-ful that his love pro-tects us, That his wis-dom all con-trols.
Till in heaven we rest re-joic-ing, Prais-ing thee for-ev-er-more.

Text: Henry Bateman, 1802-1872, alt.
Tune: George Henry Day, 1883-1966. Copyright 1942 by the Church Pension Fund. Used by permission.

404

I Would Be True

Philippians 4:8
I Timothy 4:12

PEEK 11.10.11.10.10.

1. I would be true, for there are those who trust me; I would be
2. I would be friend of all, the foe, the friend-less; I would be
3. I would be prayer-ful through each bus-y mo-ment; I would be

pure, for there are those who care; I would be strong, for
giv-ing, and for-get the gift; I would be hum-ble,
con-stant-ly in touch with God; I would be tuned to

there is much to suf-fer; I would be brave, for there is
for I know my weak-ness; I would look up and laugh and
hear his slight-est whis-per; I would have faith to keep the

much to dare; I would be brave, for there is much to dare.
love and lift; I would look up and laugh and love and lift.
path Christ trod; I would have faith to keep the path Christ trod.

Text: Howard Arnold Walter, 1883-1918.
Tune: Joseph Yates Peek, 1843-1911.

As Saints of Old Their Firstfruits Brought 405

D. and C. 46:9
Ephesians 4:1-6

NORSE AIR (No Other Plea, or Landas) C.M.D.
See 357 for a higher setting.

1. As saints of old their first-fruits brought Of or-chard, flock, and field
2. A world in need now sum-mons us To la-bor, love, and give;
3. In gra-ti-tude and hum-ble trust We bring our best to-day,

To God, the giv-er of all good, The source of boun-teous yield;
To make our life a sa-cri-fice That oth-er souls may live;
To serve your cause and share your love With all a-long life's way.

So we to-day first-fruits would bring, The wealth of this good land,
The church of Christ is call-ing us To make the dream come true:
O God, who gave your-self to us In Christ, your lov-ing Son,

Of farm and mar-ket, shop and home, Of mind and heart and hand.
A world re-deemed by Christ-like love, All life in Christ made new.
Teach us to give our-selves each day Un-til life's work is done. A-men.

Text: Frank von Christierson, 1900 - ; alt.; from *Ten New Stewardship Hymns.* Copyright 1961 The Hymn Society
of America. Used by permission.
Tune: Norse Folk Melody; arr. William J. Kirkpatrick, 1838-1921.

406 God, the Source of Light and Beauty

D. and C. 90:1a-e
I John 1:1-3

IN BABILONE 8.7.8.7.D.

1. God, the source of light and beau-ty, Grant re-sponse in sense and sight;
2. Great Mu-si-cian of the thun-der, Build-er of the moun-tain range,
3. Au-thor of cre-a-tion's be-ing, Thou hast shared our pain and loss;

Stir our minds to fol-low du-ty; Rouse our souls from earth-born night;
Paint-er of the sun-set's splen-dor, Plan-ner of the sea-son's change,
Through Christ's gal-lant life of serv-ice Shines the ra-diance of the cross.

Give us through our cloud-ed vi-sion Clear-er knowl-edge of thy will,
Help us fill our lives with beau-ty; Still the roar of guns and strife;
God, the source of light and beau-ty, Faith as-sures thy reign a-bove.

Till thine un-de-feat-ed pur-pose Through our lives thou shalt ful-fill.
Build thy king-dom of the fu-ture Here with-in our dai-ly life.
Here on earth we need thy pres-ence; Teach us how to walk in love. A-men.

Text: S. Ralph Harlow, 1885-1972.
Tune: Dutch Traditional Melody.

Yesu, Yesu, Fill Us with Your Love

407

Matthew 20:26-28
Luke 10:37-38

CHEREPONI 7.7.9. with refrain

Refrain

Ye - su,*   Ye - su,   Fill us with your love.
Ye - su   your love.
Ye - su

Show us how to serve the neigh - bors we have from you.
to serve   we have from you.

Stanza

1. Kneels at the feet of His friends, Si - lent - ly wash - es their
2. Neigh-bors are rich folk and poor; Neigh-bors are black, brown and
3. These are the ones we should serve; These are the ones we should
4. Lov - ing puts us on our knees, Serv - ing as though we are

feet, Mas - ter who acts as a slave to them.
white; Neigh-bors are near - by and far a - way.
love. All these are neigh - bors to us and you.
slaves; This is the way we should live with you.

* "Ye-su" is pronounced "Yā-soo."

408 Take My Life and Let It Be

Romans 12:8
II Nephi 14:12

HOLLINGSIDE 7.7.7.7.D.
Alternate tune: HENDON (4)*

1. Take my life and let it be Con - se - crat - ed, Lord, to thee;
2. Take my sil - ver and my gold; Naught of thine would I with - hold;

Take my mo -ments and my days; Let them flow in cease - less praise.
Take my heart, my mind, my will; Let them be thy serv - ants still.

Take my hands, my feet, my love; At thine im - pulse let them move;
Take my love; my Lord, I pour At thy feet its treas - ure store;

Take my voice and let me sing Al - ways, on - ly, for my King.
Take my - self, and I will be Ev - er, on - ly, all for thee. A - men.

* With Alternate Tune *HENDON*, divide into 4 stanzas, repeating last line of each stanza.

Text: Frances Ridley Havergal, 1836-1879; alt. by Alice Edwards, 1899-1973.
Tune: John B. Dykes, 1823-1876.

Touch Me, Lord, with Thy Spirit Eternal 409

John 17:3
D. and C. 16:4b, c

RUSSIAN MELODY 10.9.10.9.9.

1. Touch me, Lord, with thy Spir - it e - ter - nal;
2. Teach me, Lord, to walk hum - bly be - fore thee;
3. Fill me, Lord, with thine in - fi - nite pow - er;

Stir my soul to re - spond to thy call. Take my
May I has - ten thy will to o - bey. Make me
Make me firm, make me pure, make me whole. With thy

love, for I of - fer it free - ly; Hear my prayer as I
wise to see clear - ly thy pur - pose; Keep me true to my
Spir - it to strength - en and guide me, I shall serve thee with

thank thee for all. Hear my prayer as I thank thee for all.
call - ing, I pray. Keep me true to my call - ing, I pray.
all of my soul. I shall serve thee with all of my soul.

Text: R. Romanov or P. Rogozin; adapted from the Russian by Don C. Rawson, 1932 - ; alt.; adaptation copyright
1979 by Zionic Research Institute, Inc. All rights reserved. Used by permission.
Tune: Russian Melody arr. by Alexander Efimov.

410

Master, Speak! Thy Servant Heareth

Isaiah 6:8
I Samuel 3:10

CARTER 8.7.8.7.

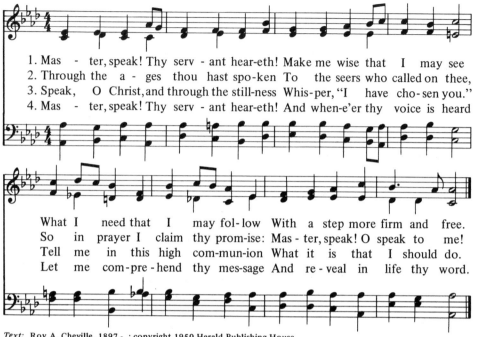

1. Mas - ter, speak! Thy serv - ant hear-eth! Make me wise that I may see
2. Through the a - ges thou hast spo-ken To the seers who called on thee,
3. Speak, O Christ, and through the still-ness Whis-per, "I have cho-sen you."
4. Mas - ter, speak! Thy serv - ant hear-eth! And when-e'er thy voice is heard

What I need that I may fol-low With a step more firm and free.
So in prayer I claim thy prom-ise: Mas - ter, speak! O speak to me!
Tell me in this high com-mun-ion What it is that I should do.
Let me com-pre - hend thy mes-sage And re - veal in life thy word.

Text: Roy A. Cheville, 1897 - ; copyright 1950 Herald Publishing House.
Tune: Edmund S. Carter, 1845-1923.

411

More Love to Thee, O Christ

Ephesians 3:19
II Nephi 13:29, 30

MORE LOVE TO THEE 6.4.6.4.6.6.4.4.

1. More love to thee, O Christ, More love to thee! Hear thou the
2. Once earth - ly joy I craved, Sought peace and rest; Now thee a -
3. Let sor - row not de - stroy, Nor grief and pain; Sweet are thy

prayer I make On bend-ed knee; This is my ear - nest plea,
lone I seek, Give what is best. This all my prayer shall be,
mes - sen-gers, Sweet their re - frain, When they can sing with me,

More love, O Christ, to thee, More love to thee, More love to thee.

Text: Elizabeth P. Prentiss, 1818-1878.
Tune: William H. Doane, 1832-1915.

Lord, Speak to Me 412

I Corinthians 2:12, 13
D. and C. 10:5

CANONBURY L.M.

1. Lord, speak to me that I may speak In liv - ing
2. O teach me, Lord, that I may teach The pre - cious
3. O fill me with thy full - ness, Lord, Un - til my
4. O use me, Lord, use e - ven me, Just as thou

ech - oes of thy tone; As thou hast sought, so
things thou dost im - part, And wing my words that
ver - y heart o'er - flow In kin - dling thought and
wilt, and when and where, Un - til thy bless - ed

let me seek Thine err - ing chil - dren lost and lone.
they may reach The hid - den depths of man - y a heart.
glow - ing word, Thy love to tell, thy praise to show.
face I see, Thy rest, thy joy, thy glo - ry share. A-men.

Text: Frances R. Havergal, 1836-1879.
Tune: Robert Schumann, 1810-1856.

413 Grant Us, Lord, the Grace of Giving

II Corinthians 9:7, 8
Matthew 5:18 (16)

STUTTGART 8.7.8.7.

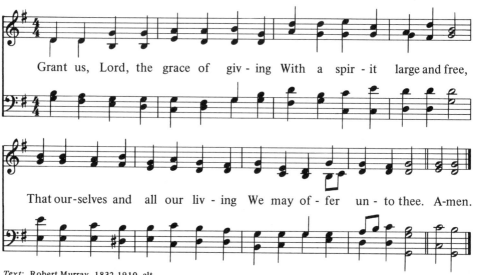

Grant us, Lord, the grace of giv-ing With a spir-it large and free,

That our-selves and all our liv-ing We may of-fer un-to thee. A-men.

Text: Robert Murray, 1832-1910, alt.
Tune: Christian F. Witt, 1660-1716, *Psalmodia Sacra*, 1715; adapt. by Henry J. Gauntlett, 1805-1876.

414 Beloved Community of God

Romans 12:1, 9-18
Ephesians 2:19-22

ST. CRISPIN L.M.

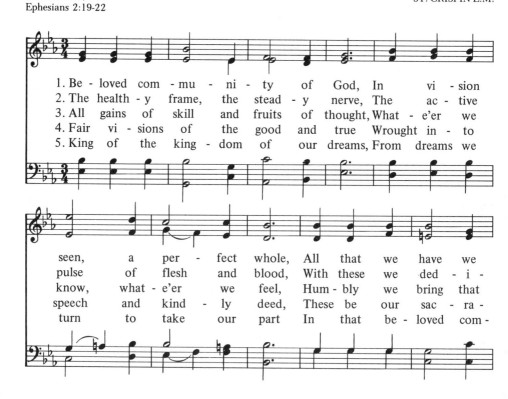

1. Be - loved com - mu - ni - ty of God, In vi - sion
2. The health - y frame, the stead - y nerve, The ac - tive
3. All gains of skill and fruits of thought, What - e'er we
4. Fair vi - sions of the good and true Wrought in - to
5. King of the king - dom of our dreams, From dreams we

seen, a per - fect whole, All that we have we
pulse of flesh and blood, With these we ded - i -
know, what - e'er we feel, Hum - bly we bring that
speech and kind - ly deed, These be our sac - ra -
turn to take our part In that be - loved com -

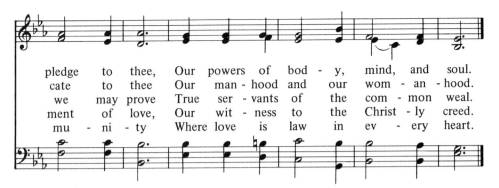

pledge to thee, Our powers of bod - y, mind, and soul.
cate to thee Our man - hood and our wom - an - hood.
we may prove True ser - vants of the com - mon weal.
ment of love, Our wit - ness to the Christ - ly creed.
mu - ni - ty Where love is law in ev - ery heart.

Text: Ernest Dodgshun, 1876-1944.
Tune: George J. Elvey, 1816-1893, alt.

Help Us Express Your Love 415

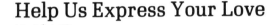

Mosiah 1:49
Romans 12:9, 10

BROOKFIELD L.M.

1. Help us ex - press your love, O Lord— Com - mit - ted
2. There is no sea - son when we dare With - hold our
3. The grace of God can flood the heart, Give love its

to one world in thee! A - bun - dant gifts en - hance our
love from hu - man - kind. Em - brac - ing earth's sup - port - ing
full - ness and its glow: Our un - con - fined and free de -

lives; Oh, free them for hu - man - i - ty!
strength, We match what - ev - er needs we find.
light Springs forth im - pelled by na - ture's flow. A - men.

Text: Cleo Hanthorne Moon, 1904 - ; copyright 1980 Reorganized Church of Jesus Christ of Latter Day Saints.
Tune: Thomas B. Southgate, 1814-1868.

416 May We Who Know the Joyful Sound

I Timothy 1:5
II Nephi 14:4-6

ST. MAGNUS C.M.

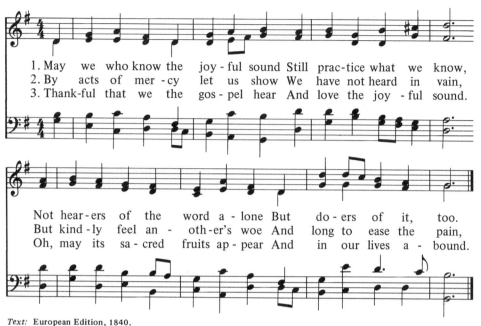

1. May we who know the joy-ful sound Still prac-tice what we know,
2. By acts of mer-cy let us show We have not heard in vain,
3. Thank-ful that we the gos-pel hear And love the joy-ful sound.

Not hear-ers of the word a-lone But do-ers of it, too.
But kind-ly feel an-oth-er's woe And long to ease the pain,
Oh, may its sa-cred fruits ap-pear And in our lives a-bound.

Text: European Edition, 1840.
Tune: Jeremiah Clark, c. 1670-1707.

417 From Isles and Continents Afar

Mosiah 1:46-49
D. and C. 4:1

DEDICARE L.M.
Alternate hymn: 418

1. From isles and con-ti-nents a-far, O'er moun-tains
2. In bus-y marts, in cit-y crowds, In qui-et
3. It is not mine to choose, O Lord, My place of
4. In strength di-vine I'll speak thy word, The bat-tle

and the storm-y sea, Of man-y rac-es,
of the coun-try-side, In hum-ble homes, in
ser-vice, nor the hour; Wher-e'er thy voice shall
join, or wait on thee; I'll go or stay, nor

man - y climes, Thy chil - dren, Lord, now call to me.
courts of kings, They wait, all those for whom Christ died.
bid me go, I shall go glad - ly, in thy power.
count the cost, Thy peo - ple serve, wher - e'er they be.

Text: Evan A. Fry, 1902-1959; alt. Copyright 1956 Herald Publishing House.
Tune: Franklyn S. Weddle, 1905 - ; harm. Evan A. Fry, 1902-1959. Copyright 1956 Herald Publishing House.

From Isles and Continents Afar 418

Mosiah 1:46-49
D. and C. 4:1

BELSIZE SQUARE L.M.
Alternate hymn: 417

1. From isles and con - ti - nents a - far, O'er moun-tains
2. In bus - y marts, in cit - y crowds, In qui - et
3. It is not mine to choose, O Lord, My place of
4. In strength di - vine I'll speak thy word, The bat - tle

and the storm - y sea, Of man - y rac - es,
of the coun - try - side, In hum - ble homes, in
ser - vice, nor the hour; Wher - e'er thy voice shall
join, or wait on thee; I'll go or stay, nor

man - y climes, Thy chil - dren, Lord, now call to me.
courts of kings, They wait, all those for whom Christ died.
bid me go, I shall go glad - ly, in thy power.
count the cost, Thy peo - ple serve, wher - e'er they be.

Text: Evan A. Fry, 1902-1959; alt. Copyright 1956 Herald Publishing House.
Tune: Louita Clothier, 1936 - .

419

God of Grace and God of Glory

I Corinthians 15:57, 58
Ephesians 6:10-17

CWM RHONDDA 8.7.8.7.8.7.7.

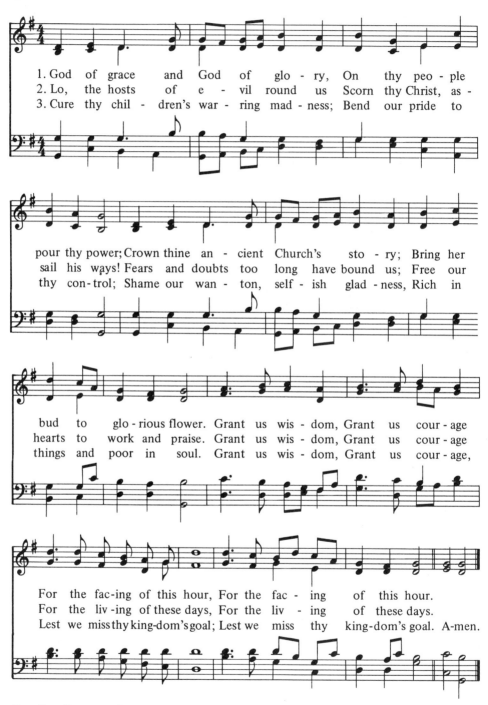

1. God of grace and God of glo - ry, On thy peo - ple
2. Lo, the hosts of e - vil round us Scorn thy Christ, as -
3. Cure thy chil - dren's war - ring mad - ness; Bend our pride to

pour thy power; Crown thine an - cient Church's sto - ry; Bring her
sail his ways! Fears and doubts too long have bound us; Free our
thy con - trol; Shame our wan - ton, self - ish glad - ness, Rich in

bud to glo - rious flower. Grant us wis - dom, Grant us cour - age
hearts to work and praise. Grant us wis - dom, Grant us cour - age
things and poor in soul. Grant us wis - dom, Grant us cour - age,

For the fac-ing of this hour, For the fac - ing of this hour.
For the liv -ing of these days, For the liv - ing of these days.
Lest we miss thy king-dom's goal; Lest we miss thy king-dom's goal. A-men.

Text: Harry Emerson Fosdick, 1878-1969. Used by permission of Elinor Fosdick Downs.
Tune: John Hughes, 1873-1932. Used by permission of Snell and Sons Ltd.

Your Cause Be Mine, Great Lord Divine

420

Philippians 2:5-12
D. and C. 10:2

RICHMOND BEACH 8.7.8.7.8.8.7.

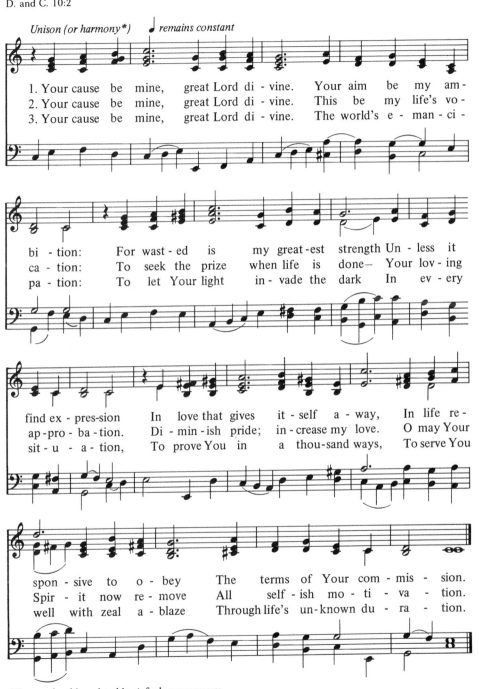

Unison (or harmony*)   ♩ remains constant

1. Your cause be mine, great Lord di - vine. Your aim be my am-
bi - tion: For wast - ed is my great-est strength Un - less it
find ex - pres-sion In love that gives it - self a - way, In life re-
spon - sive to o - bey The terms of Your com - mis - sion.

2. Your cause be mine, great Lord di - vine. This be my life's vo-
ca - tion: To seek the prize when life is done— Your lov - ing
ap - pro - ba - tion. Di - min - ish pride; in - crease my love. O may Your
Spir - it now re - move All self - ish mo - ti - va - tion.

3. Your cause be mine, great Lord di - vine. The world's e - man - ci-
pa - tion: To let Your light in - vade the dark In ev - ery
sit - u - a - tion, To prove You in a thou-sand ways, To serve You
well with zeal a - blaze Through life's un-known du - ra - tion.

*Tenors should read treble clef when necessary.

Text: Bryan Jeffery Leech, 1931 - .
Tune: A. Royce Eckhardt, 1937 - .

421
Just as I Am, Thine Own to Be

I Corinthians 6:19, 20
D. and C. 132:3, 4

JUST AS I AM 8.8.8.6.

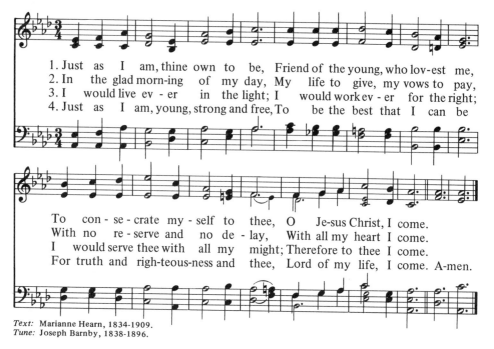

1. Just as I am, thine own to be, Friend of the young, who lov-est me,
2. In the glad morn-ing of my day, My life to give, my vows to pay,
3. I would live ev-er in the light; I would work ev-er for the right;
4. Just as I am, young, strong and free, To be the best that I can be

To con-se-crate my-self to thee, O Je-sus Christ, I come.
With no re-serve and no de-lay, With all my heart I come.
I would serve thee with all my might; Therefore to thee I come.
For truth and righ-teous-ness and thee, Lord of my life, I come. A-men.

Text: Marianne Hearn, 1834-1909.
Tune: Joseph Barnby, 1838-1896.

422
O Jesus, Master, When Today

I John 4:21
Isaiah 41:6

HEBRON L.M.

1. O Je-sus, Mas-ter, when to-day I meet a-long
2. To cheer them in their on-ward way Till eve-ning ends
3. Grant, too, that they my need may know As side by side
4. Then give our hands a touch di-vine And to our voic-

the crowd-ed way My bur-dened neigh-bors, mine and thine,
the var-ied day, To kin-dle so a grow-ing light
we on-ward go, An e-qual need of kind-ly thought
es tones like thine As side by side we on-ward go,

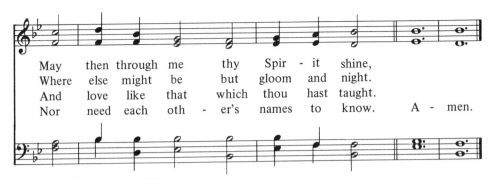

May then through me thy Spir - it shine,
Where else might be but gloom and night.
And love like that which thou hast taught.
Nor need each oth - er's names to know. A - men.

Text: Charles S. Newhall, 1842-1935.
Tune: Lowell Mason, 1792-1872.

The Bread That Giveth Strength 423

LIVORNO 10.10.10.10

Mosiah 2:22-24, 28
Galatians 6:7-10

1. The bread that giv - eth strength I want to give, The wa - ter
2. I want to give the oil of joy for tears, The faith to
3. I want to give good meas - ure, run-ning o'er, And in - to
4. I want to give to oth - ers hope and faith; I want to

pure that bids the thirst - y live; I want to help the faint - ing
con - quer crowd-ing doubts and fears; Beau - ty for ash - es may I
an - gry hearts I want to pour The an - swer soft that turn - eth
do all that the Mas - ter saith; I want to live a - right from

day by day;
give al - way: I'm sure I shall not pass a - gain this way.
wrath a - way:
day to day:

Text: W. R. Fitch.
Tune: Arthur S. Sullivan, 1842-1900.

424 Send Me Forth, O Blessed Master

Isaiah 6:8
Luke 10:2

MASTER, USE ME 15.11.15.12. with refrain

1. Send me forth, O bless - ed Mas - ter! There are
2. There are lives that may be bright - ened by a
3. There is work with - in the vine - yard; there is

souls in sor - row bowed; Send me forth to homes of
word of hope and cheer; There are souls with whom life's
ser - vice to be done; There's a mes - sage of sal -

want and homes of care, And with joy I will o -
bless - ings I should share; There are hearts that may be
va - tion to de - clare; In - to hearts that know not

bey the call, and in thy bless - ed name I will
light - ened of the bur - dens which they bear; Let me
Je - sus I would speak the sav - ing Word; Let me

take the bless - ed light of the gos - pel there.
take the bless - ed hope of the gos - pel there.
take the bless - ed joy of the gos - pel there.

Refrain

Call me forth to ac - tive ser - vice,
Call me forth, call me forth, to ac - tive ser - vice, call me forth,

And my prompt re - sponse shall be, "Here am I, send me!"

I am read - y to re - port for or - ders, Mas - ter, sum - mon

me; And I'll go on an - y er - rand of love for thee.

Text and Tune: Elisha A. Hoffman, 1839-1929.

425

God Send Us Saints

Alma 12:4, 5
D. and C. 153:9

MELROSE L.M.

1. God send us saints whose aim 'twill be, Not to de-
2. God send us saints a - lert and quick His loft - y
3. God send us saints of stead - fast will, Pa - tient, cou-
4. God send us saints with hearts a - blaze, All truth to

fend some an - cient creed But to live out the
pre - cepts to trans - late Un - til the laws of
ra - geous, strong, and true, With vi - sion clear and
love, all wrong to hate; These are the pa - triots

laws of right In ev - ery thought and word and deed.
right be - come The laws and hab - its of the state.
mind e - quipped His will to learn, his work to do.
na - tions need; These are the bul - warks of the state.

Text: F. J. Gillman, 1866-1949, alt.
Tune: Frederick C. Maker, 1844-1927.

426

Spirit of Truth, of Life, of Power

John 4:25, 26 (23, 24)
Psalm 73:25, 26, 28

HESPERUS L.M.

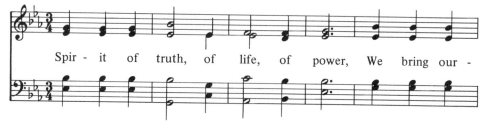

Spir - it of truth, of life, of power, We bring our-

selves as gifts to thee: Oh, bind our hearts this

sa - cred hour In faith and hope and char - i - ty.

Text: Horace Westwood, 1884-1956; copyright Beacon Press; used by permission.
Tune: Henry Baker, 1835-1910.

Lord, Here Amidst the Poor 427

Mosiah 2:43
I John 3:16-18

SOLOTHURN L.M.

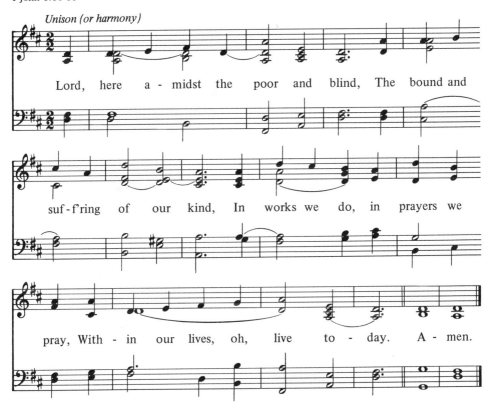

Unison (or harmony)

Lord, here a - midst the poor and blind, The bound and

suf - f'ring of our kind, In works we do, in prayers we

pray, With - in our lives, oh, live to - day. A - men.

Text: John Greenleaf Whittier, 1807-1892.
Tune: Swiss Traditional Melody; arr. Ralph Vaughan Williams, 1872-1958; used by permission of Oxford University Press.

428

Beneath the Cross of Jesus

Galatians 6:14
Hebrews 2:14-17

ST. CHRISTOPHER 7.6.8.6.8.6.8.6.

1. Be-neath the cross of Je-sus I fain would take my stand—
2. Up-on the cross of Je-sus Mine eye at times can see
3. I take, O cross, thy shad-ow For my a-bid-ing place.

The shad-ow of a might-y Rock With-in a wea-ry land;
The ver-y dy-ing form of One Who suf-fered there for me;
I ask no oth-er sun-shine than The sun-shine of his face;

A home with-in the wil-der-ness, A rest up-on the way,
And from my strick-en heart with tears Two won-ders I con-fess—
Con-tent to own no oth-er place, To know no gain nor loss,

From burn-ing of the noon-tide heat And bur-dens of the day.
The won-ders of re-deem-ing love, And my un-worth-i-ness.
My sin-ful self my on-ly shame, My glo-ry all, the cross.

Text: Elizabeth C. Clephane, 1830-1869.
Tune: Frederick C. Maker, 1844-1927.

O God, Send Heralds

429

Luke 4:18
D. and C. 151:9

WELWYN 11.10.11.10.
Alternate tune: CITY OF GOD (224)

1. O God, send her-alds who will nev-er fal-ter,
   Who dare to walk where Christ has set his feet,
   Who know the Church as bea-con and as al-tar
   Where hu-man need and your a-bun-dance meet.

2. Not to be served but on-ly to be serv-ing,
   To feed the hun-ger in the hu-man heart,
   To know that love which comes with-out de-serv-ing,
   That love which on-ly Je-sus can im-part.

3. Em-pires have come, have flour-ished and de-part-ed,
   But still your Church, as wit-ness to your way,
   Lives on in dark-ness, light of the true-heart-ed,
   And calls to ac-tion those whose feet would stay.

4. Send her-alds, then, in whom your heart re-joic-es;
   Send those who hear the call that sets us free,
   With ea-ger hearts and ju-bi-lat-ing voic-es
   Each mak-ing an-swer, "Here am I! Send me." A-men.

Text: Elisabeth Burrowes, 1883- ; alt.; from *Ten New Hymns on the Ministry*, copyright 1966 The Hymn Society of America, Wittenberg University, Springfield, OH 45501. Used by permission.
Tune: Alfred Scott-Gatty, 1847-1918.

430 All to Jesus I Surrender

Romans 6:8-14
Alma 18:14, 16, 17

HEAVENLY DOVE 8.7.8.7.

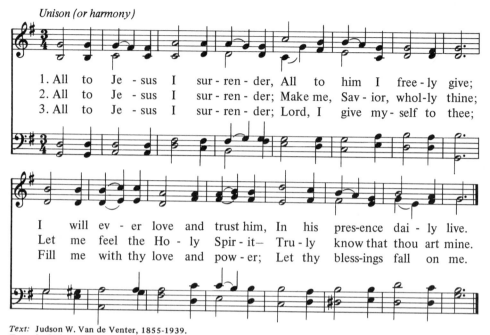

Unison (or harmony)

1. All to Je - sus I sur - ren - der, All to him I free - ly give;
2. All to Je - sus I sur - ren - der; Make me, Sav - ior, whol - ly thine;
3. All to Je - sus I sur - ren - der; Lord, I give my - self to thee;

I will ev - er love and trust him, In his pres - ence dai - ly live.
Let me feel the Ho - ly Spir - it— Tru - ly know that thou art mine.
Fill me with thy love and pow - er; Let thy bless-ings fall on me.

Text: Judson W. Van de Venter, 1855-1939.
Tune: Joel Blomquist, 1840-1930; harm. Rosalee Elser, 1925 - ; copyright 1980 Rosalee Elser; used by permission.

431 O May Thy Church Build Bridges

Ephesians 2:14, 18-22
II Corinthians 5:17-20

ST. CRISPIN L.M.

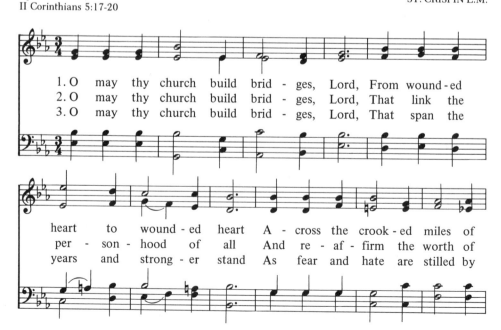

1. O may thy church build brid - ges, Lord, From wound - ed
2. O may thy church build brid - ges, Lord, That link the
3. O may thy church build brid - ges, Lord, That span the

heart to wound - ed heart A - cross the crook - ed miles of
per - son - hood of all And re - af - firm the worth of
years and strong - er stand As fear and hate are stilled by

pain That truth's dis-tor-tions still im-part.
each In spite of col-or, cult, or call.
love And Spir-it's pow-er lights the land. A-men.

Text: Evelyn Maples, 1919 - ; copyright 1980 Reorganized Church of Jesus Christ of Latter Day Saints.
Tune: George J. Elvey, 1816-1893.

If by Your Grace I Choose to Be 432

Ephesians 4:1-6
D. and C. 151:8a, 9

MENDON L.M.

1. If by Your grace I choose to be Re-flec-tion
2. If Spir-it's touch my gifts a-lign In keep-ing
3. E-ter-nal Par-ent, help me see The life-pro-

of Your Gift to me, Then sure-ly I must own my
with Your grand de-sign, Then I would all my days em-
claim-ing dig-ni-ty, The gift-ed-ness, the Spir-it

worth As part-ner in cre-at-ed earth.
ploy In shar-ing worth-af-firm-ing joy.
flame In all Your chil-dren, in Your name. A-men.

Text: Evelyn Maples, 1919 - ; copyright 1980 Reorganized Church of Jesus Christ of Latter Day Saints.
Tune: Traditional German Melody, arr. by Samuel Dyer, 1785-1835.

433

I Timothy 6:12
Jude 3

Faith of Our Fathers

ST. CATHERINE L.M. with refrain

1. Faith of our fa - thers, liv - ing still In spite of dun - geon, fire, and sword, Oh, how our hearts beat high with joy When - e'er we hear that glo - rious word! Faith of our fa - thers, ho - ly faith, We will be true to thee till death.

2. The mar-tyrs, chained in pris - ons dark, Were still in heart and con - science free; And blest would be their chil - dren's fate Though they, like them, should die for thee.

3. Faith of our fa - thers! We will love Both friend and foe in all our strife; Pro - claim thee, too, as love knows how, By sav - ing Word and faith - ful life.

Refrain

Text: Frederick W. Faber, 1814-1863; alt.
Tune: Henri F. Hemy, 1818-1888; refrain, James G. Walton, 1821-1905.

When God Created Human Life

434

D. and C. 68:4a-c
D. and C. 90:6d

ST. HYLDA L.M.
Alternate tune: HESPERUS (348)

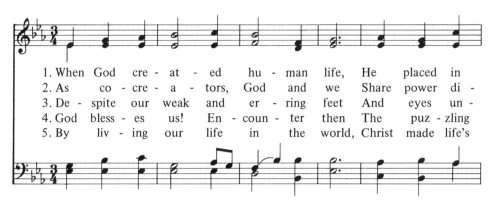

1. When God cre - at - ed hu - man life, He placed in
2. As co - cre - a - tors, God and we Share power di -
3. De - spite our weak and er - ring feet And eyes un -
4. God bless - es us! En - coun - ter then The puz - zling
5. By liv - ing our life in the world, Christ made life's

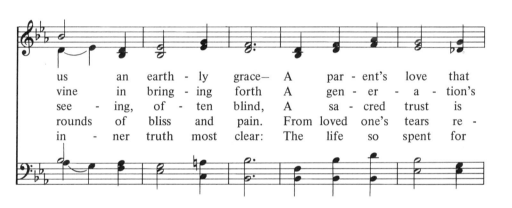

us an earth - ly grace— A par - ent's love that
vine in bring - ing forth A gen - er - a - tion's
see - ing, of - ten blind, A sa - cred trust is
rounds of bliss and pain. From loved one's tears re -
in - ner truth most clear: The life so spent for

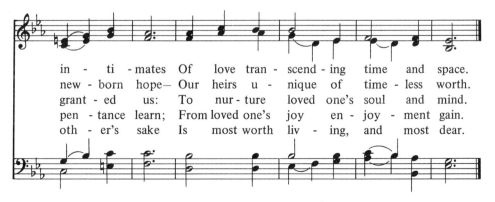

in - ti - mates Of love tran - scend - ing time and space.
new - born hope— Our heirs u - nique of time - less worth.
grant - ed us: To nur - ture loved one's soul and mind.
pen - tance learn; From loved one's joy en - joy - ment gain.
oth - er's sake Is most worth liv - ing, and most dear.

Text: Alan D. Tyree, 1929 - ; copyright 1980 Reorganized Church of Jesus Christ of Latter Day Saints.
Tune: William E. Butler, 1889-1967; copyright 1956 Herald Publishing House.

435 # O Lord of Light and Love and Power

Philippians 4:10-13
Acts 2:38, 39

BETHLEHEM (Seraph) C.M.D.

1. O Lord of light and love and power, How joy-ful life might be
2. 'Tis ne'er too late, while life shall last, A new life to be-gin;
3. Not for our-selves a-lone we plead, But for all faith-ful souls

If in thy serv-ice ev-ery hour We lived and moved with thee;
'Tis ne'er too late to leave the past And break with self and sin;
Who serve thy cause by word or deed, Whose names thy book en-rolls.

If we in all our zeal and might By thee were sanc-ti-fied
And we this day, both old and young, Would ear-nest-ly as-pire
Oh, speed thy work, vic-to-rious King, And give the work-ers might,

And ev-er found our chief de-light In work-ing at thy side!
For hearts to no-bler pur-pose strung, And pur-i-fied de-sire
That through the world thy truth may ring, And all may see thy light!

Text: Ella S. Armitage, 1841-1931, alt.
Tune: Gottfried W. Fink, 1783-1846.

Go Now Forth into the World

436

D. and C. 12:2
Matthew 20:26-28

EMERALD 7.6.7.6.7.7.7.7.7.

1. Go now forth in-to the world; Of your-selves be giv-ing.
2. Grant us wis-dom for the task; Give us broad-er vi-sion

Make dis-ci-ples of all lands; Tell them Christ is liv-ing.
Of the king-dom-build-ing plan And the Great Com-mis-sion.

Share the news that Christ makes whole Bat-tered lives and
We give praise for lives that feel God's great power, through

wea-ry souls— That his lov-ing grace up-holds All who
Christ made real. In all acts, may we re-veal Hearts a-

seek him— young and old, All who seek him— young and old.
live with mis-sion zeal, Hearts a-live with mis-sion zeal.

Text: Kenneth L. McLaughlin, 1951 - ; copyright 1980 Reorganized Church of Jesus Christ of Latter Day Saints.
Tune: Mark H. Forscutt, 1834-1903.

437

Look for the Beautiful

Philippians 4:8
D. and C. 81:4c

BELDEN 10.10.10.10.10.

1. Look for the beau-ti-ful, look for the true; Sun-shine and shad-ow are all a-round you. Look-ing at e-vil you grope in the night; Look-ing at Je-sus you walk in the light. Look for the beau-ti-ful, hon-or the right.

2. Think of the beau-ti-ful, think of the true; Thoughts like an av-a-lanche sweep o-ver you. Keep not the mul-ti-tude, sort them with care, Test-ing by pu-ri-ty, purg-ing by prayer. Think of the beau-ti-ful, think of the fair.

3. Talk of the beau-ti-ful, talk of the true; Tongues full of poi-son are whis-per-ing to you. An-swer them not with a tale-bear-ing word; On-ly in bless-ing the voice should be heard. Talk of the beau-ti-ful, talk of thy Lord.

4. Live for the beau-ti-ful, live for the true, Lift-ing the fall-en as Christ lift-ed you. Search for the jew-els im-bed-ded in sin; Bring them to Je-sus, his blood wash-es clean. Live for the beau-ti-ful, keep love with-in.

Text and Tune: Franklin E. Belden, 19th century.

Lord, Thy Church on Earth Is Seeking

438

Matthew 28:17-19 (18-20)
D. and C. 6:1, 2a, b

GENEVA 8.7.8.7.D.

Unison (or harmony)

1. Lord, thy church on earth is seek-ing Thy re-new-al from a-bove;
2. Free-dom give to those in bond-age; Lift the bur-dens caused by sin.
3. In the streets of ev-ery cit-y Where the bruised and lone-ly dwell,

Teach us all the art of speak-ing With the ac-cent of thy love.
Give new hope, new strength and cour-age; Grant re-lease from fears with-in:
We shall show the Sav-ior's pit-y; We shall of his mer-cy tell.

We would heed thy great com-mis-sion: "Go ye in-to ev-ery place—
Light for dark-ness, joy for sor-row, Love for ha-tred, peace for strife.
In all lands and with all rac-es We shall serve, and seek to bring

Preach, bap-tize, ful-fill my mis-sion; Serve with love and share my grace."
These and count-less bless-ings fol-low As the Spir-it gives new life.
All the world to ren-der prais-es, Christ, to thee, Re-deem-er, King.

Text: Hugh Sherlock, 1905 - ; alt.; used by permission of the author.
Tune: George Henry Day, 1883-1966; copyright 1942 by The Church Pension Fund. Used by permission.

439 Teach Me, My God and King

II Nephi 3:48
II Timothy 1:6, 7

CARLISLE S.M.

1. Teach me, my God and King, In all things thee to see; Teach
   me to be in ev - ery - thing All thou wouldst have me be.
2. In all I think or say, Lord, may I not of - fend. In
   all I do, be thou the way; In all be thou the end.
3. Each task I un - der - take, Though weak and mean to me, If
   un - der - tak - en for thy sake Draws strength and worth from thee.
4. Teach me, then, Lord, to bring To all that I may be, To
   all I do, my God and King, A con - scious - ness of thee. A-men.

Text: George Herbert, 1593-1633; alt. by Helen Harrington, 1909 - .
Tune: Charles Lockhart 1745-1815.

440 Teach Us, O Lord, True Thankfulness

Mark 10:42-45
D. and C. 6:4

SURSUM CORDA 10.10.10.10.

Unison (or harmony)

Teach us, O Lord, true thank - ful - ness di - vine That
gives as Christ gave, nev - er count - ing cost, That knows no bar - ri -

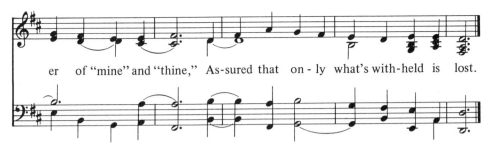

er of "mine" and "thine," As-sured that on - ly what's with-held is lost.

Text: William Watkins Reid, Sr., 1890 - ; copyright 1965 The Hymn Society of America; used by permission.
Tune: Alfred M. Smith, 1879-1971; copyright by composer. Used by permission of Mrs. Alfred M. Smith.

In Nature's Voice We Hear You, Lord 441

Mosiah 8:47-52
Romans 14:9, 17

ASHLAND L.M.

1. In Na - ture's voice we hear you, Lord. In rush - ing
2. In homes so rich or homes so poor, The cit - ies
3. Your voice we hear and an - swer, Lord; We'll ven - ture
4. New skills we'll learn, new arts we'll gain To help all

streams we hear you speak; In rum - bling clouds, in
large, the ham - lets small— Where - ev - er there is
forth to meet this need With hand and heart and
per - sons know their worth; With pur - pose strong, with

gen - tle rain, And in the tower - ing moun - tain peaks.
hu - man need We hear Your voice call out to all.
mind in - spired In thought and word and dai - ly deed.
faith re - newed To build Your king - dom here on earth.

Text: Mildred Jordan, 1918 - ; copyright 1980 Reorganized Church of Jesus Christ of Latter Day Saints.
Tune: Keith Landis, 1922 - ; harm. Jeffrey Rickard; alt.; copyright 1977 Praise Publications, Inc.; used by permission.

442

D. and C. 132:3, 4
Romans 6:6-11

Savior, Thy Dying Love

SOMETHING FOR JESUS 6.4.6.4.6.6.6.4.

1. Sav - ior, thy dy - ing love Thou gav - est me,
2. Give me a faith - ful heart, Like - ness to thee,
3. All that I am and have, Thy gifts so free,

Nor should I aught with - hold, Dear Lord, from thee;
That each de - part - ing day Hence - forth may see
Ev - er in joy or grief, My Lord, for thee;

In love my soul would bow, My heart ful - fill its vow,
Some work of love be - gun, Some deed of kind - ness done,
And when thy face I see, My ran - somed soul shall be

Some of - fering bring thee now, Some - thing for thee.
Some wan - derer sought and won, Some - thing for thee.
Through all e - ter - ni - ty Some - thing for thee. A - men.

Text: S. Dryden Phelps, 1816-1895.
Tune: Robert Lowry, 1826-1899.

Jesus' Hands Were Kind Hands

443

Matthew 10:34, 35, 38 (39, 40, 42)
II Peter 1:5-8

NOËL NOUVELET 6.5.6.5.D

1. Je - sus' hands were kind hands, Do - ing good to all,
2. Take my hands, Lord Je - sus; Let them work for you,

Heal - ing pain and sick - ness, Bless - ing chil - dren small,
Make them strong and gen - tle, Kind in all I do.

Wash - ing tired feet, and Lift - ing those who fall:
Touch me with your Spir - it Till I'm gen - tle, too,

Je - sus' hands were kind hands, Do - ing good to all.
Till my hands are kind hands, Quick to work for you.

Text: Margaret B. Cropper, 1886-1980; alt.; used by permission of Anne Hopkinson, Executor of the Margaret B. Cropper Estate.
Tune: Traditional French Carol.

444

Great God, Our Source

Matthew 5:15, 16
Mark 8:36-38 (34, 35)

GOD OUR SOURCE 8.8.8.D.

Unison (or harmony) ♩ *remains constant*

1. Great God, our source and Lord of space, O Force of all by
2. Great God of fire, in - car - nate flame, Through Christ in whom your
3. Lord of the at - om, we praise your might, Ex - pressed in ter - ri -

whose sheer power The pri - mal fires that flared and raged Were
love has burned And burns the way for our dark pace On
fy - ing light; Be - fore us rise the flames as pyres, Or

struck, blazed on, and still are made: Oh, save us, Lord, at
cos - mic routes with - in us turned: Lead us be - yond a
bursts of love— they blind our sight. Help us, our Lord, oh,

this fierce hour From threat-'ning fires that we have laid.
tom - ic night; Guide, Lord, in hope our bro - ken race.
help us see New forms of peace through suf - f'ring fires. A-men.

Text: George Utech, 1931 - ; alt.; copyright 1963 by the author. Used by permission.
Tune: Gerhard M. Cartford, 1923 - ; copyright 1963 by the composer. Used by permission.

When the Church of Jesus

445

Micah 6:6-8
Mosiah 2:28, 29, 32, 36

KING'S WESTON 6.5.6.5.D.
Alternate tune: BJORKLUND MAJOR (377)

Unison (or harmony)

1. When the church of Je - sus Shuts its out - er door
2. If our hearts are lift - ed Where de - vo - tion soars
3. Lest the gifts we of - fer—Mon - ey, tal - ents, time—

Lest the roar of traf - fic Drown the voice of prayer:
High a - bove this hun - gry, Suf - f'ring world of ours:
Serve to salve our con - science To our se - cret shame:

May our prayers, Lord, make us E - ven more a - ware
Lest our hymns should drug us To for - get its needs,
Lord, re - prove, in - spire us By the way you give;

That the world we ban - ish is our Chris - tian care.
Forge our Chris - tian wor - ship in - to Chris - tian deeds.
Teach us, dy - ing Sa - vior, how true Chris - tians live.

Text: F. Pratt Green, 1903 - ; alt.; used by permission of Oxford University Press.
Tune: Ralph Vaughan Williams, 1872-1958. From *Enlarged Songs of Praise* by permission of Oxford University Press.

446

Lord God of Hosts

Ephesians 1:3, 9, 10
D. and C. 2:1

WELWYN 11.10.11.10.

1. Lord God of Hosts, whose pur-pose, nev-er swerv-ing,
2. Strong Son of God, whose work was his that sent thee,
3. Lord God, whose grace has called us to thy serv-ice,

Leads toward the day of Je-sus Christ, thy Son,
One with the Fa-ther, thought and deed and word,
How good thy thoughts toward us, how great their sum!

Grant us to march a-mong thy faith-ful le-gions,
One make us all, true com-rades in thy serv-ice,
We work with thee, we go where thou wilt lead us,

Armed with thy cour-age, till the world is won.
And make us one in thee with God, the Lord.
Un-til in all the earth thy king-dom come. A-men.

Text: Shepherd Knapp, 1873-1946.
Tune: Alfred Scott-Gatty, 1847-1918.

Would You Bless Our Homes

447

Ephesians 3:14-19
Luke 2:51, 52

ALL THE WAY 8.7.8.7.D.
Alternate tune: NETTLETON (31)

1. Would you bless our homes and fam-ilies, Lord of life, who calls us here.
2. When our way is un-de-mand-ing, Let us use the time that's ours
3. From the homes in which we're nur-tured, With the love that shapes us there,

In our world of stress and ten-sion Teach us love that con-quers fear.
To de-light in sim-ple pleas-ures, Shar-ing joys in gen-tle hours.
Teach us, Lord, to claim as fam-ily Ev-ery-one whose life we share.

Help us learn to love each oth-er With a love that con-stant stays;
When our way is anx-ious walk-ing And a heav-y path we plod,
And through all that life may of-fer May we in your love re-main.

Teach us when we face our trou-bles Love's ex-pressed in man-y ways.
Teach us trust in one an-oth-er And in you, our gra-cious God.
May the love we share in fam-ilies Be a-live to praise your name.

Text: Walter Farquharson, 1936 - ; copyright 1977 The Frederick Harris Music Company; used by permission.
Tune: Robert Lowry, 1826-1899; alt. 1980 Rosalee Elser, 1925 - .

448   In Christ There Is No East or West

D. and C. 85:41   McKEE C.M.
Romans 8:35-39   *Alternate hymn: 449*

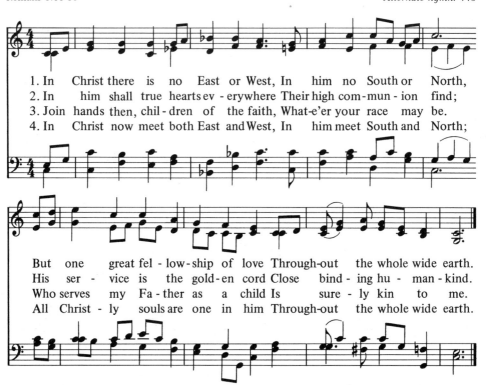

1. In Christ there is no East or West, In him no South or North,
2. In him shall true hearts ev - erywhere Their high com-mun-ion find;
3. Join hands then, chil-dren of the faith, What-e'er your race may be.
4. In Christ now meet both East and West, In him meet South and North;

But one great fel-low-ship of love Through-out the whole wide earth.
His ser - vice is the gold-en cord Close bind - ing hu - man-kind.
Who serves my Fa-ther as a child Is sure - ly kin to me.
All Christ - ly souls are one in him Through-out the whole wide earth.

Text: John Oxenham, 1852-1941; alt.; used by permission of Desmond Dunkerley.
Tune: American Folk Melody, adapted by Harry T. Burleigh, 1866-1949; copyright 1940 by Harry T. Burleigh. Used by cooperation of the Executor of the Estate of Harry T. Burleigh.

449   In Christ There Is No East or West

Colossians 3:11   ST. PETER C.M.
IV Nephi 1:17, 19   See 330 for a lower setting
         Alternate hymn: 448

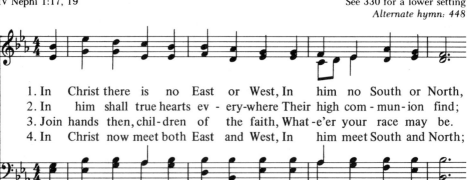

1. In Christ there is no East or West, In him no South or North,
2. In him shall true hearts ev - ery-where Their high com - mun-ion find;
3. Join hands then, chil-dren of the faith, What -e'er your race may be.
4. In Christ now meet both East and West, In him meet South and North;

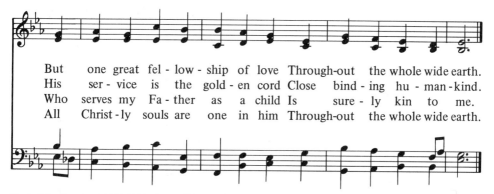

But one great fel-low-ship of love Through-out the whole wide earth.
His ser-vice is the gold-en cord Close bind-ing hu-man-kind.
Who serves my Fa-ther as a child Is sure-ly kin to me.
All Christ-ly souls are one in him Through-out the whole wide earth.

Text: John Oxenham, 1852-1941; alt.; used by permission of Desmond Dunkerley.
Tune: Alexander R. Reinagle, 1799-1877.

Unto the Calmly Gathered Thought   450

Micah 6:6-8
Alma 19:78

SOLOTHURN L.M.

Unison (or harmony)

1. Un - to the calm - ly gath - ered thought The in - ner -
2. That to be saved is on - ly this, Sal - va - tion
3. That wor - ship's deep - er mean - ing lies In mer - cy,

most of truth is taught, The mys - ter-y, dim - ly
from our self - ish - ness; From sin it - self, and
and not sac - ri - fice, Not proud hu - mil - i -

un - der - stood, That love of God is love of good;
not the pain That warns us of its chaf - ing chain;
ties of sense, But love's un - forced o - be - di - ence.

Text: John Greenleaf Whittier, 1807-1892.
Tune: Swiss Traditional Melody; arr. Ralph VaughanWilliams, 1872-1958; used by permission of Oxford University Press.

451

O Church of God, Arise

Ephesians 4:1-6
D. and C. 142:5

DENBY 6.6.6.6.D.

1. O Church of God, a-rise And take thy lamp of love,
2. Re-buke the dev-il's mart; The souls in prison re-lease;
3. In ev-ery dark-est place Let ra-diant warmth be shed

The light that nev-er dies On earth, in heaven a-bove!
Bind up the bro-ken heart; Give joy and mirth and peace.
Till in each drear-y face The joy of God is read.

With wis-dom and with truth Keep quick and straight the flame,
What-ev-er things are fair, What-ev-er things are just,
Tell all the souls on earth, The great-est and the least,

The light of love and youth, To save a world of shame.
Go, make them free as air And plen-teous as the dust!
Love calls us from our birth To share God's gra-cious peace.

Text: Annie Matheson, 1853-1924, alt.
Tune: Charles J. Dale; from the *Lutheran Hymnal.*

For the Healing of the Nations

452

Matthew 9:41, 42 (35, 36)
I John 3:14, 16-18

NEW MALDEN 8.7.8.7.8.7.

Unison (or harmony)

1. For the heal-ing of the na-tions, Lord, we pray with
2. Lead us, Fa-ther, in-to free-dom; From de-spair your
3. All that kills a-bun-dant liv-ing, Let it from the

one ac-cord; For a just and e-qual shar-ing
world re-lease, That re-deemed from war and ha-tred,
earth be banned: Pride of sta-tus, race, or school-ing,

Of the things that earth af-fords. To a life of
Men may come and go in peace. Show us how through
Dog-mas keep-ing man from man. In our com-mon

love in ac-tion Help us rise and pledge our word.
care and good-ness Fear will die and hope in-crease.
quest for jus-tice May we hal-low life's brief span.

Text: Fred Kaan, 1929 - ; copyright © 1968 by Galliard Ltd. Sole U. S. agent: Galaxy Music Corp., N. Y. Used by permission.
Tune: David McCarthy, 1931 - ; copyright 1971 by the composer. Used by permission.

453   # Father, Hear the Prayer We Offer

Psalm 50:14, 15
Romans 4:17, 20, 21

SARDIS 8.7.8.7.

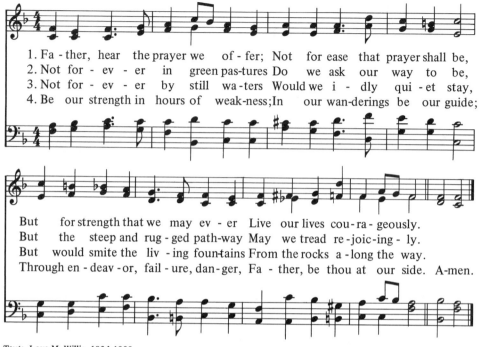

1. Fa - ther, hear the prayer we of - fer; Not for ease that prayer shall be,
2. Not for - ev - er in green pas-tures Do we ask our way to be,
3. Not for - ev - er by still wa-ters Would we i - dly qui - et stay,
4. Be our strength in hours of weak-ness; In our wan-derings be our guide;

But for strength that we may ev - er Live our lives cou - ra - geously.
But the steep and rug - ged path-way May we tread re - joic-ing - ly.
But would smite the liv - ing foun-tains From the rocks a - long the way.
Through en - deav - or, fail - ure, dan-ger, Fa - ther, be thou at our side. A-men.

Text: Love M. Willis, 1824-1908.
Tune: Arr. from Ludwig van Beethoven, 1770-1827.

454   # Open My Eyes, O Lord

Psalm 119:18
D. and C. 38:2

BREAD OF LIFE 6.4.6.4.D.

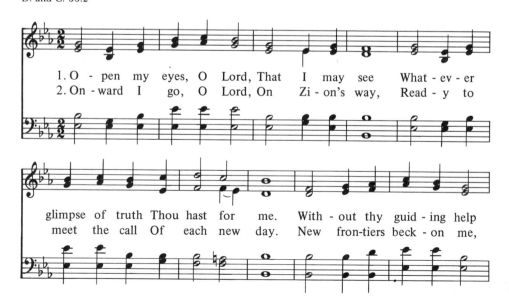

1. O - pen my eyes, O Lord, That I may see What - ev - er
2. On - ward I go, O Lord, On Zi - on's way, Read - y to

glimpse of truth Thou hast for me. With - out thy guid - ing help
meet the call Of each new day. New fron-tiers beck - on me,

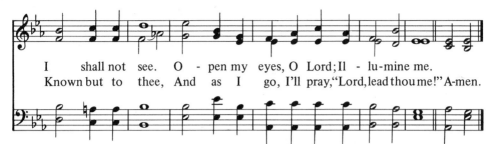

I shall not see. O - pen my eyes, O Lord; Il - lu-mine me.
Known but to thee, And as I go, I'll pray, "Lord, lead thou me!" A-men.

Text: Roy A. Cheville, 1897 - ; copyright 1950 Herald Publishing House.
Tune: William F Sherwin, 1826-1888.

O Lord, We Come in Gratitude 455

Psalm 30:1-4
Romans 12:1, 2

ST. MARGARET 8.8.8.8.8.6.

1. O Lord, we come in grat - i - tude For all the full and
2. O Lord, for - give our will - ful sins; For - give the sub - tle
3. O Lord, re - store, if this thy will, The health of bod - y,
4. In - spire a clear, en - dur - ing zeal, In all our ways with

boun-teous years. We bring our ser - vice, bring our hopes; We
sins of race. Thy bless - ing clear the coun - te - nance Where
mind, and soul. A cour - ier for thy cause re - store To
thee to stand, In life to serve, in death to yield, Rich

bring to thee our cares and fears; We bring our prayers to thee.
dwells thy love, and ra - di - ates A glow-ing love for thee.
ser - vice full and free and whole, In great-er love for thee.
in thy love and thy com-mand—This is our prayer to thee. A-men.

Text: Cleo Hanthorne Moon, 1904 - ; copyright 1956 Herald Publishing House.
Tune: Albert Peace, 1844-1912.

456

Lord of the Bronze-Green Prairies

D. and C. 150:7
Isaiah 52:7

ZOAN 7.6.7.6.D.

1. Lord of the bronze-green prai - ries, God of the pound-ing seas,
2. Give us clean hearts and val - iant, Firm wills to cher-ish all

Of shel-tered coves and ham - lets, Of or - chards, lakes and trees:
These gifts, so var - ied, splen - did. O hear us when we call

Your pulse beats in the cit - ies, Steel-ribbed and ris - ing high,
For self - con-trol and pa - tience, In - teg - ri - ty and power,

Your spir - it broods o'er moun-tains Whose stern peaks stab the sky.
That fu - ture gen - er - a - tions May know we served this hour. A-men.

Text: Grace Lane; from *The Hymn*, copyright 1972 The Hymn Society of America; used by permission.
Tune: William H. Havergal, 1793-1870; harm. Rosalee Elser, 1925 - . Copyright 1980 Rosalee Elser; used by permission.

My Lord, I Know That All My Life

457

Luke 12:29-35 (27-32)
Alma 3:58

MORNING SONG 8.6.8.6.8.6.

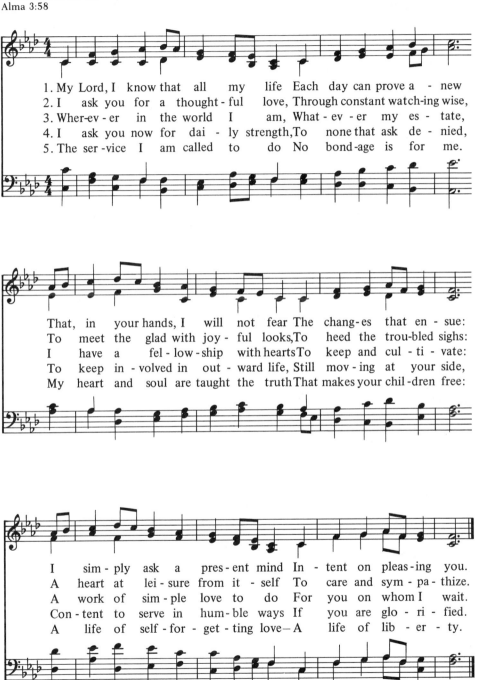

1. My Lord, I know that all my life Each day can prove a - new
2. I ask you for a thought - ful love, Through constant watch-ing wise,
3. Wher-ev - er in the world I am, What - ev - er my es - tate,
4. I ask you now for dai - ly strength, To none that ask de - nied,
5. The ser - vice I am called to do No bond-age is for me.

That, in your hands, I will not fear The chang-es that en - sue:
To meet the glad with joy - ful looks, To heed the trou-bled sighs:
I have a fel - low - ship with hearts To keep and cul - ti - vate:
To keep in - volved in out - ward life, Still mov - ing at your side,
My heart and soul are taught the truth That makes your chil-dren free:

I sim - ply ask a pres - ent mind In - tent on pleas-ing you.
A heart at lei - sure from it - self To care and sym - pa - thize.
A work of sim - ple love to do For you on whom I wait.
Con - tent to serve in hum - ble ways If you are glo - ri - fied.
A life of self - for - get - ting love— A life of lib - er - ty.

Text: Anna Laetitia Waring, 1820-1910, alt.
Tune: Wyeth's *Repository of Sacred Music, Part Second*, 1813; harm. Rosalee Elser, 1925 - ; copyright 1980 by
Rosalee Elser; used by permission.

458   Eternal Ruler of the Ceaseless Round

D. and C. 38:5a-c
Galatians 3:26-29

YORKSHIRE 10.10.10.D.

1. E - ter - nal Rul - er of the cease-less round Of cir-cling plan-ets sing-ing
2. We are of thee, the chil-dren of thy love, The fam -ily of thy well-be-
3. We would be one in ha -tred of all wrong,One in our love of all things

on their way, Guide of the na - tions from the night pro - found
lov - ed Son; De - scend, O Ho - ly Spir - it, like a dove
sweet and fair, One with the joy that break - eth in - to song,

In - to the glo - ry of the per - fect day, Rule in our hearts that
In - to our hearts, that we may be as one— As one with thee, to
One with the grief that trem-bleth in - to prayer, One in the power that

we may ev - er be Guid - ed and strength-ened and up-held by thee.
whom we ev - er tend; As one with him, our broth-er and our friend.
makes the chil - dren free To fol- low truth, and thus to fol -low thee. A-men.

Text: J. W. Chadwick, 1840-1904.
Tune: J. Wainwright, 1723-1768.

Lord, Who Views All People Precious 459

D. and C. 153:9
D. and C. 16:3b-f

PITTSFIELD 8.7.8.7.D.

1. Lord, who views all peo-ple pre-cious, Wor-thy, love - ly in your sight;
2. Heal the bruised and bro-ken-heart -ed, Those enmeshed in sin and strife;

Who, through mer - cy and com-pas - sion, Calls us for - ward in - to light,
By the Spir - it, grant your peo - ple Wholeness in this earth-ly life.

We ac - cept the great com-mis-sion. May we, strength-ened with your power,
God of re - con-cil - i - a -tion, We, your saints, give you the praise

Join with Christ in common pur-pose—Serv-ing no - bly in this hour.
For your grace and pa -tient gui-dance As this prayer, with joy, we raise. A-men.

Text: Kenneth L. McLaughlin, 1951 - ; copyright 1980 Reorganized Church of Jesus Christ of Latter Day Saints.
Tune: H. R. Mills, 1844-1933.

460 With My Substance I Will Honor

Proverbs 3:9
D. and C. 38:5c, d

SARDIS 8.7.8.7.

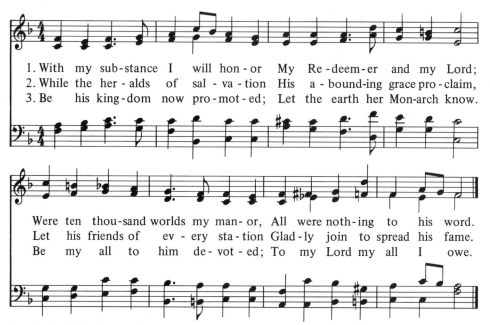

1. With my sub-stance I will hon-or My Re-deem-er and my Lord;
2. While the her-alds of sal-va-tion His a-bound-ing grace pro-claim,
3. Be his king-dom now pro-mot-ed; Let the earth her Mon-arch know.

Were ten thou-sand worlds my man-or, All were noth-ing to his word.
Let his friends of ev-ery sta-tion Glad-ly join to spread his fame.
Be my all to him de-vot-ed; To my Lord my all I owe.

Text: Benjamin Francis, 1734-1799.
Tune: Arr. from Ludwig van Beethoven, 1770-1827.

461 Let the Words of My Mouth

Psalm 19:14
Psalm 119:108

IN CORDE MEO 6.9.8.9.

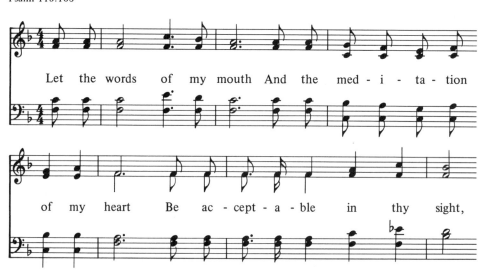

Let the words of my mouth And the med-i-ta-tion

of my heart Be ac-cept-a-ble in thy sight,

O Lord, my strength, and my re-deem-er. A-men.

Text: Psalm 19:14.
Tune: Adolph Baumbach, 1830-1880.

O Master, Let Me Walk with Thee 462

Mark 8:36 (34)
Mosiah 3:21

MARYTON L.M.

1. O Mas-ter, let me walk with thee In low-ly paths of ser-vice free; Tell me thy se-cret; help me bear The strain of toil, the fret of care.
2. Help me the slow of heart to move By some clear, win-ning word of love; Teach me the way-ward feet to stay, And guide them in the home-ward way.
3. Teach me thy pa-tience; still with thee In clos-er, dear-er com-pa-ny, In work that keeps faith sweet and strong, In trust that tri-umphs o-ver wrong,
4. In hope that sends a shin-ing ray Far down the fu-ture's broad-ening way, In peace that on-ly thou canst give; With thee, O Mas-ter, let me live. A-men.

Text: Washington Gladden, 1836-1918.
Tune: H. Percy Smith, 1825-1898.

463

Hebrews 13:6
D. and C. 22:9a, b

O Jesus, I Have Promised

WATERMOUTH 7.6.7.6.D.

1. O Je - sus, I have prom - ised To serve thee to the end;
2. O let me feel thee near me! The world is ev - er near;
3. O let me hear thee speak - ing In ac - cents clear and still,
4. O Je - sus, thou hast prom - ised To all who fol - low thee

Be thou for - ev - er near me, My Mas - ter and my Friend;
I see the sights that daz - zle; The tempt - ing sounds I hear;
A - bove the storms of pas - sion, The mur - murs of self - will!
That where thou art in glo - ry There shall thy serv - ant be;

I shall not fear the bat - tle If thou art by my side,
My foes are ev - er near me, A - round me and with - in,
O speak to re - as - sure me, To has - ten, or con - trol;
And, Je - sus, I have prom - ised To serve thee to the end;

Nor wan - der from the path-way If thou wilt be my Guide.
But, Je - sus, draw thou near - er And shield my soul from sin.
O speak and make me lis - ten, Thou Guard-ian of my soul!
O give me grace to fol - low My Mas - ter and my Friend. A - men.

Text: John E. Bode, 1816-1874.
Tune: Arthur H. Mann, 1850-1929.

Lord, I Want to Be a Christian

464

Galatians 5:22, 23, 25
Alma 3:27-29

LORD, I WANT TO BE A CHRISTIAN 14.11.6.11.

1. Lord, I want to be a Chris-tian in my heart, in my heart;
2. Lord, I want to be more lov-ing in my heart, in my heart;
3. Lord, I want to be more ho-ly in my heart, in my heart;
4. Lord, I want to be like Je-sus in my heart, in my heart;

Lord, I want to be a Chris-tian in my heart.
Lord, I want to be more lov-ing in my heart.
Lord, I want to be more ho-ly in my heart.
Lord, I want to be like Je-sus in my heart.

In my heart, in my heart,

Lord, I want to be a Chris-tian in my heart.
Lord, I want to be more lov-ing in my heart.
Lord, I want to be more ho-ly in my heart.
Lord, I want to be like Je-sus in my heart.

Text: American Folk Hymn.
Tune: American Folk Hymn; arr. Rosalee Elser, 1925 - . Copyright 1980 Rosalee Elser; used by permission.

465 We Thank Thee, God, for Eyes to See

D. and C. 59:4, 5a

I John 3:16-19

JERUSALEM C.M.D.

1. We thank thee, God, for eyes to see The beau-ty of the earth;
2. Help us re-mem-ber that to some The eye and ear and mind
3. O may our eyes be o-pen, Lord, To see our neigh-bor's need;

For ears to hear the words of love And hap-py sounds of mirth;
Bring sights and sounds of ug-li-ness And on-ly sad-ness find;
And may our ears be kept a-lert Their cries for help to heed;

For minds that find new thoughts to think, New won-ders to ex-plore;
Help us re-mem-ber that to them The world has seemed un-fair;
Make keen our minds to plan the best For one an-oth-er's good,

For health and free-dom to en-joy The good thou hast in store.
That we should strive to bring to them The beau-ty all may share.
That all the world may be at last One friend-ly neigh-bor-hood.

We Are One in the Spirit

466

John 13:34, 35
Moroni 7:52

ST. BRENDAN'S 13.13.14. with refrain

Unison (or harmony) f

1. We are one in the Spir-it, we are one in the Lord;
2. We will walk with each oth-er, we will walk hand in hand;
3. We will work with each oth-er, we will work side by side;
4. All praise to the Fa-ther, from whom all things come,

We are one in the Spir-it, we are one in the Lord;
We will walk with each oth-er, we will walk hand in hand;
We will work with each oth-er, we will work side by side;
And all praise to Christ Je-sus, his on-ly Son,

And we pray that all u-ni-ty may one day be re-stored:
And to-geth-er we'll spread the news that God is in our land:
And we'll guard each one's dig-ni-ty and save each one's pride:
And all praise to the Spir-it, who makes us one:

Refrain Dᵇ f

And they'll know we are Chris-tians by our love, by our

love; Yes, they'll know we are Chris-tians by our love.

467

Acts 10:34, 35
I Nephi 3:197

Lord of All Nations

MELROSE L.M.

1. Lord of all na-tions, grant me grace To love all
2. Break down the wall that would di - vide Thy chil - dren,
3. For - give me, Lord, where I have erred By love - less
4. Give me thy cour - age, Lord, to speak When-ev - er
5. With thine own love may I be filled And by thy

peo - ple, ev - 'ry race, And in each per - son
Lord, on ev - 'ry side. My neigh-bor's good let
act and thought - less word. Make me to see the
strong op - press the weak. Should I my - self the
Ho - ly Spir - it willed, That all I touch, wher -

may I see My kin - dred loved, re - deemed by thee.
me pur - sue; Let Chris-tian love bind warm and true.
wrong I do Will cru - ci - fy my Lord a - new.
vic - tim be, Help me for - give, re - mem - b'ring thee.
e'er I be, May be di - vine - ly touched by thee.

Text: Olive Wise Spannaus, 1916 - ; from *The Worship Supplement*, copyright 1969 by Concordia Publishing House; altered and used by permission.
Tune: Frederick C. Maker, 1844-1927.

Let Us Sing a Worldwide Anthem

468

Galatians 3:26-28
Acts 10:34, 35

AUSTRIA 8.7.8.7.D.

1. Let us sing a world-wide an-them, Ming-ling saints of ma-ny a land,
2. Let us have a world-wide chor-us, Ev - 'ry kin-dred, tribe, and tongue

In the gos-pel mo-tif join-ing, At the lead-ing of God's hand.
Sing-ing of God's love out-reach-ing, Of his min-is-try far-flung.

Though di-verse, we blend to-ge-ther In a sym-pho-ny di-vine,
Let us sing how ev-'ry per-son Can by love be well en-ticed,

As we vow un-to our Fa-ther, "We are one, for we are thine."
And be blend-ed by His Spir-it In the Church of Je-sus Christ.

Text: Roy Cheville, 1897 - . Copyright 1980 Reorganized Church of Jesus Christ of Latter Day Saints.
Tune: Franz Joseph Haydn, 1732-1809.

469   Shout the Tidings of Salvation

Philippians 2:8-11
D. and C. 1:4b-e

PROCLAMATION 8.7.8.7. with refrain

1. Shout the ti - dings of sal - va - tion To the a - ged and the young
2. Shout the ti - dings of sal - va - tion O'er the prai - ries of the West
3. Shout the ti - dings of sal - va - tion, Min - gling with the o - cean's roar,
4. Shout the ti - dings of sal - va - tion O'er the is - lands of the sea

Till the pre - cious in - vi - ta - tion Wak - ens ev - ery heart and tongue.
Till each gath - ering con - gre - ga - tion With the gos - pel sound is blest.
Till the ships of ev - ery na - tion Bear the news from shore to shore.
Till, in hum - ble ad - o - ra - tion, All to Christ shall bow the knee.

Refrain

Send the sound the earth a - round, From the ris - ing to the set - ting of the sun,

Till each gath - ering crowd Shall pro - claim a - loud, "The glo - rious work is done!"

Text: Lucius Hart.
Tune: William B. Bradbury, 1816-1868, alt.

Tell It! Tell It Out with Gladness

470

Matthew 28:17-19 (18-20)
D. and C. 6:4

HYMN TO JOY 8.7.8.7.D.

1. Tell it! Tell it out with glad-ness, God's good news on ev - ery hand,
2. Lord, we thank thee for the trea-sure Hid with - in the sa - cred page.
3. "Go and teach," thus spoke the Mas-ter, Ris - en vic - tor from the grave.

Sin for - giv - en, lives trans-fig - ured, All in God's great lov- ing plan.
We would be thy faith - ful her - alds To our deep - ly trou-bled age;
Still he gives this great com - mis - sion To his faith - ful ones, and brave.

In the scrip-tures find the wit-ness To God's might-y acts of yore;
We would pub-lish thy sal - va - tion, Ev - er on thy side to stand,
Let us know the gos - pel sto - ry Of what we through Christ can be.

Lis - ten, heed, o - bey, and serve him; Kneel be - fore him and a - dore.
Liv - ing, serv - ing, giv - ing, send-ing Life to quick-en ev - ery land.
Send it! Send it to the na - tions That God's love may set us free.

Text: Georgia Harkness, 1891-1974; alt.; copyright 1966 The Hymn Society of America. Used by permission.
Tune: Arr. from Ludwig van Beethoven, 1770-1827, by Edward Hodges, 1796-1867.

471 When Holy Ghost Shall Come in Power

Acts 1:8
D. and C. 1:4

ELLACOMBE C.M.D.

1. "When Ho - ly Ghost shall come in power, With knowledge deep, pro-found,
2. A - pos - tles, proph-ets, mar - tyrs, saints Have known him, have con-fessed
3. We would not hide the gos - pel's light, But sens - ing our great need,

Ye shall be wit - ness - es of me To earth's re - mot - est bound.
That Je - sus Christ is King of Kings, God's Son, for - ev - er blessed.
We would be wit - ness - es of Christ In life, in word, in deed.

Pro - claim my words un - to the world, To hum - ble folk and kings;
Grant, Lord, we too may see and hear And know thee as did they,
Un - til thy king-dom comes on earth, We pledge our lives a - new;

Bear wit - ness of those things ye know, The peace my Spir - it brings."
Then send us forth to tes - ti - fy Of Christ, the liv - ing way.
Till out of Zi - on light shall shine In wit - ness strong and true.

Text: Evan A. Fry, 1902-1959; alt.; copyright 1956 Herald Publishing House.
Tune: From *Gesangbuch der Herzogel, Wirtemburgischen Katholischen Hofkapelle,* 1784.

Unto God, Who Knows Our Every Weakness   472

Ether 5:28
D. and C. 132:3b, 4

CONSECRATION 10.8.10.10. with refrain

1. Un - to God, who knows our ev - ery weak - ness, With faith we
2. Though the task be great that lies be - fore us, We trust in
3. Lord, ac - cept the hum - ble con - se - cra - tion Of our lives, our

lift our hearts in prayer, Ask - ing, in hu - mil - i - ty and meek - ness,
One di - vine - ly strong, Knowing well at last we'll be vic - to - rious;
tal - ents to thy cause, Till thy word is preached in ev - ery na - tion

Refrain

For his love, his di - rec - tion, and his care.
We will pray that the time will not be long.   In these lat - ter days,
And each one has a knowl - edge of thy laws.

with songs of praise, We all must help to spread the gos - pel sto - ry,

Our ev - ery deed from sin be freed Till Zi - on we re - deem.

Text: Albert McCullough, 1901-1961.
Tune: Hawaiian Melody, arr. by Verna Schaar Gustavus, 1906 - .

473

I Love to Tell the Story

D. and C. 108:10a
Acts 1:8

HANKEY 7.6.7.6.D. with refrain

1. I love to tell the sto - ry Of un - seen things a - bove,
2. I love to tell the sto - ry; More won - der - ful it seems
3. I love to tell the sto - ry; 'Tis pleas - ant to re - peat
4. I love to tell the sto - ry, For those who know it best

Of Je - sus and his glo - ry, Of Je - sus and his love.
Than all the gold - en fan - cies Of all our gold - en dreams.
What seems, each time I tell it, More won - der - ful - ly sweet.
Seem hun - ger - ing and thirst - ing To hear it, like the rest.

I love to tell the sto - ry, Be - cause I know it's true;
I love to tell the sto - ry; It did so much for me,
I love to tell the sto - ry, For some have nev - er heard
And when in scenes of glo - ry I sing the new, new song,

It sat - is - fies my long - ings As noth - ing else can do.
And that is just the rea - son I tell it now to thee.
The mes - sage of sal - va - tion From God's own ho - ly word.
'Twill be the old, old sto - ry That I have loved so long.

Refrain

I love to tell the sto-ry; 'Twill be my theme in glo-ry,

To tell the old, old sto-ry Of Je-sus and his love.

Text: Katherine Hankey, 1834-1911.
Tune: William G. Fischer, 1835-1912.

Father, Bless Thy Word to All 474

D. and C. 34:6
Philippians 1:9-11

HENDON 7.7.7.7.7.

1. Fa - ther, bless thy word to all; Quick and power-ful
2. Thine own gra - cious mes - sage bless; Fol - low it with
3. Fa - ther, bid the world re - joice; Send, O send thy

let it prove. Oh, may sin - ners hear thy call— Let thy
power di - vine; Give the gos - pel great suc - cess— Thine the
truth a - broad; Let the na - tions hear thy voice— Hear it

peo - ple grow in love; Let thy peo - ple grow in love.
work, the glo - ry thine; Thine the work, the glo - ry thine.
and re - turn to God; Hear it and re - turn to God. A-men.

Text: Thomas Kelly, 1769-1855.
Tune: H. A. C. Malan, 1787-1864.

475

Join with Us in Sweet Accord

Matthew 28:18, 19 (19, 20)
D. and C. 11:2a, b

JOIN THE CHILDREN OF THE LORD
7.7.7.7.8.8.8.7.

1. Join with us in sweet ac-cord; Sing the prais-es of the Lord,
2. Tell the na-tions, all a-broad, Of the true and liv-ing God,

Praise un-to his ho-ly name; Ev-ery heart his love pro-claim,
Of his mer-cies, of his love, Of his com-ing from a-bove,

Send the news to ev-ery na-tion; Show the way un-to sal-va-tion;
Of his word by rev-e-la-tion, Of his works in all cre-a-tion;

Give to all this in-vi-ta-tion: Join to-geth-er in the Lord.
Give to all this in-vi-ta-tion: Join to-geth-er in the Lord.

Text: F. Christensen, alt.
Tune: F. Christensen.

O Zion, Haste

476

Romans 10:13-16 (13-15, 17)
D. and C. 62:2b

TIDINGS 11.10.11.10. with refrain

1. O Zion, haste, thy mission high fulfilling,
To tell to all the world that God is light,
That he who made all nations is not willing
One soul should perish, lost in shades of night.

2. Behold how many thousands still are lying
Bound in the darksome prison-house of sin,
With none to tell them of the Savior's dying,
Or of the life he died for them to win.

3. Proclaim to every people, tongue, and nation
That God, in whom they live and move, is love;
Tell how he stooped to save his lost creation
And died on earth that all may live above.

Refrain

Publish glad tidings, tidings of peace,
Tidings of Jesus, redemption and release.

Text: Mary A. Thomson, 1834-1923.
Tune: James Walch, 1837-1901.

477

We've a Story to Tell to the Nations

D. and C. 45:2
Luke 10:1, 2

MESSAGE 10.8.8.7.7. with refrain

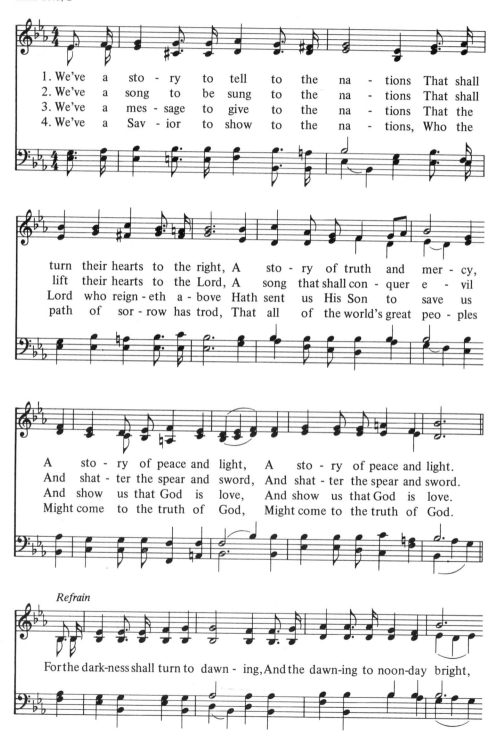

1. We've a sto - ry to tell to the na - tions That shall
2. We've a song to be sung to the na - tions That shall
3. We've a mes - sage to give to the na - tions That the
4. We've a Sav - ior to show to the na - tions, Who the

turn their hearts to the right, A sto - ry of truth and mer - cy,
lift their hearts to the Lord, A song that shall con - quer e - vil
Lord who reign - eth a - bove Hath sent us His Son to save us
path of sor - row has trod, That all of the world's great peo - ples

A sto - ry of peace and light, A sto - ry of peace and light.
And shat - ter the spear and sword, And shat - ter the spear and sword.
And show us that God is love, And show us that God is love.
Might come to the truth of God, Might come to the truth of God.

Refrain

For the dark - ness shall turn to dawn - ing, And the dawn - ing to noon - day bright,

And Christ's great king-dom shall come on earth, The king-dom of love and light.

Text and Tune: H. Ernest Nichol, 1862-1928.

Christ for the World We Sing 478

D. and C. 45:2a-d
John 3:16-17

ITALIAN HYMN 6.6.4.6.6.6.4.

1. Christ for the world we sing; The world to Christ we bring
2. Christ for the world we sing; The world to Christ we bring
3. Christ for the world we sing; The world to Christ we bring
4. Christ for the world we sing; The world to Christ we bring

1. With lov-ing zeal: The poor and them that mourn, The faint and
2. With fer-vent prayer: The way-ward and the lost, By rest-less
3. With one ac-cord, With us the work to share, With us re-
4. With joy-ful song: The new-born souls whose days, Re-claimed from

1. o-ver-borne, Sin-sick and sor-row-worn, Whom Christ doth heal.
2. pas-sions tossed, Re-deemed at count-less cost From dark de-spair.
3. proach to dare, With us the cross to bear For Christ, our Lord.
4. er-ror's ways, In-spired with hope and praise, To Christ be-long.

Text: Samuel Wolcott, 1813-1886.
Tune: Felice de Giardini, 1716-1796.

479

III Nephi 7:20
John 10:16

Still Other Sheep I Have

HAWARDEN 6.6.6.6.D.

1. "Still oth - er sheep I have," Said Christ in days of old;
2. "My voice to them shall speak, My law and gos - pel give;
3. He who is Is - rael's King Shall Is - rael ne'er for - get

"They, too, shall hear my voice And gath - er to one fold;
And Scrip - tures they shall write, Bear wit - ness that I live.
Un - til all scat - tered sheep In one great fold are met;

Of Is - rael's cho - sen seed, Through E - gypt's Jo - seph come—
Lost Is - rael, too, shall hear And write the words I speak;
One God o'er all the earth, One Christ, one king - dom, too!

In Jo - seph's land they wait For Is - rael's prom - ised One.
Then Scrip - tures, tribes, and laws Be gath - ered, one, com - plete."
The Book of Mor - mon bears This wit - ness that is true.

Text: Evan A. Fry, 1902-1959; copyright 1956 Herald Publishing House.
Tune: Samuel S. Wesley, 1810-1876.

For All the Saints

480

SINE NOMINE 10.10.10.4.4.

Ephesians 2:19-22
Revelations 19:1, 5, 6

Unison

1. For all the saints who from their la - bors rest,
2. May we thy saints, thy ser - vants true and bold,
3. O blest com - mun - ion, fel - low - ship di - vine!
4. From earth's wide bounds, from o - cean's far - thest coast,

And for all liv - ing saints who thee con - fess,
Serve as the saints who no - bly lived of old,
Saints old and new joined in one grand de - sign;
From age to age re - sounds the count - less host,

Thy name, O Je - sus, be for - ev - er blest.
The world to win and with thy love en - fold.
For all are one in thee, and all are thine.
In praise to Fa - ther, Son, and Ho - ly Ghost.

Al - le - lu - ia, Al - le - lu - ia!

Text: William Walsham How, 1823-1897; rev. Richard Clothier, 1937 - .
Tune: Ralph Vaughan Williams, 1872-1958; from *The English Hymnal* by permission of Oxford University Press.

481

This God Is the God We Adore

Colossians 1:16-18
III Nephi 4:43-45, 48

CONTRAST (De Fleury) L.M.D.

This God is the God we a-dore, Our faith-ful, un-change-a-ble friend Whose love is as large as his power And knows not be-gin-ning nor end. 'Tis Je-sus, the first and the last, Whose Spir-it will guide us safe home; We'll praise him for all that is past, And trust him for all that's to come.

Text: Joseph Hart, 1712-1768.
Tune: Early American Melody, attr. to Maria de Fleury.

Let Us Breathe One Fervent Prayer

482

Philippians 1:9-11
D. and C. 77:4

DANCER 7.7.7.7.D

1. Let us breathe one fer-vent prayer, Ere from hence our foot-steps tend,
2. Go with rev-erent pur-pose hence, Strengthened, helped, by Spir-it's power;

To the Prince up-on whose care All our hopes and joys de-pend.
Christ is help-er, strength, de-fense; Bless him for this peace-ful hour.

Look be-neath, a-round, a-bove— All is filled with bless-ed peace;
Look with chas-tened hearts be-fore; See, the clouds are sil-ver lined!

'Tis the gift of God's best love— Pray that love may still in-crease.
What as-sur-ance need we more? God is ev-er true and kind.

Text: Joseph Smith, III, 1832-1914, alt.
Tune: Norman W. Smith, 1833-1917.

483

The Lord Bless You and Keep You

D. and C. 76:2a
Ephesians 6:23, 24

THE LORD BLESS YOU AND KEEP YOU
7.10.8.10.10.10.

Text: Numbers 6:24-26
Tune: Peter C. Lutkin, 1858-1931. By permission of The Parish Press, Fond du Lac, Wisconsin.

Make Us, O God, a Church That Shares 484

Alma 19:78
Romans 12:9-18

FOREST GREEN C.M.D.

1. Make us, O God, a church that shares Thy love for hu-man-kind
2. Make us, O God, a church that cares For ev - ery hu-man need;
3. Make us, O God, a church that dares Cour - a - geous-ly to act;

That lives the truth thy word de - clares, And heeds the Mas - ter's mind.
That suf - fers when one life des - pairs, And moves to in - ter - cede.
That clothes with flesh its fer - vent prayers And makes the Gos - pel fact.

Help us reach out with lov - ing hands, In times that try the soul,
Give to our voice pro - phet-ic power That stirs each wav-er-ing heart
Now thrust us from the clois -tered halls Where we may want to hide

With sym - pa - thy that un - der-stands And makes the need-y whole.
To meet the chal - lenge of this hour And take a no - ble part.
And send us forth where du - ty calls To serve the Cru - ci - fied!

Text: Victor Kane, 1906 - ; alt. Copyright 1971 The Hymn Society of America. Used by permission.
Tune: English traditional melody, coll., adapt. and arr. by Ralph Vaughan Williams, 1872-1958. From *The English Hymnal* by permission of Oxford University Press.

485

Blest Be the Tie that Binds

I Thessalonians 3:11-13
I John 3:14, 16

DENNIS S.M.

1. Blest be the tie that binds Our hearts in Chris-tian love;
2. Be-fore our Fa-ther's throne We pour our ar-dent prayers;
3. We share our mu-tual woes, Our mu-tual bur-dens bear,
4. When here our path-ways part We suf-fer mu-tual pain;

The fel-low-ship of kin-dred minds Is like to that a-bove.
Our fears, our hopes, our aims are one, Our com-forts and our cares.
And of-ten for each oth-er flows The sym-pa-thiz-ing tear.
Yet, one in Christ and one in heart, We hope to meet a-gain.

Text: John Fawcett, 1739-1817; alt.
Tune: Arr. from Johann G. Nägeli, 1773-1836, by Lowell Mason, 1792-1872.

486

O Lord, Thy Benediction Give

D. and C. 34:6
D. and C. 85:21a, b

CANONBURY L.M.

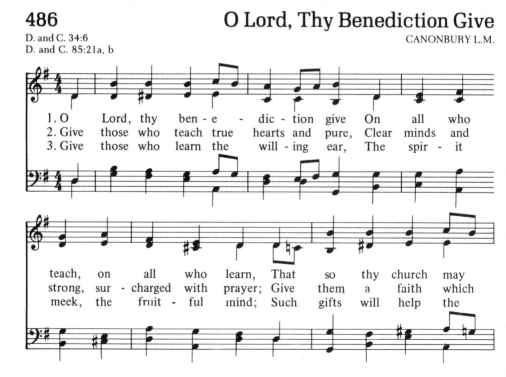

1. O Lord, thy ben-e-dic-tion give On all who
2. Give those who teach true hearts and pure, Clear minds and
3. Give those who learn the will-ing ear, The spir-it

teach, on all who learn, That so thy church may
strong, sur-charged with prayer; Give them a faith which
meek, the fruit-ful mind; Such gifts will help the

ho - lier live, And ev - ery lamp more bright - ly burn.
held se - cure Will bring a hope their stu - dents share.
low - liest here Far bet - ter than a king - dom find. A-men.

Text: John Armstrong, 1813-1856.
Tune: Robert A. Schumann, 1810-1856.

Be with Me, Lord, Where'er I Go 487

Philippians 4:4-7
Romans 12:9-18

BISHOP L.M.

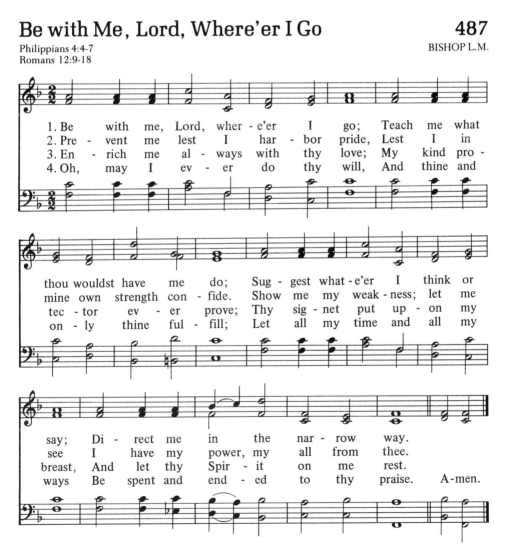

1. Be with me, Lord, wher - e'er I go; Teach me what
2. Pre - vent me lest I har - bor pride, Lest I in
3. En - rich me al - ways with thy love; My kind pro -
4. Oh, may I ev - er do thy will, And thine and

thou wouldst have me do; Sug - gest what - e'er I think or
mine own strength con - fide. Show me my weak - ness; let me
tec - tor ev - er prove; Thy sig - net put up - on my
on - ly thine ful - fill; Let all my time and all my

say; Di - rect me in the nar - row way.
see I have my power, my all from thee.
breast, And let thy Spir - it on me rest.
ways Be spent and end - ed to thy praise. A-men.

Text: John Cennick, 1718-1755.
Tune: J. P. Holbrook, 1822-1888.

488 God Be with You Till We Meet Again

D. and C. 115:1e
Alma 5:44

GOD BE WITH YOU (Deus vobiscum)
9.8.8.9. with refrain
Alternate hymn: 489

1. God be with you till we meet a-gain, By his coun-sels guide, up-hold you,
2. God be with you till we meet a-gain, Dai-ly man-na still pro-vide you,

With his sheep se-cure-ly fold you; God be with you till we meet a-gain.
Neath his wings pro-tect and hide you; God be with you till we meet a-gain.

Refrain

Till we meet, till we meet, Till we meet at Je-sus' feet;

Till we meet, till we meet a-gain, Till we meet,

Till we meet, till we meet, God be with you till we meet a-gain.

Till we meet, till we meet a-gain,

Text: Jeremiah E. Rankin, 1828-1904.
Tune: William G. Tomer, 1832-1896.

God Be with You Till We Meet Again 489

II Corinthians 13:11, 14
Alma 5:44

RANDOLPH 9.8.8.9.
Alternate hymn: 488

1. God be with you till we meet a - gain;
2. God be with you till we meet a - gain;
3. God be with you till we meet a - gain;
4. God be with you till we meet a - gain;

By His coun - sels guide, up - hold you,
'Neath His wings se - cure - ly hide you,
When life's per - ils thick con - found you,
Keep love's ban - ner float - ing o'er you,

With His sheep se - cure - ly fold you:
Dai - ly man - na still pro - vide you:
Put His arms un - fail - ing round you:
Smite death's threat - 'ning wave be - fore you:

God be with you till we meet a - gain.

Text: Jeremiah E. Rankin, 1828-1904.
Tune: Ralph Vaughan Williams, 1872-1958; from *The English Hymnal* by permission of Oxford University Press; arr. alt. with permission.

490

Lord, Let Thy Blessing Rest

Moroni 7:3
Romans 14:19

NAOMI C.M.

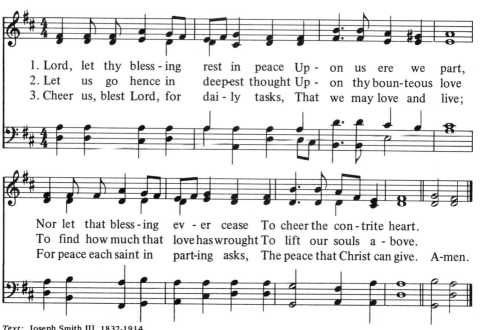

1. Lord, let thy bless-ing rest in peace Up-on us ere we part,
2. Let us go hence in deep-est thought Up-on thy boun-teous love
3. Cheer us, blest Lord, for dai-ly tasks, That we may love and live;

Nor let that bless-ing ev-er cease To cheer the con-trite heart.
To find how much that love has wrought To lift our souls a-bove.
For peace each saint in part-ing asks, The peace that Christ can give. A-men.

Text: Joseph Smith III, 1832-1914.
Tune: Johann G. Nägeli, 1768-1836; harm. Carlton R. Young, 1926 - ; harm. copyright 1964 Abingdon Press; used by permission.

491

Lord, as We Rise to Leave

Romans 12:2
I Nephi 5:59

CLOISTERS 11.11.11.5.

1. Lord, as we rise to leave the shell of wor-ship,
2. Give us an eye for o-pen-ings to serve you;
3. Lift from our life the blan-ket of con-ven-tion;

Called to the risk of un-pro-tect-ed liv-ing, Will-ing to
Make us a-lert when calm is in-ter-rupt-ed, Read-y and
Give us the nerve to lose our life to oth-ers, Be with your

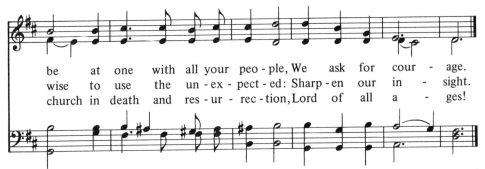

be at one with all your peo-ple, We ask for cour-age.
wise to use the un-ex-pect-ed: Sharp-en our in-sight.
church in death and res-ur-rec-tion, Lord of all a-ges!

Text: Fred Kaan, 1929 - ; copyright © 1968 by Galliard Ltd. Sole U. S. agent: Galaxy Music Corp., N. Y. Used by permission.
Tune: Joseph Barnby, 1838-1896.

Come, Gracious Lord, Descend and Dwell 492

D. and C. 85:3
FEDERAL STREET L.M.
Psalm 34:8, 9

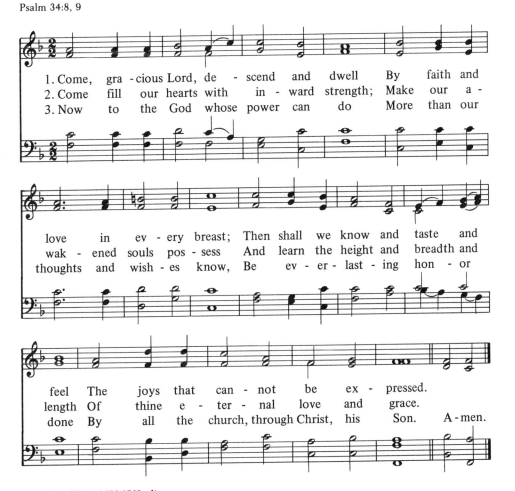

1. Come, gra-cious Lord, de-scend and dwell By faith and
2. Come fill our hearts with in-ward strength; Make our a-
3. Now to the God whose power can do More than our

love in ev-ery breast; Then shall we know and taste and
wak-ened souls pos-sess And learn the height and breadth and
thoughts and wish-es know, Be ev-er-last-ing hon-or

feel The joys that can-not be ex-pressed.
length Of thine e-ter-nal love and grace.
done By all the church, through Christ, his Son. A-men.

Text: Isaac Watts, 1674-1748; alt.
Tune: H. K. Oliver, 1800-1885.

493

Sent Forth by God's Blessing

II Corinthians 5:14-21
II Corinthians 1:21, 22

ASH GROVE 6.6.11.6.6.11.D.

1. Sent forth by God's bless-ing, Our true faith con-fess-ing,
The peo-ple of God from his dwell-ing take leave.
The sup-per is end-ed. Oh, now be ex-tend-ed
The fruits of this ser-vice in all who be-lieve.

2. With praise and thanks-giv-ing To God ev-er-liv-ing,
The tasks of our ev-'ry-day life we will face.
Our faith ev-er shar-ing, In love ev-er car-ing,
Em-brac-ing his chil-dren of each tribe and race.

The seed of his teach-ing, Re - cep - tive souls reach-ing,
With your feast you feed us, With your light now lead us;

Shall blos - som in ac - tion for God and for all.
U - nite us as one in this life that we share.

His grace did in - vite us; His love shall u - nite us
Then may all the liv - ing With praise and thanks-giv - ing

To work for God's king - dom and an - swer his call.
Give hon - or to Christ and his name that we bear.

Text: Omer Westendorf, 1916 - ; copyright 1964 World Library Publications; reprinted with permission.
Tune: Traditional Welsh Melody; harm. Rosalee Elser, 1925 - ; copyright 1980 Rosalee Elser; used by permission.

494

Hebrews 13:20, 21
John 14:27

Again, Dear Savior

CARPENTER 10.10.10.10.
See 367 for a higher setting.

1. A - gain, dear Sav - ior to thy name we raise
2. Grant us thy peace, Lord, through the com - ing night;
3. Grant us thy peace through - out our earth - ly life;
4. Thy peace in life, the balm of ev - ery pain;

With one ac - cord our part - ing hymn of praise;
Turn thou for us its dark - ness in - to light;
Peace to thy Church from er - ror and from strife;
Thy peace in death, the hope to rise a - gain;

Guard thou the lips from sin, the hearts from shame,
From harm and dan - ger keep thy chil - dren free,
Peace to our land, the fruit of truth and love;
Then, when thy voice shall bid our con - flict cease,

That in this house have called up - on thy name.
For dark and light are both a - like to thee.
Peace in each heart, thy Spir - it from a - bove:
Share with us, Lord, thine ev - er - last - ing peace. A - men.

Text: John Ellerton, 1826-1893, alt.
Tune: Keith Landis, 1922 - ; harm. Erik Routley, 1917 - ; copyright 1977 Praise Publications, Inc.; used by permission.

Now Let Our Hearts Within Us Burn 495

Isaiah 6:5-8
Luke 24:29-31 (30-32)

NORSE AIR (No Other Plea, or Landas) C.M.D.
See 357 for a higher setting.
Alternate tune: MASSACHUSETTS (360)

1. Now let our hearts with-in us burn As with a clean-sing fire.
2. As in an-oth-er time and place, A-long a for-lorn road,
3. How can we now de-ny that voice That calls us from with-in,

Your gra-cious Word has stirred in us A surge of new de-sire.
The Lord's re-new-ing grace pre-vailed Till new-born cour-age glowed;
Or blind-ly claim we need not bear An-oth-er's pain and sin?

Should vi-sion fail and cour-age yield To care-less com-pro-mise,
Our wor-ship here has lift-ed us From self-in-dul-gent care
In hearts that beat ex-ul-tant-ly Re-new your per-fect will;

Then re-di-rect our falt'-ring steps To brav-er en-ter-prise.
And strength-ened us to in-car-nate The price-less hope we share.
And send us forth, re-stored a-gain, Our mis-sion to ful-fill.

Text: Geoffrey F. Spencer, 1927 - ; copyright 1980 Reorganized Church of Jesus Christ of Latter Day Saints.
Tune: Norse Folk Melody; arr. William J. Kirkpatrick, 1838-1921.

496

Heavenly Father, Grant Thy Blessing

Mosiah 2:49
Colossians 3:15, 16

SARDIS 8.7.8.7.

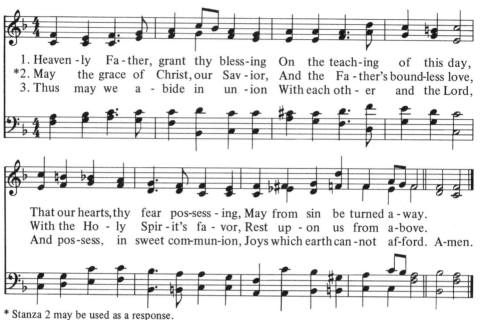

1. Heaven-ly Fa-ther, grant thy bless-ing On the teach-ing of this day,
*2. May the grace of Christ, our Sav-ior, And the Fa-ther's bound-less love,
3. Thus may we a-bide in un-ion With each oth-er and the Lord,

That our hearts, thy fear pos-sess-ing, May from sin be turned a-way.
With the Ho-ly Spir-it's fa-vor, Rest up-on us from a-bove.
And pos-sess, in sweet com-mun-ion, Joys which earth can-not af-ford. A-men.

 Stanza 2 may be used as a response.

Text: John Newton, 1725-1807, and Psalter.
Tune: Ludwig van Beethoven, 1770-1827.

497

With a Steadfast Faith

Hebrews 11:1
Helaman 5:97

EDWARDS 11.7.11.7.

1. With a stead-fast faith to-geth-er let us walk
2. With a stead-fast faith to-geth-er let us walk
3. With a stead-fast faith to-geth-er let us walk,

As we seek our Fa-ther's mind; In our dai-ly task, and
That each one on earth may know The a-bun-dant life, the
Serv-ing with a com-mon heart, Shar-ing grate-ful-ly the

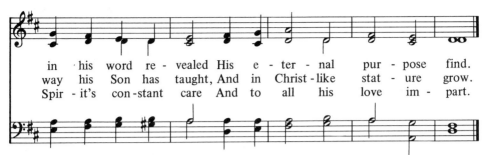

in his word re - vealed His e - ter - nal pur - pose find.
way his Son has taught, And in Christ - like stat - ure grow.
Spir - it's con - stant care And to all his love im - part.

Text: L. Wayne Updike, 1916 - ; alt.
Tune: Franklyn S. Weddle, 1905 - , and Evan A. Fry, 1902-1959; alt.
　　　　Text and tune copyright 1956 Herald Publishing House.

Forth in Thy Name, O Lord, We Go　　498

D. and C. 38:9a, c　　　　　　　　　　　　　　　　EISENACH L.M.
I Corinthians 10:31

1. Forth in thy name, O Lord, we go, Our dai - ly
2. The task thy wis - dom hath as - signed We long to -
3. Forth in thy name, O Lord, we go With gifts di -

la - bor to pur - sue; Thy mind, O Lord, we
geth - er to ful - fill, In all our works thy
verse, with hearts as one, That in our la - bors

long to know And serve in all we speak and do.
pres - ence find, And prove thy good and per - fect will.
we may grow In - to the king - dom of thy Son. A - men.

Text: Charles Wesley, 1707-1788; alt. by Roy A. Cheville, 1897 - .
Tune: Johann H. Schein, 1586-1630; harm. by Johann Sebastian Bach, 1685-1750.

499 Who Will Go Forth and Serve?

Isaiah 6:8
Acts 20:28

O'KELLEY S.M.

"Who will go forth and serve?" We speak, "O God, send us
To bring thy peace and heal - ing touch, We go now in thy name."

Text: Barbara Howard, 1930 - ; copyright 1980 Reorganized Church of Jesus Christ of Latter Day Saints.
Tune: Eleanor O'Kelley, 1934 - ; copyright 1980 by the composer. Used by permission.

500 Once More Before We Part

Ether 5:41
D. and C. 50:8e-g

TRENTHAM S.M.

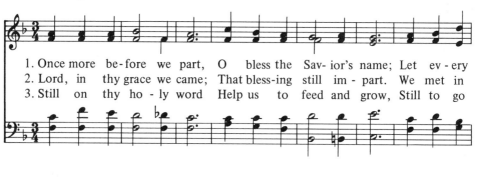

1. Once more be-fore we part, O bless the Sav-ior's name; Let ev - ery
2. Lord, in thy grace we came; That bless-ing still im - part. We met in
3. Still on thy ho - ly word Help us to feed and grow, Still to go

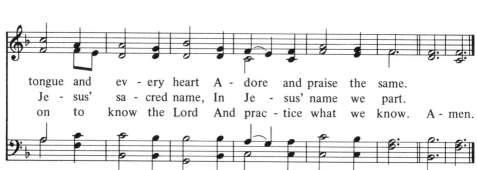

tongue and ev - ery heart A - dore and praise the same.
Je - sus' sa - cred name, In Je - sus' name we part.
on to know the Lord And prac - tice what we know. A - men.

Text: Joseph Hart, 1712-1768.
Tune: Robert Jackson, 1842-1914.

Now, on Land and Sea Descending

501

D. and C. 85:16a-e
Numbers 6:24-26

VESPER HYMN 8.7.8.7.8.6.

1. Now, on land and sea descending, Brings the night its peace profound; Let our vesper hymn be blending With the holy calm around. *Jubilate! Jubilate! Jubilate! Amen.

2. Soon as dies the sunset glory, Stars of heaven shine out above, Telling still the ancient story— Their Creator's changeless love. Jubilate! Jubilate! Jubilate! Amen.

3. Now, our wants and burdens leaving To His care who cares for all, Cease we fearing, cease we grieving: At His touch our burdens fall. Jubilate! Jubilate! Jubilate! Amen.

4. As the darkness deepens o'er us, Lo! eternal stars arise; Hope and faith and love rise glorious, Shining in the spirit's skies. Jubilate! Jubilate! Jubilate! Amen.

* "Jubilate" (ū-bǐ-lah-tā) means "Shout joyfully (to God)."

Text: Samuel Longfellow, 1819-1892; refrain added.
Tune: Dimitri Bortniansky, 1751-1825; arr. John A. Stevenson, 1761-1833.

Authors, Translators, and Sources Index

Restoration authors' and translators' names are preceded by a dot (•).

AUTHORS

Composers, Arrangers, and Sources Index

Restoration composers' and arrangers' names are preceded by a dot (•).

Tune Index

Italicized listings are alternate names by which some tunes are known.

Metric Index

Scripture Index

Where Inspired Version versification differs from other versions, the I.V. verses are listed first with the others in parentheses.

Topical Index

TOPICAL

TOPICAL

TOPICAL

Light (see also Intellect, Knowledge, Revelation, Truth)

Amazing grace 104
Come down, O Love 289
Come, Holy Ghost, our . . . 286
Dear Master in whose life . 113
God has spoken through . . 306
God of smallness, God of . . 164
God, the source of light . . . 406
Great God our source 444
Holy Spirit, truth divine . . 281
I heard the voice of 134
Immortal, invisible, God . . . 32
In the cross of Christ I 203
Joyful, joyful, we adore . . . 20
Look for the beautiful 437
Lord, in this hour 150
Lord, whose love through . . 17
My children, "hear ye 205
My life flows on in endless . 157
O God, our Source of . 301, 302
O Love that wilt not let . . . 132
O Word of God incarnate . 305
Oh, for a closer walk with . 117
Open my eyes, O Lord 454
Send forth thy light, O 317
Sometimes a light . . . 154, 155
Sovereign and 12
Spirit divine, attend our . . 288
Spirit of God, descend 181
Walk in the light 303
We limit not the truth 309
Your cause be mine 420

Lord's Day

In God's most holy 5
Lord, may our hearts be . . . 26
O help us, Lord, to keep 90
O thou who hearest every . . 16

Lord's Supper

See numbers 325-345
Break thou the bread of . . . 173
Come, ye disconsolate 166
Come, ye yourselves apart . . 84
My song is love unknown . 202
O Lord, around thine 7
O Lord, grace our 1
O thou, whose youthful . . . 207
Sent forth by God's 493
There's a spirit in the 214
What wondrous love is . . . 216
Word of God, come down . 227

Love (see also God's Love, Christ's Love)

See numbers 403-409, 447-452
Bear each other's burdens . 369
Beloved community of . . . 414
Beneath the forms of 339
Blest be the tie that 485
Breathe on me, breath of . . 179
Come, Holy Ghost, our . . . 286

Creator of sunrises 186
Every good and perfect . . . 151
Faith of our fathers 433
Father, bless thy word to . . 474
Father when in love to 116
For the beauty of the 75
God who gives to life its . . . 184
Gracious Spirit, dwell 284
Grant us, Lord, the grace . 413
Great God, as followers of . . 13
Help us accept each other . 171
Help us express your love . . 415
Hope of the world . . . 208, 209
If suddenly upon the 389
In God's most holy 5
Jesus calls us o'er the 371
Jesus, the very thought of . . 167
Joyful, joyful, we adore 20
Let us pray for one 312
Lord, I want to be a 464
Lord, let thy Holy Spirit . 346
Lord of all nations grant . . 467
Lord, thy church on earth . 438
Love divine, all loves 170
Make us, O God, a church . 484
Met in thy sacred name 2
More love to thee, O 411
My Jesus, I love thee 204
My Lord, I know that all . . 457
My song is love unknown . 202
Now let us from this table . 327
O God, from whom 367
O Jesus, Master, when 422
O Lord of heaven and 396
O Lord, thy people 352
O Lord, we come in 455
O Love that wilt not let . . . 132
O Master, let me walk 462
O may thy church build . . 431
O my people, saith the 387
O thou joyful, O thou 235
O thou, whose youthful . . . 207
Pour down thy Spirit from . 165
Prophetic Church, the . . . 293
Savior, thy dying love 442
Send forth thy light, O 317
Sing to the Lord a joyful . . . 55
Source of all gifts 400
Spirit divine, attend our . . 288
Spirit of God, descend 181
Teach me, God, to 176
The weight of past and . . . 118
Thou must be true thyself . 379
Unmoved by fear, my 131
Walk in the light 303
We are one in the Spirit . . . 466
We bring our children 348
We thank you, Lord, for . . . 78
Where beauty, truth, and . 321
With eyes of faith 122
Your cause be mine 420

Loyalty (see Commitment, Duty)

Marriage (see also Family)

Behold thy sons and 361
O God, from whom 367
O Lord, around thine 7
O perfect love 368
With a steadfast faith 497

Maturation (see Growth, Change)

Maundy Thursday (see Christ's Passion & Death)

Meditation (see also Prayer)

"Come ye apart!" 79
Come ye yourselves apart . . 84
God himself is with us 39
Lord, let thy blessing rest . . 490
Nearer, my God, to . . 138, 139
O God, in restless living . . 177
One hour with Jesus 82
Sometimes a light . . . 154, 155
Sweet hour of prayer 87
Take time to be holy 180
Unto the calmly gathered . 450
With eyes of faith 122

Memorial Services (see Eternal Life, Resurrection)

Mercy (see also Forgiveness, Grace, Repentance, Sin)

Bread of the world 329
Cast thy burden upon the . 133
Come thou fount of every . . 31
Come ye disconsolate 166
Great is thy faithfulness . . . 187
I am trusting thee, Lord . . . 127
I know not what the 126
I lift my soul to thee 110
Lead on, O King Eternal . . 374
Let us break bread 342
Let us pray for one 312
Lord, thy mercy now 114
May we who know the 416
My God, how wonderful . . 193
O how blessed are the 322
O Jesus Christ, to thee 224
O Master, let me walk 462
Pass me not, O gentle 149
The Lord's my shepherd . . 124
These things shall be: a . . . 323
We would see Jesus . . 217, 218
When Jesus wept 270
Where wilt thou put thy . . 148

Might (see Strength)

Mind (see Intellect, Knowledge)

TOPICAL

Ministry (see also Servanthood, Service)

See numbers 412-424
A diligent and grateful...362
According to the gifts that.363
As saints of old.........405
Bear each other's burdens.369
Brothers and sisters of....388
For the fruits of all......73
Help us accept each other.171
In Nature's voice we hear.441
Jesus' hands were kind....443
Lord God, we meet in....365
Lord, thy church on earth.438
Lord, whose love through..17
Make us, O God, a church.484
O Church of God, arise...451
O Jesus Christ, to thee....224
O Lord of light and love..435
Send forth thy light, O....317
The voice of God is......394
There's a spirit in the air..214
Thou must be true thyself.379
We thank thee, God, for..465
Where cross the crowded.383

Mission (see also Call, Commission, Witness)

See numbers 291-294, 474-478
A charge to keep I have...399
As saints of old.........405
Bear each other's burdens.369
Come, labor on.........384
Come ye yourselves apart..84
For bread before us......340
Forth in thy name, O.....498
"Go, make of all.........392
Go now forth into the....436
God is working his......324
Hark! The voice of Jesus..381
In Nature's voice we hear.441
Leave we now the table of.326
Lord, thy church on earth.438
Make us, O God, a church.484
Now let our hearts within.495
O Church of God, arise...451
O Master Workman of the.219
O may thy church build..431
O my people, saith the....387
Rise up O saints of......378
Sent forth by God's......493
Shout the tidings of......469
The bread that giveth....423
The church's life is built..297
The Spirit of God like a....33
The vision of a life to.....349
The voice of God is......394
Though anxious and.....380
Thy love, O God, has all..163
When the church of Jesus.445
Yesu, Yesu, fill us with...407
Your cause be mine......420

Morning

Holy, holy, holy.........56
Lord of all hopefulness...185
Morning has broken......22
Thank You for giving me...74
When morning gilds the...35

Motherhood (see Parents)

Music

Earth and all stars........49
Hallelujah! Hallelujah!....53
Let us sing a world-wide..468
My life flows on in endless.157
Sing songs of joy.......241
These things shall be: a...323
This is my song.........315

Mystery

Amazing grace.........104
Beyond the mist and 152
Crown him with many...228
Father in thy mysterious..141
Go to dark Gethsemane...266
God of earth and planets..198
I wonder as I wander.....251
Immortal, invisible, God...32
Jesus, the very thought of..167
My song is love unknown.202
Mysterious Presence,.....169
O Christ, my Lord, create.174
O Jesus, thou art........385
O little town of.........248
O Lord, how can it be....332
O love of God, how..188, 189
O Sacred Head, now.....262
Unto the calmly gathered.450
What wondrous love is...216
You satisfy the hungry....345

Nations (see also Peace—National and World, World)

All hail the power of...70, 71
Faith of our fathers......433
For the healing of the.....452
From all that dwell below..50
God has spoken through..306
God of our fathers......191
God send us saints whose..425
Join with us in sweet.....475
Let us pray for one.......312
Let us sing a world-wide..468
Lord of all nations grant..467
My soul, praise the Lord!..61
O Church of God, arise...451
O come, O come.......211
O God of every nation....175
O Zion, haste.........476
The church's life is built..297
This is my song.........315
Thy kingdom come, O....320
We gather together.......11
We've a story to tell to....477

Nature (see also Beauty, God the Creator)

All creatures of our God...72
All things bright and......18
Creator of sunrises......186
Day is dying in the west....45
Earth and all stars........49
Earth with her ten.......194
Eternal Ruler of the......458
Fairest Lord Jesus.......226
For the beauty of the......75
God of creation.........395
God of earth and planets..198
God of the earth, the sky...65
God, the source of light...406
God, who touchest earth..172
Great is Thy faithfulness..187
Heaven and earth and sea..51
In Nature's voice we hear.441
Joyful, joyful, we adore....20
Lord of the bronze-green..456
Morning has broken......22
My soul, praise the Lord!..61
O sing the mighty power...42
Praise ye the Lord!.....62, 63
This is my Father's.......52
We thank thee, God for...465
When morning gilds the...35
With happy voices ringing.29

Neighbors (see also Community, Fellowship)

Brothers and sisters of....388
For the fruits of all......73
Help us accept each other.171
In Christ there is no..448, 449
Let us pray for one......312
Let us sing a world-wide..468
Lord of all nations......467
O God of every nation....175
O Jesus, Master, when....422
O may thy church build..431
Teach me God to wonder.176
The weight of past and...118
These things shall be.....323
We thank thee, God, for..465
We thank you, Lord, for...78
Yesu, Yesu, fill us with...407

New Life

See numbers 170-174, 349-357
Angels roll the rock......277
Beneath the forms of.....339
Father, when in love to...116
Forgive our sins as we....108
Good Christian friends,...275
Hail to the Brightness of..318
Hark, the herald angels...252
Heir of all the waiting....253
How can creation's voice.300
How shall we come before.106
Let God be God.........197
Let us give praise to the...398

TOPICAL

TOPICAL

First Lines Index

Italicized listings are alternate names by which some hymns are known.

FIRST LINES

FIRST LINES